D1234027

Before
the BOMB

Before the BOMB

HOW AMERICA APPROACHED THE END OF THE PACIFIC WAR

John D. Chappell

THE UNIVERSITY PRESS OF KENTUCKY

Scholarly publisher for the Commonwealth,
serving Bellarmine College, Berea College, Centre
College of Kentucky, Eastern Kentucky University,
The Filson Club, Georgetown College, Kentucky
Historical Society, Kentucky State University,
Morehead State University, Murray State University,
Northern Kentucky University, Transylvania University,
University of Kentucky, University of Louisville,
and Western Kentucky University.

Editorial and Sales Offices: The University Press of Kentucky
663 South Limestone Street, Lexington, Kentucky 40508-4008

01 00 99 98 97   5 4 3 2 1

Library of Congress Cataloging-in-Publication Data
Chappell, John D. (John David), 1961-
    Before the bomb : how America approached the end of the Pacific
War / John D. Chappell.
        p. cm.
    Includes bibliographical references and index.
    ISBN 0-8131-1987-1 (cloth : alk. paper)
    1. World War, 1939-1945—Public opinion.   2. World War, 1939-1945—
United States.   3. Public opinion—United States—History—20th
century.   I. Title.
D810.P85U53   1996
940.53—dc20   96-31070

Contents

Illustrations

This work is dedicated to
JOHN E. AND EDIE CHAPPELL

Acknowledgments

The debts one accumulates in the process of writing a book are so numerous that the appropriate expressions of gratitude are difficult to list, let alone properly acknowledge. I must first extend my appreciation to the late John E. Wilz for his guidance during the early stages of my research. Joan Hoff's insightful commentary was a tremendous help. In their respective critiques of the manuscript, Christian Appy and Craig M. Cameron pointed out various errors and provided valuable suggestions for sharpening arguments. Thanks also to Paul Murphy for sharing his ideas about public opinion.

I am indebted to numerous archivists at the Modern Military Branch of the National Archives and the Library of Congress. At the Truman Library, Randy Soell was friendly, attentive, and perceptive. Ginger Greenfield kindly furnished the copy of the V-E Day edition of the *Harrisburg (Illinois) Daily Register.* Mary and Anastasio Gianoplus offered gracious hospitality during two of my research trips to Washington, D.C.

I can never express sufficient thanks to my parents, John and Edie Chappell, for their enduring love and unwavering support. Finally, loving gratitude goes to Juliana Kate Greenfield. Her challenging criticism of the manuscript improved it immeasurably and her generous love helped sustain me in this difficult task.

Introduction

In 1990 the Buick division of General Motors published a large advertisement dominated by a photograph of Gen. Douglas MacArthur af-
fixing his signature to the surrender documents that officially ended
World War II. "Once Again, the Japanese Must Come to Terms With an
American Leader," proclaimed the accompanying caption, the wording reminiscent of prevailing attitudes during World War II. "While we
Americans have always been willing to sit down and listen to the other
side," continued the advertisement's text, "we prefer to deal from a position of strength." The Buick LeSabre, the automobile featured, was
described as more reliable and economical than comparable Japanese
models. According to the advertisement, the LeSabre ranked "number
one" in the "battle for performance and value. And that's something
we won't negotiate under any terms."[1]

Produced at a time when U.S. automakers were still enduring de-
pressed business, in part because consumers were purchasing greater
numbers of what they considered better quality Japanese cars, the advertisement hinted that by technologically surpassing the Japanese, automakers could dictate terms of competition. Its blatant exploitation
and revival of a wartime motif also suggested that memories and images
associated with the Pacific War remained emotional touchstones some
forty-five years after the Allies defeated Japan in the epochal year of
1945.[2]

"With confidence in our armed forces—with the unbounding de-
termination of our people—we will gain the inevitable triumph—so
help us God."[3] So vowed President Franklin D. Roosevelt the day after
Japan's infamous Sunday morning aerial assault on Pearl Harbor on
December 7, 1941, which plunged the United States into World War II.
Despite the bleakness of the situation, few citizens doubted that the
United States would eventually triumph.

In early May 1945 Germany surrendered and the massed forces of
the Allies—mainly American—converged on Japan. Awareness that
the United States held a position of overwhelming strength vis-a-vis

the enemy in the Pacific did not alleviate the concerns of U.S. citizens or their leaders. As U.S. forces drove closer to Japan, casualties rose. Indeed, casualties during the battle on Iwo Jima in early 1945 were the highest of the war up to that time, surpassed only by the brutal struggle to capture Okinawa that lasted from April until late June. Although obviously defeated, the Japanese persisted with suicidal defense at Iwo Jima, Okinawa, and in the Philippines.

With Germany's surrender additional forces could be transferred from Europe for the final onslaught against Japan. After lengthy debate the Joint Chiefs of Staff agreed upon a strategy of sustained bombing and blockade of Japan followed by an invasion of Kyushu, the southernmost of the four main islands. Several American leaders wondered whether a political solution to the conflict could be reached, one acceptable to the Japanese while satisfying the Allied demand for unconditional surrender. By the time of Germany's capitulation a few Allied leaders knew that atomic bombs would be ready for use against Japan before the summer's end. U.S. political and military leaders shared a growing concern about the public's endurance for a prolonged war and also feared citizens' tolerance for victory achieved at the cost of casualty rates such as those on Okinawa.

Historians have produced overviews of the war against Japan, numerous studies of particular battles, and several works about the American home front during World War II. Scholars have also studied the influence of prejudices and racial hatreds on the conduct of the war. The war's conclusion has also received extensive scholarly attention, most of it focused on the decision to use atomic bombs against Japan.

Neglected in the literature are the attitudes, opinions, and perceptions on the home front during the final chaotic months of the war. What did Americans think about the prospect of invading Japan? What opinions were expressed on the home front about the strategies of siege and assault? Was the public as enthusiastic about the war effort as it was exhorted to be? What was the response on the home front to the campaign on Okinawa? Were people as unanimously supportive of unconditional surrender as American leaders claimed? Did opinions on the home front influence the policies of the U.S. government? How were the views of leaders, commentators, and citizens alike or dissimilar?

In this study I assess the commentary of newspaper editors, syndicated columnists, and other prominent commentators regarding the important events and issues related to concluding the war against Japan. Also included are examples of the thoughts of citizens. In addition, the policies for ending the war are evaluated, with attention to the consideration, or lack thereof, of American leaders to public concerns. I appraise the information available to the public in the war's final months, to determine if public attitudes—or leaders' perceptions of those attitudes—influenced the conduct of the war in its closing stages. Also analyzed are military decisions never subjected to public debate, such as the use of atomic weapons.

Dispositions toward the Japanese that had been common throughout the war remained pervasive after V-E Day. The Japanese were considered inherently savage, hopelessly irrational, and often depicted as animals. Susceptible to these stereotypes because of racial prejudices and general ignorance about Japan, many people sought vengeance for Japan's surprise attack on Pearl Harbor and for atrocities committed against American troops by Japanese soldiers. Even after more than three years of war, the print media abounded with analyses that attempted to explain the Japanese. Most of these were superficial efforts that only reinforced stereotypical perceptions. Enlightened opinion about the Japanese was also scarce among U.S. leaders, many of whom shared the common views of Japanese as the "Other."

Government and military leaders urged Americans to remain dedicated to the war effort and warned of the possibility of an extended struggle. Yet numerous leaders joined the ongoing discussion among editors, columnists, radio commentators, and citizens about the best strategy for ending the war expeditiously while minimizing casualties.

The published accounts of the battle for Okinawa have devoted less attention to the reaction on the home front to that bloody campaign. One columnist's criticism of the tactics used provoked considerable controversy. As the fighting on Okinawa continued, U.S. military leaders reconsidered using poison gas against the Japanese. Commentators and citizens expressed sharp differences of opinion over the morality of chemical warfare, and supportive arguments resembled later justifications for the dropping of atomic bombs.

The United States remained committed to achieving Japan's unconditional surrender. Although several top officials recommended alteration of the policy, President Harry S. Truman proved reluctant to modify it. Several historians have claimed that fear of hostile public and congressional reaction influenced Truman's attitude. Yet thousands of people wrote letters to members of Congress, the State Department, and the White House urging clarification of unconditional surrender.

Historians have neglected the vigorous discourse on the home front about these issues. Citizens wanted to expedite the war's end but expressed approval of a longer war that minimized casualties. They disputed the necessity of invading Japan, discussed the morality of incendiary bombing of Japanese cities, debated whether the Japanese should retain their imperial system of government, and disagreed about the ethics and practicality of chemical warfare.

The war's final months were marked by confusion, anxiety, fear, and expectation among Americans and their leaders. The ideas of commentators, citizens, and leaders created a dissonant cacophony of divergent and overlapping views. Although the government admonished people to remain focused on the war, advertisements in the mass media offered visions of postwar affluence and promoted a distracting array of consumer products that would be available when the war ended. The advertisements celebrated an idealized, predominantly Caucasian, male-dominated society where, despite their work-related war efforts, women would be relegated exclusively to domestic duties as mothers and homemakers.

Any explanation of the end of the war against Japan must acknowledge the complexities of the time. Events in the war's final months, and perceptions of those occurrences at the time, were marked by contradiction, uncertainty, misunderstanding, random insight, and much irrationality. The attitudes of U.S. citizens and their leaders and the policies those leaders pursued defy simple explanation.

In an effort to evaluate the information and rhetoric available to the public, I have devoted more space to the public statements of officials, without neglecting their private thoughts or utterances. Records consulted included those of President Harry S. Truman, the Joint Chiefs of Staff, the State Department, and papers of several government and military officials.

A variety of newspapers, magazines, journals, and radio commentary captured popular perceptions. Americans were still a reading public in 1945, and larger cities often supported several newspapers. It was still the golden age of radio too, and the commentaries by broadcasters such as H.V. Kaltenborn and Raymond Gram Swing remained important sources of information. The communications media do not completely capture the elusive concept labeled "public opinion" but are indispensable for evaluating the national mood inasmuch as it provides hints about general perceptions. The commentary in the print media often reflected popular attitudes toward the war but also frequently tried to shape public opinion.

I have evaluated a variety of printed sources, including conservative and liberal newspapers from various regions of the country, popular magazines, scholarly journals, as well as specialized religious publications. The variety of magazines includes those devoted to a broad, general audience, major news magazines, radical publications, and magazines that targeted male and female readers respectively. Consultation of major African-American publications revealed that the editorial content devoted most of its attention to ongoing racial injustice in the United States. However, these sources also provided fascinating examples of all-too-rare evaluation of the racial overtones to the Pacific War.

However deep one delves into these sources, one still cannot claim to completely comprehend or define "public opinion." Yet one must make generalizations based on the sources available and what is known of their audiences. Characteristics of public opinion elude commentators, advertisers, and policymakers even when they attempt to understand the concept. In part, this is because the term "public opinion" is a misleading one developed in and for a mass society in an effort to find a neat, cohesive entity that does not really exist. My method is to acknowledge this fact, look at carefully selected sources, while trying to remain aware of the vital interest of these sources in this chimera called public opinion.

In the war's closing months, most people recognized the inevitability of Japan's defeat. Yet that realization did not ease the concerns about quickly achieving that triumph with minimal loss of life. At the heart of the debate was the policy of unconditional surrender. American leaders said that winning the war required Japanese compliance with that policy. In May 1945, gaining that adherence loomed as a formidable task.

1

A War Half Won

There is only one road to Japan's total defeat—a long, hard road necessarily marked by death and destruction.[1]

At approximately 9:35 A.M., EST, Monday, May 7, 1945, the people of the United States, via radio news bulletins, learned of the surrender of Nazi Germany. The brutal war that had convulsed Europe, spread to the Soviet Union and Northern Africa, and spilled into the rolling waters of the Atlantic since September 1939 had ended. For weeks the American press had publicized rumors of Germany's imminent capitulation. Erroneous broadcasts two days earlier claimed Germany had surrendered. Both the CBS and NBC radio networks carried that news, although announcers stressed that it remained unconfirmed. The Mutual network made several brief announcements of the item, and the "Blue Network" passed it on as authentic. The reports also fooled newspaper editors; in several major cities presses rolled out extra editions carrying the word of a German surrender. Then, within hours of its release, President Harry S. Truman issued a denial of the story.[2]

Most citizens acknowledged the announcement of May 7 with relief rather than exultation. Japan's continued defiance tempered popular response to news of victory over Germany. Germany's final defeat had been expected for some time and, in fact, a journalistic controversy concerning disclosure of the capitulation received nearly equal media coverage. German officials signed the surrender documents on May 7 at Rheims, France, in a small brick schoolhouse that for months had been the headquarters of the supreme Allied commander in Western Europe, Gen. Dwight D. Eisenhower.[3]

In churches across the country people attended special memorial services and offered prayers of thanks for the cessation of hostilities in Europe. In Atlanta, newspapers noted, citizens welcomed the news calmly. A brief celebration ensued in Boston, but in Los Angeles no public demonstrations took place. Dallas was described as being "as quiet as Arbor Day," and it was reported that the news hit Cleveland "with the impact of a feather." Denver, too, was still. An Indianapolis newspaper disclosed that in Indiana's "Capital City" there "wasn't so much as a single 'whoopee!' nor a single festoon of ticker tape, and telephone books remained intact." In St. Louis, reaction was likewise subdued, and throngs of servicemen who crowded the waiting room of Union Station received the news thoughtfully, perhaps remembering comrades killed or pondering battles that appeared to lie ahead in the Pacific. About the only demonstration in St. Louis occurred at a downtown department store where a few employees tossed confetti onto a sidewalk.[4]

In Washington, D.C., a restrained response prevailed as well, and most churches announced special services of thanks for the official V-E Day, Tuesday, May 8. Government employees reported for work as usual that morning, and at the Brentwood Terrace Citizens Association's V-E Day meeting an official from the American Legion remarked that the war against Japan could be shortened by using poison gas.[5] A report from the British Embassy noted, "The mood here is one of sober triumph: even this mercurial nation is for the moment at least made grave by the thought of Pacific ordeals yet to come."[6]

Outbursts of revelry transpired in a few cities. In San Francisco, exuberant civilians and servicemen looted liquor stores and overturned taxis. Tons of paper cascaded from the windows of downtown office buildings in Detroit as workers welcomed the news, and crowds surged through the streets until Mayor Edward Jeffries, Jr., asked people to refrain from "unwarranted celebration." More than eight hundred policemen assembled for extra duty in downtown Chicago to erect barricades in front of store windows and prevent a repetition of the Armistice Day celebration of 1918 that had left six people dead, hundreds injured, and resulted in a million dollars in property damage. Heavy rain curtailed the throwing of ticker tape in downtown thoroughfares of the "Windy City," but the brief merrymaking did not compare with the wild glee of November 1918. As in Detroit, authorities in Chicago proclaimed that all liquor stores would be closed for twenty-four hours following the official Victory in Europe announcement on Tuesday, May 8.[7]

Only in New York did citizens give themselves over to sustained jubilation on May 7. From 10:00 A.M. to 5:00 P.M., more than a million New Yorkers danced, shouted, and sang in the streets. After the first news bulletin reporting the surrender of Germany at about 9:35 A.M., people tossed tons of paper and, in the garment district, bales of textiles into the streets from upper-story windows. Within an hour, over eight inches of multicolored fabrics covered Sixth, Seventh, and Eighth

Avenues and Broadway. Several women happily hurried off with complete dresses and slips thrown by exultant garment workers. The shower of paper was described as the heaviest in New York since the reception the city accorded Charles A. Lindbergh, Jr., following his epic trans-Atlantic flight in 1927. Joining the throngs, servicemen gladly accepted offers of kisses, liquor, and cigarettes. However, one wounded veteran sitting beside the Paramount Theater remarked, "What are they hollering about? It ain't over." Thousands of celebrants gathered in Times Square, which in the initial moments of the festivity provided a stage for some two dozen Hitler and Mussolini impersonators. Three sailors led one of the Hitler mimics through the crowd with a noose around his neck as onlookers jeered and laughed.[8]

New York's inimitable mayor Fiorello La Guardia stifled much of the fanfare when, at 3:15 P.M., in what one reporter described as a "high-pitched and unusually emotional" voice, he made an announcement that boomed through the WYNC public address system in Times Square, imploring people to return to their jobs or homes. A small contingent of the suddenly subdued throng booed La Guardia's plea but stopped when he appealed on behalf of the men still fighting and dying in the Pacific. La Guardia closed by saying, "Let's be patient for just a few more hours and behave in a manner befitting the great people of a great democracy." Almost immediately the crowds began to disperse.[9]

The response in New York City to the news of Germany's surrender was an exception to the expressions of simple thankfulness that prevailed across the nation. As one former congressman remarked, "It is a time for dedication, not dissipation; for gladness, not gaiety; happiness, not hilarity."[10] One woman disapproved of the celebrations in a letter to her husband, a pilot in the Army Air Forces: "While I think we should thank God that the European war is over, I can't see any excuse for these wild demonstrations."[11] A public announcement posted in the small southern Indiana community of Oakland City informed citizens that businesses would close after the official V-E announcement and requested that townspeople attend a planned memorial service. "This is not the time for hilarious-carnival celebration," read a portion of the placard, "so it is your duty to discourage in all ways this type of celebration." The program for the service included a reading of the names of local men killed in action, prayers for their families, as well as the singing of the songs "America" and "When the Lights Go on Again All Over the World."[12]

Somewhat anticlimactically, at about 8:35 A.M. on Tuesday, May 8, before a large group of reporters in the Executive Office of the White House, President Harry S. Truman issued the formal announcement of

Germany's surrender to the United Nations and said he would relay the news to the nation via radio at 9:00 A.M. Clad in a dark blue suit, his service button from World War I pinned to the lapel, and flanked by his wife, Bess, his daughter, Margaret, members of the cabinet and Congress, as well as ranking military leaders of both the United States and Great Britain, Truman simply read the official announcement. The day marked Truman's sixty-first birthday, and after stating that "the flags of freedom fly all over Europe," he smiled and added, "It's celebrating my birthday today, too."

Truman also read a release, not included in his subsequent radio broadcast, in which he said that fighting in the Pacific would continue until Japan surrendered unconditionally. For the Japanese people, Truman explained, unconditional surrender would mean the return of peace and the end to military leadership of Japan. "Unconditional surrender does not," he concluded, "mean the extermination or enslavement of the Japanese people."[13]

After his meeting with the press Truman adjourned to the radio room in the White House for his broadcast. As he began speaking solemnly in his flat Midwestern accent, Truman expressed the wish that Franklin Delano Roosevelt had lived to see this day. Calling the occasion "a solemn but glorious hour," Truman cautioned that rather than rejoicing, people should remember American casualties. "If I could give you a single watchword for the coming months, that word is—work, work, and more work. We must work to finish the war. Our victory is but half won." That evening, for the first time since December 9, 1941, the lights of the U.S. Capitol were lit, and the beautiful dome glistened against the evening sky.[14]

Since the fateful Sunday morning of December 7, 1941, when Japanese planes swooped down upon the U.S. fleet at Pearl Harbor, Americans had achieved an unprecedented sense of unity and shared purpose. Delivered without warning, the Pearl Harbor attack knocked out numerous ships, damaged or destroyed hundreds of aircraft, and killed 2,400 servicemen. The daring Japanese strike initially shocked U.S. citizens, but stupefied surprise quickly turned to resolute anger and vindictive determination.

During the remainder of 1941 and into 1942, people pulled dusty atlases from shelves or removed unused world maps from closets to follow the rapid advance of the Japanese forces that overran Malaya, Burma, and the Dutch East Indies. Hong Kong, Singapore, and previously unheard of islands fell, and Japanese troops advanced into the Philippines, where the names Bataan and Corregidor became synonymous with heroic resolve and frustrating defeat for Allied forces.

In 1942 the Japanese suffered setbacks. The Battle of the Coral Sea of May 1942, the first major carrier battle of the war, halted the advance of Japanese forces toward Australia. Then, U.S. naval forces inflicted a stunning blow upon the Imperial Japanese Navy at the Battle of Midway in June. The Japanese fleet never recovered from the crippling loss of four aircraft carriers and hundreds of its most skilled pilots. By 1943 U.S. forces were engaging the Axis powers over much of the globe. From 1943 through 1944 more hitherto unheard of places became familiar to U.S. citizens as the location of costly battles: Kasserine Pass, Salerno, Anzio, Guadalcanal, Tarawa, Omaha Beach, and Saipan.

By the dawn of 1945 momentous events were occurring with dizzying rapidity as the Allies approached victory over Nazi Germany. The German offensive through the Ardennes forests of December 1944 had been blunted, and from February through April 1945, Allied armies relentlessly drove toward the German heartland. There, on April 25, American and Soviet troops met near Torgau on the Elbe River seventy miles south of Berlin. In the Pacific, meanwhile, the Allies pressed the offensive against the Japanese. In February, marines invaded the tiny volcanic isle of Iwo Jima, and the bloody, month-long struggle that ensued produced the highest casualties of the war up to that time.

Scarcely had the battle for Iwo Jima ended before U.S. Army troops and marines on April 1 assaulted the Japanese island of Okinawa in the Ryukyus. While the battle for Okinawa raged, on April 12 President Roosevelt, serving an unprecedented fourth term, died suddenly at Warm Springs, Georgia. Visibly worn when he returned from the Crimean city of Yalta, where in February he conferred with the Soviet leader Joseph Stalin and the British prime minister Winston Churchill, his death nonetheless shocked Americans.

Vice President Harry S. Truman succeeded Roosevelt. An unpretentious man, fiercely proud of his roots in rural and small-town Missouri, he had almost no experience in diplomacy or foreign affairs. A onetime farmer and haberdasher, Truman entered politics as a minor cog in the Pendergast political machine in Kansas City, and those connections propelled him to election to the U.S. Senate in 1934. Before his selection as Roosevelt's running mate in 1944, Truman's major achievement was his work as chairman of the Special Committee to Investigate the National Defense Program, popularly known as the Truman Committee.[15] As president, Truman believed in tackling problems decisively, although he sometimes equated resolution with speed of deliberation.

With the exception of cabinet meetings, Truman met with Roosevelt only twice before his death and deeply resented being uninformed about policy.[16] Some of Roosevelt's advisers doubted the new chief executive's ability to successfully cope with the complex issues he confronted.[17] Certain fighting men felt apprehension about Truman's ability to manage the war. "We surely didn't want someone in the White House who would prolong it one day longer than necessary," recalled former marine E.B. Sledge.[18] Although he initially considered Truman a "bush-leaguer" and questioned his competency, Chief of Staff Adm. William D. Leahy—and other advisers—soon developed respect for the new president.[19] Still, a month into the Truman presidency, one White House reporter commented on the incongruity of attending press conferences and not seeing Roosevelt seated behind the executive desk. Surveying the sparse decor of the oval office in the White House, he noted the absence from the walls of Roosevelt's seascapes and the once crowded bookshelves, now almost barren. "The place looks new, bare, uncertain like the new President's own policies," he remarked.[20]

Truman presided over a nation composed of forty-eight contiguous states and an assortment of overseas territories, populated, according to the 1940 census, by 132 million people of which 118 million were white and 13 million black.[21] It was an era when male students at the Illinois Institute of Technology elected an eighteen-year-old secretary as "Girl We'd Most Like to Dictate To."[22] Cole Porter's song "Don't Fence Me In," from the film "Hollywood Canteen," was the top hit of the 1944-1945 season according to a survey of radio stations, having received an estimated 700 million listenings on the four major radio networks.[23] On Broadway, the play "Life with Father" surpassed two thousand performances, and Kathleen Winsor's risque novel *Forever, Amber* remained a best-seller.[24] Newly released films in the war's final months included "Salome, Where She Danced," starring the Hollywood newcomer Yvonne "She's An Eyeful" DeCarlo. Or one could see "Hotel Berlin," billed as "Amazing! Shameless! Shocking!" and "The Hottest Story to Ever Hit the Screen!"[25]

Such escapist fare provided Americans welcome respite from the war. In some respects they experienced what the oral historian Studs Terkel later labeled the "Good War."[26] Of course, the war brought unfathomable heartache and sorrow to families, relatives, and friends of the hundreds of thousands of servicemen killed, maimed, wounded, or held captive. Tragically, the U.S. government forcibly moved more than 100,000 Japanese Americans from their homes to primitive detention camps in desolate locations in seven western states. Despite the prevalent image of a unified America, racism and gender stereotypes endured. The government also imposed censorship on the motion picture industry.

The civilian population of the United States was spared the horrors of bombing or invasion. Although the government rationed gasoline, tires, shoes, and numerous food products, citizens never suffered serious deprivation. The booming war industries offered new job opportunities for millions of people, including women and African Americans. Full employment mitigated the inconvenience and annoyance of consumer product shortages. After the world economic depression, massive unemployment, farm foreclosures, factory shutdowns, bank failures, and general societal disruption of the 1930s, many Americans during the war years were fired by an invigorated sense of national community. They saw themselves as fighting a noble and just war against the barbarism of Nazi Germany and sought revenge against Japan for the attack on Pearl Harbor.

Animated by a unity of purpose and an impulse to self-sacrifice, Americans' national spirit soared in the three and one-half years following Pearl Harbor. Civilian energies were channeled into tasks that gave everyone, even people not directly involved in war-related work, a sense of contribution to the war effort. The government encouraged homemakers to give collected grease and fats to butchers for the manufacture of explosives and ammunition. Drives for collecting scrap metal, paper, and rubber became commonplace, with active participation by children who organized "Junior Commandos," "Uncle Sam's Scrappers," and "Tin Can Colonels" groups for such campaigns. People grew some of their own food in "victory gardens," participated in massive war bond drives, and joined the ranks of the civilian defense forces as air-raid wardens, fire fighters, auxiliary police, and nurses' aides.[27]

One man who served as an air-raid warden in Philadelphia later recalled of the war, "Everybody had certain obligations, and doggone it, they fulfilled them." A boy who grew up in Portland, Oregon, during the war remembered "a solidarity, a unity, . . . a feeling that we're all in this together, and by God, through our technological know-how and our determination and our downright good Americanism, we were going to win." A young woman in Long Beach, California, recollected that the war years generated "a kind of team atmosphere and team spirit," and another woman later reminisced, "We all pulled together in a way I have never seen happen any other time in this country."[28]

By May 1945 this robust spirit of all for one and one for all had weakened.[29] The sense of triumph over defeating Germany remained tinctured with foreboding about what might lie ahead in the Pacific. Undoubtedly, many citizens had tired of sacrifices, shortages, casualty lists, and rising prices. The perception of everyone pulling together became frayed as the war dragged on. Crime reflected shortages, as items such as meat, liquor, and cigarettes became targets for thieves.[30] Encouraging a sustained collective effort in a society that had always admired and acclaimed individual initiative and personal gain proved extraordinarily difficult. As the threat of attack or invasion vanished and eventual victory became certain, people returned to more traditional behavior and looked out for themselves. Personal problems again took precedence over mutual concerns.[31] Indeed, in a Gallup poll of February 1945, 64 percent of the respondents said they had not made any real sacrifice for the war.[32]

War weariness may partially explain the inordinate degree of attention the press lavished on Gertie, a gray mallard hen that became a national celebrity after she built a nest and laid eggs on a rotted bridge piling in the midst of downtown Milwaukee along the city's busiest street. Christened "Gertrude the Great," or "Gertie" for short, the media chronicled the duck's exploits through May and early June of 1945. Groups of schoolchildren visited the site, guards protected the nest, and firemen extinguished one blaze that resulted when a careless onlooker flipped a cigarette into Gertie's domicile. One Milwaukee newspaper assigned four reporters and five photographers to cover Gertie, who eventually became the heroine subject of a book. On Memorial Day, Milwaukee radio stations flashed the news that Gertie's first offspring had hatched, and later bulletins announced the births of four siblings. Thousands visited the babies, and five days later two hundred spectators watched Gertie and her family swim in a park lagoon where they would spend the summer. Park workers kept track of Gertie by dabbing her with a yellow stripe.[33] Amidst a world still convulsed by war, the miracle of new life appeared wondrous. And interest in Gertie mirrored a renewed veneration of motherhood in print advertisements.

The conclusion of fighting in Europe brought some changes to the home front. Many cities temporarily lifted curfews. Racing at horse and dog tracks briefly resumed, some additional gasoline became available, limited manufacturing of washing machines and refrigerators for civilian consumption began, and it was hoped that new cars would appear within a few months. Despite a continuing scarcity of new clothes, it was expected that inexpensive clothing would soon be more plentiful. The forty-eight-hour week remained in place at factories producing implements of war but gradually disappeared elsewhere. Yet war mobilization director Fred M. Vinson asserted that "all out effort toward war, and toward production, will be needed up to the last instant." Large Army draft calls continued, as did wage and price controls.[34]

The redeployment of troops from Europe to the Pacific meant passenger trains would remain crowded, and in June the government required that reservations for passenger trains be made no more than five days in advance, rather than the customary thirty days.[35] After July 15, the government barred civilians from sleeping cars on trains traveling 450 miles or less in order to free space for servicemen. Due to the shortage of Pullman cars, only troop trains making journeys that lasted more than twelve hours received Pullmans. Yet many trips lengthier than twelve hours lacked sleeping cars, and thousands of soldiers traveled coast to coast crammed three to every two seats in decrepit, hot, squalid coaches.[36]

The end of warfare in Europe did not ease annoying shortages of numerous goods. In St. Louis, a scarcity of toilet paper was alleviated when the local district manager of the War Production Board secured five extra railroad cars of tissue.[37] Some residents of Michigan were amused, others angered, when a senator from that state publicized a letter he had received from a wholesale dry goods firm claiming that the paucity of textiles had prompted numerous men in the Detroit area to purchase women's underpants.[38] In Jacksonville, Florida, a drugstore was damaged when more than one thousand customers rushed the doors in response to a sale on soap flakes.[39]

The rationing of food continued because 10 percent less food was available than in 1944.[40] Published reports warned of more severe food restrictions and speculated that by August 1945 the diet of the average American would be largely vegetable.[41] In June the government announced a 20 percent reduction in allotments of meat for most hotels and restaurants for July and August.[42] The Office of War Information (OWI) urged the public to conserve sugar and store fresh peaches, which might be the only plentiful fruit of the summer. The OWI also implored citizens to enlist appropriate breeds of dogs in the Army K-9 corps, and encouraged butchers, chefs, and bakers to consider working one voyage on a troopship bringing soldiers home from Europe.[43] Food shortages, high food prices, and the lack of travel space on trains remained major topics of conversation.[44]

Certain of victory, people became increasingly fearful about the human cost of defeating Japan, particularly in light of the alarming losses recently suffered capturing Iwo Jima, where total casualties numbered nearly 27,000. After learning of the toll on Iwo Jima one woman wrote to the Navy Department: "Please for God's sake, stop sending our finest youth to be murdered on places like Iwo Jima. It is too much for boys to stand. It is driving some mothers crazy. Why can't objectives be accomplished some other way? It is most inhuman and awful—stop, stop!" Uncounted citizens probably shared similar thoughts.[45] Indeed, Elmer Davis of the OWI, in a meeting with the Joint Chiefs of Staff in February 1945, suggested that given the general concern about casualties, preparatory broadcasts to brace the public for severe losses might be necessary before Allied armies invaded Japan.[46] Fighting continued in several regions of the Pacific theater, the heaviest on the island of Okinawa. On V-E Day newspapers disclosed that American losses on Okinawa up to May 3 numbered 2,337 dead, 11,432 wounded, and 514 missing.[47]

With the end of fighting in Europe, the Allied military effort could be concentrated on Japan. Americans had recognized the importance of defeating Nazi Germany, but most felt greater emotional involvement in the war against the Japanese. By May 1945, numerous commentators on the home front still expressed uncompromising hatred toward the Japanese yet desired that the war be ended quickly. A report from the British Embassy in Washington noted that Americans had long awaited the surrender of Germany "in order to throw themselves with all their strength upon the hated Japanese savages, and in that sense this is more of America's own war than the great world conflict with its climax on German soil."[48]

Despite the general loathing of the Japanese, government leaders and the media admonished the public to avoid any letdown in their support for the war, a motif exemplified by President Truman's exhortation for continued work. The members of the Joint Chiefs of Staff, in remarks broadcast on V-E Day, urged people to sustain their efforts for the war. Gen. Henry H. "Hap" Arnold, commander of the Army Air Forces, called the victory over Germany the conclusion of a battle rather than a war and cautioned, "Remember, although a great battle has been won . . . your war, goes on!"[49] Joseph C. Grew, the former ambassador to Japan and then acting secretary of state, echoed the president's entreaties when he proclaimed that citizens must "dedicate ourselves with redoubled energy to the unfinished business in the Pacific."[50]

Speeches by members of Congress reiterated the theme of rededication to the war effort. F. Edward Hébert (D-La.) warned that any slackening of effort on the home front would cause needless casualties. Rep. Charles A. Plumley (R-Vt.) proclaimed that victory over Germany "should not be permitted to sap or weaken our determination to carry on unrelentingly until the great day comes when the stars and stripes shall fly over the Imperial Palace in Tokyo."[51]

In rather contradictory remarks, Democratic House Majority Leader John W. McCormack of Massachusetts referred to the war as only half finished but declared the hardest part completed. "We could have licked Japan 1 or 2 years ago," he contended. Despite his assertion that the most difficult part of the war had transpired, McCormack called for Americans to "go forward with grim determination . . . toward the early defeat of . . . the vicious Jap."[52]

Several members of Congress disputed McCormack's pronouncement.[53] In an appeal to expel the uncivilized from civilization, John E. Rankin (D-Miss.) said that the war must be pursued "until that bunch of ruthless savages" was defeated and "driven from the society of civilized nations." Likewise, Philip J. Philbin (D-Mass.) summoned people to use all available resources "against the ruthless Jap enemy and smash it mercilessly until this despicable menace to our free institutions is brought to its knees and its evil influence removed once and for all from the civilized world."[54]

Editorials in major newspapers also warned against diminution of the war effort. "It would be a blunder worse than a crime for Americans to assume that, with Germany beaten, we can afford to relax," stated a typical editorial in the *Washington Post*.[55] Editors urged citizens to endure continued shortages of food and gasoline.[56] "The war with our savage and malevolent Japanese enemy must be pressed with even greater energy to a victorious finish," declared the editors of the *St. Louis Post-Dispatch*.[57] The editors of *Time* published a statement in more than 100 newspapers "to remind Americans everywhere in this hour of victory that we still have another major war to fight."[58]

Advertisements expressed gratitude for victory over Germany but reminded readers of further toil ahead. In Washington, D.C., a haberdashery published a large advertisement picturing the slashed faces of Adolf Hitler and Benito Mussolini beside a grinning Japanese officer. "Two Down, One to Go!" read the caption. A shoe store's full-page advertisement depicted Albrecht Durer's famous "Praying Hands" and called upon the public to forego rejoicing and adopt "a sense of solemn obligation."[59]

Comparable advertisements appeared in newspapers throughout the nation. In New York City, department stores and specialty shops published large displays reminding readers of the job ahead.[60] In Chicago, Marshall Field and Company department stores printed a two-page spread of a panicked Japanese soldier with ape-like hands and face, cowering in the enormous shadow of a bomber. "Little men, what now?" asked the caption.[61] A furniture store in Indianapolis published an advertisement that exhorted, "We've Got to Lick Japan!"[62]

Similar advertisements appeared in newspapers in smaller communities as well. In the southern Illinois city of Harrisburg, the *Daily Register*, as did numerous newspapers, published a special V-E Day edition containing advertisements reflective of common themes regarding the war and the Japanese.

and NOW it's YOUR turn, HIROHITO!

YOU figured it was in the bag, Hirohito!

Yes, sir, by this time—so you said—your buck-toothed boys would be marching up Pennsylvania Avenue, your fried-egg flag would be flying from the Capitol. And, you figured, the luxury-loving, so soft Yankees would be bowing low before your begoggled troops.

So sorry to disappoint! So sorry that honorable time-table has upset!

Yes, you figured that while your rug-chewing pal in Berlin kept us busy in the Atlantic, all **you** would have to do would be to follow up the Pearl Harbor stab with island hops that would bring you clear to our West Coast—and from there it would be just a sleeper jump to Washington.

Well, Hirohito, you know what's happened to Adolf. And now it's your turn. What you've gotten so far—in the Coral Sea, Midway, the Solomons, the Aleutians, Tarawa, the Philippines, Iwo and Okinawa—is just a pink tea to what's coming.

Because **now,** you're going to get the works . . . and fast! You're going to learn what it feels like to get in front of the biggest battle fleet in the world. You're going to learn—as Berlin learned—how it feels to watch your dreams of empire go up in the flame and smoke of four-ton block-busters. You're going to learn what it means to take a swipe at Uncle Sam when his back is turned.

You're going to wish you had never even heard of Pearl Harbor!

Fashion Palace

In its V-E Day edition, the *Harrisburg (Illinois) Daily Register,* like newspapers across the country, published advertisements that called for unrelenting warfare against Japan.

That Japan's attack on Pearl Harbor remained unavenged was a common theme in the media. *Harrisburg (Illinois) Daily Register.*

The fervent hope that an abundance of weaponry would enable the United States to quickly conclude the war was expressed in a display for the Hi-Way Tire Recapping Company, which said, "Let's shove the men, the ships, the guns, and the planes over there in an overwhelming, irresistible, avenging flood that will wind up this Jap business fast, once and for all!" Typifying the frequent admonition that the Japanese expected the United States to tire of fighting, another advertisement depicted three grotesque-looking Japanese officers drinking toasts to such an occurrence. The local Elks lodge sponsored an exhortation that compared the Japanese to rodents: "We're going to knock out Hirohito but it won't be easy. We must fight warily and wisely before our enemy is crushed. Rats are dangerous to the last corner."[63]

Avenging Pearl Harbor remained a prominent theme. One illustration in the *Daily Register* showed a muscular Uncle Sam, rolling up his sleeves as he stepped away from the body of a German soldier toward a terrified-looking, diminutive caricature of Emperor Hirohito. The caption claimed that Hirohito had vowed that his "buck-toothed boys would be marching up Pennsylvania Avenue" while the "luxury-loving, so soft Yankees would be bowing low before your begoggled troops. So sorry to disappoint! So sorry that honorable time-table has upset!" The advertisement threatened, "You're going to learn what it means to take a swipe at Uncle Sam when his back is turned. You're going to wish you had never even heard of Pearl Harbor!" The display for Mac's Goodyear store also emphasized vengeance with a large illustration of a memorial stone labeled, "Fallen at Pearl Harbor." Beneath the words "The Unavenged," it called for unrelenting war: "The shame of Pearl Harbor must be wiped out in blood."[64]

In an allusion to the prominence of fire in conducting the war, one illustration showed a large hand, presumably belonging to an enormous Uncle Sam since it protruded from a star-ornamented sleeve, holding a screaming Japanese over flames.

BUY BONDS
BURN TOKYO

Leo Richmond

This display bluntly reminded readers that fire had become an important weapon in the Pacific War. *Harrisburg (Illinois) Daily Register.*

"NOW! Let's Put the Heat on Hirohito. Buy Bonds. Burn Tokyo." In another advertisement a GI bayonetted a Japanese soldier. "He's still in there fighting. ARE YOU?" inquired the accompanying heading.[65]

So the media inundated people with exhortations to continue laboring for victory. In St. Louis, workers in area war production plants enlisted in "On to Tokyo Clubs" where they pledged to remain at their jobs until Japan surrendered.[66] The playwright Robert E. Sherwood composed a brief, poignant essay for *Collier's* in which he declined an invitation to a friend's V-E Day party, saying that thinking about the tough job of defeating Japan did not put him in a celebratory mood.[67]

Thus the government and the media attempted to gird citizens for the continuing struggle against the detested Japanese. All the martial rhetoric was probably numbingly familiar by 1945. Captious about the worn appeals for renewed dedication to the war, conservative columnist David Lawrence, writing in the Washington, D.C., *Evening Star* lamented the staging of victory celebrations while the war continued and faulted General Eisenhower for accepting invitations to large parades and receptions held in his honor in Washington, D.C. and New York City.[68]

He's still in there Fighting

ARE YOU?

Victory in Europe

Yes, there is peace in Europe tonight, but the battle is still raging in the Pacific . . . lives are being lost . . . boys are being maimed and ruthlessly shot down. Peace has come to Europe, but not to our boys in the Pacific. It is up to you to prove during the 7th War Loan Drive that you're still in there fighting, too . . . crushing Japan will be a big order, for us as well as our fighting men!

Let us continue to buy Bonds until TOTAL victory is ours.

WILEY'S AUTO SERVICE

This illustration exhorted readers to toil for victory. *Harrisburg (Illinois) Daily Register.*

One author later said that following Germany's defeat "there was a heady optimism in the air." The national mood was more accurately described at the time as "war weary, restless, irksome." *Newsweek* resisted characterizing the public as complacent, yet noted, "But upon too many millions. . . the hard, cold fact of the war still to be won in the Pacific lay lightly."[69]

From V-E Day until the war's conclusion Americans received contradictory messages about the issues related to ending the Pacific War. President Truman, members of Congress, government and military leaders warned citizens to brace for the arduous task of defeating Japan. Yet House Majority Leader John W. McCormack's remarks indicated that some people believed the most onerous period of the war had ended. The government also undercut its appeals to concentrate on winning the war. While leaders urged continued support of the war effort, the Department of Commerce sponsored an exhibit of models and drawings of forthcoming railroad passenger cars.[70]

No one doubted the certitude of victory. But the ferocity of Japanese resistance gave no indication of abating. Troubled by the rising casualty rates in the Pacific, most citizens dreaded the prospect of invading Japan and hoped that the war would end before such an assault occurred.

After the defeat of Germany, the most threatening and powerful member of the Axis coalition, civilians quite naturally gave more thought to the postwar world. With few exceptions, however, they greeted the news of Germany's surrender with restraint, in part because they had anticipated Germany's downfall for some time. They also recognized that Germany's defeat did not signal the end of America's responsibilities in Europe. Of course, the continuation of the Pacific War also inhibited celebratory response to Nazi Germany's capitulation. Newsreel footage of the festive cavorting by New Yorkers and the partially liquor-induced mayhem that occurred in San Francisco after the first reports of Germany's surrender have helped perpetuate a distorted view of reaction to the news.[71] The presence of newsreel cameras in Times Square probably contributed to the carnival atmosphere there that differed from the subdued response in most of the country. Those expressions of glee contrasted sharply with the more common reaction of quiet thankfulness that war in Europe had ceased.

The country was weary of war. As the great global conflict shifted to an effort directed entirely against Japan, Americans grew more apprehensive about the cost of achieving Japan's unconditional surrender. But they also began thinking more about domestic concerns and their postwar lives. They expectantly anticipated the war's conclusion, the return of millions of men and women from the armed forces, and the reuniting of families and loved ones.

The Japanese, however, remained defiant. Politicians, military leaders, and commentators tried to sustain public morale by reminding citizens of the formidable chore remaining, namely, winning final victory over Japan. Indeed, the exhortations in speeches, editorials, and advertisements resonated as entreaties one would hear at the beginning of a conflict. Of course, few foresaw that Japan would surrender by August 1945. Yet the urgency of the appeals that people remain dedicated to the war effort reflected the general concern about the public's morale.

Americans knew that the tremendous forces of the Allies could be redeployed to strike Japan. Yet with Japan now isolated and fighting alone, the moment appeared opportune to reevaluate the enemy in the Pacific. Indeed, in the war's final months dozens of articles and essays in the print media attempted to explain the nature of the Japanese. But endeavors to encourage more enlightened commentary about the Japanese had to contend with the dominant attitudes of U.S. citizens and their leaders, many of whom regarded the "Japs" as a uniquely fanatical enemy.

2

Images of the Enemy

He knew that Japan was an island off the coast of Asia inhabited by a preposterous musical comedy species of humanity.[1]

Shortly before his death on the isle of Ie Shima in 1945, Ernie Pyle, one of the most popular chroniclers of the war, wrote about American attitudes toward the Japanese. Making his first tour of the Pacific, Pyle quickly learned that "the Japanese were looked upon as something subhuman and repulsive; the way some people feel about cockroaches or mice." Listening to marines' accounts of combat affected Pyle, who described a group of Japanese prisoners "wrestling and laughing and talking just like normal human beings. And yet they gave me the creeps, and I wanted a mental bath after looking at them."[2]

Pyle's observations exemplified the intense loathing that Americans generally felt for the Japanese. His desire to cleanse himself after a mere glimpse of the enemy reflected widespread perceptions of the Japanese as particularly diabolical, savage foes. Although engaged in normal activity, the Japanese prisoners Pyle observed made him uneasy, and his prose conveyed the impression that he had confronted something alien. He vicariously confirmed the emotions of the many citizens who had never seen a Japanese person, yet considered "Japs" inherently cunning and brutal.

During the war, civilians' antipathy for the enemies in Europe often focused on individuals such as Adolf Hitler, Benito Mussolini, and prominent Nazis. Not so with regard to the Japanese. Although commentators and cartoonists ridiculed and scorned Japanese leaders such as Gen. Hideki Tojo, prime minister of Japan from 1941 to 1944, and Emperor Hirohito, hatred of the enemy in the Pacific tended to be directed against the Japanese people.[3] Similar castigation of Germans only occurred after the full disclosure of the horrors and depravity of the "Final Solution"—the German campaign to exterminate the Jews of Europe—following the liberation of German concentration camps by Allied armies.

Despite the enormity of the brutalities committed by Nazi Germany, Americans seldom regarded Germans as inherently treacherous or evil as they did the Japanese. Allied propaganda tended to differentiate between good and bad Germans, with atrocities portrayed as Nazi acts rather than behavior representative of the German people. Japanese cruelties also had greater impact because they more frequently victimized Americans than German abuses did.[4] Indeed, respondents to a Gallup poll published in June 1945 deemed Nazi leadership more responsible for German crimes than the German people. Conversely, 63 percent of those polled considered the Japanese people completely accountable for the abuse and killing of prisoners of war and regarded Japanese as intrinsically more cruel than Germans by a 5 to 1 margin. "In short," the poll concluded, "most Americans apparently think of the Japanese people as a barbaric lot, beyond the pale of civilized behavior, but consider the German people less so."[5] Wartime Hollywood films reflected the different attitudes toward the respective enemies. Although they frequently portrayed Nazis as sadistic, filmakers seldom ascribed them the malevolent savagery reserved for the Japanese.[6]

In an essay published shortly after the war, historian Allan Nevins discussed the enmity of Americans for the Japanese. "Probably in all our history no foe has been so detested as were the Japanese," he wrote. "Emotions forgotten since our most savage Indian wars were reawakened." Nevins believed the attack on Pearl Harbor engendered such feelings, adding that subsequent reports of atrocities committed against American prisoners of war further stimulated public anger.[7]

Nevins's reference to North American Indians acknowledged the racist ideology evident in American history from the colonial period onward. White Americans tended to categorize Native Americans and blacks racially as homogeneous groups and later associated various Asian nationalities likewise. Americans adopted the European legacy of fascination with images of an exotic Orient and fear of a sinister "Yellow Peril."[8] An editorial published in *Life* in May 1945 stated, "Americans had to learn to hate Germans, but hating Japs comes natural—as natural as fighting Indians once was."[9] This passage illustrated the wartime practice of likening the Japanese to peoples previously considered inferior savages, who also had to be eliminated.[10]

Racism influenced attitudes and perceptions of the Japanese, who were frequently described as subhuman or nonhuman and continually depicted as animals, most commonly rodents or apes.[11] When American soldiers discovered evidence of cannibalism among isolated Japanese troops on Leyte, Gen. Robert L. Eichelberger did not attribute it to severe deprivation but deemed it confirmation of his conviction that the Japanese "are much nearer the animal stage than one would suspect who has only traveled through Japan and seen the beauties of the place."[12]

Americans regarded Japanese in terms of the "Other." Japanese and Americans defined themselves and justified the war by portraying their enemy as a polar opposite. In characterizing the Japanese as primitive, militaristic, irrational savages with illogical thought patterns, Americans implicitly accepted the contrasting images of themselves as thoroughly modern, rational people guided by a basic devotion to peace and democracy.[13]

The fury roused by the Japanese attack on Pearl Harbor cannot be overestimated. It "provoked a rage bordering on the genocidal among Americans," historian John W. Dower has remarked, and remained the most frequently cited example of Japanese treachery throughout the war.[14] "Remember Pearl Harbor" became an instant rallying cry.[15]

Immediately after the attack, newspaper editorials exhibited stereotypical characterizations that became prominent during the war. The editors of the St. Louis Post-Dispatch delineated the war as pitting civilization against savages. They equated the assault to "a murderer in the dark, stealing upon his quarry unawares . . . The issue is force versus reason, savagery versus civilization." A few days later the editors said, "The little yellow men know now that the grim gray ships of an aroused Uncle Sam will seek them out and exact fearful vengeance."[16]

A surprise attack launched at dawn on a Sunday morning was thus transformed into a vicious murder stealthily committed in darkness. By describing the Japanese as lilliputian "yellow men" who would be methodically pursued by Uncle Sam's navy, the editors depicted the Japanese as a diminutive people to be picked off individually by more technologically advanced U.S. forces. Portrayals of the Japanese as "little men" remained common throughout the war, as did the theme of American technological superiority, expressed in this instance by ships seeking Japanese as if hunting them.

The editors of the Chicago Daily Tribune expressed a theme that became a staple perception of the Japanese: "The Japanese high command has outwitted itself. Its slant-eyed scrutiny of American psychology will prove to be very costly to the military government which sought a military advantage without counting the ultimate cost."[17] Calling the attack on Pearl Harbor illogical, this editorial employed a common motif that the Japanese mind was backward or upside-down. The phrase "slant-eyed scrutiny" fit with the stereotypical illustration of the Japanese that became a fixture in wartime cartoons, which often depicted Japanese wearing thick glasses. These portrayals implied both a physical and mental myopia that contributed to and epitomized the idea that the Japanese were inherently irrational.

The print media described Japanese as fanatical, ruthless, and diabolical. *Time* recounted the overwhelming civilian response to Pearl Harbor as "Why, the yellow bastards!"[18] The intense reaction resulted from the success of the attack, shock that American territory was struck, and anger over the deaths of a substantial number of servicemen. Humiliated at being caught unprepared and enraged that the assault came without warning, editorialists immediately characterized the Japanese as unscrupulous savages who neither gave nor asked for quarter. The rapidity with which such expressions of hatred occurred testified to Pearl Harbor's profound impact. Vengeful hostility combined with racist attitudes became a fundamental component of American dispositions toward the Japanese. Commentators told citizens that the United States faced an enemy beyond the pale of civilization, which implied the acceptability of any method of combating such a deviously savage foe.

Pearl Harbor remained an emotional touchstone throughout the war. Government leaders, military commanders, and commentators frequently described exacting retribution for the attack as a war aim. What constituted sufficient reprisal remained unclear, but nearly every military action was deemed retaliation for Japan's initial assault. Numerous speeches by government and military leaders on V-E Day invoked the bitter memory of Pearl Harbor as a means of rousing public support for the war ahead.[19] Rep. H. Carl Andersen (R-Minn.) said that the occasion marked "the beginning of the end for the Japanese Empire in just repayment for its scurrilous attack at Pearl Harbor." Rep. Charles A. Plumley (R-Vt.) declared: "Nothing but retributive justice can or will ever square the account we have to settle with those treacherous, barbaric, inhuman yellow devils, who, owing all that they had ever been and were or hoped to be, to us and our endeavors to make them civilized and prosperous, for 20 years and more prepared and waited for an opportunity to stab us in the back as they did at Pearl Harbor."[20] A former congressman warned, "More tough fighting must come before the Jap serpent that struck at Pearl Harbor has been beheaded."[21] An editorial published in *Life* in May 1945 reasoned, "Moreover, revenge is sweet; we have much to avenge since Pearl Harbor and Bataan."[22] Indeed, the *Indianapolis Star*, in a description of the dropping of the atomic bomb on Hiroshima, in August 1945 stated, "It left a wake of death and rubble as terrible vengeance for Pearl Harbor."[23]

The use of the pejorative terms "Jap" and "Nip" was omnipresent. Dehumanization of the Japanese continued unabated after V-E Day.

Hardly a rallying point by 1945, dehumanization appeared more a justification for killing any and all Japanese, soldiers or civilians.

Related to dehumanization was the continued comparing of combat against the Japanese to hunting. An article published in the *Washington Post* about Japanese stranded on Guam related, "Yank riflemen improve their aim by periodic Japanese hunts in the hills. It is about like jack rabbit hunting. You'd better get in your first shots because after that the prey has scurried."[24] Lt. Gen. Simon Bolivar Buckner, Jr., killed in action on Okinawa, characterized the struggle to drive Japanese soldiers from caves and underground fortifications on the island as "'prairie dog' warfare."[25] Journalists and military commanders also compared the Japanese to moles.[26] The journalist Fletcher Pratt labeled Japanese troops "the most persistent and effective burrowing animal the war has produced."[27] One Army officer said that, in contrast to German soldiers who slept at night, "the Jap is a night-crawler."[28]

Naval warfare against the Japanese was also compared to hunting. At the end of July 1945, Adm. William F. "Bull" Halsey, the most openly racist of American commanders, said, "What's left of the Jap navy is helpless, but just for good luck we will hunt them out of their holes."[29] Likening warfare against the Japanese to hunting underscored faith in American technological superiority by depicting U.S. forces in pursuit of a quarry that, like a hunted rodent, could only burrow and hide.[30]

In a graphic, moving article published in June 1945, the reporter Edgar L. Jones recounted the battle on Iwo Jima. He compared the bodies of dead Americans and Japanese, writing of the former, "The smell of one's countrymen rotting in the sun is a lasting impression." He considered the sight and smell of the Japanese corpses endurable, "mostly I think because a dead Japanese does not look quite human." He noted, "The yellow darkens and the bodies seem unusually small and characterless, like figures in a wax museum. One cannot look at them and be unmoved, but they lack the personal quality which grips the soul of an observer."[31]

Jones's nearly macabre reflections provided a grotesque example of dehumanization; he portrayed dead Japanese as less human than American bodies. The morbidity of making distinctions between two peoples by comparing corpses did not provoke letters of disapproval from readers of the journal that published Jones's article. Lt. Gen. Holland M. "Howlin' Mad" Smith, who boasted of his reputation as the worst "Jap hater" in the Marine Corps, expressed similar thoughts more crudely when he said, "When you see the little stinking rats with buck teeth and bowlegs dead alongside an American, you wonder why we have to fight them and who started this war." He added, "The Japanese smell—they don't even bleed when they die," although he claimed his loathing would be just as intense "if they bled like pigs."[32] Smith thus characterized Japanese as bloodless rodents.

Advertisements routinely dehumanized Japanese by using caricatures to convey patriotic themes and encourage continued support for the war. The Sperry Corporation promoted "The gunsight that 'thinks' faster than humans . . . or Japs!"[33] A widely reprinted advertisement for the seventh war bond drive in 1945 featured a picture of a smug-looking Japanese officer above the caption, "So sorry, please . . . still think *Yankees* are *inferior race!*" and exhorted civilians to make this bond drive "the one that *smashes* the savages!"[34] Similar displays frequently showed individuals posed as Japanese officers, sometimes grappling with American soldiers, and nearly always with crazed expressions.[35]

Advertisements also employed more subtle anti-Japanese imagery. In an advertisement captioned "Old Enemy Invades Home Anew," Revere Copper and Brass implored consumers to purchase new plumbing fixtures for their homes after the war. The accompanying illustration depicted a man and woman cowering from huge drops of water with Asian faces falling from the ceiling of their home.[36]

Even more bizarre was an advertisement for Skat mosquito repellent that portrayed an enormous mosquito, with a face both Asian and devilish, grinning maliciously as it menacingly hovered above a group of potential victims. The insect's forelegs resembled arms and ended in a pair of hands rubbing together in a gesture suggestive of nefarious intent. The mosquito's remarkably long proboscis looked like a samurai sword. Oblivious to the peril was a picnicking family. "Ready to STRIKE but . . . SKAT will drive them away!" proclaimed the accompanying caption.[37] The plural pronoun implied that more mosquitos lurked nearby. With its depiction of an idyllic American family engaged in peaceful activities while unknowingly threatened by an impending aerial assault, the advertisement served as a visual metaphor for the Japanese attack on Pearl Harbor.

Major newspapers endorsed the common characterizations of the Japanese. In June 1945 the *Washington Post* printed a photograph of a Japanese prisoner of war who had protruding front teeth and wore round glasses and the small cap of the Japanese army, all of which caused him to resemble the stereotypical Japanese depicted in war-time cartoons. The photograph's caption said, "Japs Really Look Like This."[38] In the war's final months, then, a respected newspaper tried to validate the accuracy of familiar caricatures by providing a living example.

Hostile attitudes toward the Japanese influenced subjects unrelated to the war. Beneath a headline suggestive of extermination, "Farm Agency Tips to Wipe Out Jap Beetle," a gardening column in the *Washington Post* offered suggestions for protecting plants from the Japanese beetle.[39] A similar article about Japanese beetles in the *Atlanta Constitution* declared that the state entomologist was leading a campaign "against the Jap menace on the home front in Georgia."[40] Both pieces likened Japanese to the insect bearing the name and equated precautionary measures for this pest to combat against the Japanese.

The often abominable behavior of Japanese soldiers throughout Asia—and the abuse of American prisoners in particular—angered Americans and reinforced stereotypical views of all Japanese as bestial savages. Earlier in the war the U.S. government prevented the publication of eyewitness reports of Japanese abuse. When an American escapee from a Japanese prison camp sold an option on a narrative of his experiences to the *Chicago Daily Tribune*, the army's Bureau of Public Relations warned the newspaper's editors that printing the account "would be contrary to public interest."[41] President Roosevelt and the Joint Chiefs feared that disclosure of Japanese atrocities might jeopardize ongoing efforts to send food and medical supplies to prisoners or even worsen their treatment. However, Roosevelt requested that the Joint Chiefs recommend "as to the moment when I should inform the country of the mistreatment of our nationals."[42]

Gen. George C. Marshall, chairman of the Joint Chiefs of Staff, believed that the problem required "the most careful handling." He suggested that the "storm of bitterness which will arise, once the public is aware of the brutalities and savagery displayed by the Japanese toward our prisoners, should be directed along carefully thought out lines rather than left to dissipate itself in a lurid press and unpredictable reactions." Secretary of War Henry L. Stimson proposed further gathering of facts regarding

Poised to attack, this gigantic mosquito with its distorted Asian features provided a visual metaphor for the assault on Pearl Harbor. Skol Company, *Life,* June 18, 1945, p. 106.

alleged atrocities, "free from the hysterical emotions that have attended the narrations thus far."[43]

The War Department belatedly instructed theater commanders to suppress atrocity accounts after officers of the Army Air Forces circulated a memorandum in November 1943 that graphically described the event soon known as the Bataan death march. The Office of War Information's (OWI) department on censorship objected, and OWI director Elmer Davis pressed the Joint Chiefs for complete disclosure. Davis feared that a letdown in public morale after Germany's defeat could generate support for a negotiated peace with Japan. He argued that "the Japanese enemy is much less widely understood" and claimed the widespread perception that the Japanese were "incomprehensible" made it "more difficult to demand of the nation the exacting sacrifices necessary to win the kind of victory that can be expressed in comprehensible terms." Revealing Japanese mistreatment of Americans, he believed, would help stiffen morale and perhaps prompt improved treatment of prisoners by the Japanese to avoid more adverse publicity.[44]

After further consideration the Joint Chiefs concluded that the release of the information would have a beneficial effect on public opinion and recommended publication of verified atrocity accounts. Roosevelt agreed, and the first reports of the infamous Bataan death march appeared in late January 1944.[45] During this grisly ordeal in April 1942, captured Americans and Filipinos, many already weakened by hard fighting, lack of food, and disease, endured a grueling march up the Bataan peninsula in the Philippines to prisoner of war camps. Japanese guards shot, beheaded, or bayoneted hundreds of Americans and thousands of Filipinos who collapsed from exhaustion or illness along the tortuous sixty-five-mile route.

The anger that these reports roused among ordinary citizens can perhaps be gauged by the rhetoric they evoked from the reserved General Marshall, who proposed a blistering public statement. "These brutal reprisals upon helpless victims," Marshall's draft said, "evidence the shallow advance from savagery which the Japanese people have made." He declared; "We serve notice upon the Japanese military and political leaders as well as the Japanese people that the future of Japan as a nation, in fact the future of the Japanese race itself, depends entirely and irrevocably upon their capacity to progress beyond their aboriginal barbaric instincts."[46]

After V-E Day the print media produced a veritable flood of articles about Japanese atrocities. The appearance of these stories at a time when national leaders feared a public letdown in the war effort was certainly not coincidental. Indeed, an editorial in the *New York Herald*

Tribune advised readers to maintain their morale by recalling "that Japanese atrocities, so incredibly bestial, are as bad or worse than anything of which the Germans, evil as they are, have been guilty."[47] Many of the reports concerned events from years earlier, and particular newspapers also printed articles about local servicemen who had witnessed atrocities or personally suffered abuse.[48]

Accounts of mistreatment provided by former prisoners of war now received prominent coverage.[49] A former captive recuperating in a naval hospital recalled the gruesome litany of beatings and beheadings he had witnessed, adding: "There are worse things I'd rather not tell. I don't think you could print them anyhow. Stories of personal mistreatment and cruelty. Beyond anything you could imagine. The Japanese aren't human."[50] Liberated airmen recounted deprivations they had observed and personally endured. Newspaper articles reported all manner of atrocities and described the horrid conditions of Japanese prison camps in explicit detail.[51] Japanese atrocities against native populations also received substantial publicity.[52]

Magazines and newspapers published photographs depicting atrocities. The most publicized, purporting to show a Japanese soldier preparing to behead an Allied airman, appeared in *Life*. Reprinted in newspapers across the country, it prompted one person to ask, "What in God's world can possess us to treat these beasts like human beings!" Another objected to the release of such graphic photographs, while one letter writer questioned the picture's authenticity.[53]

A few commentators criticized the publication of atrocity accounts. An editorial in *Atlantic Monthly* disapproved of "the effort to maintain our willingness to fight by atrocity stories, by viewing Japanese conduct of the war as stemming from racial barbarity or exotic peculiarity" and claimed that the reports obscured the principal reason for fighting Japan—to halt "totalitarian militarism and aggression."[54] Willis Church Lamott, a missionary in Japan before the war, argued that the Japanese were not inherently "warlike, cruel, cunning, unreliable, crafty, and generally loathsome people." For the sake of future peace, he contended, Americans must "stop thinking of them as being, racially, subhuman devils, monkeys without tails, or something slimy that crawled from under a rock."[55]

Dwight Macdonald, the editor of the radical journal *politics*, lamented the perpetuation of the image of "70 million bucktoothed grinning apes, whose totalitarian uniformity is only exceeded by their political fanaticism" and insisted that "the Japanese are people, not apes."

In a rare instance of a journalist evaluating the racial overtones to the Pacific War, George S. Schuyler, the associate editor of the *Pittsburgh*

Courier, one of the nation's leading African-American newspapers, charged that the enthusiasm for the war against Japan was "based largely on race hatred."[56] Likewise the journal *Crisis*, published by the National Association for the Advancement of Colored People, cautioned that as a "white-minded nation," Americans tended to demean people of color. "If we continue to maintain this attitude in the Pacific war," the editors said, "we may send more American boys to their deaths than we should."[57]

Summons for vengeance outnumbered appeals for reason. The *Washington Post* published excerpts of a letter purportedly written by an unidentified nun, recently escaped from China, who described the torture and execution of three captured U.S. fliers that she claimed to have witnessed in the city of Hankow. "There is nothing we can ever do to those Japs that is sufficient to pay back for what they are doing to our people," she declared. "I sincerely hope the people at home will not weaken and try to make our leaders give Japan an easy peace. It will be one of the most costly mistakes we ever made."[58] The letter captured the sentiments of numerous people on the home front. Even a nun could admonish the public to avoid any decrease of martial spirit and enthusiasm, and affirm that no punishment meted out to the Japanese equaled the retribution they deserved.

Atrocity accounts reconfirmed the belief of innate brutality in all Japanese, angering Americans and probably reinforcing the approval of any means of waging war against them. Indeed, the government cited atrocities as justification for incendiary bombing and later for the use of atomic bombs. This gave the atrocity accounts a rather ritualistic quality that tended to diminish the plight of those who suffered the abuse.[59] Of course, one cannot ignore the fact, as the historian John W. Dower has remarked, that the atrocities committed by the Japanese "frequently were so grotesque, and flaunted in such a macabre manner, that it is not surprising they were interpreted as being an expression of deliberate policy and a calculated exhibition of some perverse 'national character.'"[60]

General ignorance of Japan and its people made citizens more susceptible to embracing stereotypes. In a book published in 1944 that evaluated public opinion and attitudes toward a variety of issues related to the war, psychologist Jerome Bruner stated, "Probably never has a modern nation fought an enemy about which she knew so little as we do of Japan."[61] "Our press has been so busy hating the Japanese as an alien race that it has failed to provide us with any information as to what Japan and the Japanese are really like," complained Dwight Macdonald.[62] An Army publication of May 1945 concluded that "inadequate understanding" of the Japanese based upon "lack of interest

and lack of information" remained a problem for U.S. citizens and soldiers.[63] Indeed, even after more than three years of war, commentators
appeared baffled by the Japanese. "To most Americans the vast and
teaming lands of the Orient are still terrae incognitae," concluded an
editorial in the *New York Times*.[64]

The genesis of the idea that the Japanese were an inscrutable
people whose thinking was backwards or upside-down can be traced
to the writings of Jesuit missionaries in the sixteenth century. Anthropologists, historians, diplomats, and journalists with knowledge of
Japanese history, society, and culture often sustained this perception
in the twentieth century. Several anthropologists and psychologists
produced studies during the war that characterized the Japanese as a
collectively unstable, childlike people who possessed a primitive or
tribal mentality. As an explanation of Japanese aggression, numerous
anthropologists postulated that all Japanese possessed an inferiority
complex.[65] American journalists referred to this inherent inferiority
complex as a staple trait of the Japanese and an obstacle to peace.[66]

The idea that all Japanese possessed a backward or illogical mind
was evident in news accounts of the war. *Newsweek* called the appeals
by the Japanese government for all Japanese to form themselves into
suicide corps ludicrous but contended that they might appear logical
in a nation where "white is the color of mourning and black the color
of ceremony, where newspapers are read from right to left."[67]

Newsweek published a seven-part series by Maj. Compton Pakenham, a British military officer raised in Japan who spent six months
attached to a Japanese army regiment before the war. The editors introduced him as an "expert" on Japan and posited that the series intended
"to analyze the most important features of the Japanese mind and their
relationship to the war." The editors admitted that Americans had difficulty understanding "remote peoples" such as the Chinese, Indians, or
Arabs but argued that the "ideas and social systems of these peoples
have enough in common with our own so that there can be some comprehension at least." Japan, however, was "an absolutely unique nation," so different from any other "that nearly every action of the Japs
requires skillful interpretation." According to the editors, the "peculiar
Japanese mentality" influenced the nature of the war as much as military and geographic factors.[68]

In his first installment, Pakenham addressed what he called the
"suicidal streak in the Japanese character." Some paragraphs read like
passages from a wildlife guidebook: "In his native habitat the Jap is
roughly kind, hospitable, considerate, and generous. His humor is animal, and he loves laughter, gambling, and drinking." In characterizing the Japanese as coarsely affable creatures, Pakenham evoked a de-

piction applicable to the typical resident of a fraternity house on almost any college campus in the United States. His use of the term "native habitat" implied an inherent savagery lurking within every Japanese and portended his explanation of how that barbaric soul was animated: "But introduce the simple formula of unquestioned loyalty to the emperor and you have a grim fanatic... whose mind stops working."[69]

According to Pakenham, the typical Japanese soldier, once sent abroad in the name of the emperor, "begins by slapping the faces of white women and ends up a devil incarnate, boasting of what he did at Nanking, Hong Kong, and Manila."[70] It is revealing that Pakenham chose a white woman, suggestive of Western womanhood in general, as the representative initial victim of Japanese brutality. Sexual fears constituted an underlying theme in the "Yellow Peril" anti-Japanese rhetoric prevalent early in the war when the rapidity and scope of Japanese conquests stunned the Allies, and the threat of rape and actual rape by Japanese was a recurring motif in several wartime Hollywood films.[71] One of the most memorable "This Is the Enemy" posters published in *Life* magazine portrayed a lecherously grinning Japanese officer, brandishing a pistol and carrying a naked white woman over his shoulder.

The reference to Nanking reminded readers of the "rape of Nanking," a six-week rampage of looting, raping, and murder by Japanese forces after they entered the Chinese city in December 1937. Pakenham's allusion implied that the average Japanese soldier inevitably progressed from face slapping to rape.[72]

Other articles in the series discussed the psychological outlook of the Japanese and its influence on their conduct in the war. Pakenham's observations rested on the assumption that all Japanese shared a common psychology. When he discussed the Imperial Army's influence on Japanese society, Pakenham revived the timeworn concept of Asian inscrutability, saying that the army's power helped explain "the otherwise unexplainable nature and discipline of the enemy we are fighting."[73]

In further exploration of "the warped psychology" of the Japanese, Pakenham said that the war pitted the Allies against "a way of life, a set of unhealthy mental processes, an ingrained fixation by which a race has hypnotized itself." He warned that beyond defeating the armed forces of Japan, the Allies must disprove the myth of Hirohito's divinity. He described the Japanese as practitioners of a unique propensity for disregarding facts. This trait, which he considered the most troubling aspect of "the Jap mentality," made it nearly "impossible for a foreigner to exchange opinions or reach an understanding with a Jap."[74]

Under the guise of elucidating readers, Pakenham's essays re-inforced notions of the Japanese as incomprehensible, innately primi-tive foes. His ideas reflected aspects of American thought, but the editors of *Newsweek* apparently also intended to shape opinion to an extent by publicizing the views of a person they presented as an au-thority on Japan. They introduced Pakenham as a kind of wartime Sherlock Holmes, an experienced sleuth adept at deciphering the mystifying thought process of the Japanese and fashioning patterns from their otherwise inexplicable actions. According to Pakenham, rational discussion with Japanese was impossible; by implication, an enemy possessing the characteristics he ascribed could only be an-nihilated.

Japanese propaganda, which received extensive coverage in the American media, sometimes ostensibly affirmed dominant opinions of the Japanese. Representative of numerous similar broadcasts, an edi-torial from the *Nippon Times* read on Radio Tokyo cautioned that the Japanese people "cannot be defeated by any such tactics as the Ameri-cans may conceive upon premises of their own psychology."[75] The American media cited these and other statements as confirmation of the inherent irrationality and inscrutability of the Japanese.

To be sure, the content of broadcasts by Radio Tokyo often bor-dered on fantasy by attempting to portray adversity as advantageous. Not surprisingly, Americans responded incredulously when Japanese propagandists claimed that the destructive incendiary bombing of Japanese cities actually raised civilian morale by relieving individuals of concern about their personal belongings.[76] Yet the ridicule of this propaganda in the American print media through contemptuous head-lines and sarcastic prose now appears unusual when one considers how favorably the war had progressed.[77]

A representative example of the continued mockery of the Japanese occurred in late May 1945 when the War Department officially con-firmed what a number of people in several states already knew. Since late 1944, bomb-laden balloons launched from Japan had landed in the United States. In one tragic incident six people died after the bomb attached to a balloon they discovered exploded.[78] A Japanese army spokesman threatened further assaults from piloted balloons and charged that the U.S. government had not revealed the full extent of the resultant damage.[79] Response to this insignificant threat was often vitri-olic and derisive. An editorial in the *New York Herald Tribune* argued that the "desperate character" of the Japanese "suggests an insane hysteria, madder even than the Nazis" and concluded that the vision of manned balloons "leaves no doubt that only death or a straitjacket can render the hysteria harmless."[80]

The editors of the Washington, D.C., *Evening Star* described the balloons as "quaint and ineffectual to the point of being silly." Considering the effort indicative of Japan's technological inferiority to the United States, they compared the aerial assaults to "a bow and arrow trying to compete against modern guns" and dismissed them as "another example of Japan's peculiar tendency to do things too queer to be comprehensible to our western minds."[81] Such a comparison implied that Japanese resistance, like that of North American Indians in former times, was futile, technologically primitive, and ultimately incomprehensible.

Similar rhetoric dominated accounts of the shelling of Japan by the U.S. Third Fleet in July and August 1945. Rather than assess the military results of these operations, the media produced encomiums about the supposed psychological effects of the assaults on the Japanese. *Newsweek* pridefully noted it was the first time "the sacred soil of Japan" was shelled since 1864.[82] The *New Republic* also praised the "indignity" of shelling Japan's "sacred soil," a gesture that "struck at the walls of the enemy's stronghold, within sight of the firing slits in his coastal defenses."[83] The *Evening Star* cited the bombardment of Japan's "sacred soil" as proof that "their revered gods are no longer on the job."[84]

Whatever their psychological impact on the Japanese, these actions apparently provided a psychic boost for Americans. The exultant approval of the desecration of the enemy's inviolate ground, which confirmed the bogus nature of his deities, made the shelling commensurable to warfare of the Middle Ages. Carrying the analogy further, the *New Republic* compared the shelling to bombarding an enemy castle. For the media, the bombardment provided dramatic, bold proof of American military, technological, and cultural superiority.

Commentators and military leaders commented on the differences between Americans and Japanese. The columnist Robert Quillen, of the *Atlanta Constitution*, evaluated the mentality of Japanese and Japanese-Americans. He believed "the Jap" differed from whites "mentally as much as he differs physically. He not only has different ideas, but his mind works in a different way." Quillen said the atrocities committed by the Japanese "make the Jap seem almost sub-human. Trusting him with the white man's destructive inventions was almost like trusting an ape with a pistol." Although he conceded that Japanese soldiers fought with skillful courage, Quillen claimed that "a cornered rat" possessed the same qualities.[85]

Quillen then posed two questions that composed "the mystery" Americans must solve. "If the Jap in Japan is a stone-age brute, despite his cleverness in imitating white men, are the Japs in America a different species? Are they typical Americans, inside as well as outside?"

Quillen claimed that if one described all Japanese as similar, critics would denounce it as racial prejudice. He contended that individuals of any race "seem much like typical Americans if they are brought up in this country, not among many of their own kind but in a typical American environment, surrounded by all of America's advantages." Before the war, according to Quillen, Japanese-Americans, whom he called "American Japs," were worthy members of society. But he argued that was true of "every Jap in Japan who has tortured or murdered American boys. The beast didn't show until war gave it an opportunity. Who can know what was and is in the hearts of American Japs, or how their minds work?[86]

Quillen not only differentiated the Japanese from Americans in general, but distinguished them mentally and physically from Caucasians. He regarded Japanese as illogical and inhuman. He employed the two most pervasive animalistic depictions of the Japanese, apes and rats, finally simply calling them beasts. Insinuating that the Japanese could only mimic white men, he then questioned whether these inherent traits might ever be changed, even in Japanese-Americans who adopted all the advantages of a "typical" American upbringing. Quillen did not list the attributes of the surroundings that he considered superior, although one can assume he meant at least a middle-class, white lifestyle. By declaring that American society possessed benefits Japanese culture lacked, Quillen ignored the problem of racism in the United States, exemplified by the racist attitudes that permeated his writing.

One of the most unique examples of conjecture about Japanese mentality and behavior by a military leader came from Vice Adm. John S. McCain, who declared that Japanese men needed tougher women. Known for sporting the most ostentatious headgear of any naval commander, McCain praised American women for making their husbands do chores around the home like helping clean dishes. "That's the kind of thing that keeps our feet on the ground," he declared. Conversely, he believed Japanese men treated their spouses as domestic menials. Calling Japanese men "braggarts without brakes," he added, "They have no one to convince them of their unimportance and when we puncture their balloon it's too much for them. We're lucky we have the kind of women in America who take the starch out of us occasionally."[87] Probably unintentionally, McCain refuted the caustic assertions of author Philip Wylie, who three years earlier bemoaned the overprotection of young males by domineering, dictatorial "Moms."[88]

An editorial in the *New York Times* was indicative of American ignorance about Asia in general and Japan in particular. "We must study this unknown Orient," it said, "and we must try to understand the psychological tides that rise and fall there." The editors also contended that citizens should learn about "the crafty enemy" because postwar stability in Asia depended in part on "an enlightened opinion and understanding here at home."[89] The editorial exemplified the dilemma of common attitudes by calling for heightened understanding of the Japanese while simultaneously characterizing them as inherently devious.

Stereotypical depictions of the Japanese remained pervasive after V-E Day. The emphasis on vengeance did not make clear when the war could be ended or whether it helped achieve lasting peace. The government would have done better to emphasize, as some observers contended, the importance of abolishing Japanese militarism rather than contributing to the belief that all Japanese were inherently savage and equally complicit in Japan's expansionist policy. Characterizing the war as a battle against irrational fanatics implied that the war could not be ended on rational terms. The publication of photographs purporting to prove that Japanese really resembled the caricatures of them and the continual deprecation of Japanese as technologically primitive indicate that by 1945 most people gave these commonplace stereotypes little thought.

Providing Maj. Compton Pakenham, a British officer, the forum of a major news magazine to express his "expert" opinions about Japan demonstrated the interlocking of American attitudes with those pervasive in Western thought toward Asians. The media also perpetuated stereotypes in its reporting of Japanese propaganda broadcasts. Rather than evaluate these statements as propaganda, the media ridiculed them as proof of Japanese irrationality and simultaneously cited them as accurate reflections of Japanese attitudes and intentions. Citizens who enjoyed the derision of Japan's bomb-laden balloons probably would have been surprised to learn that earlier in the war President Roosevelt had approved a project to attack Japan with bats carrying small incendiary bombs.[90]

Isolated examples of dissent appeared amidst the predominant opinions. Coexistent with the persistent hatred of the Japanese was an impatience for the war's end. Numerous government and military leaders, aware of these competing societal tensions, feared that the public lacked the fortitude necessary for accomplishing Japan's final defeat. Commentators, government officials, and military leaders discussed the issue of the war's duration. It was a contradictory dialogue, shaped by, and often warped by, the pervasive stereotyped attitudes toward the Japanese.

3

How Long Will This War Last?

Victory in Europe had been won, but peace seemed far away.[1]

By V-E Day the United States had been at war for nearly forty-one months. It was the nation's longest conflict since the Civil War and the lengthiest against an overseas enemy since the War for Independence. Concerned about a letdown in morale after Germany's surrender, American leaders and numerous commentators tried to bolster public fortitude by cautioning that achieving Japan's unconditional surrender could take considerable time. Yet leaders feared that a war of indeterminate duration might undermine public support. Warnings of a prolonged struggle only encouraged supposition about the war's length.

Throughout the war, leaders in Washington doubted Americans' ability to endure a long conflict.[2] In 1944, the Joint Chiefs of Staff received complaints about various political and military leaders who predicted impending surrenders by Germany or Japan. The White House subsequently issued a memorandum to the heads of numerous federal agencies, instructing them to discourage speculative statements about the war's duration.[3] Admiral Ernest J. King, chief of naval operations, was particularly concerned about public support for the Pacific War. One of the journalists with whom King held regular informal discussions later recalled that the exacting commander worried "that pressure at home will force a negotiated peace, before the Japs are really licked."[4] Gen. George Marshall, head of the Joint Chiefs of Staff, later contended that a democracy cannot tolerate a lengthy war. He said that in order to sustain public morale, the Allies had to devise and meet timetables that demonstrated continual progress toward victory.[5]

By May 1945 the Allies had decimated Japan's naval and air forces. Incendiary bombing was steadily reducing Japanese cities to ashes. Yet bitter fighting continued. Unlike the end of the war against Germany, which culminated with Allied armies converging on the ruins of the Third Reich, the land combat against Japan involved smaller forces engaged in battles of attrition. The campaigns on Okinawa and in the

Philippines proceeded without the prospect of rapid advances. The military commentator Hanson W. Baldwin, writing in the journal *Foreign Affairs* observed, "Japan has already lost the war in the Pacific, though we have not yet won it."[6]

Commentaries in the print media that described the Japanese as irrational fanatics also expressed frustration at Japan's continued defiance. An editorial in the Washington, D.C., *Evening Star* surmised that the Japanese comprehended the hopelessness of their situation. Yet it lamented that their resistance was "becoming fiercer than ever—grim, unyielding, wildly fanatical, a terrible business of battling to the death, with no quarter asked and none given."[7]

The war's slowing pace and its remoteness from the national heartland contributed to apprehension about the public's patience. Former New Deal adviser Raymond Moley, a columnist for *Newsweek*, urged "using every possible means to crack into the Jap mind" out of concern for "what may happen in this country if, as is likely, things go more slowly and more bitterly in our war effort." He added, "Mutterings of appeasement are already audible."[8]

An Army booklet published in May 1945 declared that the nation faced the most dire morale problem in its history.[9] In late May, Fred Vinson, the director of the Office of War Mobilization and Reconversion, told the Joint Chiefs of Staff about a prevailing sense of "restlessness and nervousness that does not augur well." Vinson, who claimed he "never saw the people in their present frame of mind before," believed that distress about the war and concern over reconversion, unemployment, and food shortages fostered the agitation.[10] The Joint Chiefs, who did not agree about when the war might end, did not offer solutions for public discontent. Privately, Chief of Staff Adm. William Leahy noted that he did not anticipate Japan's unconditional surrender in 1945.[11] However, General "Hap" Arnold, commander of the Army Air Forces, anticipated Japan's imminent collapse. By May 1945, he later wrote, the war with Japan was "in the bag, as far as creative work was concerned."[12]

Implored to stay dedicated to the war effort so that Japan could be quickly defeated, the public was simultaneously warned to expect a war of indefinite length. Commentators reiterated the idea that the peculiar psychology of the Japanese and their tenacious resistance made it nearly impossible to predict the war's end. Acting Secretary of State Joseph Grew, the former ambassador to Japan, claimed that his previous diplomatic experience provided him a unique understanding of the Japanese mentality. Rather than being discouraged by Germany's surrender, he asserted, the Japanese "are capable of finding a mad sense of glory in fighting alone," and he cautioned that Allied forces "have a tough and bloodstained road ahead." Grew proclaimed that the Japanese were prepared to fight a solitary total war, and he said that all of them, even women and children, remained dedicated to killing Americans.[13]

Other leaders also predicted further savage fighting. Admiral Leahy's comments resembled remarks made by fellow members of the Joint Chiefs around V-E Day when he warned that the United States had "a long road to travel before victory."[14] In a speech delivered in July 1945, Under Secretary of War Robert P. Patterson declared, "We must prepare ourselves to win our war with Japan the hard way—by killing Japanese soldiers right thru the ruins of Tokyo and thruout the home islands."[15] His remarks suggested that despite the devastation that Allied forces had inflicted on Japan, the war could only be ended by the methodical elimination of all Japanese troops.

Several members of Congress stressed the unpleasant prospect of protracted war.[16] Speeches intended to sustain public support for the war were not new. However, by emphasizing further military action against Japan, government officials and military commanders engendered rather than quelled conjecture about the war's length.

Numerous essays and editorials admonished the public to expect an extended war, a theme expressed in the title of a representative editorial from the Saturday Evening Post: "If We Expect a Long War, Let's Act That Way!"[17] "Too many people still consider the Japanese war a minor-league fray, one which can be ended without straining," observed an editorial in the Atlanta Constitution.[18] When he returned from a tour of the Pacific in May 1945, correspondent Kyle Palmer said that civilians should steel themselves for further fighting: "If there is even the slightest slackening of the war effort at home it will mean the needless loss of American boys." In a talk a few days after his initial interview, Palmer estimated that between 500,000 and one million more American fighting men would probably die before the war's end. This estimate subsequently appeared in other articles and was cited by both Secretary of War Stimson and President Truman after the war as influencing the decision to use atomic weapons on Japan.[19]

Public events reflected citizens' concerns. At the annual "I Am an American" celebration in Chicago in May 1945, a crowd of forty thousand assembled in Soldier Field listened to patriotic speeches and viewed a reenactment of the raising of the American flag on Mount Surabachi on Iwo Jima. Numerous veterans' organizations participated in the ceremony, as did several movie stars including Lauren Bacall and Humphrey Bogart. Gen. Alexander A. Vandegrift, commandant of the

U.S. Marine Corps, told the crowd, "If Japanese war leaders can detect any lessening of our fighting spirit, any willingness to lose heart in our task, they will have a ray of hope."[20]

Vandegrift reiterated an omnipresent theme: the Japanese would interpret signs of war weariness as a signal that the United States was ready to quit the war and negotiate. Americans often heard that the Japanese considered them a soft, decadent people, unable to endure the bloodshed and sacrifice required of a prolonged conflict. Indeed, the public could appreciate the sentiments of Carey Orr's cartoon "Endurance Contest," published in the *Chicago Daily Tribune*, in which Uncle Sam repeatedly struck a rooster dubbed "Japan" on a chopping block labeled "Hope of Tiring Out America," with a hatchet inscribed, "One Defeat After Another." "If You Can Stand It—I Guess I Can!" exclaimed the determined Uncle Sam.[21]

The editors of the *New York Times* lashed out against public complacency. In one commentary they said that reports indicating civilians' preoccupation with their own concerns made "good propaganda for the Japanese and encourages them to think that we may not pay the bitter cost of exacting unconditional surrender." Using the contradictory rhetoric frequently applied to the Japanese, the editorial characterized them as a formidable yet inferior foe, adding, "By temperament the Japanese have more patience than we have; they can afford to wait." The implication that a more technologically advanced nation lacked the forbearance of a less mechanized society reflected the public's sense of frustration that Allied superiority in weaponry did not appear to be accelerating the war's pace. The editorial, which called the Japanese "our personal enemies," was intended to jolt the "comfortable security" of citizens and linked public steadfastness with successful prosecution of the war.[22]

Several syndicated military commentators cautioned readers not to assume that Japan's capitulation was impending. Hanson W. Baldwin said that years of protracted combat could lie ahead and posited that Japan might attempt to negotiate when its leaders believed American morale had reached its nadir. Resolute determination, he concluded, would dissuade the Japanese from believing that the United States sought a bargained settlement.[23] The military writer Fletcher Pratt faulted the public for its impatience to return to "the business of putting two cars in every garage.'"[24] In June, *Newsweek* announced that it would continue publishing the "War Tides" column written by the retired admiral William V. Pratt, who said that he welcomed the opportunity to counter the opinions of those who believed Japan would soon fall.[25]

The War Department disclosed that the redeployment of troops from Europe to the Pacific would require several months.[26] One report described the task as the most logistically difficult and the most demanding on public morale in the nation's history.[27] Gen. Brehon Somervell, the caustic chief of the army's Services of Supply, pointed out that the fourteen thousand miles separating the European and Pacific theaters constituted a far greater distance than soldiers were transported prior to the invasion of France in 1944, a process that required two years. Referring to the high casualty rate on Iwo Jima, he compared its 8 square miles to the 148,000 square miles of the Japanese home islands, which he implied must be captured. Somervell emphasized the length of time needed to transfer men and supplies to the Pacific. Yet he argued that the longer the United States waited to "hit Japan with everything we have, the more time the Japanese will have to prepare for us and the more Americans will die."[28]

Computations of the amount of territory held by Japan, such as those by General Somervell, served as grim measures of the expanse that Allied forces had yet to conquer. Frequently these estimations did not distinguish effectively isolated areas and included regions the United States was unlikely to invade, such as northern China and Korea. In May 1945 the Foreign Economic Administration announced that the Allies had captured less than 7 percent of the nearly three million square miles controlled by Japan. Its report also cautioned that the "inner zone" consisting of Japan, Korea, Manchuria, and northern China contained numerous industries and substantial stockpiles of strategic materials.[29] The ABC radio network commentator Raymond Gram Swing cited the account as proof that, despite the devastation caused by bombing, Japan could continue fighting for some time.[30]

A Gallup poll reported that 42 percent of the respondents expected the war to last until 1946, while 20 percent anticipated it would continue until 1947 or beyond.[31] In July 1945, Gen. Douglas MacArthur reportedly concurred with predictions that the war would rage until the end of 1946.[32] The journalist Mark Gayn predicted fighting until 1947.[33] As late as the first week of August 1945, Lt. Gen. Alexander M. Patch, commander of the Fourth Army, admonished against optimism that Japan might suddenly capitulate. He said citizens remained confused because "they know in their minds that we are still at war. But in their hearts they find it hard to believe we have not already won."[34]

The public understood that the transfer of men and supplies to the Pacific would take several months. However, implications that the war would be in a holding pattern in the meantime belied ongoing combat and contributed to public impatience. Media commentators, politicians, and military leaders often described the juncture as a lengthy interlude, which only stimulated conjecture about how to speed the war with available forces.[35]

An editorial in the *Atlanta Constitution* acknowledged the necessity of moving forces from Europe to the Pacific but recognized a competing tension: the public's desire for rapid victory.[36] A similar editorial published in the *New York Times* called for steadfastness in "this terrible battle for American independence" and admitted, "Victory relieves the anxiety that spurs a nation on."[37]

Forewarning the public to expect a lengthy conflict while simultaneously calling for a timely triumph, leaders and commentators offered rather contradictory pleas for citizens to remain focused on the war. Emphasizing speed undercut appeals for endurance, as several members of Congress exhorted civilians to work for an early victory.[38] Rep. A. Leonard Allen (D-La.) called expeditiously ending the war "an obligation we owe to our heroic dead." Americans, said Rep. Charles M. LaFollette (R-Ind.), must remain disciplined "if we honestly wish to honor the dead and the permanently crippled."[39]

This rhetoric resembled entreaties made since man first initiated the tragedy of war. It linked public support and public sacrifice as integral components of the national effort to attain victory. Infusing death in combat with a higher meaning harkened to venerated oratory such as Abraham Lincoln's address at Gettysburg. Rapidity was emphasized because no one desired a prolonged war. Combining the traditional theme of victory in honor of the dead with speedy triumph as homage to those who had died marked an important change. These statements outlined a morality in which actions considered immoral in peacetime, such as incinerating civilians, became deeds that fulfilled the aims of a contrasting morality: decisive, quick victory that honored the deceased. An article in the *St. Louis Post-Dispatch* matter-of-factly expressed such sentiments when it declared "everything possible will be done to bomb, burn and starve the Japanese to defeat."[40]

Optimism that Japan might suddenly surrender, perhaps sustained in part by the belief that the Japanese were unpredictable, could not be entirely suppressed.[41] H.V. Kaltenborn, radio commentator for NBC, remarked on V-E Day, "The end for Japan may not be as far off as we once thought."[42] In June, Clarence Cannon (D-Mo.), the chairman of the House Appropriations Committee, averred that certain "military authorities" had informed him the war would be of long duration only if Japan did not surrender within 90 days.[43] Columnist David Lawrence predicted that Japan would capitulate by Christmas.[44]

Of equal import to speed of triumph was its cost. One article quoted an unidentified but "famed" military leader who described the nation's task as defeating Japan "without bleeding us to death."[45] Leaders and commentators endorsed using technology to minimize casualties. Throughout the war the government and popular culture had lauded American prowess in manufacturing massive quantities of weaponry and supplies. Numerous documentary films produced by the military diminished the plight of soldiers and instead emphasized the sheer volume of weaponry which provided the firepower that overwhelmed the Axis forces. This antiseptic depiction of war removed the elements of human suffering and death.[46]

Popular culture sometimes likened American fighting men to machines.[47] Advertisers contrasted Japanese reliance on "picks and shovels, baskets and little ricksha carts" with American supremacy in machines such as the bulldozer. In one advertisement, a soldier praised a power shovel he dubbed "Faith" because of its ability to "move mountains." "Bring on your Japs," the GI challenged, "Faith'll fix 'em!" Fondness for technology exemplified the "American way," celebrated by advertisers.[48] In a series of advertisements produced by Nash-Kelvinator, fictional servicemen proclaimed their love of engines and factories. "I never had a girl," gushed an aircraft mechanic in one illustration, who proclaimed that at age sixteen he fell in love with an engine. That first paramour had been replaced by a newer, more powerful motor "waiting for me now back home." Despite his embrace of technology, with its obvious implication of modernization and change, the man longed to return to his hometown, "where I want *everything* just as I left it." A pilot praised the engine of his plane as "this friend, this almost human thing" and yearned for "the noise and the heat, the beat and pace of the factory," where after the war he would help produce even more advanced motors.[49]

Citizens accepted the extensive use of flamethrowers and napalm against entrenched Japanese forces as means of minimizing casualties and hastening the war's conclusion. Commentators cited these weapons as further proof of American technological superiority. In a newspaper photograph headed "Squirting Hell" that showed a soldier firing a flamethrower, the caption explained, "The flame completely covers the pillbox and the dying screams of the burning Jap end another milestone on the road to Tokyo."[50] The prose approvingly noted the weapon's thoroughness and resembled the text of wartime advertisements that lauded products for their efficiency in killing Japanese.

Numerous commentaries in the media considered overwhelming firepower the best means of shortening the war and reducing casualties. The greater the amount of weaponry and supplies built up in the Pacific, observed an editorial in the *New York Times*, "the more quickly the war can be won and, what is more important, the more cheaply it can be done in human lives."[51] "Everyone agrees that the Japanese military position is hopeless," stated an editorial in the journal *Commonweal*. "Defeat is a mere question of time. But that time is measured in terms of lives."[52]

Thus, victory became defined as ending the war swiftly with minimal casualties. Rep. Edward H. Rees (R-Kans.) called for fortitude and prayers so that U.S. forces could "conquer this last stronghold of barbaric aggression with minimum casualties."[53] At a press conference held shortly after V-E Day, Secretary of War Henry Stimson vowed, "We intend to make sure that our men in this theater have all the advantages of superiority in numbers and in weapons . . . thereby the war against Japan will be brought to a swifter end and our casualties will be kept down."[54]

Depicting an enormous steamroller, the "Allied War Machine," which bore a banner emblazoned with Remember Pearl Harbor, moving toward a tiny Japanese, a concurrent cartoon in the *New York Herald Tribune* captured the idea of reliance on technological abundance. Although a soldier was seated at the steamroller's controls, the machine appeared to be moving on its own momentum. Other soldiers on the steamroller looked diminutive in comparison to the machine. Materiel abundance diminished the fighting men, who in this portrayal occupied an ancillary role as they sped onward aboard a mechanized juggernaut.[55]

President Truman emphasized speed at the beginning of his special message to Congress on June 1. "The primary task facing the Nation today is to win the war in Japan," he declared, "to win it completely and to win it as quickly as possible. For every day by which it is shortened means a saving of American lives." Truman cautioned that despite efforts to provide fighting men superiority in weaponry and supplies there was "no easy way to win" against "strongly entrenched and fanatical troops." Still, in point three of a four-point policy for defeating Japan he called for "massive concentrations" of supplies and weapons to "gain victory with the smallest possible loss of life."[56] The editors of the *New York Times* applauded Truman's vow to fight the war as efficiently as technologically possible, saying that the strategy would save lives.[57]

The War Department's supply bill, containing a pledge by the army to hasten Japan's defeat by "an overwhelming application of force," went to the floor of the House of Representatives in late June 1945. In contrast to previous years when most testimony before the Appropriations Committee remained secret, the government published a considerable amount of General Marshall's and General Arnold's remarks. Marshall stressed speed as the uppermost concern: "Economy in lives and material, as well as the psychology of the American people, demand that we mount a swift, powerful offensive forcing a victory at the earliest possible date."[58]

The incendiary bombing of Japanese cities combined with the naval blockade of Japan prompted conjecture about whether the Japanese could long withstand such severe destruction and deprivation.[59] An article based on conversations with unidentified U.S. military strategists commented that Japan would surrender when its military defeat became "obvious," although the article cautioned this might not occur until Japan was invaded. In addition, the war's duration would be determined by Japan's leaders.[60]

Citizens often read and heard that the war's length depended both on their perseverance and the endurance of Japanese leaders. No one pointed out the contradiction of awaiting a decision by enemy leaders portrayed as irrational and unpredictable. Victory was frequently defined as convincing the Japanese that they were beaten. An editorial in the *Los Angeles Times* stated, "There is nothing to indicate the Japs are ready to throw in the sponge, but it is a question how much more pressure the Jap mentality can stand."[61] "It is almost incredible that even the Oriental mind can be so lacking in understanding as to prefer national hara-kiri to surrender and an opportunity for national survival," bemoaned an editorial in the *Indianapolis Star*.[62]

Columnist Gladstone Williams, of the *Atlanta Constitution*, frequently addressed the issue of the war's duration. In spite of his habitual assertions that the Japanese were inherently illogical, Williams thought incendiary bombing combined with the prospect of starvation should "bring the Tokyo warlords to their senses. . . . It just does not make sense that a nation of people, however strange and uncivilized they may be, can commit themselves to total destruction."[63] He contended that despite the peculiarities of the Japanese mind, intelligent Japanese must recognize that the war was lost. If "an ounce of brains" remained among Japan's leaders, they would surrender before Japan was destroyed.[64] Williams overlooked the fallacy of his conclusion that force constituted the only method of compelling people to behave as he expected.

Other commentaries offered similar observations. The editors of the Washington, D.C., *Evening Star* called the Japanese mad to continue fighting.[65] Commentators simultaneously described Japanese as insane, unpredictable barbarians and deduced that Japanese leaders would make reasonable judgments, because failure to do so constituted madness.

Mindful of prevailing perceptions of Japanese irrationality, other observers remained less certain about Japan's leaders making temperate decisions. "Nobody knows what the Japs are going to do," declared the correspondent Kyle Palmer. "They're an unpredictable lot." Palmer implied that the Allies would eventually have to employ any available weapon to defeat Japan.[66] Rep. Jed Johnson (D-Okla.) said that he, and he believed, most people, hoped for Japan's immediate unconditional surrender but did not expect it.[67] Japanese mentality was regarded as a Gordian knot. "But how long can this mental attitude be maintained?" asked an editorial in the *Evening Star.* "Nobody knows. The Japanese mentality is difficult to understand."[68]

An editorial in the June 1945 issue of *Fortune* summarized the problems of analyzing the Japanese psyche and argued that "common sense" dictated that Japan surrender immediately. For the Japanese, the editors observed, the issue of peace involved the "highly dissimilar" Japanese society and "the Japanese mind that holds the society together." Unlike the Germans, the editors said that the Japanese did not understand the concept of capitulation. "What Japan needs," they wrote, "is a symbolic act in tune with high and ancient Japanese tragedy." The editors concluded that no one could predict the actions of Japan's leaders and that the Japanese were most concerned with "the survival of the Japanese mind with all its paradoxes of exaggerated restraint and extreme excess, all its wild dreams of an evanescent moment of blood and glory."[69]

Belief in an unfathomable Japanese mentality resistant to reason spawned conjecture that the Japanese would have to be annihilated. Journalist Jesse F. Steiner queried, "Will the war end only when the entire nation is annihilated?"[70] "It may be stated very flatly that no nation is so psychologically prepared to fight to the bitter end of annihilation," said an editorial in the *Washington Post.*[71] An essay in the *Atlanta Constitution* apocalyptically proclaimed that there was "nothing to indicate that we won't literally have to eliminate them from the face of the earth before they ever cease fighting."[72] Rep. Dean P. Taylor (R-N.Y.) declared in a V-E Day speech, "As Americans, we must realize how very important it will be to our future welfare to totally annihilate the Jap."[73] "They are a brutal, savage, vicious race," remarked Adm. Frederick C. Sherman, "and I think the world would be a lot better off if a good many of them were exterminated."[74] The *Los Angeles Times* lauded a local regiment that was helping, its commanding officer remarked, "to exterminate the Japs."[75]

Given the options of annihilation or surrender, the columnist Merlo Pusey said that most civilians believed the Japanese would choose annihilation.[76] A cartoon, originally published in the *Buffalo Evening News*, showed a bedraggled Japanese officer in a scorched uniform standing amidst flames asking, "To Be or Not To Be?" as he held a paper labeled "Capitulation or Annihilation?"[77]

The reporter Edgar L. Jones, who described the war in Europe as gentlemanly in comparison with combat in the Pacific, deemed the Pacific War a Manichean struggle for survival: "The Pacific war is not so much between two armed forces as between two peoples. . . . it is a war of extermination between Americans and Japanese. The showdown battle is not being fought for political, economic, or social theories, but for survival."[78] A letter printed in the Washington, D.C., *Evening Star* contended that in this "war to the death" the United States' existence depended on Japan's destruction: "There can be no compromise with those subhuman fiends. Earth is too small for that. Ultimately either we or they shall perish. Their islands must be isolated, bombed, burned and starved until the Japs are exterminated. God help us if we turn soft."[79]

Because civilians in Japan had become targets such remarks contained a pungency lacking earlier in the war. Exasperated by negative public reaction to casualties at Tarawa in 1943, the correspondent Robert Sherrod had charged that Americans simply did not grasp the horrific realities of modern war. He said that the Japanese could only be defeated "by extermination."[80] In 1943, such statements applied to Japanese soldiers. By 1945, they encompassed all Japanese.

Commentaries relied on assessments of Japanese temperament and character to predict the war's length. Japanese soldiers, whom an editorial in the *New York Herald Tribune* said possessed a "strange, medieval armor of fanaticism," received scrutiny as did Japanese civilians.[81] Responding to rumors that Japan might attempt a negotiated peace, an editorial in the *New York Times* admonished readers to remain resolute in their disdain for the Japanese. The United States faced "a nation more savage, more fanatical, more cunning, more indoctrinated with the notion of its own racial superiority, more impregnated with hatred of all foreigners, and above all far more ready to fight to the last man and die than the Germans ever were."[82]

Described as exceeding that of the Nazis, Japanese fanaticism was frequently cited as a cause for the war's duration. An editorial in the *New York Times* noted that although the Japanese lacked the numerical strength of Germany's armed forces, "the individual Japanese is imbued with a religious fanaticism such as was shown only by the most insane Nazis, and he has nearly always fought to the death."[83] A military summary in the *New Republic* said that "a Japanese force becomes most dangerous and inflicts the heaviest casualties at precisely the point where a German army begins to break up into mass surrenders."[84] The journalist Brooks Atkinson argued, "Japanese warfare can be as baffling as the warfare of the American Indian which bewildered the well-trained British troops. Even when his situation is hopeless he kills until he is killed. Although he is less modern than the Nazi he is far more fanatical."[85]

Despite the tenacity of Japanese resistance, some observers denigrated the character and fighting ability of Japanese soldiers. The aforementioned Maj. Compton Pakenham explored the relationship between his concept of inherent Japanese psychology and the behavior of Japanese troops. As an officer in the British army before the war, Pakenham was attached to an infantry regiment of the Imperial Army for six months. He consistently expressed a low opinion of all Japanese and regarded Japanese army officers as coarse and provincial. He depicted the typical Japanese "military mind" as one "blandly confident in its destiny."[86]

In an essay entitled "How the Jap Learns to Fight as He Does," Pakenham described the grueling training of Japanese soldiers, which centered around ceaseless marching and drilling. During the lengthy marches in which he participated, he found the Japanese officers "merciless, perpetually driving their men and not above using physical force—a slap on the face or an occasional kick." When the column fell out, Pakenham noted that officers "became nurses, tending a blister, shifting a pack, or helping an exhausted man to a drink." He prided himself on resisting surreptitious offers of extra water or rides on a colonel's horse because acceptance would have caused him to "lose face." By calling Japanese officers nurses Pakenham implied that they possessed an inherent weakness of character, a femininity that he deemed unsuited for the masculine art of soldiering. He viewed this "overdone paternalism" as an advantage for the Allies and believed Japanese troops lacked initiative. The training of recruits, he noted, emphasized attack rather than defensive preparations.[87]

Pakenham considered Japanese troops completely dependent on their superior officers. "When the command throws in the sponge," he declared, "the bewildered soldiery is lost. The resourceless conscript can only hole up like a rat and pray for a quick but expensive end." He did not explain the obvious discrepancy of soldiers he deemed incompetent organizing staunch resistance in every campaign in the Pacific. Commenting on Allied firepower during the campaign on Okinawa, he observed that the "effect on the child mind of the Jap conscript . . . must have been devastating. That this putty-minded clod held out through weeks of concentrated bombardments . . . shows the stubbornness of the resistance our men have been up against." Although he did not address the contradiction of denigrating troops trained only for offensive combat while admitting they displayed defensive tenacity, Pakenham concluded that Japan's breaking point must be first reached at the top. Once Japan's leaders accepted defeat "and ceremonially degutted themselves, the natural docility of the people will reassert itself and they will try to find their own way out."[88]

Ultimately, then, Pakenham relied on the perception of the Japanese as violent, wayward children to conclude that all Japanese would surrender when their leaders capitulated. This contrasted with claims that all Japanese would fight when Allied forces invaded Japan. He did not clearly explain how the United States should convince Japanese leaders that Japan was defeated. Published evaluations of Japanese troops by American officers concurred with some of Pakenham's assertions. Barrett McGurn, an army sergeant, complimented Japanese soldiers for their stamina, bravery, and adept use of camouflage. He considered Japanese equipment inferior and also believed that the average Japanese soldier lacked initiative.[89]

Harold J. Noble had lived in Japan, Korea, and Manchuria for twenty years, spoke Japanese, and served as an intelligence officer in the Marine Corps. In the essay "Give the Devils Their Due," he contested the notion of Japanese troops being mere fodder, describing them as intelligent, well trained, and well equipped. Noble lapsed into views akin to those of journalist Edgar Jones when he said that because dead Japanese, with their "buck teeth grinning in the sun," resembled "the bodies of some subhuman race," American troops tended to consider them dangerous but incipient savages. He argued that Japanese also held peaceful aspirations. Their harsh treatment of prisoners resulted, he believed, from differences between beliefs based on "a Greco-Christian civilization" and an "Oriental" mindset untouched by humaneness. He cited examples of approval of American troops who refused to surrender as proof that reverence for those killed in battle was not unique to Japan.

Like Pakenham, Noble considered Japanese officers rather parochial, but he admired their skillful exploitation of terrain, which to him indicated thorough training and resourcefulness rather than animalistic instinct. In short, the Japanese comprised a "first-class enemy," and although he disavowed being pro-Japanese, Noble insisted that if the Japanese were "the ignorant fanatics some writers would have had us believe we should have been in Tokyo a long time ago."[90]

The temperament, mentality, and character of Japanese civilians received similar analysis. Concurrent evaluations of them by journalist Jesse F. Steiner and correspondent Bernard Seeman, who served as a special consultant on Japan for the Office of War Information, agreed that because the majority of Japanese were accustomed to meager diets, cramped houses, and low incomes, they would accept "with remarkable docility" the severe conditions imposed on them by the war. Seeman believed that the Japanese could quickly adjust to "conditions which would seem unendurable to the average American." Neither bombing nor scarcity of food, he argued, had diminished their determination, and their "hysterical resolve" would only increase as Allied forces closed on Japan.[91]

Steiner deemed "the volatile temperament of the Japanese" and their "lack of emotional balance when faced with a great calamity" as important determinants in predicting the war's length. Unlike the British, who had stoically withstood bombing according to Steiner, the Japanese remained "too excitable, too easily swayed by emotion to endure a similar ordeal." He did not mention that the destruction inflicted on Japan far exceeded the damage suffered in Britain. Because he considered the Japanese more fanatical and fragile in temperament than Westerners, Steiner expected Japan's defeat soon, without "the destruction of the major portion of a population resisting savagely to the end like an animal at bay."[92]

Perhaps the most unusual basis for predicting the war's conclusion came from the economist Roger W. Babson, who said the Pacific War would end earlier than most people anticipated. Because he had employed Japanese house servants for twenty-seven years, Babson claimed to know the Japanese temperament, and like other commentators he believed in a universal Japanese disposition. He argued that only a minority of Japanese, "who, as a whole, are human like ourselves," preferred death to surrender. Babson described the typical Japanese as brave, obedient, and incapable of adjusting to unexpected events or changing conditions. "As a nation, they are wonderful copyists, but they lack originality." He based his conclusions on behavior he claimed to have witnessed in his home, where he bragged of hosting superb dinners for up to twenty people provided that he allowed "my Jap" a week to prepare for the event. According to Babson, if he brought home merely one unexpected guest, his Japanese servant became agitated. "They prosper on success, but cannot stand failure," Babson reasoned. "Hence, I feel certain that their collapse will only be a question of months."[93]

The military commentator George Fielding Eliot continually reprised the question that he first posed in May 1945, "How Long—Japan?" He thought the war's length depended on Japan's leaders, whom he described as inscrutable.[94] Eliot said, "We just don't know enough about how Jap minds work, singly and in mass" to judge when

Japan might capitulate. Japanese leaders might abruptly surrender or continue fighting until only "a few scattered survivors of the Jap race" survived in the "blackened wilderness" of Japan. He said that "no Western mind" could understand "Jap psychology. We can only keep plugging away until they surrender, or until they are utterly destroyed."[95]

Perhaps thoughtful readers questioned the dismissive quality of Eliot's observations. Figuratively throwing up his hands and saying that the Japanese existed beyond the boundaries of Western comprehension, Eliot decided that the war's duration depended on leaders whose minds he regarded as warped and feudal. Proposing continued pounding as a solution to this dilemma hardly sounded rational. Yet Eliot's arguments offered few options.

After Germany's surrender most civilians probably supported appeals for continued sacrifice and dedication, but none welcomed predictions of lengthy combat. Entreaties to remain focused on the war did not prevent commentators, government officials, and military commanders from speculating about the war's length themselves. Numerous editorials and essays urged additional military pressure beyond the ongoing bombing and blockade. Reminders about technology's limitations against a primitive foe tempered promises that technological superiority would reduce casualties. The demands that military pressure against Japan be increased during the transfer of additional forces to the Pacific reflected more than impatience for the war's end. Various commentators expressed anxiety because they knew that these forces were being assembled for the invasion of Japan, which most citizens and observers wanted to avoid.

Commentators contended that the war involved a struggle against a sinister mindset, an alien way of thinking shared by all Japanese. This argument implied that there must be a fundamental alteration of Japanese society. Such reasoning led to discussion of annihilation. Japanese fanaticism was described as religious and perhaps seemed even more dangerous because major religions of Japan remained mostly unknown in the United States. Even Joseph Grew, who privately disputed the notion that all Japanese shared a warped outlook, publicly portrayed them as infantile, violent, and obedient people. Other observers, such as the columnist Gladstone Williams, who also considered the Japanese an irrational people, thought that military pressure would force them, despite their inherent strangeness, to behave sensibly and surrender.

Some of the commentary contained telling admissions, as when unconditional surrender was described as a bitter rather than a noble duty. The numerous speeches and commentaries that emphasized speed implied that a more industrialized society lacked the patience of one less mechanized. The assertion that Japanese possessed more patience than Americans also reflected a widely accepted belief that Japanese, in common with other Asians, thought in terms of millennia and centuries rather than decades and years.[96]

The prevailing perceptions of the Japanese biased the discussion about the war's duration. Commentators repeatedly speculated about the actions and motives of people they admitted they did not understand. Those concessions produced few efforts to rethink the dominant stereotypes that abounded in editorials, essays, and commentaries about the war's length. No one acknowledged the contradictions of declaring that the war's duration depended on the fortitude of Americans and the decisions made by Japanese leaders who were described as irrational. Neither did commentators address the discrepancy of urging quick victory while warning of a protracted conflict. The pervasive ignorance about Japan was reflected in the binary oppositional descriptions of the Japanese—savage and docile, panic-prone and fanatically persistent.

4

Visions of Abundance

An American returning from the battle zones looks at current advertisements with a fresh eye—and finds a large number of them cheap
and shoddy, insultingly presumptuous and incredibly far below the
awe-inspiring challenge of this tragic struggle. To one who comes back
filled with inexpressible emotions from the spectacle of young Americans fighting and dying, it is like hearing a popcorn-man's penny
whistle jarring the climax of a mighty symphony.[1]

While Americans were admonished to remain dedicated to the war
effort the media abounded with visions of postwar affluence. Advertisers promised consumers improved versions of existing goods, tantal-
izing them with descriptions of myriad new products. Advertisements
frequently depicted the war as a distant annoyance delaying a pro-
fusion of merchandise. As fighting men endured hellish combat in the
Pacific, advertisers extolled a blissful postwar milieu in which women
worked as housewives and homemakers, people enjoyed increased leisure time, and families prospered in isolated splendor amidst their possessions.

Advertisers had expected that the war would cause a decline in
the standard of living as well as shortages of basic goods and services.
Yet advertisers wanted to preserve their traditional purpose of enticing
consumers to purchase products they did not necessarily need, an especially arduous prospect at a time when the diversion of materials from
the production of consumer goods to implements of war became paramount.[2]

Advertisers lobbied government agencies with claims that advertising could promote the war and elucidate war aims. Advertisers also
sought to publicize individual products, glorify consumerism, laud
the free-enterprise system, and celebrate ideals that constituted "the
American way." As advertising executive Walter Weir phrased it, advertising could defend "*why* the American way of life—with its bathtubs
and pop-up toasters and electric refrigerators and radios and insu-

lated homes—is worth sacrificing anything and everything not only to preserve but to take forward into a future more glorious than ever."[3]

Advertisers often neglected ennobling the war and simply honored consumerism.[4] Numerous companies sold the war itself, simultaneously keeping their products conspicuous. Advertising became increasingly patriotic as various companies identified brand-name goods with the war. Almost any product could be associated with the war, as evidenced by the truss manufacturer that declared, "To the Four Freedoms add a Fifth. Freedom from Rupture."[5]

In the era before television, advertisements in the print media appeared primarily in popular magazines such as *Life*, the *Saturday Evening Post*, and *Collier's*. News magazines such as *Newsweek* and *Time* often published the same advertisements. Occasionally, photographs accompanied advertisements, and color paintings that frequently resembled the work of the popular artist Norman Rockwell remained the most common form of illustration. Didactic in comparison to modern print advertisements, those of the 1940s featured more explanatory text.

Advertisements for war-related products remained evident in the war's final months.[6] Items such as boxes, thread, and broadcasting equipment were still depicted as crucial to the war effort.[7] Some advertisers used lurid depictions of wounded or dead soldiers to reiterate the theme of everyone remaining focused on the war.[8]

By mid-1945 advertisements that referred to pending prosperity and affluence outnumbered those related to the war.[9] Some advertisements supported the war while hinting of coming good times. In one illustration a war correspondent savored a highball as he lounged beside a pool and lectured his friend about the dangers of a letdown on the home front.[10] The relaxed setting undercut the endorsement of the war effort and implied that ongoing fighting delayed the day when people would have more time to relax and enjoy a superior highball.

Peace itself became a selling point subtly instilled within advertisements heralding the future as serene.[11] Equating the war's end to new life and rebirth, General Electric declared that while listening to FM radios, "Judy Garland's songs will come to you like a breath of Spring."[12] Companies that manufactured war-related products also began mentioning postwar production. Boeing touted its B-29 bomber as "Double trouble—for Japs" and noted that Boeing's expertise would also be applied to peacetime aircraft.[13] Railroad companies emphasized that they continued hauling cargoes for the war but also promised more powerful locomotives and superior passenger cars after the war.[14]

Because the destructive effects of World War II remained distant from the American heartland, it was easier for advertisers to portray the war as an endeavor that could lead citizens to a prosperity unknown since the 1920s. According to advertisers, consumers would reap the benefits of wartime technological developments. Bendix contended that the knowledge gained from the development of radar and radio equipment for the armed forces would be applied to the production of postwar radios, phonographs, and televisions, providing "an entirely *NEW* world of entertainment."[15]

Advertisements described pending products, as one contemporary said, "in nearly utopian tones" and praised forthcoming goods as improvements over those presently available.[16] Even transparent adhesive tape, according to Scotch, would surpass what was produced for the military.[17] Companies promoted substances such as Velon, a fabric for car interiors, luggage, shoes, and hats touted by Firestone.[18] Revere Copper and Brass publicized portable sewing machines, lightweight washers, wheelbarrows, and lawnmowers made of magnesium.[19] Several companies advertised televisions.[20] DuMont Laboratories said that television would "topple the walls of misunderstanding and intolerance—the Tower of Babel of our time," because it appealed to the eye, "which discerns truth far more quickly than the ear."[21] Radio and phonograph manufacturers boasted of improved quality and greater variety in postwar models.[22] Makers of cameras, beer, and tires described them as products "of tomorrow," reinforcing the theme that technological advances had rendered current goods obsolete.[23] The theme of inevitable progress reached an apogee when the Anheuser-Busch brewery, summarizing research to develop more nourishing foods, claimed, "Americans are going to Eat Better . . . Feel Better . . . Look Better."[24]

Advertisers emphasized the allure of vacationing, implying that increased leisure time awaited Americans after the war. Automobile manufacturers promised new features and advanced designs.[25] A succession of advertisements for the Lincoln nameplate featured scenic locations to be explored in cars "filled with wanderlust." "Peace will put an end to your stay-at-home days," assured the soothing text, "the gypsy in you will call out."[26]

Other companies that linked travel with companionship also put forth ideas about the respective positions of men and women in postwar society. Greyhound advertisements emphasized reunited spouses exploring the country.[27] Just as they had served together in the nation's armed forces and toiled collectively in factories during the war, "so they will one day rediscover the magnificent land for which they have fought . . . *still side by side!*"[28] The wording reinforced the notion of stability in the postwar home and implied that despite their contributions outside the home during the war, women would once again take their place beside their men in the postwar era.

The airline industry promoted air travel as so affordable after the war that people would feel like "citizens of a new world!"[29] Advertisements also promoted ownership of private aircraft. Goodyear, which claimed that "legions" of Americans would own planes after the war, publicized a small craft called the "amphibian" that could land on water and carry four passengers "in limousine comfort." The advertisement suggested that helicopters might become widely available for private use as well as "a half-plane, half-auto that takes to highways and skyways alike."[30] Firestone displays also featured families traveling in hybrid car/helicopters.[31]

In their depictions, advertisers characterized males as the molders of postwar society, the architechts of forthcoming products, and placed men in a variety of occupations. In representative gendered references, advertisements for Seagram's Whiskey depicted the "Integrated Transportation Center by Men Who Plan beyond Tomorrow"—a combined air, train, and bus terminal, and "The Super Market of the Future by Men Who Plan beyond Tomorrow"—an automated store where customers registered grocery lists and awaited delivery of the order in their car.[32] The visionary men who designed these structures would, of course, drink Seagram's, the whiskey of the future.

Idealized portrayals of home and family became more conspicuous in the myriad idyllic depictions of postwar society. Advertisements frequently focused on returning veterans, the subsequent reuniting of families, impending marriages, and the formation of new families. Some illustrations showed women expectantly and compliantly awaiting the return of men eager for sex, although the allusions to sex often remained indirect. Occasionally advertisers presented males' courtship of women in terms of conquest by comparing it to military campaigns. Motorola promoted its portable "Playmate" radio with an illustration of a man and woman lying on a beach. "After the war there will be *quieter* and *lovelier* beachheads to take and hold," the text promised, implying that women would cheerfully and submissively accept the pursuit of returned veterans eager for sex.[33] It also suggested women's obedient return to traditional roles.

Advertisers frequently portrayed women as anxiously awaiting marriage proposals from returning servicemen.[34] An advertisement for International Silver entitled "Sometimes I almost tell him," featured a uniformed man, whose countenance was unseen, caressing the face of a woman who stared up at him with an expression of hopeful joy.

In the last months of the Pacific War an increasing number of advertisements depicted women eager to marry returning servicemen. International Silver Company, *Life*, May 7, 1945, p. 23.

The soldier's anonymity reinforced the theme that he could be anyone, while the woman remained an ideal, albeit one awaiting any veteran.[35]

Oneida, makers of Community silver, produced a series of similar advertisements. Entitled "Back Home for Keeps," they depicted young wives and their returned servicemen husbands breathlessly embracing. Accompanying text expressed themes also found in advertisements for appliances, where a woman's existence centered on her husband and the secluded environment of their dream home. The Oneida advertisements spawned a pinup craze, as the illustrations decorated walls in the dormitory rooms of women's colleges, the interiors of high schools lockers, and soldiers' barracks. Oneida prepared fifty thousand reprints for anticipated requests from housewives, the primary targets of the campaign. By May 1945, however, the company had mailed over one million. A "Back Home for Keeps" club was formed, and a song of the same title recorded.[36]

In recognition of an expected increase in the birthrate after the war, companies extolled the virtues of their goods in helping raise children properly. Magnavox boasted that its phonographs could further a child's musical knowledge and cautioned that the sensitive ears of children must not be exposed to "poor or distorted reproduction."[37] Appealing to even more affluent consumers, Freed-Eisenmann esteemed the child raised in "a home enriched by great music and fine art," with classical music played on one of the company's radio-phonographs.[38]

Despite the fact that unprecedented numbers of women worked in factories during the war, the illustrations in advertisements in 1945 placed women almost exclusively in domestic settings. Several historians have examined the public's ambivalence about the millions of women who entered the work force during the war. The number of working women increased by nearly six million from 1941 to 1944, when more than nineteen million women populated the labor force. Hundreds of thousands of women also served in various branches of the armed forces. Popular culture of the 1940s—films, advertisements, magazine articles, and short stories—reflected the widespread admiration for women's contributions during the war but also emphasized their femininity and eventual return to domestic roles. Women's actions were viewed as a temporary, patriotic response to an emergency situation. By 1944 government propaganda and popular culture publicized the pending departure of women from the work force and their return to the household.[39]

To convince women of the scope of work awaiting them at home, companies encouraged women to remodel their homes, especially kitchens and bathrooms, where it was apparently expected that women would spend most of their time after the war. Advertisements presented postwar kitchens as women's domains. Bright, renovated kitchens full of new appliances would provide women a sense of freedom by making cooking easier and more pleasurable. Advertisements featured illustrations of smiling, apron-clad women wearing dresses, earrings, and high-heels, removing huge meals from an oven while a husband, just returned from work, looked on approvingly.[40] Numerous companies offered booklets to acquaint women with new kitchen styles and designs.[41]

Advertisers usually made women the initiators of remodeling and men the benefactors of delicious meals prepared in these renovated kitchens. The methods women used to design their kitchens in advertisements exemplified dominant attitudes. In one display a woman, holding a length of string before her mother, exclaimed, "This string is all I need to plan my NEW kitchen! Anybody can do it!"[42] Employing the fairy tale of Cinderella, the Crane company suggested that a woman could be literally transformed by planning a new kitchen.[43] Other depictions only endowed women with the ability to dreamily imagine alterations to their kitchens.[44] One advertisement featured an apron-clad woman, holding a mixing bowl in her lap with a pan at her feet, in a pose reminiscent of Auguste Rodin's sculpture "The Thinker." A group of male architects hovered over blue-prints in a smaller illustration. The text promised "more *fun*, more *freedom*" in "scientifically designed" kitchens that would even eliminate fatigue.[45]

Advertisements presented kitchens as rooms in which women could dwell. The American Gas Association pledged that gas appliances made the kitchen a "beautiful, *livable* place."[46] Companies promised to liberate women with new appliances that simplified cooking.[47] Noteworthy for its comparison of cooking to bondage, Gibson promised "Freedom From Hot-Stove Servitude" with its electric range that offered deliverance from "kitchen slavery."[48] Yet advertisements implied that the increased ease of kitchen chores would prompt women to spend even more time there.[49]

Certain advertisements showed entire families celebrating technological improvements for kitchens. A fatuous display from General Electric featured a family visiting a model kitchen where they marveled over the garbage disposal, a device which so intrigued one daughter that she pleaded to scrape leftover food into it. The wife thrilled over the kitchen's cleanliness, while her husband admired the dishwasher that would emancipate him from helping wash dishes. Even the baby, conspicuously named Faith, uttered an approving gurgle.[50]

By 1945 advertisements seldom mentioned women involved in war-related work. An exception was a Westinghouse advertisement in which women praised various electric appliances that helped them manage their daily tasks. Although the text described two of the women as factory workers, they were not clothed as "Rosies." Their attire—dresses and high-heels—symbolized their imminent return to domesticity.[51] According to appliance manufacturers, women's chores would no longer constitute work. As the smiling apron-clad woman of one advertisement stated, approvingly watching her identically clothed daughter work with a miniature beater and bowl, "Housework will be play for me too." And by implication, the next generation of women would continue the tradition.[52]

Advertisements depicted appliances as fulfilling women's dreams and desires, and Westinghouse deemed them "As Precious As Rare Jewels."[53] Advertisements for other appliances reiterated the themes of liberation and satisfaction. Washing clothes would become an effortless job according to General Electric, which claimed that its clothes dryer would keep women smiling, while its electric iron would prompt them to burst into song.[54]

Nash-Kelvinator produced the most sentimental advertisements for kitchen appliances. In one illustration a man in an army uniform sat

During the war's final months more advertisements showed women expectantly awaiting forthcoming household products. Landers, Frary, and Clark, *Parents Magazine*, June 1945, p. 101.

behind a house with a white picket fence, his arm around his daughter, as his wife benignly watched from a window. The text, written as if composed by the woman, was a glorious testimony to her happiness living in "a world of our own." The woman emphasized the allure of a "kitchen for me that's *full* of magical things."[55]

Amidst these advertisements one looks in vain for women devising plans with instruments more complex than a pencil and ruler. Some advertisements portrayed women as incapable of using even these utensils and had them rely instead on more manageable tools such as pieces of string. The woman who planned her kitchen with string as she joyfully proclaimed "anybody can do it!" left unstated the obvious implication: "Even a dumb woman like me!" As depicted, women produced simplistic and superficial sketches of kitchens hastily scrawled on scrap paper or the backs of envelopes, and male architects and engineers transformed this crude, fragmentary scribble into intricate blueprints. As the advertisements made clear, men intended to turn women's "dreams" into reality by manufacturing sparkling new kitchen appliances that made the kitchen a "livable" place. The Kelvinator advertisements presented the end result: a completely contented woman with a husband and children, a home with a white door denoting the purity contained within, and a white picket fence that demarcated the boundary between the idyllic home and the outside world. Joyous of her role as housewife and mother, a woman could be completely fulfilled by existing with her family in "a world of our own."

Advertisers attempted to appeal to the sense of purpose that many women derived from their work outside the home during the war by promising them more control within their homes. Advertisers implied that women's aspirations should be channeled into domestic roles as a substitute for loss of power outside the home. Thus, the new ambition many working women experienced during the war would not be taken from them at the war's conclusion, according to advertisers, but merely redirected where it belonged—in the home.

Along with remodeled kitchens, numerous companies promoted renovated bathrooms. Looking today at these illustrations for kitchens and bathrooms one is struck by the inherent sterility of the streamlined decor. Perhaps intended to convey modernity, the post-art deco appearance resembled the modern style of the 1920s and 1930s. The aseptic depictions of bathrooms also presaged the emphasis on cleanliness and modesty evident in much of the advertising directed toward women in the 1950s.[56] One advertisement by a maker of bathroom fixtures showed a smiling woman in a glistening bathroom cheerfully drying off her beaming, golden-haired daughter with a fluffy towel. The caption simply stated, "Among the Durable Satisfactions of Life," which presumably encompassed the new sink and bathtub, raising children, and a woman's role as mother and housewife.[57]

Targeted at women, advertisements for bathroom products claimed that fashionable bathrooms helped parents instill important values in their children, such as "the training of your children in habits of health and cleanliness."[58] To accomodate the anticipated increase in children after the war, companies suggested enlarging bathrooms or constructing additional ones.[59] Advertisements for new bathrooms also emphasized abundance. In one display a woman dreamily admired her ultra-modern bathroom, stocked with enough towels for a small motel.[60] Whether a refrigerator bulging with food, or a household bathroom overstocked with towels, advertisers depicted a postwar environment of lavishness in which food rationing and fabric shortages would be merely unpleasant memories.

The advertisements for renovated bathrooms also explained that the suggested refinements would appeal to men. This theme, combined with the idea of women anxiously awaiting marriage, reinforced the motif of female subservience in the postwar years. According to advertisers, women would not only derive satisfaction from modernized kitchens and bathrooms but could also be gratified knowing that the improvements benefited their men. For example, one advertisement showed a woman looking at a photograph of her serviceman husband cheerfully scrubbing in an outdoor shower in the Pacific. Concluding that he would desire a modern bathroom after the war, she immediately drew a design for one. Its features included a series of racks beneath the counter—because "he *hates* my stockings on his towel rack"—and "folding doors down the middle so he'd have plenty of privacy—even from me!"[61]

In stressing the importance of a man's privacy, the advertisement echoed concurrent advice for women considering marriage. One author reminded potential brides to remember that "privacy is a basic requisite of a happy marriage" and cautioned that "a possessive woman, by invading her husband's fundamental right of privacy, will eventually destroy the basic dignity of their relationship." The article did not mention whether men were expected to observe a similar measure of respect for the privacy of their wives.[62]

Although the depictions of servicemen in advertising engendered criticism earlier in the war, advertisers frequently used fighting men as integral components of their pitch. Usually presenting idyllic combat as a prelude to postwar consumerism, these sanitized depictions implied that even the grueling combat of the Pacific War would not alter the basic wholesomeness of U.S. soldiers, whose Americanism was preserved by access to uniquely American products like jukeboxes and refrigerators.[63] In a typical illustration, a soldier dreamily leaned against a palm tree, after the "last lurking Jap has been cleaned out of the jungle," gazed toward the starry sky, and hummed Hoagy Carmichael's song "Star Dust." The sentimental text described combat as the equivalent of a hard day's work. The soldier was comforted in the knowledge that forthcoming Wurlitzer musical instruments and jukeboxes would benefit from numerous wartime technical improvements.[64]

In contrast to the images of women expectantly awaiting the return of fighting men, the servicemen in advertisements appeared less ardent about seeking female companionship. More frequently, illustrations showed them fighting for technological advancement, which was associated with masculine ideals of consumerism.

Numerous advertisements portrayed fighting men as grateful for a particular product, be it the tires on a jeep or the specific brand of engine in a plane.[65] In many advertisements soldiers eagerly awaited word of new goods. Why the assembly of cars or boats would excite men risking death in combat was never explained. In one advertisement a soldier in a Pacific locale clutched a newspaper clipping while he claimed to be "watching the news" of developments about automobiles at Graham-Paige. The text added that many servicemen had expressed interest in rototillers and farm tractors as well, implying that the thought of postwar products boosted soldiers' morale.[66] A boat manufacturer claimed that fighting men from all over the world had inquired about postwar models.[67] The Buick division of General Motors contended that victory in Europe permitted the nation to devote more attention to consumer products, with one advertisement promising that new Buicks would be "all that returning warriors have dreamed about."[68]

Advertisers insisted that fighting men, having received training in war-related technology, also wanted technological improvement at home. Texts in advertisements used gendered phrases that in part reflected the traditional male practice of referring generally to cars, locomotives, planes, or machinery in feminine terms such as "she." The gendered expressions also conveyed a sense of male dominance in the postwar world through prose and illustrations that often contained sexual overtones. Nash Motors expressed these themes in advertisements entitled "Waiting for You," which said that veterans longed for a new car to drive on "wide highways that beg your car to spread her wings and fly."[69]

The Nash advertisements depicted a postwar United States reassuringly stable, homogeneous, and familiar. Hackneyed text and idyllic illustrations lauded the reuniting of men and women separated by war in a manner that emphasized women's place in the postwar world. One senses that a man's reunion with an automobile took precedence over returning to his mate, as the text in one Nash advertisement said all would be right with the world "when you and your car are together again with the girl you've come so far to see." In another illustration for Nash, a couple sped along in a convertible bathed in the light of a full moon. The man eagerly peered ahead while the woman dreamily rested her head on his shoulder. Familiar with the technology of war and now seated at the controls of the latest automobile, males literally looked to the future while accompanying females remained passively contented companions.[70]

Advertisers presented reunion with an automobile as a masculine form of freedom and power. A Caterpillar advertisement entitled "Pattern for Tomorrow" showed a cloverleaf interchange on the Pennsylvania Turnpike. The accompanying text described the thoughts of the typical American soldier, who while "sweating it out in a slit trench," dreamed of driving a car over "broad, smooth concrete" that would allow him to "push the accelerator to the floor and keep it there."[71] The sexual metaphor of this advertisement moved from combat to postwar images of a powerful, fast car that was equated to sexual dominance, freedom, and omnipotence.

By placing women solely in domestic roles, advertisers presented a postwar world of unlimited opportunity for males. The aforementioned masculine drive and ambition could also be channeled into a successful career. Various companies used illustrations that espoused the idea of postwar society offering boundless opportunity for returning veterans.[72] The Union Pacific railroad promoted this theme in a series of colorful advertisements entitled "Your America," which recalled the pioneer spirit of exploration and a wide-open western frontier.[73] In one of the most ridiculous displays, the airline industry depicted two grinning soldiers in full combat gear seated inside a transport plane. One remarked to the other, "Tomorrow, Joe, we'll have this speed and cushions too!" A larger illustration showed the same men later as successful businessmen in crisp suits, nestled in the cushy seats of an airplane as a smiling stewardess offered them food.[74]

Automobiles, highways, the ideal of success through personal initiative, constituted venerated cultural symbols and values and reinforced the theme of pervasive prosperity in the postwar years. In a Rockwellesque advertisement that captured the theme of the war preserving basic American goodness, a man in a small town read the posted names of local servicemen. He reflected that a small community was "a good place to grow up . . . a place with a little old bandstand in the square, and lawns and gardens around the houses . . . a place close to the ground. Makes no difference if it's in Connecticut or Kansas. It's America."[75] Thus, veterans would return to a bountiful, prosperous nation where new products and careers awaited them. Despite the technological advancements touted by advertisers, the United States would remain a combination of new and old. Traditional values would endure and coexist with rampant consumerism and technological improvements.

Few criticized the utopian visions promoted by advertisers. One journalist did state that by focusing on the "fairyland" of postwar consumer goods advertisers had "conspired to take our minds off a relatively shabby present and project them into an entirely Hollywood future."[76] In a satirical summary of advertising methods, another

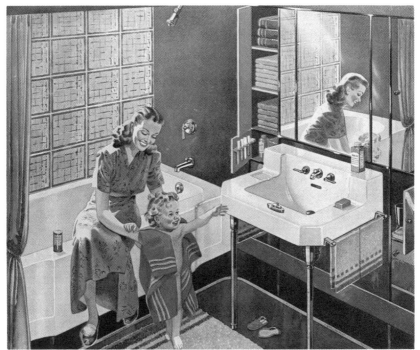

AMONG THE DURABLE SATISFACTIONS OF LIFE

Advertisements that urged women to make plans for remodeling kitchens and bathrooms after the war often venerated motherhood. Courtesy of Kohler Company.

author speculated that in the future he would commute to work in a helicopter, don clothes made of "spun glass," and ogle women wearing stainless steel stockings.[77]

Advertising attempted to exploit the public's contradictory emotions of supporting the war while anxiously awaiting its conclusion. The success of its efforts is difficult to measure. Advertisers relied on established techniques and themes while promising an imminent bonanza of radically new postwar goods. Indeed, promoting the obsolescence of products marked a return to a motif that advertisers used in the 1920s when they had increasingly emphasized style.[78] Presenting appliances as the tools of liberation also reintroduced an earlier advertising practice.[79] Even the idea of airplanes transforming society harkened to the enthusiasm for aviation, the spirit of "airmindedness," that existed prior to World War II.[80]

Accentuating forthcoming consumer products while the war raged probably disgusted people cognizant of the disparity between celebra-

tions of consumerism and appeals that the public remain fixated on defeating Japan. Of course, advertising then, as now, frequently did not
reflect reality, and some people must have scoffed at aspects of the fu-
turistic world depicted by advertisers.

On the other hand, many citizens probably hoped and even believed that American technology, values, and ideals would reign supreme in the postwar period. By 1945, the heady vision of a peaceful
postwar world shaped by the benevolent omnipotence of the United
States—a prospect expressed by *Life's* colorful publisher Henry Luce in
his essay "The American Century," published in 1941—appeared to
be attainable. Advertisers appealed to these sentiments, even presenting white bread as a cultural icon in an illustration where gaunt former prisoners of war gratefully received white bread from American
troops. With its religious overtones the advertisement depicted American civilization as a kind of salvation, with white bread serving as a
symbol of freedom from disease and famine.[81] It was also emblematic
of the "American way" that advertisers acknowledged and glorified.

Americans have a historic fondness for inventions and technological advancement. Advertisers exploited this trait and linked it with the
traditional advertising technique of encouraging discontent with current possessions.[82] The postwar society promoted by advertisers was
male-oriented, predominantly white, and placed women in a subor-
dinate position rather than one of equity. According to advertisers,
technology would uphold traditional roles and values rather than
transform them. Women would work in the home, liberated to an extent by new products that would ease the traditional female chores
of cooking, cleaning, and washing, and houses would be modernized
into bastions of abundance.[83] In an illustration that joined the images of
women desiring matrimony with their longing for new appliances, one
advertisement showed a smiling bride, equally joyous about her marriage and her electric kitchen.[84]

Advertisers reiterated the theme that women bore the responsibility of rehabilitating returning servicemen, who, after the anonymity
of the armed forces, needed to feel important. One article on the
subject published in early 1945 said that a woman's most important
duty—as the advertisements for new kitchens and bathrooms often
conveyed—in rehabilitating a man was "to fit his home to *him*, understanding why he wants it this way, forgetting your own preferences.
After all, it is the boss who has come home."[85]

The aforementioned types of advertisements seldom appeared in
major African-American publications. Yet an article in the *Pittsburgh
Courier* reinforced the theme of women remaining in the home by claim-

Advertisements frequently depicted American fighting men anticipating products such as new cars. Courtesy of Chrysler Corporation.

ing that thousands of wives had dated other men while their husbands served overseas. The piece warned women to "get things in order before Johnnie comes home" and said that veterans would "tolerate no foolishness or double talk when they return." "We suspect there's going to be a number of black eyes anyway," the article closed, "but don't say we didn't warn you."[86]

Although unique in its endorsement of the implied threat of violence against women, this article reiterated the idea that women's primary responsibility was maintaining order in the home; in advertisements this explicitly included raising children and performing tasks deemed women's work. The article also bluntly conveyed a message often implicitly communicated by advertisers—that a woman must keep her husband sexually satisfied. Married women accounted for the greatest percentage of the total increase in working women during the war, and half of all servicemen's wives worked. However, this article implied that with men absent, women became promiscuous. Ignoring the role of males in the scenario of wives dating other men it inferred that independent women constituted a sexual threat. By keeping women in domesticity, men could make women focus on household duties and control their sexuality—forcibly, if necessary.

Placing women in the home as the rehabilitators of returning veterans also reflected certain concerns on the home front. Some commentators and citizens feared a return of economic depression when the war ended. The economist John Kenneth Galbraith said that Americans retained what he called "the Depression psychosis," a fear that the Great Depression never really ended and would return after the war.[87] Women composed nearly one-third of the wartime work force of almost sixty million people. The message that these women must forsake their wartime jobs stemmed from the belief that returning veterans should have work available for them.

Citizens also worried about the readjustment of veterans to civilian life. Several books and articles portrayed returning veterans as a potentially disruptive threat to American society.[88] Few people actually regarded veterans as dangerous, yet advertisements that emphasized the domestic role of women in postwar society implied that women had an important duty in helping veterans acclimate themselves by surrounding them with items reassuring and familiar.

In their depictions of women, in often pastoral, sentimental illustrations, advertisers presented a fantasy world. "It was as though the nation were clinging in desperation to the memory of an innocence lost," one author later stated.[89] And yet advertisers also championed a modernized world of mass consumption, "A Nation of Shoppers," as one company phrased it, composed primarily of women who "have learned to choose and examine, to question and select before buying." That expertise, coupled with "America's enterprising industry" that had "learned to serve this nation of shoppers that tell and are not told what they want," would produce "a new high standard of living."[90] As they would in the 1950s, advertisers stressed the importance of women as consumers yet diminished the idea of women working as producers outside the home to earn money for the products they supposedly needed to be superb mothers and wives.[91] Advertisers simultaneously appealed to perceptions of earlier values—women as homemakers, veneration of the frontier, celebration of rural settings and small town life—while promoting new technology that prophesied epochal change.

Advertisers conveyed the idea that basic values and institutions perceived as American would remain unchanged after the war. The Nash-Kelvinator advertisements of a family living in joyful isolation from the outside world celebrated the idyllic image of the American home and nuclear family. Advertisers confirmed an ideal expressed in the popular film "Since You Went Away," from 1944, which was billed as taking place inside a representative example of "the unconquerable fortress: the American home."[92]

After the Great Depression and more than three years of war, countless Americans undoubtedly hoped that the war's end would bring a new prosperity. However, in the decades after the war, they learned that technological advancement did not guarantee a more placid society or a more peaceful world. Ironically, at the same time that advertisers began offering more depictions of postwar society, Americans were engaged in the bloodiest battle of the Pacific War.

5

Okinawa

For those who do the fighting it is a war in which every advance is paid for in torn flesh and shattered bones.[1]

Far from the home front across the vast Pacific Ocean, Americans fought and died in the spring and summer of 1945. Citizens followed the course of battles that continued in the Philippines on the island of Luzon, as well as on southern and central islands of the archipelago, where thousands of Japanese resisted until the war ended.[2] The largest-scale combat persisted on and around the island of Okinawa. There, marines, soldiers, sailors, and airmen grappled with Japanese forces in a ghastly struggle that resulted in the highest American losses of the war. The human cost of capturing Okinawa engendered criticism of U.S. tactics and prompted several military leaders to reconsider using chemical weapons against the Japanese. Commentators on the home front offered a variety of interpretations about the campaign's significance and several observers said that similar struggles must be avoided in the future. The battle did not produce heroic iconographic images like those from the previous amphibious assault on Iwo Jima.

Okinawa is the largest of the Ryukyu islands that stretch in a curving arc between Kyushu, the southernmost of the four main Japanese islands, and Formosa. Located approximately in the center of the chain, Okinawa totals 485 square miles—roughly one-third the size of Long Island.[3] Japan had annexed the island in 1879, and the majority of Okinawa's 435,000 inhabitants engaged in small-scale agriculture.[4]

On Easter Sunday, April 1, 1945, an invasion force of more than 1,200 ships assembled for the assault on Okinawa, the final component of the strategic plan approved by the Joint Chiefs of Staff in October 1944 that had included the invasions of the Philippines and Iwo Jima. The amphibious operation involved more than 180,000 soldiers and marines. Only 350 miles from mainland Japan, with room for air bases and sheltered bays ideal for naval anchorages, Okinawa would serve as a staging area for the planned invasion of Japan itself.[5]

The more than 100,000 Japanese troops on Okinawa, led by the adroit Lt. Gen. Mitsuru Ushijima, did not contest the amphibious landing. Instead, Ushijima concentrated his forces around a succession of strong defensive perimeters inland from the beaches. The Japanese made skillful use of caves and pillboxes connected by an intricate system of tunnels.[6]

Lt. Gen. Simon Bolivar Buckner, Jr., commanded the marines and soldiers that splashed ashore against light resistance on April 1. The son of a Confederate general, Buckner believed in defeating enemy forces through the steady application of superior strength and firepower. Later, the "old man of the mountains," as some called him, would be criticized for not fighting a more inventive campaign.[7]

The sporadic opposition encountered after the main landings on Okinawa's west coast prompted some correspondents and commanders to optimistically predict a brief campaign with few casualties.[8] Troops quickly captured two important airfields. The first sustained heavy fighting occurred when soldiers reached Japanese positions on Kakazu Ridge near the town of Machinato, north of the port of Naha.[9] The Japanese made expert use of hills, ridges, and escarpments where they established labyrinthine defenses.[10] Thus, the fighting became a vicious struggle to secure high ground defended by concealed strong points.

Relying on superior numbers of aircraft, artillery, and tanks, augmented by the tremendous firepower of the supporting naval task force, U.S. forces methodically blasted the Japanese from their fortifications. Using flamethrowers extensively, American troops also pumped mixtures of gasoline and napalm into caves and underground bunkers. They then used bullets, satchel charges, or grenades to ignite the liquid—General Buckner dubbed it the "blowtorch and corkscrew" method of combat—either incinerating or suffocating those inside, because the flames often consumed the oxygen in smaller caves.[11]

When news of V-E Day reached them, marines and soldiers were moving against the formidable Japanese defenses centered around the ancient city of Shuri. Although navy warships fired off three thunderous rounds in celebration of the announcement of Germany's surrender on May 8, the reaction of fighting men ashore was more subdued. Marine E. B. Sledge later remembered the comment "So what" as a typical response among American fighting men.[12] An Associated Press release said that the din of combat obscured portions of the V-E Day announcement. "It was V-E day everywhere, but on Okinawa the forests of white crosses grew, and boys who had hardly begun to live died miserably in the red clay of this hostile land."[13]

The numerous bloody clashes on Sugar Loaf Hill, first attacked by marines on May 12, typified the combat on Okinawa. Described by the newspaper correspondent Homer Bigart as a "red clay mound, scarcely 500 yards long and 300 feet high," Sugar Loaf was initially regarded as so inconsequential that it did not appear on standard military maps. But the accuracy of Japanese artillery fire there spawned a rumor among marines that German gunners were directing the shelling.[14] Nearly three thousand American casualties resulted during the struggle for Sugar Loaf, roughly the same total as in the entire battle for Tarawa in 1943.[15]

Meanwhile, the naval forces offshore came under the heaviest aerial suicide attacks of the war. The first organized kamikaze aerial suicide assaults by the Japanese had occurred in October 1944 during the Battle of Leyte Gulf. The term kamikaze, meaning "divine wind," referred to the typhoon that drove off the fleet of Emperor Kublai Khan in the thirteenth century thereby sparing the Japanese from invasion.

Beyond the protection of American air bases, the waters around Okinawa were within range of enemy airfields in Japan and on Formosa. From early April until late June, the U.S. fleet endured an estimated 1,900 suicide sorties; suicide strikes sunk 26 U.S. ships and damaged 164 vessels.[16]

Heavy rains that began in mid-May worsened conditions for troops ashore. Tanks and jeeps bogged down as the dirt roads of the island turned to thick ooze forcing soldiers and marines to manhandle supplies to the front lines, often under enemy fire. The downpours exacerbated the already deplorable sanitation.[17]

Soldiers also contended with hordes of lice, fleas, mosquitos, and swarms of flies, and thousands suffered from "immersion foot," the discomforting result of continuously damp feet. Ringworm and dysentery plagued thousands of men, and an outbreak of typhoid occurred.[18]

While attempting to crack the Japanese positions near Shuri, troops experienced some of the bloodiest, most brutal combat of the war. A marine later recalled that he could smell the front's putrid stench behind the lines and described the area of heavy fighting as "a monstrous sight, a moonscape."[19] An army colonel who visited the front later remembered the ceaseless cacophony. Smoke completely screened the sky and the odor of gunpowder burned his nostrils, producing a smell "almost overcome by the stench of rotting flesh while the sting and stickiness of the flies became almost unbearable."[20] A common greeting among troops of the Sixth Marine Division was "Hell, you still living?"[21]

Eugene Sledge later described the battlefield near Shuri similarly as a place of desolation. Shell fire had destroyed all trees and churned the muddy ground into a cratered wasteland of decaying corpses and abandoned equipment. He recalled thinking death preferable to his experiences in a setting where "we were surrounded by maggots and decay. Men struggled and fought and bled in an environment so degrading I believed we had been flung into hell's own cesspool."[22]

After encountering the formidable Japanese positions around Shuri, some of General Buckner's subordinates advised him to launch an amphibious assault behind the Shuri defenses on the beaches near Minatoga, on the southeastern coast of Okinawa, close to the location of previous diversionary landings. Buckner refused, insisting that opening another front would strain his lines of supply.[23]

Earlier in the campaign Adm. Chester W. Nimitz, the overall commander of operations in the Central Pacific, became impatient about the slow pace of the advance on Okinawa, wondering if army commanders intended to reduce their casualties at the expense of the sailors contending with kamikaze attacks. During one conference with Buckner, Nimitz threatened to find a new ground commander if the advance did not accelerate.[24]

By mid-June, Japanese morale began to crack. Even Radio Tokyo described the plight of Japanese troops as "truly desperate." U.S. planes dropped leaflets behind Japanese lines urging General Ushijima to enter surrender negotiations, but he deemed it beneath the dignity of a Japanese warrior to even consider such an absurd request. Radio Tokyo claimed that General Buckner suffered "the embarrassment of a formal rejection" of his entreaty.[25]

American interpreters fluent in Japanese and cooperative Japanese prisoners exhorted trapped Japanese to surrender, but thousands ignored the appeals and committed suicide. Efforts at inducing surrender did contribute to the capture of more than 7,400 Japanese prisoners, the largest number of the war, although conscripted Okinawans constituted about half of this total.[26]

General Buckner was killed early in the afternoon of June 18, while observing combat near the southern tip of Okinawa.[27] Within a few days General Ushijima committed suicide. Okinawa was declared secured on June 22, but a "mop-up campaign" lasted until June 30 during which nearly nine thousand Japanese were killed and almost three thousand taken prisoner. U.S. forces suffered more than seven hundred casualties.[28]

The losses in the Okinawan campaign were staggering. Total American casualties numbered 49,151, including 12,520 killed or missing, and 36,631 wounded. The army recorded 15,613 nonbattle casualties, the marines 10,598. Naval casualties totaled 4,907 killed or missing, and 4,824 wounded. Twenty percent of the navy's personnel losses in the war against Japan came in this single campaign. Thirty-six ships were sunk and 368 damaged. Japanese losses numbered approximately 110,000 killed.[29] Caught in the violence that engulfed their island, Okinawan civilians suffered terribly, and estimates of their casualties range from 80,000 to more than 160,000.[30]

As the battle on Okinawa continued, U.S. citizens learned previously withheld information about Japanese tactics. Until April 1945, the Navy had blocked disclosure of the suicidal attacks by Japanese planes so that the Japanese would not know the extent of the damage inflicted. Despite denigration of the tactics by several commanders and a few journalists, most civilians came to realize that the kamikaze raids posed a serious threat.[31] Adm. William Halsey dismissed them as a "damned nuisance rather than a menace," although *Newsweek* observed that the figures for naval casualties contradicted Halsey's bluster.[32] Admiral Nimitz referred to the "negligible effects" of the kamikazes.[33] However, Adm. Raymond Spruance candidly admitted that the destruction from kamikaze attacks constituted "the greatest naval casualties encountered in any of our operations to this time."[34] In one of the most dispassionate articles about the kamikazes, writer John Hersey emphasized that despite the "sanguine and breezy" deprecation of the raids by several naval commanders, the resultant damage was extensive.[35]

Typically, editorials tended to belittle the kamikazes. An editorial in the *New York Times* claimed such fanaticism resulted from the Shinto religion, which gave the Japanese a motivation "far beyond" Western ideals of patriotism and instilled in them "a religious fanaticism which finds its incarnated symbol in the Japanese Emperor."[36] The editors of the *Evening Star* of Washington, D.C., admitted that the suicide attacks could not be discounted but called them "quite as futile as they are macabre."[37] An article in the *Saturday Evening Post*, using an animalistic metaphor, noted that the old story about the enraged dog that bit himself to death "has a curious real-life parallel today in the air forces of the Japanese Empire."[38] Several fighting men claimed that female pilots flew some of the kamikaze planes. Shortly after the publication of these reports, Radio Tokyo announced that American aircraft with female crews had been downed over China.[39]

Controversy surrounded the conduct of the Okinawa campaign, as military leaders and journalists questioned the army's tactics. Indeed, radio commentator H.V. Kaltenborn remarked in a broadcast on May 28, "For all practical purposes, the part of Okinawa we really need is already ours."[40] Gen. Douglas MacArthur conveyed similar thoughts to several officers and journalists to whom he lamented the heavy casualties at Okinawa. He argued that following the capture of enemy air-fields during the early stages of the campaign, troops should have been placed into defensive positions to await any attempted counterattack rather than clearing Japanese from the entire island.[41] However genuine his concerns, MacArthur undoubtedly relished the opportunity to favorably compare his losses to those suffered in the area of Nimitz's command and thereby bolster his claim that forces under his own leadership should spearhead the invasion of Japan.

A dispute arose toward the end of the campaign when columnist David Lawrence, who wrote for the *Evening Star*, faulted commanders for not ordering an amphibious assault behind the intricate Japanese positions near Shuri. Lawrence based his first column on a dispatch filed by Homer Bigart, the correspondent for the *New York Herald Tribune* on Okinawa. In his report, Bigart opined that an amphibious landing behind the Shuri front would have hastened the battle's conclusion. "Our tactics were ultra-conservative," Bigart charged. "Instead of an end-run we persisted in frontal attacks. It was hey-diddle-diddle straight down the middle."[42] Lawrence suggested that a commander more experienced in amphibious operations than General Buckner should have led the ground forces and proposed that a military tribunal investigate the conduct of the campaign.[43]

In a subsequent column Lawrence dubbed the battle a "military fiasco," an example of ineptitude worse than Pearl Harbor. The slow pace of combat on Okinawa, Lawrence said, kept the supporting fleet offshore, vulnerable to kamikaze attacks. He criticized army commanders for their reliance on frontal assaults and contended that if the tactics used on Okinawa were to be repeated in an invasion of Japan, people should prepare for a extended war with heavy casualties.[44]

In an unprecedented response, Admiral Nimitz held a press conference on Guam on June 17, where he defended the strategy of the campaign and replied specifically to Lawrence's criticisms. Reading a prepared statement, Nimitz said that supplementary amphibious landings would have increased casualties and complicated the problems of supplying troops. He declared that U.S. forces were "magnificently led" and cautioned that citizens must not permit "malicious gossip" to undermine the confidence of their fighting men. In extemporaneous remarks Nimitz contended that David Lawrence was manipulated "by someone with an axe to grind." The admiral described the casualty rates as serious but acceptable.[45]

A biographer of Nimitz later claimed that the controversy ended because of widespread esteem for the admiral, but this appears too simplistic.[46] Although he was dissatisfied with the deliberate pace of the operation, Nimitz hoped to quell any interservice rivalries, especially with the invasion of Japan looming. He certainly did not want a repetition of the rancorous controversy that erupted the previous year during fighting on Saipan. In that dispute, a marine commander, Gen. Holland M. Smith, relieved an army counterpart, Maj. General Ralph Smith, for what the former considered poor performance by troops under the latter's direction. This sequence of events prompted a series of verbal and written recriminations between various commanders.[47] Buckner's death the day after Nimitz's press conference also contributed to the dropping of the matter.

It is noteworthy that Nimitz directed his comments at David Lawrence rather than Homer Bigart. Although he agreed with Lawrence that U.S. forces should have attempted landings behind the Shuri front, Bigart did not regard the campaign as a fiasco.[48] Respected for his precise composition and methodical preparation of reports based on persistent questioning, Bigart was an experienced correspondent whose career lasted through the wars in Korea and Vietnam. Previously, he had traveled with Allied forces in Italy, during which he incurred the anger of the British commander Field Marshal Sir Harold Alexander for critical articles about the Allied landings at Anzio.[49]

Apparently, both Nimitz and Adm. Ernest J. King believed someone had leaked to Homer Bigart that commanders had discussed additional landings.[50] The source of the leak, if any occurred, was never determined. Perhaps Bigart speculated about further landings on his own initiative. In his response, Nimitz ignored the fact that Bigart's initial dispatch was cleared by military censors. Lawrence, who professed respect and admiration for Nimitz, said that the admiral was "grossly misinformed" about the content of the columns.[51]

The editors of the New York Herald Tribune asserted that neither Lawrence nor Nimitz emerged untainted from their acrimonious exchange. They criticized Lawrence for drawing improper conclusions from Bigart's dispatch and disapproved of Nimitz's unsubstantiated accusation that Lawrence was somehow manipulated.[52]

Other commentators vigorously defended the military's tactics. William V. Pratt, a retired admiral who wrote a column on the war for Newsweek, considered Nimitz's explanation sufficient and argued that Lawrence's stricture sabotaged morale in the military and on the home front. He faulted critics for second-guessing the tactics of the deceased commander when Buckner's strategy brought victory.[53] Pratt avoided the principal point of contention, for Lawrence never asserted that Buckner's tactics would fail but instead questioned the pace and costliness of the campaign.

CLEANING UP THE PESTS IN THE VICTORY GARDEN

This cartoon by the *Chicago Tribune*'s Carl Somdal, published in June 1945, reflected public frustration over the rising casualties and slowing pace of the Pacific War. © Copyrighted Chicago Tribune Company. All rights reserved. Used with permission.

The military commentator Hanson W. Baldwin ridiculed comparisons of Okinawa to Pearl Harbor, although he conceded that an additional landing might have been attempted.[54] Columnist Maj. George Fielding Eliot observed that Americans typically displayed impatience with prolonged combat. He respected the commentary of Homer Bigart but reproached David Lawrence for using that critical analysis as the basis for describing the campaign as a debacle.[55]

David Lawrence later responded that issues such as minimizing casualties must not be regarded as personal disputes between commentators and commanders. The parents of those killed and wounded deserved access to informed critique of strategy, he argued.[56] In letters to the editors, some readers of the *Evening Star* questioned Lawrence's qualifications for evaluating military tactics. One woman wrote, "This Chinese-American girl feels that we have far more important things to do . . . than to hurl barbed shafts of criticism at the men who are doing the fighting in the field" and suggested that Lawrence "discuss whether Hirohito should be hanged or shot."[57] *Time* contended that "hair-trigger critics" should remember that the real cause of difficulties on Okinawa was the "implacable resistance of a fanatical enemy."[58]

During the campaign, commentary on the home front expressed apprehension about the battle's length and the increasing American casualties. Editorials in the *New York Times* and the *Pittsburgh Courier* exhibited pride in the valor of American fighting men as well as distress about casualties.[59] Some commentary expressed cautious praise for the Japanese.[60] Correspondent Bruce Rae commended the skill and tenacity of Japanese soldiers yet simultaneously denounced them for fighting "with total disregard of all the rules and with the trickiness that characterizes the Japanese and copperheads."[61]

Some published accounts considered Okinawa an example of the type of battle that would ensue when Allied troops invaded Japan.[62] That theme intensified concern about casualties in future operations. In his broadcast two days prior to Memorial Day, radio commentator Raymond Gram Swing quoted a journalist who had queried, "If nearly 10,000 Americans are dead or missing so far in Okinawa, what will the invasion of the homeland cost?"[63] A wounded soldier told a reporter from his hometown newspaper, "American invasion of the Japanese homeland will touch off the bloodiest struggle ever experienced by human beings."[64] Employing animalistic imagery, the editors of the *New York Times* said that Okinawa provided "a springboard . . . to attack the enemy in his last lair." They also asked, "If it took almost three months to conquer Okinawa, how much life, treasure and time must we expend to conquer Kyushu and Honshu?"[65]

A thoughtful editorial in the *Washington Post* said that the only way Japanese leaders could maintain their public's martial spirit was to convince citizens that the Allies intended to exterminate them. This message, the editors admitted, could be abetted with unfortunate remarks from American "saber-rattlers." The editorial called for further efforts to persuade the Japanese that the United States did not intend to enslave or annihilate them.[66]

An editorial published in the *St. Louis Star-Times* lashed out against conjecture about pending military operations and advised readers to instead devote themselves "to contemplating the cost of final victory." It suggested envisioning the agonized screams of wounded men along with "mud and blood, and stench, and hell's own noise, and the explosion that makes an end to living and loving, learning and dreaming, hoping and praying." The editorial chastised a public it portrayed as preoccupied with jobs, rationing, bond drives, and taxes, "the periphery of war," whose concerns seldom "get to the heart of it—the killing."[67] Some observers, like the columnist Barnet Nover, considered Okinawa an antidote for public complacency about the war.[68] In an attempt to make the lengthiest battle of the Pacific War more tolerable, the editors of the Los Angeles Times evaluated the laborious struggle as ultimately a means of hastening the war's conclusion.[69]

Laudatory of the battle's outcome, H.V. Kaltenborn, the dean of American radio commentators, nevertheless admitted that he found the prospect of "other Okinawas" disheartening. He cited Allied technological superiority as cause for optimism that casualties might be minimized in forthcoming campaigns.[70] Ironically, Kaltenborn called island-hopping, the tactic that strategists had devised to spare lives and hasten the Allied advance in the Pacific, a "slow and costly process." He regretted that the capture of Okinawa, which he inaccurately described as "tiny," resulted in more casualties than the liberation of the Philippines, contending that commanders must try to avoid such battles. "There are other ways of defeating Japan," he said, referring to bombing and blockade. "It may take a little longer, but if we can save a hundred thousand American lives, a few extra months will be well invested."[71]

Kaltenborn expressed the conflicting thoughts of those who deemed invading Japan a more expeditious strategy than siege, yet dreaded the anticipated casualties. His comparisons of Okinawa to combat in the Philippines neglected the fact that fighting also continued in that archipelago. Still, his message probably appealed to listeners disgruntled about the war's slowing pace. Cartoonist Carl Somdal of the Chicago Daily Tribune produced a rendering in early June captioned "Cleaning Up the Pests in the Victory Garden," which showed a GI thrusting his bayonet toward snakes, rats, and vermin labeled "Jap Fanatics." "It's the job of digging 'em out that takes time," the soldier exclaimed.[72] The illustration captured public frustrations in its depiction of a technologically superior American soldier slowed by a dehumanized yet dangerous foe. Ironically, the GI was using the bayonet, a weapon associated with Japanese treachery throughout the war. The image implied that U.S. troops had been forced to adopt more primitive methods in order to defeat the Japanese. With its "Victory Garden" heading, the cartoon suggested that achieving a more peaceful world required only a final, albeit laborious, cleansing of vermin.

Despite the recriminations over strategy, the revelation of Japanese suicide tactics, and the heavy casualties, many civilians remained somewhat sheltered from news about Okinawa. The death of President Roosevelt on April 12, the end of the war in Europe in early May, subsequent disclosures about the enormity of Nazi crimes, and the drafting and signing of the United Nations charter in San Francisco in May and June sometimes relegated stories concerning combat on Okinawa, which the editors of the *New York Times* called "a utilitarian battle," to the inner pages.[73]

An editorial published in the *New York Herald Tribune* welcomed the end of the campaign as good news for citizens anxious to purchase new automobiles. "It is easy to see," the editorial concluded, "even looking through a cracked windshield, that the capture of Okinawa, for instance, has brought a new car nearer to every two-car garage in New York, or in forty-seven other motor-hungry states."[74]

The responses to Okinawa reflected the contradictory sentiments on the home front in the spring and summer of 1945. The aforementioned editorial, which claimed that victory presaged the eventual arrival of new automobiles, expectantly anticipated the war's end. More frequently, commentators regarded the campaign as a frightful prelude to the final battle for Japan and possibly an indication that the war could last for several months. The ferocity of particular aspects of the battle appeared to hinder commentators' ability to grasp its awful scope, and the attention accorded the kamikaze attacks produced commentary that focused on the damage done to ships more than the casualties suffered by naval personnel.

Several factors contributed to the manner in which the campaign unfolded. Intelligence underestimated the number of Japanese troops on Okinawa and failed to realize the depth and strength of Japanese defenses.[75] Aerial reconnaissance before the invasion proved difficult because the nearest Allied bases were 1,200 miles away, and thick clouds hampered the missions flown to photograph the island. The first maps of Okinawa issued to U.S. troops contained large blank areas.[76]

The descriptions of the battlefield along the Shuri front are reminiscent of those of the Western front in World War I. Indeed, with its slow battering of entrenched positions, the fighting more closely resembled the Great War than any previous campaign in the Pacific. With an overwhelming superiority of supplies, dominance of the air despite the kamikaze raids, and complete control of the seas around Okinawa, the fact that U.S. commanders relied on continual pounding and costly advance against enemy positions is perplexing. In retrospect, trying to eliminate all Japanese forces on the island, as General MacArthur noted then, appears rather wasteful in time and lives.

To an extent, the battle for Okinawa was overshadowed by the amphibious invasion of Iwo Jima that preceded it and by the later dropping of atomic bombs. The struggle on Iwo Jima produced the most famous American image of the Pacific War—Joseph Rosenthal's Pulit-

Joe Rosenthal's photograph of marines raising the flag on Mount Saribashi on Iwo Jima remains the most enduring American image of the Pacific War. National Archives.

zer Prize-winning photograph of the raising of the American flag on Mount Suribachi. Published in newspapers across the nation, reproduced on war bond posters, and reenacted at bond rallies, the image of these marines working toward a common goal was adopted as a heroic embodiment of the entire nation's resolve.[77]

Since the twenty-seven thousand casualties on Iwo Jima were the highest up to that time, it is not surprising that the government exploited the dramatic photograph. The fact that Rosenthal's picture recorded the second flag raising was lost in the blitz of publicity that followed its publication. The photograph became an icon that rallied citizens and helped justify the casualties on Iwo Jima by presenting American boys erecting "Old Glory" on the isle's highest point.

No peak surmounted Okinawa as Mount Suribachi dominated Iwo Jima. Yet marines on Okinawa staged a flag raising on June 21 on a cliff overlooking the ocean, where they assumed the poses of the men in Rosenthal's picture. As the authors of a book about the legacy of the Rosenthal photograph later observed, the imagery associated with Iwo Jima validated the conclusion of combat on Okinawa.[78] The gesture reflected the measure of glory that some observers seemed to believe the Okinawan campaign lacked. Troops did not seize a soaring pinnacle that could be cited as representative of their valor like the taking of Mount Suribachi. Instead, they bravely clawed their way to the tops of dozens of deadly, small hills that they named.

On the home front, the capture of Okinawa produced more concern than praise, in part because the casualty rate surpassed that on Iwo Jima and because it came so soon after that campaign. The dichotomy of commentators praising the island's seizure while imploring that similar battles be averted in the future helps to explain why Americans have retained stronger memories of the battles at Midway, Guadalcanal, and Iwo Jima. Okinawa was not a dramatic turning point like Midway. It did not prove that U.S. forces could defeat the Japanese in jungle combat as the struggle on Guadalcanal confirmed. Nor did it produce enduring iconography as happened at Iwo Jima.[79] Instead, commentators cited it as an example of what must be avoided in forthcoming assaults.

Many citizens probably agreed with H.V. Kaltenborn that the United States should rely on its abundance of firepower and technology to win the war while minimizing casualties. However, the Allied dominance in ships, aircraft, weaponry, and supplies at Okinawa proved that known technology did not offer an easy solution for ending the war. Yet the idea of using technology enticed many people. These beliefs, combined with vengeful attitudes toward the Japanese enflamed by racial prejudices, the prevalent dehumanization of the Japanese, and the suicidal Japanese resistance contributed to the acceptance of incendiary bombing of Japanese cities and ultimately the use of atomic weapons.[80]

As mentioned previously, various commentators and leaders warned that all Japanese would resist an invasion and implied that troops would face the task of killing Japanese soldiers and civilians. Encounters with Okinawan civilians elicited a variety of responses from American troops, who both pitied Okinawans and regarded them warily; children easily won the soldiers' trust. Japanese troops exploited Okinawans by posing as civilians, using them as cover to aid in escaping. The number of civilian casualties on Okinawa shows that U.S. troops frequently could not or did not differentiate Okinawans from Japanese. Yet the complexities of the interaction between Americans and Okinawans suggests that it was easier for those on the home front to group all Japanese into one fanatical mass to be annihilated.[81]

The battle for Okinawa also worried U.S. leaders. The casualties troubled President Truman and contributed to the Joint Chiefs' delay in reaching an accord on operations scheduled to take place following Okinawa's capture. Some officials within the Truman administration began discussing the possibility of modifying unconditional surrender, while several military leaders opposed any clarification of terms until Okinawa was secured. Indeed, there is evidence that certain analysts in the War Department considered the campaign a psychological victory of sorts for the Japanese.[82]

Commanders attributed the high casualties of the campaign and its pace to the laborious task of destroying myriad underground fortifications. Even before Okinawa, various commanders and some commentators had suggested the tactical use of poison gas in the Pacific. The struggle for Okinawa helped spur interest in untried weapons that could minimize casualties. Coinciding with renewed appeals to use poison gas, the campaign helped revive discussion about chemical warfare. Periodically mentioned earlier in the war, the idea of using chemical weapons received renewed scrutiny from military leaders and prominent commentators in the summer of 1945.

6

The Sinister Cloud

The moment between 1918 and the present when the use of chemical weapons looked most promising came in the summer of 1945.[1]

From April 1945 onward, vigorous discussion occurred on the American home front as various columnists, radio commentators, and editors assessed issues related to ending the war against Japan. Arguments about chemical warfare in the war's closing months constituted a portion of a larger debate about the best strategy for securing victory with minimal casualties. Interest in chemical warfare peaked in the war's final months when several commentators argued that using poison gas could shorten the war, save lives, and possibly force Japan to surrender.

World War II witnessed concentration camps, genocide on an unprecedented scale, massive bombing of civilians, kamikazes, and the first use of atomic weapons. It is somewhat surprising that poison gas, a major weapon of World War I, was never extensively used. The absence of chemical warfare in the Pacific is particularly noteworthy considering the bitter nature of the fighting there, the intense American hatred of the Japanese, and the tenacious Japanese resistance that relied on caves and other natural barriers in defense of assorted islands. The high number of casualties suffered by American forces in capturing such positions prompted several military leaders to propose the use of chemical weapons. Still, the United States never used lethal gases in the Pacific.

The United States entered World War II lacking a definite chemical warfare policy. International law did not prohibit the United States from engaging in chemical warfare. The government had signed the Geneva Protocol of 1925 outlawing the use of poison gas in combat, but the Senate never ratified it. However, U.S. presidents pledged to abide by the accord. Little development of chemical weapons occurred in the U.S. Army during the 1920s and 1930s. When President Franklin D. Roosevelt vetoed a bill initiated by the War Department and passed by Congress in 1937 that would have changed the name of the army's

Chemical Warfare Service to the Chemical Corps, he characterized the use of chemical weapons as "inhuman and contrary to what modern civilization should stand for."[2]

In a secret memo composed shortly after the Japanese attack on Pearl Harbor, Secretary of State Cordell Hull urged that the administration declare its opposition to the use of poison gas. Secretary of the Navy Frank Knox concurred, but Secretary of War Henry Stimson disagreed. Stimson warned that Germany and Italy had prepared for chemical warfare, and he believed the reports of Japanese dispersal of gas against Chinese forces. Any statement supportive of the Geneva Protocol could raise troubling "domestic, political, and moral issues," Stimson argued, which would only hinder necessary preparations and be viewed by Axis leaders as "an indication of National weakness." He preferred unpublicized readiness for chemical warfare, arguing that treaties notwithstanding, "the only effective deterrent is fear of retaliation." He equated the prevention of negative statements about chemical weapons to tacit acceptance of their possible use.[3]

The United States gradually developed a declaratory policy regarding chemical weapons. Roosevelt issued his first remarks concerning chemical warfare in 1942, when he warned that the United States would retaliate if Japanese forces continued using poison gas in China.[4] That same year the Combined Chiefs of Staff of the United States and Great Britain issued a directive that became the foundation of Allied chemical warfare policy. It stipulated that gas warfare could only be ordered after approval by the highest government authorities in Washington, D.C., and London.[5] In 1943, Roosevelt further defined American policy when he said that the United States would only use poison gas in reprisal for chemical assaults by the Axis powers.[6]

During the war the budget for the Chemical Warfare Service (CWS) and the number of its personnel steadily increased. It was involved in preparing for both chemical and bacteriological warfare, producing various gases as well as incendiaries, flamethrowers, smoke pots, and chemical mortars. The Special Projects Division of CWS managed the development and manufacture of various biological warfare agents and weapons. The division studied diseases such as anthrax, glanders, brucellosis, plague, botulism, several plant contagions and tested a number of anthrax and botulism bombs.[7]

Chemical warfare contingency plans provided for retaliatory assaults against enemy positions with overwhelming quantities of gas dispersed by aerial spraying and bombardment. One report discussed dropping mustard-gas bombs on Japanese cities. If the bombs were used, it recommended dropping them with incendiaries and high explosives to increase casualties, complicate the repair of damage, spoil stored foods, and pollute water supplies.[8] Army Air Forces Intelligence listed several targeted Japanese cities in ranked order.[9] An Army Air Forces report of 1944 favored surprise aerial gas raids. It recounted the development of an incendiary bomb, described as probably most effective against "centers of population on the Japanese islands," which produced a lethal toxic smoke intended to hamper the efforts of firemen.[10]

Officers of the CWS continuously recommended offensive chemical warfare against the Japanese. Gen. William H. Porter, chief of the CWS, argued that using poison gas could minimize casualties. He contended that enemy troops in caves or concrete pillboxes could be killed with nonpersistent gas or, under proper conditions, by a persistent agent such as mustard gas.[11] Porter believed that the jungle canopy, high temperatures and humidity, and the calmness of prevailing Pacific winds would enhance the effectiveness of mustard gas and that the lower quality protective clothing and gas masks issued to Japanese troops provided insufficient protection from chemical assaults.[12]

In remarks to officers of the CWS, Brig. Gen. Alden H. Waitt, assistant chief of CWS for field operations, called gas "a powerful offensive weapon" and reiterated that climate, topography, inferior Japanese protective measures, and the nature of Japanese defenses made chemical warfare particularly appealing. Considering Japan's inability to attack the United States or retaliate effectively against U.S. troops, Waitt posited that "their distance from our homes while we draw steadily nearer theirs" had "profound implications." He added that the Japanese had "given us enough provocation to use gas or any other weapon on them."[13]

Refinement of Allied chemical warfare policy continued during the war.[14] A report by the Joint Intelligence Committee from mid-1944 speculated that chemical weapons might be particularly effective against Japan because of Japanese "national characteristics" that favored heroism in combat. It said that chemical attacks represented "one of those aspects of war to which there is no obvious response of 'formal' bravery and which the Japanese may well find flustering."[15]

American strategists aspired to preserve their independence in strategic planning against Japan. An appraisal of a British proposal to further limit the potential for independent use of poison gas by the United States considered whether retaliatory plans should be prepared "against the Axis or the Jap." This passage severed the Japanese from the Axis coalition.[16] One study opposed to further restraints on the use of gas acknowledged the unique problems of initiating chemical warfare, yet argued that gas might prove a valuable weapon at the proper time: "Furthermore, if we or any of the United Nations initiate gas warfare under existing policies, the grave political and psychological reactions, domestic and external, would necessitate propaganda of justification. (Security considerations would prohibit an extensive program of justification prior to using gas.) It appears from the above that our policies on gas warfare are effective only in the "preventative" sense. This condition, however, understood as it must be by our enemies, may be good "insurance" against Japan initiating gas warfare upon us and good "cover" for offensive use of gas by us at the proper time." The document repeated previous arguments that the United States possessed the advantage over Japan in chemical combat and said that the use of poison gas against Japan, "at the correct psychological moment," might cause Japan's collapse.[17]

Because of the risks of exposure for friendly civilian populations in China and the Philippines, the Joint Chiefs deemed widespread retaliatory use of gas in areas outside Japan proper "hardly conceivable," although use for "tactical purposes" remained possible. Plans for strategic retaliatory chemical warfare focused on the home islands of Japan, including the Ryukyus and Bonins.[18]

Despite concerns that Japan might initiate chemical warfare, Japanese production of chemical agents, so it was disclosed after the war, was rather small; less than five thousand tons of mustard and Lewisite gas were manufactured from 1930-1945.[19] Allied intelligence considered widespread chemical warfare by Japan unlikely.[20]

On the home front meanwhile, books about chemical weapons portrayed them as either potentially decisive or more threatening than effective.[21] Some articles in the media offered only superficial summaries about poison gas, while others attempted thoughtful evaluation of the morality of using poison gas and questioned its value as a weapon. Articles that informed readers about precautionary measures in the event of a chemical assault usually characterized poison gas as primarily a panic-inducing weapon. For example, a piece in Collier's said that fewer casualties would result from an aerial gas raid than from a conventional bombing attack but admonished that "any dolt can get himself killed or badly hurt by staying deliberately in a gassed area." A similar feature published in Good Housekeeping advised against trying to indentify gasses by smell.[22] A subsequent article in Collier's claimed that the Allies were better prepared for gas warfare than the Axis. "We can hustle it overseas in jigtime, if that's the way the other side wants to play."[23] In a speech to the New York City branch of the American Association of University Women in early 1943, a physician belittled poison gas as "an overrated weapon."[24]

Although some essays reassured citizens that poison gas was more frightening than lethal, top officers in the Chemical Warfare Service promoted it as a valuable weapon. In an article printed in *New Republic* in 1942, the aforementioned Alden H. Waitt, then a colonel in the Chemical Warfare Service, predicted widespread use of gas. Although he did not directly advise that the Allies initiate chemical warfare, Waitt implied that doing so might prove advantageous. He argued that the United States could not properly fight a war when constrained by a "national delusion that we can play the part of the 'white knight . . . when opposed by a gang of international cutthroats."[25]

Responding to such predictions *Time* attacked assertions that gas was more effective or less sinister than conventional weapons, calling poison gas "the most fearful horror of war" and "the weapon of last resort, when all other known military means have failed to force a decision."[26] In a concurrent article published in *Newsweek* a retired general disagreed, characterizing poison gas as a more humane weapon than commonly believed because it wounded or disabled more often than it killed.[27]

More articles endorsing the use of chemical weapons against the Japanese appeared in the print media after the battle for Tarawa in November 1943. The carnage of Tarawa shocked citizens, as newspapers printed photographs of dead marines, among the first published of American casualties. More than one thousand marines died and two thousand were wounded in three days of ferocious fighting to capture an area of less than three square miles.

On the day the battle commenced the *New York Daily News* editorialized, "We Should Gas Japan."[28] The *Times-Herald* of Washington, D.C., subsequently printed two similar editorials, "We Should Have Used Gas at Tarawa" and "You Can Cook 'Em Better With Gas." The latter, published after the release of information about the Bataan death march, argued that Japanese atrocities made clear that "these barbarians" had no regard for ideals of decency and humanity. "To limit ourselves voluntarily to weapons only the equal of theirs would be chivalrous but idiotic," the editorial contended. The editors said that atrocity reports should "nullify the squeamishness any American may have had about using gas or any other weapon that promises to slaughter Jap fighting men."[29]

The military commentator Hanson W. Baldwin called the atrocity accounts "cumulative and incontrovertible evidence of the decadence and bestiality of the enemy we fight." These were not isolated incidents, Baldwin argued, but measures reflective of Japanese character and mentality intended to terrorize their enemies. The disclosure of the atrocities, he reasoned, had probably eroded some of the opposition to use of poison gas.[30] Columnist Ernest K. Lindley, a regular contributor to *Newsweek*, described Japanese island outposts as ideal targets for gas. "To our enemies this is a war of survival or extermination," he wrote. "Are we fighting it as such? Or are we, by an anachronistic devotion to the code of the duel, committing thousands of our bravest youth to avoidable death?"[31]

Articles promoting the use of poison gas provoked denunciations. Norman Cousins, the editor of the *Saturday Review of Literature*, castigated proponents of chemical warfare. He believed that the Allies must uphold certain standards of humanity, and he considered poison gas an inhumane weapon.[32] Saying that Americans should not regard poison gas as an apocalyptic weapon, *Time* reminded readers that just as in World War I the lethality of poison gas depended on variables such as wind and weather. The editors of *Time* believed that Americans should stop debating the morality of particular weapons and instead consider their practicality.[33]

In the final months of the Pacific War various military commanders and commentators renewed arguments for initiating chemical warfare. With the surrender of Germany in early May 1945, the deterrent of chemical retaliation in Europe by the Axis powers vanished.[34] Rising casualty rates in the Pacific greatly concerned American military leaders, several of whom doubted the public's fortitude for achieving Japan's unconditional surrender. The battle to capture Iwo Jima also prompted editorial comment in favor of using poison gas.[35]

By 1945, strategists had devised more varied chemical warfare plans. Earlier in 1945, the War Department sent the Joint Chiefs of Staff information about a plan devised by George W. Merck, chairman of the U.S. Biological Warfare Committee and special consultant to the Secretary of War, to destroy crops grown by Japanese forces on isolated islands. The substances involved, "LN" chemicals, consisted of dichlorophenoxyacetic acid, a common weed killer, combined with tributyl phosphate and then mixed with oil. General Porter of the Chemical Warfare Service proposed spraying rice crops in the Japanese home islands as well. General Marshall requested further study to determine whether the Japanese could justly claim that the dispersal of these agents constituted chemical warfare. Maj. Gen. Myron C. Cramer, the army's judge advocate general, concluded that crop-destroying agents neither violated international law nor constituted chemical warfare as long as the chemicals only killed crops.[36]

In May 1945, General Arnold of the Army Air Forces received a plan for using the chemical ammonium thiocyanate to destroy rice crops in

Japan. The study proposed the spraying of chemicals over rice-growing regions near Japan's six largest cities. It also suggested mining and bombing areas along the coast of Japan to kill large schools of fish, thereby exacerbating the food shortages in Japan. V.E. Bertrandias, the plan's author, described it as "a quick knockout of Japan from the air by concentrating on sources of food." He argued that the United States could not be accused of using "gas warfare" because the proposed chemical was not "externally harmful to humans." However, if the United States did adopt gas warfare, the study asserted, mustard gas would be even more lethal against rice crops.[37] Submitted to the Joint Target Group for further consideration, the plan was discounted as tactically unsound, although no one offered moral objections to it. Strategists discussed environmental warfare against Japan's sources of food until the war ended.[38]

As the struggle on Okinawa continued, several military leaders advocated offensive use of chemical weapons. General Marshall, General Arnold, General MacArthur, and Gen. Joseph W. Stilwell all supported using poison gas against Japanese forces. Each of these commanders qualified their endorsement of chemical warfare. MacArthur had spoken favorably of chemical warfare in conversations with Arnold in June 1945.[39] Stilwell proposed it in the event Japan was invaded.[40] Brig. Gen. William A. Borden, director of the New Developments Division of the War Department's General Staff, also endorsed the use of chemical weapons if the Allies invaded Japan.[41] One week after V-E Day, Borden met representatives of various Army branches, including Operations (OPD) and the Chemical Warfare Service, to discuss Stilwell's recommendations.[42] Subsequently, an Army program called Project SPHINX tested poison gas against caves. One of the summary reports concluded that poison gas was the most promising weapon for neutralizing cave defenses and rated the flamethrower as the most effective nongas weapon.[43]

General Marshall suggested using poison gas against pockets of entrenched Japanese to diminish American losses. Talking with Henry Stimson and Assistant Secretary of War John J. McCloy in late May 1945, Marshall broached chemical warfare as the three discussed methods of minimizing casualties. According to the summary memo of the meeting, Marshall supported development of "new weapons and tactics" to negate the "last ditch defense tactics" of the Japanese. He wanted to avoid more battles of attrition and suggested that selective use of mustard gas could speed the war's pace and decrease casualties. Marshall admitted that public opinion might present an obstacle, but he believed this could be resolved.[44] In mid-June, John McCloy suggested evaluating the pros and cons of initiating chemical warfare—in case the public demanded it because of rising casualties.[45]

In June 1945 Gen. George A. Lincoln, chief of the Army Strategy and Policy Group, and Marshall's top strategist, directed the Strategy Section to study offensive chemical warfare. This marked a departure from previous contingency plans for the retaliatory use of chemical weapons. One memorandum recommended aerial dispersal of chemical agents over Japan and listed several potential targets including urban areas. The memo admitted, "It might take a good deal of effort to 'sell' this measure to the public."[46]

The study itself provided a detailed analysis of chemical warfare possibilities and urged that measures be taken to ensure the support of citizens. It even suggested that for "public and governmental acquiescence to Army use of gas warfare, it might prove necessary to stage some sort of incident to be cited as reason for beginning gas warfare."[47]

The proposal of a contrived incident troubled some strategists. Col. Max S. Johnson, chief of Strategy Section, reiterated to Lincoln that with regard to offensive use of gas, "Roosevelt damned it pretty thoroughly." Johnson urged that careful consideration be given to the opinions of citizens, the soldiers engaged in chemical combat, the Allies, and the rest of the world. "An incident could undoubtedly be created or merely alleged and we could insist that our use of gas is retaliatory only," Johnson continued, "but the probability that our decision to adopt gas warfare could be long hidden under the cloak of a framed incident is small."[48]

A subsequent memo from Marshall emphasized that strategy remained bound to achieving "the quickest conclusion" against Japan at minimal cost. Marshall described poison gas as "the one single weapon hitherto unused which we have readily available and which assuredly can greatly decrease the cost in American lives and should materially shorten the war." His memo said that planes could also keep various communication centers in Japan "continuously saturated with gas." The widespread dispersal of gas over Japan would, the memo argued, convince the Japanese that they faced "extermination" if they did not surrender. Of course, this contradicted Truman's assurances that the United States did not intend to exterminate the Japanese. While acknowledging prevailing opinion against chemical warfare, Marshall reasoned that if arguments supportive of it could be "put to the people properly, they should approve." The memo proposed that the Joint Chiefs agree to initiate "all-out gas warfare" against Japan by the target date of Operation OLYMPIC, the planned invasion of Kyushu, and secure President Truman's approval. Marshall suggested that Truman discuss the matter with Joseph Stalin and Winston Churchill at the forthcoming Potsdam Conference scheduled for July 1945.[49]

Marshall sent the report to other military chiefs, but the available record does not disclose Admiral King's response.[50] Chief of Staff Adm. William Leahy, Truman's personal military adviser, believed that Roosevelt's previous statements had precluded offensive use of chemical weapons "beyond the probability of change." But he did not object to anyone discussing a reversal of the policy with Truman.[51] The documentary record does not reveal General Arnold's reaction to the study either. An undated memo in Arnold's papers from the summer of 1945, sent to several subordinates, outlined various points to be discussed with President Truman in a pending meeting. Arnold wrote, "You should also present forcefully that now is the time to either use poison gas or at least threaten Japan with its use if she does not surrender unconditionally."[52] An Army briefing paper prepared prior to the Potsdam Conference said that the Joint Chiefs agreed that any change in policy would have to come from "the highest level."[53] Apparently Marshall never broached the topic with Truman. The lack of agreement among the Joint Chiefs and the impending test of the atomic bomb at Alamagordo, New Mexico, probably deterred Marshall from pressing the matter.[54]

The army brief also discussed methods of justifying offensive chemical warfare to the public. To overcome public opposition it recommended "a program of education," similar to the one suggested by Marshall. The brief argued that the assault on Pearl Harbor and Japanese atrocities meant Japan had "forfeited her rights to treatment as a civilized nation." By restricting the first use of poison gas to combat situations, it explained, "we could hold out the threat of extending its use to the Japanese civilian population." To counter any stigma the Allies might bear for starting chemical warfare, the memo suggested that it could be defended as an appropriate response to previous Japanese actions.[55]

Those who endorsed the dropping of the atomic bombs later used similar justifications. Threatening Japanese civilians was consistent with the rationale that they were accountable for the actions of Japanese soldiers. Although concluding that gas would be helpful in defeating Japan, the army memo recognized that the views of the American public and the world must be taken into account. The arguments supportive of chemical warfare resembled the claims of the Chemical Warfare Service that gas constituted a decisive weapon.

On the home front it appeared that there was some support for using chemical weapons. In a poll from June 1945, 40 percent of the respondents endorsed the use of gas if it meant saving the lives of American troops.[56] Debate over chemical weapons reappeared in the print media. Col. Frederic Palmer, writing in the Washington, D.C., *Evening Star*, suggested dispersing poison gas over airfields in Japan used by suicide squadrons.[57] The syndicated military commentator Maj. George Fielding Eliot also favored using poison gas against the Japanese and said that chemical warfare was not worse than the ongoing incendiary bombing of Japanese cities.[58]

Opponents of chemical warfare also spoke out. C.G. Paulding, the editor of the Catholic journal *Commonweal*, admitted that Eliot was technically correct. "When aviation fuel jelly . . . roasts men alive it might even be kinder to let them gasp quickly and die," he wrote. But Paulding countered that Eliot's logic proved that the decision to use poison gas should not be left to "technicians or military commentators." "To the Orient we are bringing the latest inventions of our civilization," Paulding noted. "There is only one that we have not brought. It is gas. If we use that, we will have brought them all. Gas is no worse than flame. It is only that it is one more weapon. The last one we have to use. Until we invent a new one." Paulding believed that the moment had arrived "when nothing more can be added to the horror if we wish to keep our coming victory something we can use—or that humanity can use."[59]

In letters to the *Evening Star* readers of Eliot's column also disagreed with him. One veteran feared that the United States was forsaking Christian principles in its conduct of the war. Another reader, who argued that even the Nazis did not engage in chemical warfare, accused Eliot of regressing "to the bad judgment he showed around the time of Pearl Harbor when he felt all we had to do to the Nipponese was a few weeks of mopping up." One reader said that the United States would permanently tarnish its reputation by using chemical weapons. "We cry out in horror when we hear of the inhuman acts of the Japanese. Do we wish to descend to their level, rather than be a pattern for the entire civilized world?"[60]

Raymond Gram Swing, commentator for the ABC radio network, expressed ambivalence about using poison gas. He considered the arguments in favor of chemical weapons persuasive but said that a portion of the public wanted to avoid additional wartime horrors. He believed citizens could be convinced to support chemical warfare and said that opposing the use of poison gas while accepting incendiary bombing was illogical.[61] *Time* contended that only "the people themselves" should decide whether the United States should use chemical weapons.[62]

Gladstone Williams, a columnist for the *Atlanta Constitution*, said that an invasion of Japan would be a repetition of Okinawa, with potentially "staggering" losses. He believed that using poison gas would save American lives. "What is the difference," he asked, "between killing a man by frying him in burning gasoline, as our flamethrowers do, or disemboweling him with an artillery shell, and asphyxiating him?" Pressing his argument, Williams wrote: "In putting a sick monkey to death, or a dog, you don't pour burning gasoline on him or blast off his limbs one at a time. Far easier to give him a shot of gas. Why not treat the Japanese monkeys the same way? It would shorten the war and save us countless casualties." Contending that the use of poison gas might prevent a prolonged war, Williams said that citizens had a right to demand that their military leaders use it.[63]

The respective columns of Maj. George Fielding Eliot and Gladstone Williams reiterated the familiar arguments that chemical warfare might spare American lives and expedite the war's pace. Both of them defended chemical warfare by saying that the Japanese would launch it if it was to their advantage. Perhaps cynics of the time noted the irony of these two essayists justifying potential U.S. actions by claiming that an enemy they had both described as barbaric would do the same. Their commentaries reflected the racial emotionalism directed toward the Japanese in the media throughout the war. Eliot referred to burning "hides," and Williams bluntly described the Japanese as monkeys, implying that Americans could use poison gas with a clear conscience, since dispensing it against the Japanese did not differ from gassing an animal. He thereby portrayed the use of poison gas as a more humane form of killing, just as putting a sick animal to sleep would be more merciful than shooting it.

The *Atlanta Constitution* subsequently printed an editorial that opposed chemical warfare. The editors admitted that using poison gas might save lives and shorten the war, but declared that because the United States was "the moral leader in this war" and remained "a Christian nation" despite numerous faults, it should not initiate chemical warfare.[64]

Some readers of the newspaper disagreed. In a letter to the editor one person argued that "those whose sons and brothers face the task of exterminating these barbarians" would dispute such moralism. The reader scoffed at "mawkish religious sentimentality," saying that if using gas saved even one American life, "let's throw Puritanical scruples out the window and turn the chemical warfare service loose on Hirohito & Company. War is no prep school basketball game, and all that counts is results, so what are we waiting for?" Another reader, who called the Japanese "yellow rats," argued that speeding the war's end and saving "our boys from death and/or fates worse than death at the hands of those barbarians" constituted good reasons for using gas. "If there are still Americans that believe there is anything humane about the Japanese," he wrote, "then may God help them."[65]

Obviously, commentators and citizens held diverse views on the subject of chemical warfare. The dropping of the atomic bombs in early August 1945 ended the debate on the home front about using poison gas in the Pacific.

Numerous constraints deterred chemical warfare by the United States during World War II. Historians have generally considered President Roosevelt's declaration that the United States would use poison gas only in reprisal for first use by the Axis the most important.[66] The British, in particular, feared German retaliation, and American military leaders recognized that chemical warfare might spread to regions occupied by Japan and expose friendly civilian populations to chemical agents.[67] Roosevelt's pronouncements carried considerable weight, but their import has probably been overemphasized. He might have annulled stated policy had he been advised that chemical warfare was a necessity for shortening the war and saving lives. Earlier in the war he had remarked in a letter, "In fighting Japanese savages all previously accepted rules of warfare must be abandoned."[68] Conceivably, President Truman could have reversed Roosevelt's policy, but he never received concerted pressure to do so. The most important inhibition to chemical warfare was that no military leader ever said that the use of poison gas was indispensable for achieving victory.

The logistical problems of shipping and storing chemical weapons made them more problematic than conventional munitions.[69] Preparing for chemical warfare required compiling quantities of gas masks and protective clothing, which added to the existent logistical logjam. Complete readiness for chemical warfare would have required the manufacture of quantities of chemical bombs, which in turn would have reduced the production of bomb casings for the incendiaries that had proven extremely effective during firebomb raids over Japan.[70] Stockpiling enough chemical weapons for offensive chemical warfare would have taken up space needed for moving troops and conventional supplies to Pacific staging areas for the planned invasion of Kyushu.[71]

The perception among military strategists that a significant number of civilians perceived gas to be a diabolical weapon also served as a constraint on chemical warfare. If the sentiments of citizens did not prevent chemical warfare, the army still believed that prevailing opinion opposed it, and strategists recognized the necessity of justifying chemical warfare should it occur.[72]

As noted, commentators expressed a range of views about chemical warfare. Those who supported the use of poison gas argued that it might shorten the war, save lives, and exact further retribution for Pearl Harbor and Bataan. Those who opposed chemical warfare deemed it worse than incendiary bombing. In general, critics of chemical warfare have considered it more insidious and inhumane than traditional forms of killing.[73]

Had the United States followed through with operation CORONET, the invasion of Honshu in 1946, the pressure for using chemical weapons may have become irresistible. One of the final studies of chemical warfare advised against the use of poison gas in the invasion of Kyushu but recommended it, both tactically and strategically, in support of CORONET. The plan discussed gas attacks against Japanese cities, where it anticipated vast civilian casualties. High explosives would be dropped along with mustard gas bombs. "Casualties could be expected to be so heavy," the report stated, "that the whole population would be put in a state of panic."[74]

One author later singled out the summer of 1945 as the one period after 1918 when chemical weapons received serious consideration as decisive weapons. This occurred at a time when most commentators, military leaders, and citizens hoped to gain Japan's unconditional surrender without an invasion. According to author Michael Mandelbaum, "A shock, to persuade the Japanese that holding out would be not only futile but catastrophic, was required—a shock that could be administered without risk to Americans."[75]

Rising casualties and lengthening campaigns, culminating with the costly struggle on Okinawa, caused people within and outside the military to consider untried methods of combating the increasingly suicidal Japanese resistance. The legacy of Pearl Harbor, accounts of Japanese abuse and execution of Allied prisoners, racial prejudices, and climbing casualties had eroded nearly all compassion for the Japanese, soldiers or civilians. Before there was widespread knowledge of the atomic bomb within the military, or any awareness of its development among the public, military planners and various commentators sought a weapon that could accomplish the goals of expeditiously ending the war and saving lives. Those who favored using poison gas frequently mentioned its value in having a "shock" effect on the supposedly panic-prone Japanese, sufficient to make them quit the war. Proponents of the atomic bomb later made similar remarks about its shock value. Poison gas was the known available weapon, but it remained a weapon of disrepute.

By July 1945 a new weapon, possibly capable of achieving the aims Americans desired, unencumbered by the sinister attributes ascribed to chemical weapons, and logistically simple to move, was ready. The atomic bomb fit the circumstances of the time and was not subject to public debate. Numerous scientists knowledgeable about the bomb's development raised objections to its unannounced use, but the project's secrecy effectively excluded commentators and the public from making any contribution to the issue. The debate over the use of poison gas offers, on a smaller scale, a glimpse of what might have occurred had citizens known about the atomic bomb.

7

Assault or Siege?

The question is whether we face the rather appalling necessity of killing 3,600,000 armed men to put an end to the war. Any strategy that will produce the surrender rather than the extermination of a substantial number of these men is desirable—not for humanitarian reasons, but because the extermination process involves heavy casualties to us.[1]

"I have to decide Japanese strategy—shall we invade Japan proper or shall we bomb and blockade? That is my hardest decision to date. But I'll make it when I have all the facts."[2] President Harry S. Truman made this notation in his diary the day before he conferred with the Joint Chiefs of Staff to discuss plans for invading Japan. Actually, the Joint Chiefs did not present Truman with these alternatives. Instead, they sought his approval of Operation OLYMPIC, an invasion of Kyushu, the southernmost main Japanese island. Their plans represented a compromise, based in part on perceptions of public morale, that combined the strategies of siege and invasion. In the last months of the war, commentators and military leaders expressed conflicting opinions about whether assault or siege offered the best method of defeating Japan.

During the 1920s and 1930s American stategists envisaged a war against Japan as primarily a naval struggle that would culminate in a blockade of the Japanese home islands. As concepts of air power developed, bombing was included in the strategic plans.[3]

After the United States entered World War II, the Allies' "Europe first" policy hindered the development of overall strategy for the Pacific War.[4] The Allied demand for unconditional surrender also affected plans. In comments he later described as extemporaneous, Franklin Roosevelt first announced the policy in January 1943 at Casablanca, where he had traveled to meet Winston Churchill as American and British military staffs discussed future operations. Roosevelt said that peace could be achieved only by the unconditional surrender of the Axis powers.[5] Although his remarks were not as spontaneous as he claimed, he appears to have thought little about the military implications of unconditional surrender.[6]

Initial plans for the Pacific War did not regard an invasion of Japan as inevitable.[7] Early strategic studies posited that the blockade and bombing of Japan might achieve victory without an invasion.[8] The conditional timetables of one of the first Allied strategic plans projected bombing of Japan and invasion by 1947 or later, emphasizing the importance of expeditiously defeating Japan after Germany's surrender because the public would be "considerably exhausted" from several years of war.[9] American strategists objected to such lengthy forecasts. An Army Air Forces planner believed the public would not tolerate the war lasting until 1947, and a navy counterpart said that if Japan fought that long, civilian morale might be so enervated that Japan "would have won the war."[10]

In a directive of June 1944 the Joint Chiefs of Staff emphasized speed, contending that relying solely on siege would cause an objectionable protraction of the war, possibly prompting criticism from Congress and the public.[11] The Combined Chiefs of Staff approved a proposal to defeat Japan within twelve months of Germany's surrender. General Marshall remarked that although Japan's defeat might be achieved by siege, "this would probably involve an unacceptable delay."[12]

The Joint Chiefs agreed that the United States should avoid "costly land campaigns."[13] Eventually, army and navy strategists recommended attacking Kyushu, preliminary to invading Honshu. One directive described the invasions of Kyushu and Honshu as complementary and proposed that the latter be launched within three months of the former. It stated that the assaults "cannot be treated as separate, unrelated operations but rather are two coordinated steps in a single, integrated offensive in the decisive area."[14]

Sustained bombing of Japan by newly developed B-29 bombers began in mid-1944. By 1945 the Army Air Forces had consolidated these operations on bases in the Marianas islands. Dissatisfaction with the damage results of high-altitude bombing with conventional explosives helped renew interest in incendiary bombing, a tactic espoused by Army Air Forces personnel as early as the 1920s.[15]

Shortly after he assumed control of the bomber groups based in the Marianas in January 1945, Gen. Curtis LeMay prepared for nighttime firebombing of Japanese cities. On March 9 and 10, more than three hundred B-29s attacked Tokyo, causing unprecedented destruction. Reconnaissance photographs showed nearly sixteen square miles of the city gutted. The U.S. Strategic Bombing Survey later estimated that the assault killed nearly 88,000 people, injured almost 41,000, and left more than one million homeless.[16] From May to August 1945, U.S. planes firebombed fifty-eight Japanese cities.[17]

In the meantime, the Joint Chiefs deliberated future operations. Army commanders vigorously opposed Admiral King's proposals for landings in islands off the coast of China after the capture of Okinawa.[18] The army believed that delaying a direct assault on Japan would only lengthen the war. Gen. John E. Hull, chief of the army's Operations Division, said King's ideas guaranteed more costly battles on small islands, whereas invading Kyushu, a larger island, would allow room for maneuver and thereby diminish losses.[19] Marshall's primary strategist, Gen. George A. Lincoln, castigated the idea of "tangential operations" that might leave the United States unprepared to invade Japan when the Soviet Union entered the Pacific War. "Won't the Russians say we have welched?" Lincoln queried. "If they mop-up the Japs themselves while we are fooling around in the Yellow Sea, won't the Russians take all the credit for the victory and ask for the spoils?"[20]

Concerned about ending the war quickly, the army deemed siege a less attractive option. A Joint Intelligence Committee study of April 1945 said that a siege would progressively weaken Japan's "will" to fight. However, it noted that estimates of the time required for siege to force Japan's surrender ranged from a few months to several years.[21] A memo from the Joint Chiefs from April 1945 characterized siege as a strategy that might result in a negotiated peace. It considered invasion the strategy most likely to achieve unconditional surrender, although then and later not all the Joint Chiefs agreed on this point.[22] General Marshall was the most ardent supporter of invasion. In April 1945 both General MacArthur and Admiral Nimitz informed Marshall that they endorsed an invasion of Kyushu after the capture of Okinawa. On May 25, 1945, the Joint Chiefs instructed them to begin planning for OLYMPIC, the invasion of Kyushu, scheduled for November 1, 1945.[23] Admiral King, and other naval commanders, expected Japan's collapse before an invasion.[24]

These decisions did not entirely resolve the issue. President Truman requested a meeting with the Joint Chiefs in June to discuss strategy. Historians have disagreed about whether Truman was more concerned with ending the war quickly or sparing American lives.[25] Truman later wrote that a speedy resolution of the war remained his primary concern, and predictions by military advisers that the Pacific War would continue for another eighteen months did not deter him from emphasizing rapidity.[26] Certainly casualties worried Truman. Admiral Leahy notified the Joint Chiefs prior to the meeting that the president wanted projected timetables and casualty estimates for the respective strategies of siege and invasion. Leahy's memo said that Truman would consider foremost "economizing to the maximum extent possible . . . the loss of American lives. Economy in the use of time and in money cost is comparatively unimportant."[27]

Truman desired a timely end to the war and wanted to avoid more battles of attrition. He equated speed with the sparing of life in the opening lines of his message to Congress of June 1, 1945, which proclaimed the nation's most important goal as quickly ending the war.[28] Leahy emphasized time constraints over casualties, yet closed his memo by stressing the importance of minimizing casualties. The contradictions probably reflected his awareness of Truman's desire to fulfill both aims.

General Marshall requested casualty estimates for an invasion of Kyushu from MacArthur. Correspondence between the army command in Washington and MacArthur made clear that Truman was "very much concerned" about casualties. For the three-month period allotted for OLYMPIC, MacArthur's staff predicted 50,800 casualties during the first thirty days, 27,150 in the next thirty-day period, and 27,100 for the final thirty-day span. In a memo to Marshall, MacArthur said that a section of his staff compiled these "purely academic and routine" forecasts without his input. He did not expect such high losses.[29] Marshall provided considerably lower figures when he met with Truman.[30]

The president, Secretary of War Henry Stimson, Secretary of the Navy James Forrestal, and Assistant Secretary of War John J. McCloy met with the Joint Chiefs on June 18 at the White House. Marshall, who dominated the meeting, characterized OLYMPIC as "the only course to pursue." He described the capture of Kyushu as fundamental to a strategy of "strangulation" and a necessary precursor to an invasion of Honshu. Marshall said that MacArthur gained objectives with reasonable losses, and he read a memo from MacArthur in which the commander heartily endorsed OLYMPIC. Cognizant of Truman's concerns about casualties, MacArthur called the capture of Kyushu "the most economical one in effort and lives that is possible." Supporting Marshall's views, Admiral King said that further study had convinced him of Kyushu's strategic value. He considered its possession essential to the success of siege.

Admiral Leahy again raised the topic of casualties and pointed out that the casualty rate on Okinawa had been 35 percent. He reasoned that a sound estimate of casualties could be derived by applying this percentage to the total of 766,700 troops slated for OLYMPIC. King argued that the geography on Okinawa had limited strategic options.

Ironically, he then cited the army comments that the larger area of Kyushu would permit forces to avoid frontal assaults and thereby sustain fewer casualties than on Okinawa. Leahy did say that possession of Kyushu would provide more bases for bombing Japan.

Stimson concurred with planning for an invasion. However, he believed that many Japanese wanted to end the war, and he thought the United States should try to encourage them. Stimson said that such measures must occur prior to an invasion, which he believed would unify the Japanese. After listening to the discussion Truman approved OLYMPIC saying "we can do this operation and then decide as to the final action later." He reiterated his desire to prevent "an Okinawa from one end of Japan to the other."[31]

Throughout the meeting the Joint Chiefs resisted precise discussion of casualties. To allay Truman's concerns they referred to the casualty rates in the Philippines rather than the higher totals on Okinawa. Truman did not press Leahy's point that a comparison with Okinawa was a more valid collation.

Implicitly, although unstated, concern about public morale underlay the talks. Marshall said that an invasion was more likely to achieve unconditional surrender within a reasonable period of time. Yet if one applied the 35 percent casualty rate of Okinawa to the attack on Kyushu, casualties would total roughly 268,000. The effect on the public of losses of such magnitude justifiably worried Truman. Predictions of one million American casualties resulting from an invasion of Japan soon appeared in the press.[32] Public opinion polls from the war's final months indicated that citizens favored a lengthier war if it meant fewer casualties.[33]

The options presented a dilemma. At the risk of incurring heavy casualties, invasion would apparently avoid diminishing public support for a war of indeterminate length. Siege meant fewer casualties, yet it was perceived by several commentators and certain commanders as increasing the likelihood of an indefinite war. To some, siege appeared a more passive strategy that placed the United States in the position of awaiting Japan's surrender rather than forcing it by invasion. Several leaders remained concerned that citizens might not tolerate casualty rates that surpassed those of Okinawa.

In the discussions of June 18, the Joint Chiefs intimated the hope that CORONET, the invasion of Honshu, would not be necessary. Their remarks about intensifying bombing after the seizure of Kyushu disregarded the claims of Army Air Forces commanders who said there would be few remaining targets in Japan by November 1945.[34]

With Truman and the members of the Joint Chiefs making statements about weighing options after the capture of Kyushu, OLYMPIC was really a hybrid of invasion and siege. Obviously, it was hoped that taking Kyushu would induce Japan's unconditional surrender. Marshall and King described OLYMPIC as essential to the success of siege in statements that forsook the plans of 1944 which considered the assaults upon Kyushu and Honshu as components of a single operation. Indeed, in a later diary entry, Leahy distinguished between the landings on Kyushu and further invasion plans, which he considered too costly.[35]

On the home front, bombing remained the most publicized component of the siege strategy. With their descriptions of hundreds of planes wreaking destruction on Japan, the media accounts of incendiary assaults contrasted dramatically with those of the tortuous campaign on Okinawa. In June 1945, on the anniversary of the first B-29 raid on Japan, the *New York Times* published a chart reminiscent of a scorecard that recounted all previous bombing missions, listed the intended targets, the approximate number of planes involved in each raid, and the number of bombers lost.[36] Bombing undoubtedly helped satisfy the enduring American desire for revenge against the Japanese, and Army Air Forces commanders assumed that most citizens heartily endorsed it. Still, the Army Air Forces diligently kept track of public opinion on the issue.[37] Bombing provided the public a vicarious satisfaction beyond the defeat of Japan's armed forces because it inflicted suffering on Japanese civilians.[38] Certainly numerous citizens and commentators shared the conviction that the Japanese deserved whatever punishment they received. A cartoon published in the *Chicago Daily Tribune* captioned "He's Asking for It" showed huge planes flying over Japan's coastline, while an enormous bomb labeled "Total Destruction" hurtled toward a typically diminutive, ridiculous looking Japanese.[39]

Reports about bombing seldom mentioned civilian casualties, even when describing a Japanese city as "a flaming caldron."[40] By 1945 most people accepted the bombing of urban areas, especially Japanese cities.[41] The lack of reference to civilian losses also reflected the pervasive notion that incinerating civilians, however regrettable, was justifiable if it ultimately saved American lives. One editorial described Tokyo as transformed from "a beehive of activity" to "little more than a desert of ashes and desolation," and concluded that such ruination must be making unconditional surrender a more attractive option to the average Japanese.[42] Despite public disclaimers that bombing cities did not constitute warfare on civilians, an Army Air Forces intelligence report from July 1945 described Japan's major cities as "largely ashheaps" and admitted that "the numbers of citizens interred in those ashes must be staggering."[43]

A few articles expressed whimsy about bombing. Summarizing a broadcast by Radio Tokyo that recounted a Japanese government plan to limit the size of urban populations, an Associated Press story approved the use of firebombs "to get Tokyo's population down to more seemly proportions" and made mocking estimates of the amount of vacant land beneath the ashes and debris within the Japanese capital.[44] Announcing forthcoming local events scheduled on Air Forces Day, an article in the *Los Angeles Times* commented that the observance would be worldwide in scope, "although Japanese participation will be purely as targets."[45] In a knowing acknowledgement that fire had become the principal weapon against Japan, Jack Tarver, associate editor of the *Atlanta Constitution*, composed a short piece entitled "Keep 'Em Frying," in which he characterized ongoing war bond drives as a way "to keep the home fires burning in Tokyo."[46]

More commonly, editorials expressed ambivalence about the incendiary bombing. A few essays conveyed revulsion and occasionally remorse about the destruction, yet the majority of thoughtful compositions defended bombing as an unsavory necessity that might shorten the war.[47] A representative editorial from the *Washington Post* called incendiary bombing "terror bombing, something we have condemned when it was practiced by our enemies. It makes no distinction between soldier and civilian, between the guilty and the innocent, between the adult and the child." Although this editorial described bombing as regrettable, it repeated the military's argument that the dispersal of Japanese industry made it nearly impossible to distinguish military targets from civilian residences.[48]

Army Air Forces commanders contended that incendiary bombing intended to raze the myriad small workshops in Japan's urban areas that produced war-related products. These scattered industries could only be obliterated, as an editorial in the *New York Herald Tribune* phrased it, "by spreading seas of flame over large areas." In an oblique reference to the deaths of Japanese civilians the editorial acknowledged that "fires destroy far more than factories, of course."[49] In a rare admission, another editorial in the *New York Herald Tribune* recognized that the bombing took its "toll of women and children" but argued that modern warfare provided no allowance for "civilian life when it gets in the way of military objectives."[50] This defense of bombing, a kind of "ritual denial," as historian Michael Sherry later called it, justified civilian deaths as an unintentional result of striking legitimate targets.[51] One commentary believed that the destruction of "household factories" offered "one of the quickest and cheapest methods" of achieving victory. In addition, the tremendous number of casualties might cause Japan to surrender.[52]

In his study of American bombing in World War II, historian Ronald Schaffer concluded that the incendiary bombing seriously damaged Japan's economy, yet the more flammable areas of cities did not contain the most important factories. He also pointed out that some of the workshops could not have contributed to the war effort in any case, because the Allied blockade had cut off their flow of supplies and prevented the Japanese from shipping what they produced. According to Schaffer, incendiary bombing did not interfere with Japan's ability to defend the home islands.[53] Thus, the commentary in 1945 that explained incendiary bombing as a kind of insurance that guaranteed fewer casualties when the Allies invaded Japan was inaccurate.

Several commentators contended that no true civilians inhabited Japan.[54] Certain commanding officers of the Army Air Forces shared this view. One of them, wing commander Col. Alfred F. Klaberer, suggested bombing Japan until it resembled "a beautiful desert" and declared that Japan must surrender or be "put through our meat grinder." He said that the bombing of urban areas was not directed against civilians because only infants and the elderly did not actively contribute to the Japanese war effort; his remarks assumed that bombs and flames somehow distinguished between those employed in the war effort and those not.[55] In July 1945 an Army Air Forces officer announced, "There are no civilians in Japan."[56] *Life* proclaimed that "the war-making power of every Japanese resource, every Japanese man, woman and child, must be destroyed."[57] Adm. Jonas H. Ingram, the outspoken commander of the U.S. Atlantic Fleet, said, "If it is necessary to win the war, we shall leave no man, woman or child alive in Japan and shall erase that country from the map."[58] No one noted that such commentary contradicted Truman's statements that the United States did not intend to exterminate the Japanese. The radio commentator H.V. Kaltenborn, mentioning Ingram's remarks, did say that the Japanese might surrender sooner "if we were more skillful propagandists."[59]

Other observers anticipated that bombing might cause widespread panic in Japan. In a rather contradictory piece, writer Bernard Seeman asserted that because all Japanese possessed "a hysterical resolve to go down fighting," people should prepare for an extended conflict. Yet he thought that incendiary bombing could shock the Japanese due to their pervasive fear of fire, which he called "a national phobia."[60] Raymond Moley, writing in *Newsweek*, also believed that the Japanese possessed an inherent "tendency to become panicky." He hoped the bombing would activate this trait and thus end the war.[61]

These opinions demonstrated how people could become inured to human destruction over the course of the war. Categorizing all Japanese as fanatical war supporters ignored the complexities of civilian experience under an authoritarian regime in wartime. Equating Japanese civilians with Japanese soldiers, and holding the former responsible for the deeds of the latter, offered little alternative to annihilation. If one accepted the conventional wisdom of all Japanese as zealous fighters, one wonders whom Moley and Seeman expected to panic. Commentaries simultaneously portrayed Japanese as mystic fanatics who could only be destroyed and victims of a unique psychological disposition that made them more likely to panic because they could not endure bombing as stoically as Westerners.[62]

Public condemnation of bombing, in truth, was rare. The editors of the *Indianapolis Star* acknowledged the receipt of letters expressing concern that by "rejoicing over these human bonfires," Americans were becoming as inhumane as the Nazis. In reply, the editors admitted that the war had become a "ghastly and inhuman affair," yet countered that the "time has come to fight fire with fire" inasmuch as the Japanese understood only force.[63]

The few outright denunciations of the bombing of Japan usually came from sources such as the pacifist journal *Christian Century*, which repeatedly condemned it. After the large firebomb raids in the final weeks of May 1945, when aviators could see the resultant fires in one city two hundred miles out at sea, an editorial in the journal stated, "There was too much smell of roasting flesh in the communiques to make anyone feel like celebrating." The editors expressed their conviction that American Christians, repulsed by the barbarous nature of the war, pitied Japanese civilians, especially the women and children.[64] When a spokesman for General LeMay described a portion of Tokyo as "one of the happiest combinations of inflammability and congestion," the editors of *Christian Century* wondered whether those sentiments reflected the thoughts of the bomber crews. "If so," they concluded, "then God have mercy on us, for before the world's harvest of hate is fully gathered we will certainly have need of his mercy."[65]

Other Protestant publications also criticized unrestricted bombing of cities. The biweekly journal *Christianity and Crisis*, founded by the theologian Reinhold Niebuhr in 1941 with the intention of countering pacifistic religious views, accepted bombing of "strategic centers" as an unfortunate necessity. But it objected to the "obliteration bombing" of Japanese cities "crowded with their helpless populations" and deemed it "morally wrong and politically dangerous" to allow military strategy to dominate overall planning.[66] A few Catholic writers also condemned the bombing of urban areas.[67]

The public's apparent apathy to such carnage troubled radio commentator H.V. Kaltenborn. In a Memorial Day broadcast, he contrasted the public's horrified reaction to the German bombing of London in 1940 with the casual acceptance of the deaths of tens of thousands of

Japanese women and children. "So accustomed have we become to the killing of civilians in this war," Kaltenborn noted, "that no one even thinks of protesting what we ourselves declared to be willful violation of the rules of war."[68] His sober message failed to acknowledge that World War II had obliterated the anachronistic idea that global conflict remained governed by so-called rules of war.

Commanders of the Army Air Forces believed bombing would force Japan's capitulation.[69] General Arnold contended that the Japanese lacked "the ingenuity to put their industries underground or decentralize them as the Germans did."[70] His comments contradicted his own claims that Japanese cities had to be burned down to demolish the industries dispersed throughout them. General LeMay believed that bombing would destroy Japanese industry and thus the nation's ability to wage war. Asked whether there would soon be a lack of targets he replied, "Yes, and we are going to be fresh out of Japs, too."[71]

Accounts of bombing raids often reported negligible Japanese opposition for which government officials and military commanders issued contradictory explanations. Adm. Aubrey Fitch thought it proved the impotency of Japan's air forces. Under Secretary of War Robert Patterson countered that view when he said the Japanese were holding planes in reserve for the anticipated Allied invasion.[72] Gen. George Kenney, the commander of the Army Air Forces under General MacArthur, attributed Japanese aerial inactivity to paucity of fuel and pilots, lack of spare parts, and "stupid leadership."[73]

Commanders endorsed bombing with a variety of analogies. General Kenney likened the aerial assault to an earthquake.[74] A cartoon entitled "Everything Seems to Be Losing Face in Japan" published in the *Chicago Daily Tribune* also compared bombing to a natural calamity. It depicted two simian-faced talking volcanoes in Japan surveying the damage caused by U.S. bombers. One remarked, "They Make Us Look Like a Couple of Sissies."[75] One naval commander compared bombing to "a great symphony."[76] An editorial in the *Washington Post* used a similar musical metaphor when it described bombing as a "crescendo of doom."[77] Lt. Gen. Barney Giles of the Army Air Forces paralleled bombing to boxing when he declared Japan would be bombed into submission. "It's as though I were fighting Jack Dempsey," he remarked, referring to the brawling heavyweight champion of the 1920s. "I wouldn't have a chance."[78] In June 1945, General Arnold announced that within eighteen months, by the end of 1946, all significant targets in Japan would be destroyed.[79] By July, General LeMay claimed that the Army Air Forces would lack targets by Christmas 1945.[80] The media did not evaluate the implication of these statements, which unintentionally revealed the inherent problems of relying on a military strategy disconnected from other methods of inducing a defeated enemy's surrender.

The members of the U.S. Strategic Bombing Survey questioned the assumption that bombing urban centers would end the war. In July 1945 they completed a report based on their study of Allied bombing of Germany, which contained a prioritized list of five target categories for Japan. The transportation network was listed first, urban areas last. They even ranked the dispersal of defoliants on rice crops above the bombing of cities. However, the Army Air Forces' Joint Target Group continued to assign higher priority to incendiary attacks on cities.[81]

Despite the general approval of bombing there was widespread doubt that it would force Japan's surrender.[82] Because he considered the Japanese less resourceful than the Germans, radio commentator Raymond Gram Swing reasoned that bombing might end the war. Yet he deemed the prospect of defeating Japan solely by aerial assault slim. "The GI will have to clinch it," Swing said. "It is clear we are going to invade the Japanese home islands."[83] Their belief in an inherent Japanese fanaticism caused some commentators to regard bombing as an insufficient strategy for winning the war. If Japanese civilians were "as tenacious as their soldiers," bombing would not prompt Japan's surrender, cautioned the editors of the New York Times. Yet they supported bombing because it might achieve "the least costly victory a nation ever won." If bombing did not induce Japan's capitulation, it provided a necessary precursor to invasion.[84]

The foregoing aside, army and naval aircraft pounded Japan throughout the war's final months. As the number of important targets declined, the Army Air Forces increasingly turned to a sort of psychological warfare by attempting to spread defeatism among Japanese civilians. In July 1945, aircraft dispersed leaflets over several Japanese cities, warning that various urban areas listed on the leaflets would soon be destroyed. The following day planes firebombed six of the cities.

The Associated Press praised the tactic, which was repeated twice, as "a gesture of contempt for the enemy war leaders and their ability to defend Japan."[85] General LeMay considered it effective psychological warfare against the Japanese and a refutation of the charges of critics who claimed that bombing indiscriminately killed civilians.[86] Columnist David Lawrence dismissed the policy as "a good publicity stunt" and believed that warning the Japanese would only help them better prepare their defenses.[87] A concurrent cartoon captioned "Calling His Shot" depicted LeMay playing billiards with a profusely sweating Japanese officer. The balls on the table each bore a letter that in combination spelled "Jap Cities," and the abnormally large cue ball was labeled "B-29's." With his cue stick, LeMay gestured toward a corner pocket labeled "Destruction" and remarked, "All of Them...*Right Here!*"[88]

One columnist equated the leaflet campaign to the famous story of Babe Ruth pointing to the spot where he would hit a home run in Chicago's Wrigley Field during the 1932 World Series between the New York Yankees and the Chicago Cubs.[89] This unusual comparison made a point, nevertheless. Likening the actions of the Army Air Forces to a famous bit of sporting lore confirmed American military prowess. Just like Ruth, U.S. forces could effect a prediction.

Discussion about the necessity of invading Japan coincided with the ongoing debate over the efficacy of bombing. Despite repeated statements that preparation for an invasion of Japan would require considerable time, the strategy of assault was often equated with ending the war expeditiously. An editorial in the *Washington Post* argued against hurried military actions. In the final months of war in Europe, it claimed, speed had been essential because *"Germany was outstripping the Allies technologically."* In view of the casualties suffered on Okinawa and Japan's technological inferiority, the editorial posited that military planners should consider ending the war by siege rather than invasion.[90] One anonymous citizen, writing to the Washington, D.C., *Evening Star*, questioned the transfer of troops to the Pacific and compared the "present stampede-minded psychology" to the Crusades. "The people, long drenched with machine propaganda, seem to have lost their power of independent thought. 'Brass rules.'"[91]

Various observers deemed invasion a strategy of last resort. Columnist Gill Robb Wilson advocated a year of bombing to render Japan "unrecognizable as a nation or a habitable country." An invasion must not be attempted, he said, "until not one house stands or one field can be harvested." The columnist and former naval commander William V. Pratt also believed an invasion should be postponed until bombing had reduced Japan "to rubble."[92] Several commentators observed that if siege did not cause Japan's defeat, it remained a necessary forerunner to invasion.[93]

Other commentators regarded invasion as inevitable. Editorials in the *New York Times* contended that siege alone had never won a war.[94] A correspondent who witnessed combat in the Pacific cautioned that siege would not weaken the determination of Japanese troops.[95] Columnist Maj. George Fielding Eliot compared the apprehension of invading Japan to public misgivings about invading Europe prior to 1944. He concurred with the comments attributed to Adm. Thomas C. Kinkaid, who had been quoted as remarking, "Of course, you've got to send in troops to meet 'em, fight 'em and kill 'em. There's no easy way out."[96] Foster Hailey, writing in the *Yale Review*, called an invasion of Japan "the greatest amphibious venture ever undertaken. Bloody as it may be, hard as it is to face the prospect of the casualty lists, we must steel ourselves to fight the Battle for Tokyo."[97] Many people believed that an invasion of Japan would bring resistance from all Japanese. Gen. Joseph Stilwell, the acerbic veteran of the China-Burma-India theater, told the Joint Chiefs to expect "the fanatical opposition of the entire population, who will resort to any extremity to oppose us."[98] Journalists admonished that U.S. troops would face "a hostile, drilled populace ready and eager to help defend its homeland" and declared "every man's, woman's and child's hand will be actively against us."[99]

Propaganda broadcasts by Radio Tokyo that received attention in the media abetted this belief. Radio Tokyo announced that a volunteer corps numbering more than forty-six million people stood ready to repel invaders. Premier Kantaro Suzuki boasted that even 500,000 enemy troops would be met by forces "five or ten times superior." One broadcast vowed that Japan would never accept unconditional surrender, despite Truman's assurances that it did not mean the enslavement of the Japanese. "The Japanese-American war can only be terminated through the ghastly landing operation of the American forces on the homeland of Japan," proclaimed one announcer, "where they will bury mountains and rivers of Japan with their dead bodies and paint beaches of Japan crimson with their own blood." Other pronouncements declared that a vast network of underground fortifications had made Japan "an impregnable fortress."[100] Throughout the war's final months, Radio Tokyo broadcast the texts of newspaper articles and speeches which reiterated that an invasion of Japan would result in casualties so vast that the Allies would decide to stop the war.[101]

Some observers hoped that the Japanese could be starved into surrendering.[102] Cartoonist Carey Orr of the *Chicago Daily Tribune* produced an illustration entitled "Our Ally" in which a likeness of the grim reaper labeled "Famine" stepped ashore in Japan saying "You Furnish the Transports—I'll Do The Landing."[103] Starvation-induced capitulation remained an unlikely scenario, however, and one not suited to the public's impatience or the timetables of strategists.

Three generals, two army and one marine, publicly said that siege could not win the war.[104] When a reporter asked Admiral Nimitz whether he believed an invasion would be necessary, he replied, "I don't know how much the Japs can take. All I do know is that it is necessary to go through with the planning of the invasion of Japan."[105]

Certain military leaders minimized the danger of invading Japan. Vice Adm. Daniel E. Barbey said that Allied forces could invade Japan or China "without a bit of difficulty."[106] Lt. Gen. Roy S. Geiger of the Marine Corps described Japan's defeat as "just a question of wading in and finishing it," surprising remarks from a veteran of Guadalcanal, Bougainville, Guam, Peleliu, and Okinawa. His professed belief in the cowardly nature and inherent inferiority of the Japanese apparently prompted his declamation; he described them as mentally deficient, weak in character, and lacking the physical stamina of Americans.[107] In light of the casualties on Okinawa, these comments must have struck even the most optimistic Americans as wide of the mark.

Some commentators speculated that China might be invaded instead of Japan. H.V. Kaltenborn conjectured that General Stilwell's appointment as commander of the Tenth Army suggested subsequent landings would occur in China because Stilwell had been the onetime military adviser to Chiang Kai-shek.[108] Adm. Kinkaid, however, publicly dismissed the possibility of landings there. Referring to these comments, an editorial in the Los Angeles Times remarked, "The Japs, of course, will not know whether to believe him or not. The chances are the admiral is being quite frank, but with an adversary whose mental processes are Japanese, frankness is perhaps the most effective form of deception."[109]

Broadcasts over Radio Tokyo referred to relocating the Japanese government and major industries to northern China and Manchuria. The American media treated these reports more seriously than Japanese boasting about an array of suicide weapons that would amaze the world and repulse an Allied invasion.[110] Spokespersons for the army and navy dismissed the accounts as "pure propaganda," and editorial reaction ranged from cautious to dismissive. However, various military leaders and members of Congress did fear the consolidation of Japanese forces in Manchuria.[111] In his typically searing fashion, columnist Gladstone Williams characterized the reports as desperate propaganda intended to deter the United States from the task of demolishing Japan. He believed bombing would make Japan "a barren waste, a shambles of destruction. Then we will move in for the final kill."[112]

The columns of Hanson W. Baldwin, arguably the most respected commentator on military affairs, reflected widespread ambivalence about an invasion of Japan. He hoped for—but did not expect—a Japanese surrender prior to an invasion.[113] Baldwin increasingly focused on the psychology of the Japanese as the most important but least understood factor influencing the war's length. Fundamentally, he concluded, the war's duration depended on the resolve of the Japanese.[114]

Although he expressed concern about the destruction of Japan, Baldwin did not offer alternatives to the continual pounding of a people he admitted he did not comprehend. For Baldwin, the bombing's psychological impact on the Japanese psyche outweighed its military significance.[115]

Perceptions of the Japanese permeated the evaluations of the strategies of siege and invasion. Commentators characterized the Japanese as prone to panic yet so inherently fanatical that they might not succumb to bombing. A contradictory strain appeared in the critiques of these strategies, although no one addressed it at the time. As mentioned earlier, numerous commentators who evaluated Japanese psychology called it a hindrance to Japan's leaders acknowledging their obvious defeat. But many of these same commentators neglected this in their assessments of strategy. If, as they claimed, Japan had lost the war, it would appear logical to apply that knowledge to Allied strategy and seek a resolution to the conflict that did not obligate more fighting men to die in a war already won.

Hatred of the Japanese, however, and notions about their illogical nature led certain commentators back to endorsing military means—siege, invasion, or both—to end the conflict. Siege was regarded as a fundamental precursor to an invasion, and certainly many people hoped siege would cause Japan's surrender. Americans and their leaders remained frustrated by mounting casualties from the fanatical resistance of a defeated foe. Time remained an important consideration. By 1945 citizens were definitely weary of war, but military leaders probably underestimated the public's fortitude. One public opinion poll from June 1945 tallied 43 percent of the respondents preferring a longer war if it meant saving American lives, while slightly more than 33 percent wanted to conquer Japan quickly.[116]

The media often presented the strategic choices as invasion or siege. Truman framed the options similarly in his diary, but neither he nor the Joint Chiefs ever approved the overall invasion plans. He endorsed OLYMPIC, the assault of Kyushu, which was presented as a combination of invasion and siege. Most military leaders did not regard siege and assault as mutually exclusive options, although several military commanders publicly described them as such.

An editorial in the Washington, D.C., *Evening Star* proclaimed that aerial and naval bombardment had created a "doomsday picture" for the Japanese. Citing the opinion of an unidentified "expert," the editorial concluded that Japan was "so badly battered" that "no objective in it . . . is worth a thousand plane raid, even though the time is at hand when it will be possible to visit the country with 3,000 land-based bombers in a single day, not to mention carrier aircraft." "The picture is an awesome one," the editorial said. "Never in the history of the world has there been anything like it. Never has any country faced such concentrated fury as Japan faces now."[117]

Amidst these celebratory phrases the editors praised the array of available force and, simultaneously, described its use as impractical because Japan was so battered that deploying additional weaponry could not enhance the existent destruction. Numerous citizens and several leaders began questioning the strategy of continued devastation.

8

Unconditional Surrender

It is easy to start a war; it is difficult to stop one before one side has been knocked out.[1]

In spite of the continued virulent anti-Japanese sentiment on the home front in 1945, a number of people expressed a desire for a diplomatic resolution to the war. Those who advocated the use of diplomacy usually did not endorse the idea of negotiating with Japan. Instead, they preferred trying to end the war through the issuance of cogent surrender terms, which meant clarifying the policy of unconditional surrender.

Various studies have judged the United States' rigid adherence to unconditional surrender a hindrance to concluding the war. Yet even authors critical of the policy have said that public and congressional support of unconditional surrender hampered efforts to revise it.[2] Indeed, there was widespread support of unconditional surrender on the home front. President Truman, to rousing cheers in Congress, had emphatically endorsed it.[3] Still, the arguments that American leaders resisted clarifying terms out of fear of a hostile public response disregard the diversity of opinion on the issue in 1945. Commentators, organizations, and citizens who did not consider unconditional surrender appropriate for the Pacific War implored government leaders to explain the Allied terms of surrender, in the hope of ending the war before an invasion of Japan.

Intriguing, albeit fragmentary reports of Japanese peace initiatives appeared in the American media from May through July 1945. These stories provided incomplete accounts of contacts that actually occurred in the summer of 1945. Through intermediaries, Japanese diplomatic officials and military attaches in Switzerland and other locations in Europe evinced a willingness to surrender on conditional terms. Some of these messages indicated that a guarantee about the emperor remained the only point of contention, but others suggested additional terms. Allen Dulles, the head of the Office of Strategic Services (OSS) in

Europe, responded on one occasion that he believed that the imperial system would be sustained if Japan surrendered. However, the Japanese who initiated these feelers did so without the support of their government, and the overtures elicited little response from the United States.[4]

Newspapers published fairly accurate—as well as erroneous—descriptions of these events. Several news accounts alleged Japanese willingness to withdraw from all captured territory and allow the occupation of Japan in return for the United States ending the war. U.S. government spokespersons denied certain stories and discounted others as inaccurate. Unidentified sources claimed that the United States had either ignored offers for peace talks or replied negatively. Some observers considered the rumors encouraging indications of Japan's weakening resistance and argued that the United States must increase the tempo of its military blows to force Japan's unconditional surrender.[5]

Skepticism about the sincerity of Japanese intentions also prompted dismissal of the reports in the media. The editors of the *Los Angeles Times* cautioned that such sketchy information should not dissuade the United States "from the job of administering Japan a thorough licking." They described Japanese peace initiatives as efforts "to divide and bamboozle us into accepting something less than total victory." "It is an old trick of Japanese wrestlers to stumble and pretend to be falling in order to get the adversary off guard so he can be tripped," the editorial warned. "It may be the Japs are making use of a similar trick in their international relations."[6]

Broadcasts by Radio Tokyo rebuffed the accounts of peace offers as enemy propaganda and noted that Japanese children had received training in the use of grenades to help repel an invasion.[7] However, stories that hinted at Japanese willingness to negotiate probably contributed to discontent with unconditional surrender in the United States.

Immediately after V-E Day, requests for clarification of surrender terms appeared in the print media. The editors of the *Washington Post* endorsed the Cairo Declaration of December 1943, in which the Allies stipulated that Japan would be stripped of the territory it had occupied or conquered since 1914, as the basis for peace. They feared that recent statements threatening the extermination of the Japanese by such "fire-eaters" as Admiral Halsey and Paul V. McNutt, the head of the War Manpower Commission, would only encourage Japan to continue fighting. "What we are suggesting, to be sure, is conditional surrender. What of it? Unconditional surrender was never an ideal formula."[8] The editors of the *Washington Post*, and other critics of unconditional surrender, often lamented the policy's vagueness, and throughout the summer of 1945, editorials urged further explanation of terms, calling unconditional surrender a "purely rhetorical and meaningless phrase."[9]

Essays in other publications endorsed the idea of explaining surrender terms. "If the ill-matched communication systems between Japanese and American minds could somehow be bridged," argued *Time*, "the war might be shortened."[10] The editors of *Life* sought to define unconditional surrender in a series of essays which said that the Japanese were not "alien freaks" but a "strange" people whose "inscrutable devotion to suicide gives them a kind of negative control over their own destiny—and ours—beyond both reason and force." They recommended that before launching an invasion of Japan, U.S. leaders must be certain "that we are not being unnecessarily inscrutable, even a little suicidal, ourselves" and precisely define the terms of surrender.[11]

Columnist Hanson W. Baldwin said that unconditional surrender must be enhanced with more positive policies that contributed to a stable peace.[12] Walter Lippmann, the doyen of political commentators, argued that in determining war aims, U.S. leaders should choose the minimum essential terms rather than preferred but unnecessary maximum terms.[13] Even the rabidly anti-Japanese columnist Gladstone Williams initially endorsed a more complete explanation of terms. He claimed that given "the peculiar operations of the Japanese mind," Japanese leaders might interpret unconditional surrender as the equivalent of the conditions they would impose. Pondering hypothetical Japanese terms was enough "to make every red-blooded American want to see them exterminated as a race completely," according to Williams. However, because Americans were more civilized than the Japanese, he reasoned that unconditional surrender should be explained.[14]

The radio commentators H.V. Kaltenborn and Raymond Gram Swing also questioned the usefulness of unconditional surrender. According to Kaltenborn, a growing number of citizens believed that if the United States offered Japan "half a chance to save face on our unconditional surrender demand," satisfactory peace terms could be quickly concluded. In July 1945 he told listeners that a reliable source had informed him that Allied soldiers also wanted more definite terms.[15] Swing contended that victory might be gained more quickly and cheaply if the Allies provided Japan with more specific terms.[16]

A wide spectrum of organizations and individuals requested elucidation of unconditional surrender. The socialist leader Norman Thomas called for "prompt enunciation" of surrender terms. "Is it possible," he queried, "that even the President does not know what terms to offer and masks his uncertainty behind a supposedly popular slogan?" Thomas cited racism as a major reason for the continuation of "this costly war of annihilation." He claimed that the bombing of Japanese cities risked permanently embittering the Japanese and might create an environment where "the ultimate victor will be Stalin and his Communist party." The destruction of Japanese militarism meant little while "white imperialism lives on," Thomas charged.[17]

Writing on behalf of the pacifist Fellowship of Reconciliation, longtime peace advocate A.J. Muste called for the pronouncement of specific terms. The Women's International League for Peace and Freedom also exhorted Truman to further explain unconditional surrender, and a letter from its California chapter said that clarifying terms could shorten the war by dividing the Japanese people from Japan's militarists.[18]

Matthew Woll, a vice president of the American Federation of Labor, also believed that better terms might expedite the conclusion of what he called "a war of annihilation" in which American soldiers were dying "for ends not clearly stated." He said that the war victimized Japanese women and children, and he criticized the U.S. government's failure to counter the statements of those who called for Japan's destruction. The failure to refute such declarations enabled Japanese extremists to claim there was no choice but to continue fighting, Woll argued. Like Norman Thomas, Woll opposed furthering "white imperialism" in Asia. "I am confident," he added, "that the American people will not want their sons to die to transfer Port Arthur from Japanese to Russian hands or to reestablish a shabby French empire in Indo-China."[19]

Other published endorsements of more specific terms came from Stanley Washburn, a veteran of military intelligence service, and the erstwhile New Deal adviser Raymond Moley, then a columnist for *Newsweek*. Moley opposed a policy of "appeasement" toward Japan, but he believed surrender terms should not interfere with Japan's religions or the imperial institution.[20] The editors of the Catholic journal *Commonweal* called for lucid war aims. They believed that insistence on unconditional surrender meant "a war of mutual extinction."[21] Various Protestant and Catholic leaders, as well as people considered experts on the Far East, said that the ruination of Japan would leave a power vacuum in Asia.[22] Several observers warned of the threat of the Soviet Union expanding its influence there, arguing that the longer the war lasted, the greater the cost for the United States to rebuild Japan. The editors of the journal *Catholic World*, fearful of a return to economic depression, claimed such massive assistance would increase the national debt and lower the standard of living. They also noted the potential for an additional one million American casualties "by protracting a war which appears to have been already won except for skillful handling in the field of diplomacy."[23]

Other commentaries described further defining of unconditional surrender as a moral responsibility. The editors of *Christian Century* believed that clarified terms might halt the "war of extermination." They admitted that many citizens wanted Japan "pulverized" but doubted that few of that opinion had sons in the service or faced combat themselves. The editors deemed the United States "morally bound" to announce terms by which it would accept Japan's surrender.[24] A letter signed by twenty-four people who attended a regional conference of Executive Secretaries of Councils of Churches and Church Federations requested more explicit terms to hasten the war's end and "enhance America's moral leadership in social and political reconstruction throughout the world."[25] An editorial published in theologian Reinhold Niebuhr's journal *Christianity and Crisis* said that demanding unconditional surrender would lengthen the war and make Japanese leaders "delay an ultimately inevitable decision through fear of unnamed consequences."[26]

On June 18, 1945, sixty religious and educational leaders published a pronouncement that called on President Truman to explain unconditional surrender. The statement said that continued fighting ignored Christian principles and meant the senseless deaths of U.S. troops. The manifesto recommended a halt to the bombing of Japan, requested the immediate issuance of cogent surrender terms, and urged that the government make an effort to halt the vilification of all Japanese.[27]

Reaction to this petition in the media was hostile, and some newspapers did not even report it.[28] A critical editorial in the *New York Herald Tribune* declared that the United States could either pursue a negotiated peace, which would allow Japan to later renew its aggression, or accept "the relatively low price of her complete subjugation now."[29] The newspaper did print letters from several people in general agreement with the manifesto. One reader predicted increased discontent with the war, especially from the parents of fighting men, if the government did not define terms. "Until we do that," the writer warned, "we are bound to witness a growing domestic cry of 'What are we fighting for?'"[30]

Others staunchly opposed the manifesto. A minister criticized the statement as appeasement. "What these men are actually asking is that America sacrifice millions of its young men by storming Japan with the infantry without having blotted out the resistance in front of them by bombing," he argued.[31] A navy chaplain faulted "this pacifist group of ministers" for "doing the church a real disservice."[32] "They don't know what the hell the score is," a serviceman remarked, adding that if those who signed the petition had witnessed the results of Japanese atrocities, their opinions would change.[33] Columnist Robert Quillen expressed incredulity that people could protest the bombing of Japanese cities. "If the Japs will not quit," he said, "they must be destroyed."[34]

In June 1945, the editors of *Christian Century* printed and circulated a petition which urged that Truman, in concert with the Allies, make a proclamation of terms by which peaceful relations with Japan could be restored. The suggested conditions included the withdrawal of Japanese forces from regions outside Japan's home islands, the demobilization of Japan, Allied administration of Japanese finances and industries, the right to try Japanese charged with war crimes, and a pledge by the Japanese people to establish representative government. Paul Hutchinson, the journal's managing editor, informed the White House that he intended to present the petition in early August 1945 and predicted that it would contain more than twenty-five thousand signatures.[35]

The editors of the *Chicago Daily Tribune* commended the petition: "We hope our state department will take advantage of all such suggestions to bring this war to a speedy and satisfactory conclusion."[36] Rep. Howard H. Buffett (R-Nebr.), a onetime critic of unconditional surrender, introduced the petition into the Congressional Record.[37] In reply to a letter from Bishop Herbert Welch, of the Committee for Overseas Relief, concerning the petition, the acting secretary of state Joseph Grew said that the Allies wanted to avoid a repetition of events in Germany following World War I. He cautioned that Japanese psychology was such that if the United States agreed to a negotiated peace, the Japanese could argue—as some Germans had after World War I—that Japan had not been completely defeated.[38]

After his return from Japan in 1942, Grew made public statements regarding his belief that all Japanese possessed an atypical mindset. In response to Bishop Welch, Grew reinforced his previous remarks, and undermined them as well. His argument—that the abnormal outlook of the Japanese would induce them to respond as the people of a Western nation—did not fit with the contention that the exclusivity of the Japanese made them unpredictable. Yet Grew's assertions resembled a stereotypical trait commonly attributed to the Japanese—by the columnists Roger Babson and Gladstone Williams among others—that Japanese were imitative of Westerners. As characterized during the war, the Japanese became both sui generis and master mimics. Grew's reply to Bishop Welch demonstrated the malleability and the shallowness of common perceptions about the Japanese.

Ordinary citizens sent letters to members of Congress, to the State Department, and to the White House, in which they proposed modification of unconditional surrender.[39] Mrs. David L. Lares of Minneapolis, who said that she had not previously written a senator, enclosed a self-addressed stamped envelope in the hope of receiving a reply to her appeal for full disclosure of any Japanese peace offers. "I can't understand why our free, intelligent America should not at least hear about these peace offers and voice our opinion."[40]

After the reports of Japanese peace feelers in May 1945, letters and telegrams to the White House requested confirmation or denial of the stories. Most of these messages advocated prompt pursuit of peace. Citing one account of Japanese peace initiatives, Mrs. Priscilla Hopkins, writing from Oskaloosa, Iowa, argued that the terms, if accurate, "exceeded anything we've ever asked of Japan." She lamented the "bad effect that killing by flame torches, decapitating, knifing, bombing civilians, taking no prisoners has upon the thinking and reaction patterns of the men who have to do the work of war. For these reasons, I ask you, what are we fighting for now?"[41]

"There is a growing sentiment in this country against adhering to the policy of 'unconditional surrender,'" wrote Miss Lottie B. Owen of Milwaukee, who favored terms in the spirit of the Atlantic Charter.[42] "You know that next to the boys themselves, the mothers suffer most in this war," wrote Marie E. Osborne, a mother of two sons in the service, from Massillon, Ohio, in her handwritten letter to Truman. She urged him to seek a diplomatic resolution to the war.[43] A couple from Oneonta, New York, praised Truman for "interpreting unconditional surrender so that the Japanese people may have hope" and they asked him to further define surrender terms and negotiate with Japan. "I hope you will go on to state specific war aims based on justice," advised Elizabeth T. Johnson, from Pottsville, Pennsylvania. "We do not want softness," she said, "but we do want justice."[44] In a telegram, Dr. Edwin O. Kennedy of Englewood, New Jersey, beseeched Truman to immediately announce peace terms in order to sustain morale on the home front and to reassure the families of fighting men that the government intended to shorten the war.[45] Worried that unconditional surrender would require an invasion of Japan, Guille B. Goldin, an attorney from New York City, said that the government could devise "an 'out' or 'face saving' mechanism for the Japanese war-lords."[46] Merlin G. Miller of North Kansas City, in Truman's home state of Missouri, asked why the war should continue if, as some reports claimed, the Japanese had indicated their willingness to surrender and withdraw from occupied regions.[47] Ruth P. Whitcomb from Corvallis, Oregon, who called herself "a common citizen in a small city," also favored immediate clarification of terms for Japan. "It seems to me," she wrote, "most reasonable that this could be done, and unreasonable that it should not be tried at once. Are we not losing a thousand men a day under our present policy?"[48]

Academicians advocated revision of Allied terms. James R. Ware, an associate professor of Chinese at Harvard, wrote Truman that the moment was precipitous for negotiations to spare the United States "the preposterous adventure of occupying Japan." Asians always compromised, according to Ware, and he believed that the Allies should do likewise.[49] In a reversal of the comparisons of Japanese to savages, one professor feared that rather than seeking a just peace, the United States appeared intent on vengeance that condemned all Japanese "with a savagery reminiscent of the tribal warfare of the past."[50]

Republicans in Congress became increasingly outspoken about the need for surrender terms.[51] On July 2, 1945, Sen. Wallace H. White, Jr., of Maine, the Republican leader of the Senate, said that clearer terms might end the war, adding that unconditional surrender had never been sufficiently explained to Americans or Japanese. He endorsed the disarming of Japan, the withdrawal of Japanese forces from all occupied regions, and punishment of war criminals. He opposed, however, the destruction of Japanese society and religious institutions.[52]

Ten days later the recently elected Sen. Homer E. Capehart (R-Ind.), who had earlier charged that the government was concealing legitimate peace offers from Japan, proposed the announcement of explicit terms. Saying that he opposed a "soft" peace, Capehart remarked that if the emperor's retention was the necessary "face saving" that Japanese leaders required, "then I for one advocate permitting Japan to save that much 'face.'" Senate Majority Leader Alben W. Barkley (D-Ky.) defended the administration. He contended that it was "a little unusual" for a nation winning a war to initiate discussion of terms for capitulation. However, Sen. Robert A. Taft (R-Ohio) reminded Barkley that during World War I, Woodrow Wilson had offered the Fourteen Points prior to any request for terms from the Central Powers. Capehart said that he agreed with Barkley that peace must be reached on Allied terms.[53]

Senator White's remarks provoked both supportive and critical comment.[54] "What is soft about that?" queried the columnist Ernest K. Lindley, after other commentators assailed White and Capehart for advocating a "soft peace." Lindley believed that the terms proposed by White guaranteed the national security of the United States. When Japan did capitulate, "we are unlikely to exact much more than that," Lindley said.[55] The editors of *Christian Century* claimed that "soft peace" was a term heard "most frequently and loudly from non-combatants, for whom this has certainly been a soft war."[56] *Time* reaffirmed its support for issuing more definite terms. The editors argued that Truman's assurances that the United States did not intend to destroy or enslave the Japanese were insufficient. "U.S. military policy is clear," declared *Time*, "blow upon blow until all resistance is crushed. But the application of shrewd statesmanship might save the final enforcement of that policy—and countless American lives."[57] "Senator White has voiced the view of many, if not most, thoughtful people in this country," wrote Robert Gray Taylor of Philadelphia, a professedly loyal Democrat, in a letter to Secretary of State James F. Byrnes.[58]

The columnist Dorothy Thompson considered White's efforts laudatory and futile. She deemed Truman's prior statements meaningless in a world in which the terms "extermination" and "enslavement" remained as ambiguous as "free elections." She also noted what she considered a troubling irony: As delegates from the Allied nations convened in San Francisco to draft the charter of the United Nations, Truman had reassured the world that the United States did not intend the destruction or enslavement of another nation. Thompson believed that a concise pronouncement of surrender terms had not been issued because American leaders did not know their aims. Since the Casablanca Conference, Thompson said, the Allies had pursued a war of ill-defined objectives, and she predicted "an international arms race between the victors" after the war.[59]

Calls for modifying the policy of unconditional surrender caused concern within the U.S. government. In July 1945, the Office of War Information initiated a radio campaign to counteract the "sentiment, either latent or expressed, which favors a peace with Japan short of unconditional surrender."[60] The government officially responded to the reports of Japanese peace efforts on July 10, 1945, when Joseph Grew issued a statement in which he said that "in no case has this government been presented with a statement purporting to define the basis upon which the Japanese government would be prepared to conclude peace." Grew described various unofficial contacts made by the Japanese and characterized them as attempts to encourage dissent within the United States. He said that thoughtful people who recalled Pearl Harbor and Japanese atrocities could not regard the reports as credible and warned that citizens must avoid the temptation to accept less than Japan's unconditional surrender.[61]

Senator Capehart complimented Grew for the disclosures but noted that the State Department had issued similar denials before Italy's surrender in 1943.[62] "Mr. Grew argues that every peace feeler is nothing more than an attempt to divide our public opinion," said the radio commentator H.V. Kaltenborn, "but it may also be a sincere attempt to escape the ignominy of unconditional surrender."[63] Dismissing Grew's reasoning, the editors of the *Washington Post* speculated that the government's reluctance to announce categorical terms stemmed from not having formulated them.[64] Radio Tokyo continued denying that Japan had initiated peace feelers, and cited Grew's remarks as evidence of war weariness in the United States.[65]

Grew received numerous letters regarding the government statement. Ernest Caldecott, a Unitarian minister from Los Angeles, called unconditional surrender a "barbaric and archaic" phrase and said the government had a responsibility to its citizens to declare specific terms of surrender.[66] W.H. Rayner, a professor of engineering at the University of Illinois, turned Grew's remarks about the Japanese being inherently different against the diplomat. He lectured Grew that the centuries-old mindset of the Japanese people differed so fundamentally from "American" ways of thought "that it would be a tragic mistake to suppose that they will react to our demands as we would react under similar circumstances." He argued that failure to attempt a negotiated end to the war was "just plain dumb."[67] Paul E. Johnson, of Edgartown, Massachusetts, described unconditional surrender as "impossible and unreasonable" and asked Grew, "By what right do we demand the lives of countless more American soldiers and of Japanese women and children subject to obliteration bombing?"[68] Shaken by his visit to an Army "psychopathic ward" where he observed patients he termed "the living dead," a medical student from Chicago told Grew that the United States should seek a conditional peace to spare further bloodshed.[69]

As journalists and citizens evaluated unconditional surrender, numerous commentaries supported the policy. The editors of the *New York Times* repeatedly stressed the uselessness of trying to reason with the Japanese.[70] "Evil has to sign on the dotted line, without conditional escape," declared an editorial published in the *Atlanta Constitution*.[71] Columnist David Lawrence preferred continued bombing, and the intervention of the Soviet Union, before the announcement of specific terms.[72] Several members of Congress warned that anything less than unconditional surrender would increase the likelihood of another war against Japan in the future.[73] Advocates of unconditional surrender reiterated the government line that Japanese leaders would interpret a direct overture as confirmation that the United States had lost its will to fight.[74]

Columnist Gladstone Williams reversed his previous support for explaining terms and said that revising unconditional surrender would allow Japanese militarists to revive Hitler's "stab-in-the back" argument.[75] Thus, Japanese leaders could claim that the Imperial Japanese Army was never defeated but forced to capitulate due to flagging support at home. "Now, the Germans are obviously a far more enlightened people than the half-civilized Japs," Williams argued. "If it was possible to sell them a phony bill of goods of the kind, what can we expect of the Japanese?"[76]

Maj. Compton Pakenham, British military officer and author of articles on Japan for *Newsweek*, expressed pessimism about a diplomatic solution to the war. Hindering the chances of such a settlement, Pakenham said, was the Japanese propensity to disregard facts while preserving "faith in transparent but convenient fictions." This trait made it "almost impossible for a foreigner to exchange opinions or reach an understanding with a Jap." "If the Jap mind were merely devious," he reasoned, "it might offer some hope, but its intransigence is reinforced by deliberately adopted formulas to explain away aggression." Pakenham said that when evaluating the leadership of Japan, "one must scrap the familiar labels—dictator, fascist, warmonger, liberal, democrat, moderate. Fundamentally all think as one."[77]

Some observers said that clarifying terms was not incompatible with the policy of unconditional surrender.[78] A public opinion poll of June 1945 indicated overwhelming support for an occupation of Japan as a condition of Japan's surrender. However, more respondents favored a longer war if it meant saving the lives of U.S. troops.[79]

Entwined with the issue of defining surrender terms was the eventual fate of Emperor Hirohito. During the war he had been vilified as the equivalent of Hitler and ridiculed by others as merely a pathetic figurehead. The public knew little about Hirohito except that the Japanese venerated him as a deity. In a Gallup poll of June 1945 one-third of the respondents endorsed executing the emperor. Indicative of general ignorance about Japan, 46 percent did not know his name.[80] A Honolulu newspaper which requested suggestions for the emperor's fate received responses that he be forced to retrace the route of the Bataan death march and that he earn a living performing menial work.[81] Some commentaries satirized Hirohito's ultimate fate. When Radio Tokyo announced that American bombing had prevented the emperor's customary horseback rides, an editorial in the *Atlanta Constitution*, alluding to the image of Japanese as inherently panicky, mocked, "The Hon. Enemy has caused the admirals and the generals to rush so frequently to Hon. Hirohito with distressing news and apologies that the horse has nothing to do but eat his oats and give the horse laugh to the Emperor." When Japanese citizens came to their senses, the editorial claimed, "they will bury the Emperor and eat the horse. Which makes more sense than their present course."[82]

On a more serious note, two authors who published books in 1945 that addressed the issue of postwar Japan, said that the Allies could not forcibly abolish the imperial institution. The journalist Wilfrid Fleisher, who called Hirohito "the feeble-minded marionette of the Japanese war lords," thought that the emperor should be deposed. Yet he admitted that the Allies could not impose a republic upon the Japanese. The author William C. Johnstone said that the Japanese should be encouraged to abandon their imperial government.[83]

The editors of the *New Republic* argued that after the United States occupied Japan, it should halt the practice of worshipping the emperor. Yet they doubted that the Allies could achieve this unilaterally. Such foreign interference, they feared, might only increase devotion to the emperor. Eventually, the editors reasoned, the Japanese themselves would have to decide the fate of the imperial institution.[84] The ABC radio commentator Raymond Gram Swing said that the United States did not need to commit to permanently preserving the monarchy. As part of a program of "aggressive democracy," Swing favored convincing the Japanese that abolishing the monarchy would be in their own interest. If the Japanese wished to retain the emperor, he considered it "their affair and their tragedy."[85] The columnist Ernest K. Lindley endorsed the idea of allowing the Japanese to vote on the emperor's retention and said that in a disarmed Japan, the emperor's continued presence would make little difference.[86]

Some observers questioned the wisdom of continuing the war to achieve Hirohito's downfall. One published account claimed that the Japanese government had offered to surrender if the Allies allowed Japan to keep the emperor. The editors of the *Chicago Daily Tribune* concluded that the reputed fraudulence of the report was the only possible justification for its rejection. "If we fight on with nothing more to gain than the person of the mikado we convict ourselves of placing as high a value on his carcass as the Japs themselves do," they argued.[87]

Certain commentators deemed Hirohito the only person capable of compelling Japanese militarists to abide by unconditional surrender.[88] The editors of the *Washington Post* suggested that Hirohito could help end the war and subsequently assist in preserving order in Japan.[89] "Emperor Hirohito has the power to save his people from this hideous nightmare," wrote columnist Merlo Pusey.[90] "With a stroke of his hand he could replace the militarist regime with a new cabinet of his own choosing which would be amenable to our terms of peace," claimed Gladstone Williams.[91]

In July 1945, three Republican senators, Homer Capehart of Indiana, Kenneth S. Wherry of Nebraska, and Alexander Wiley of Wisconsin, urged that Hirohito be allowed to retain his throne. Wiley also wanted Hirohito tried as a war criminal. Wherry and Capehart insisted that interfering with Hirohito constituted meddling in another nation's religion.[92] Some citizens shared this view. A woman from Connecticut wrote to Sen. Brien McMahon (D-Conn.), commenting that because worship of the emperor was an important component of Japanese religion, "it is understandable that they should be as unwilling to relinquish it as we should our religion."[93]

At the same time, numerous commentaries advocated abolishing the imperial system in Japan. An article in *Time*, which described the Japanese mind as "an entity utterly alien . . . and almost as uncontemporary . . . as Neanderthal man," said that the Japanese belief in the emperor's divinity represented the most peculiar aspect of Japanese mentality. In sum, *Time* characterized Hirohito as the embodiment of all the perceived paradoxes of the Japanese: "reeking savagery and sensitivity to beauty, frantic fanaticism and patient obedience to authority, brittle rituals and gross vices, habitual discipline and berserk outbursts." The editors of *Time* concluded that the current Japanese system of government must be destroyed, and that the Allies should plan for the "post victory task of remolding the Japanese mind."[94]

Several commentators claimed that Hirohito bore partial responsibility for Japan's aggression. The columnist Robert Quillen criticized those who spoke of retaining Hirohito as a "stabilizing force." He said that Hirohito would "stabilize and perpetuate the sun-god hoax that has made the Japs a race of fanatic killers, lusting to conquer the world and convert it with fire and sword as the followers of Mohammed did."[95] "History will expose the divinity of the Emperor hoax as one of the greatest rackets of all time," declared publisher and editor Miller Freeman. "Hitler and Mussolini were pikers by comparison," he added.[96]

The journalist James R. Young equated Hirohito to Japanese militarists and discounted the idea that killing the emperor would lengthen the war by stiffening Japanese resistance. "Let's cut the hokus-pokus respect for the Emperor and wake up to his true military status," Young wrote.[97] Sun Fo, the son of the Chinese leader Sun Yat Sen, said that if the Allies intended to abolish Japanese militarism, "the Mikado must go."[98] Columnist Thomas L. Stokes argued that Americans did not oppose Hirohito out of vengeance but because of their traditional dislike of rulers associated with divinity. "So we say: To hell with the Emperor!" Stokes wrote.[99]

Mark Sullivan, writing in the *Washington Post*, described Hirohito as merely "a symbol and an automaton," yet he feared that any proclamation of intent to harm the emperor might increase Japanese resolve.[100] Other commentators believed that the United States had accorded Hirohito too much respect by not intentionally bombing the Imperial Palace. The editors of the *St. Louis Post-Dispatch* wanted his residence blasted to shatter belief in his divinity by demonstrating that neither the emperor nor his domicile were impervious to bombs.[101] Indeed, the columnist Herbert R. Hill criticized the "pussyfoot policies of some old-school diplomats in Washington" for sparing the palace.[102]

If Hirohito had not cooperated with Japan's military leaders, he certainly had not resisted them, argued critics. They also contended that if Hirohito had opposed the war but lacked the power to prevent it, he had no chance of convincing Japan's militarists to end hostilities. "There is nothing that could make the Japanese fighters and ruling class any more fanatical than they are," insisted an editorial in the *Charleston* (W.Va.) *Gazette*. "And America demands," declared the editorial, "that we keep right on bombing until we blast Hirohito's 'sacred' hide out of existence and thus put an all-time end to an evil dynasty."[103] An editorial printed in the *Dayton News* said, "The war will be fought in vain unless it brings a clear break with all the forces that went into its making—and these forces were emperors and appeasers, kings and cartellists, fuehrers and fawners, field marshals and fifth columnists, colonels' cliques and collaborationists."[104]

Critics of the emperor also castigated the Shinto religious faith of Japan. More important than targeting Hirohito's palace, according to the columnist Herbert R. Hill, was bombing Shinto shrines. "Shintoism is the religious hocus-pocus which permits a ruthless oligarchy to shackle a terrible slavery on the Japanese masses," he said, claiming that the ignorant Japanese would lose respect for their "medicine men" if the United States bombed Shinto shrines.[105] Writing in the *New Republic*, D.C. Holton declared that nothing would "clear the air and overturn false gods and false ideals like the winds of disaster that are already beginning to blow strongly across Nippon."[106]

In a letter to Joseph Grew, a former missionary blamed the Western powers and U.S. missionary boards for acquiescence regarding the spread of Shintoism. He believed the religion had encouraged Japanese expansion and convinced Japan's military leaders that Americans were decadent. A minister warned Grew that vigorous measures must be taken to prevent Shintoism from replacing Christianity in areas that had been under Japanese control.[107] Grew countered that militarism had perverted the Shinto religion. Once the Japanese people realized this, Grew said, "State Shinto will soon fall of its own weight, provided we do not arrest the process of disillusionment by too overt attack on the 'religion' or its symbols."[108]

The news that President Truman would travel to Germany to consult with Joseph Stalin and Winston Churchill in mid-July 1945 encouraged those who hoped for a more definitive declaration of war aims. After Truman's departure, Sen. Kenneth Wherry of Nebraska, the Republican whip, announced that a "high military source" had compiled a list of conditions under which Japan could be induced to surrender. Wherry said that these terms, which included allowing Japan to retain the imperial system, could end the "slaughter" in the Pacific.[109] In a speech to the Senate, Wherry noted the "rising flood of demands for a definition of our terms to the Japanese."[110] However, critics accused Wherry of encouraging the Japanese.[111]

Extensive discussion and debate occurred on the home front over unconditional surrender and the fate of the emperor. Commentators and citizens recognized the imprecision of unconditional surrender. Few suggested direct negotiations with Japan, but many people obviously considered unconditional surrender insufficient incentive for encouraging the Japanese to capitulate. Some letters from the parents of fighting men suggested that they did not oppose negotiations with Japan. It appears that most of those who critiqued unconditional surrender preferred clarifying the policy rather than abandoning it. They argued that the United States could offer fair and firm conditions without appearing weak.

The correspondence received by the White House, the State Department, and various members of Congress indicated that sentiment supportive of clear terms spread across a diverse segment of the population. Liberals, conservatives, socialists, religious and labor leaders, academics, lawyers, businessmen, students, women, men, sent messages in favor of definite terms. Their reasons ranged from a desire to quickly end the war and spare American lives to the belief that the explanation of terms constituted a moral obligation. Some expressed concern about the potential for Soviet influence in Asia if the war continued. Unfortunately, American leaders thought almost exclusively in military terms when they discussed methods of ending the war, even though many citizens and commentators believed that diplomacy might end it just as expeditiously and preclude further combat.

Those opposed to alteration of unconditional surrender equated any deviation from it to appeasement, a word fraught with negative connotations as the label for the policy of Britain and France toward Nazi Germany in the 1930s. They likened modification of unconditional surrender to softness and intimated that any leniency toward Japan would increase the chances of another war later.

Despite the prevalence of opinion that regarded the Japanese as uniquely sinister, various commentators applied lessons to them based on events that occurred in Western nations. Amidst the enduring hatred of the Japanese, and the sustained desire for retribution, many commentators and citizens expressed a growing awareness that the United States should devise a cogent political policy for ending the war.

As with other issues pertaining to the war, prejudicial attitudes and uninformed opinions about the Japanese shaped the debate over unconditional surrender. Supporters of unconditional surrender used the belief in the inherent irrationality of the Japanese to buttress their arguments that trying to reason with savages was a waste of time.

Several of the letters pertaining to unconditional surrender also reflected uneasiness about the increasingly destructive course of the war. Those who considered clarification of terms a moral responsibility recognized that the war had eroded moral and ethical constraints on warfare. Americans wanted to minimize casualties, yet many remained troubled by incendiary bombing, discussion of chemical warfare, and threats that all Japanese would be wiped out despite Truman's assurances to the contrary. The U.S. government endeavored to discourage public interest in reports of Japanese peace feelers. Several leading Republicans suggested revising terms, but their efforts remained partisan critique rather than a concerted effort to alter unconditional surrender.

Although they paid little attention to the diverse opinions of ordinary citizens, various diplomatic and military leaders who favored clarification of terms for Japan attempted to forge a declaration of war aims. Their efforts coincided with the final developmental stages of a new weapon that appeared to offer a means of increasing the blows against Japan without risking American lives.

9

Resolution

"This is the greatest thing in history."[1]

As commentators and citizens evaluated unconditional surrender, the U.S. government resolutely supported the policy. Yet various governmental, diplomatic, and military leaders endorsed the idea of offering Japan specific terms. The War Department and the State Department disagreed about when such a pronouncement should be released and whether it should include a pledge to preserve the emperor. These disputes, Truman's reluctance to modify unconditional surrender, and the continued ferocity of Japanese resistance all hindered the development of precise terms. Achieving Japan's unconditional surrender remained problematic, although by any reasonable standard Japan was defeated. Of course, the potential for using atomic bombs overshadowed the deliberations about altering unconditional surrender.

The U.S. government's postwar preparations included assessment of unconditional surrender and discussion about Japan's imperial institution. State Department postwar planning committees advocated "a careful middle course" between denouncing the emperor, which might strengthen his support among the Japanese, and not criticizing him at all, which could alienate Americans. One planning committee concluded that a document signed by the emperor would be the optimal form of unconditional surrender.[2] By early 1945, army strategists began thoroughly assessing the policy of unconditional surrender. Concluding that the literal meaning of unconditional surrender was "foreign" to most Japanese, the army suggested modifying it to a formula that the Japanese could comprehend as an admission of defeat. Army analysts also said that Japan's capitulation might be more easily accomplished with the emperor's approval.[3]

The Joint Intelligence Committee endorsed the idea of clarifying unconditional surrender.[4] Belief that they fought for national survival, not a unique disposition "toward national suicide," motivated Japanese resistance, according to one intelligence study. Japanese leaders and citizens must be convinced that unconditional surrender did not mean "national annihilation."[5] A report for the Joint Chiefs from April 1945 also proposed that unconditional surrender be explained. "Unless a definition of unconditional surrender can be given which is acceptable to the Japanese," it concluded, "there is no alternative to annihilation and no prospect that the threat of absolute defeat will bring about capitulation."[6]

Leaders outside the Truman administration suggested issuing an ultimatum to Japan. In May 1945 members of General MacArthur's staff used connections with the Hearst newspaper chain to send the White House a proposed ultimatum. The statement warned Hirohito that his failure to order the surrender of Japan's armed forces made him responsible for the war's continuation and possibly a war criminal. Joseph Grew, the acting secretary of state, received an earlier draft of the statement. He considered it "politically undesirable" to directly address Hirohito. He feared that a bellicose statement might undermine Hirohito's authority, thereby jeopardizing the chance of securing his assistance in achieving unconditional surrender.[7]

Former president Herbert Hoover, who hoped to forestall Soviet influence in Asia, submitted two drafts of his plan to end the war. He proposed Japanese withdrawal from China, restoration of Manchuria to China, the ceding of various Japanese-controlled islands to the Allies, and the disarmament of Japan. Hoover recommended allowing the Japanese to maintain the imperial system and also suggested granting Japan control of Korea and Formosa. All of this, Hoover argued, would help prevent an invasion, thereby sparing the lives of up to one million American troops.[8] In their critique of Hoover's papers, War Department analysts opposed Japanese control of Formosa and pointed out that the Cairo Declaration had promised a degree of freedom for Korea. Unless the U.S. Army occupied Manchuria, Soviet interests in that vast province would have to be recognized. They deemed Hoover's casualty estimates as "entirely too high."[9] Disputing Hoover's assertion that there were large numbers of liberal Japanese, the War Department strategists nevertheless concluded that explaining unconditional surrender "has definite merit if it is carefully handled." They preferred a firm declaration that did not encourage bargaining, which they feared would impair public support of the war. The War Department proposed that a pronouncement be coordinated with Soviet entry into the war when the bombing of Japan reached a peak, probably between mid-August and early September 1945.[10]

Differences of opinion existed among Truman's advisers with regard to clarifying terms of surrender. Joseph Grew espoused immediate explanation of unconditional surrender to avert an invasion and preclude Soviet participation. Like Hoover and Secretary of War Stimson, he believed moderates in Japan wanted to end the war.[11] Throughout May and June 1945, Grew advised Truman to announce more definite terms. He told Truman that the primary obstacle to Japanese acceptance of unconditional surrender remained their belief that it meant the dismantling of the imperial institution. In late May, Grew provided Truman with a draft of a surrender offer and suggested that Truman include it in a Memorial Day speech scheduled for May 31. The genesis of the subsequent Potsdam Declaration, the statement included terms previously issued in the Cairo Declaration. It tacitly approved Japan's right to establish a postwar government that included a constitutional monarchy. Truman indicated general agreement with these ideas, but he told Grew to discuss them with Henry Stimson, General Marshall, Secretary of the Navy James Forrestal, and Admiral King.[12]

Grew did outline his proposals at what Stimson later described as an "awkward meeting" where several people remained ignorant of "the real feature which would govern the situation"—the atomic bomb. Stimson, Marshall, and Forrestal agreed with the basis of Grew's plan but citing undisclosed military reasons said the announcement was premature. Truman's Memorial Day message merely warned of further destruction if Japan did not surrender unconditionally.[13]

In mid-June, with the end of the campaign on Okinawa apparent, Grew again advised Truman to issue terms of surrender and gave the president a second proposed announcement. Threatening to abolish the imperial institution, according to Grew, would prolong the war, and preservation of the emperor constituted "irreducible" terms for the Japanese. By publicizing the importance of ending the war before an invasion, commentators would help overcome public disapproval of allowing the Japanese to determine their political future, Grew added. Truman later said that he had carefully considered the statement but preferred to first discuss it with Stalin and Churchill.[14]

Henry Stimson also believed that further defining of terms might end the war. Then seventy-seven, Stimson was an enervated man by mid-1945. His diary contained numerous references to his persistent fatigue and his need for naps to refresh himself. He concentrated most of his dwindling stamina on keeping abreast of the development of the atomic bomb.

Since 1941 the massive, top-secret effort to construct the atomic bomb, called the Manhattan Project, had forged ahead despite immense obstacles. It became the largest, most expensive weapons research and development project of the war. The government constructed huge facilities at Oak Ridge, Tennessee, and Hanford, Washington, to produce two necessary ingredients, fissionable uranium and plutonium. Scientists and engineers at Los Alamos, New Mexico, worked on the problems of detonating the material. The entire project involved more than 120,000 people working at thirty-seven different installations in nineteen states and Canada. It cost more than two billion dollars.[15]

Stimson and Grew met regularly as part of the Committee of Three, which also included James Forrestal. They appraised overall strategy and discussed the potential for Soviet intervention. Stimson considered all of these issues "powerfully connected with our success with S-1," the code designation for the atomic bomb.[16] Grew and Stimson wanted to avoid an invasion. Grew thought that diplomatic efforts might end the war before the use of new weapons; Stimson was less concerned about the immediacy of a clarifying statement. "My only fixed date," he wrote in his diary, "is the last chance warning which must be given before an actual landing of the ground forces in Japan, and fortunately the plans provide for enough time to bring in the sanctions of our warning in the shape of heavy ordinance bomb attack and an attack of S-1."[17]

Stimson speculated that an atomic blast could enhance the force of an ultimatum. Almost possessive of "S-1," or "my secret" as he alternately referred to it in his diary, Stimson endorsed planning for an invasion but hoped that the bomb would make one unnecessary. In one diary entry he mentioned presenting Japan with an ultimatum "after she had been sufficiently pounded possibly with S-1." He considered whether the Soviets would declare war and "when and how S-1 will resolve itself" as the two major uncertainties of the war.[18]

Grew, Stimson, and General Marshall favored modification of unconditional surrender, but they disagreed about when it should occur. Certain army analysts preferred the immediate release of a declaration, while navy counterparts wanted to wait until Okinawa was secured. The Military Intelligence Division supported a surrender demand because it said the intensified bombing would only increase Japanese resolve. Admiral Leahy and Stimson favored delaying any pronouncement until Okinawa was captured.[19]

In June 1945, the Joint Chiefs approved a study that recommended a demand for Japan's unconditional surrender when the outcome of the Okinawa campaign was certain. The report said that a declaration by the United States would preclude any Japanese offer of conditional surrender. Citing war weariness among citizens, the study warned that a Japanese peace proposal, if released before the redeployment of U.S. troops to the Pacific, might adversely affect public support of the war.[20]

Stimson suggested altering U.S. policy from unconditional surrender to the "complete defeat and permanent destruction of the war making power of Japan."[21] Rather than trying to rephrase Allied objectives, General Marshall desired a more lucid explanation of unconditional surrender. He advocated "enlightened direction" in the composition of public statements intended for Japanese leaders, with less emphasis on unconditional surrender, "which we all agree is difficult to define," and the issuance of "more definitive statements which indicate our war aims with more exactitude." Marshall feared that deviation from the policy of unconditional surrender might prove unpopular. Instead, it should be replaced with definite terms that did not invite negotiations.[22]

War Department documents prepared for Truman noted Stimson's and Marshall's concurrence about discouraging use of the phrase unconditional surrender. One report said that announcing more precise terms would help to sustain public morale. The War Department tacitly approved the emperor's retention since Japan's surrender remained a possibility "attractive enough to the U.S. to justify us in making any concessions which might be attractive to the Japanese, so long as our realistic aims for peace in the Pacific are not adversely affected."[23]

When Truman met with the Joint Chiefs on June 18 to discuss the plans for invading Kyushu, Stimson and Admiral Leahy spoke favorably about changing unconditional surrender. Leahy disagreed with the notion that altering it meant tarnishing the eventual victory. Insistence on unconditional surrender, he said, would likely increase American casualties. Assistant Secretary of War John J. McCloy suggested allowing Japan to retain the emperor and issuing an explicit warning about the atomic bomb. Truman claimed to have "left the door open to Congress to take appropriate action with reference to unconditional surrender," adding that he could not "take any action at this time to change public opinion on the matter."[24]

Marshall's main strategist, Gen. George Lincoln, worked with McCloy to draft a proposal that combined Grew's and Stimson's ideas. Lincoln knew of the Joint Chiefs' concern that the widely reported Japanese peace offers might become more difficult to refuse. On the other hand, Japanese rejection of an Allied demand for surrender could be used to convince the public that there was no alternative to Japan's utter defeat. Lincoln also wanted to permit the Japanese to retain their imperial system. Frustrated with certain state department officials who opposed this, Lincoln charged that they only wanted terms that would not provoke criticism in the United States.[25] Dean Acheson and Archibald MacLeish, assistant secretaries in the State Department, fought against altering unconditional surrender. Neither possessed expertise on Asia. MacLeish complained to the newly appointed secretary of state James F. Byrnes that permitting Japan to preserve the emperor diverged from unconditional surrender.[26]

Meanwhile, in early July Stimson presented Truman with his version of a statement for Japan. He told Truman that it must be issued prior to an invasion to allow time for evaluating the Japanese response. Stimson favored letting the emperor remain in power. His paper, more of an ultimatum than Grew's drafts, did not mention the atomic bomb, but he did say that the declaration would have to be revised "to conform with the efficacy of such a weapon if the warning were to be delivered, as would certainly be the case, in conjunction with its use."[27]

Stimson's comments revealed the disparity between prevailing views of the Japanese and the publicly unexpressed opinions of government leaders such as himself and Grew. He told the president that contrary to the majority of media reports, the Japanese were reasonable. He dismissed the notion of them being "mad fanatics of an entirely different mentality from ours."[28] Truman listened to Stimson's advice, although he still wanted to discuss all aspects of any pronouncement with Allied leaders at the forthcoming conference at Potsdam.

At this time, James Byrnes exerted more influence over Truman than Grew or Stimson. As the director of the Office of War Mobilization, Byrnes had learned the details of the Manhattan Project in 1944. In early May 1945, Truman appointed Byrnes as his personal representative on the Interim Committee, organized by Stimson to discuss the eventual use of the atomic bomb. In July, Truman named Byrnes secretary of state. Byrnes won Truman's confidence by spending long hours with him in the initial chaotic days of his presidency, explaining Roosevelt's foreign policy in blunt, plain terms that appealed to Truman.[29]

When Truman met with Stalin and Churchill at Potsdam in mid-July, Stalin, as Truman had hoped, vowed to declare war on Japan in August. The United States, Britain, and China released the Potsdam Declaration, which demanded that Japan immediately surrender unconditionally. Byrnes persuaded Truman to omit any overt reference to the emperor. The lack of detailed records of their conversations on this issue have prevented historians from reaching definitive conclusions on why Truman and Byrnes made this decision. It appears that Byrnes regarded any assurances about the emperor as politically risky. Before the conference at Potsdam, he had telephoned the former secretary of state, Cordell Hull, and read Stimson's draft statement to him. Hull said that the remarks about the emperor smacked of appeasement. Whether political concerns strongly influenced Truman and Byrnes remains a point of contention.[30]

In its final form, the Potsdam Declaration of July 26, 1945, said that Japan's leaders had brought their country to "the threshold of annihilation," although it vowed that the Allies did not intend to enslave the Japanese or destroy them as a nation. It repeated the terms of the

Cairo Declaration that Japan must disarm and relinquish conquered territory. The statement called for eliminating the power of those who had led Japan into war and promised stern justice for war criminals. It did not mention the emperor, the pending declaration of war by the Soviet Union, or the recently tested atomic bomb.[31]

Rumors of imminent peace abounded following the release of the Potsdam Declaration.[32] Response to the announcement was positive in the American press.[33] Columnist David Lawrence praised the pronouncement as a refutation of the idea that there were no "decent Japanese."[34] The terms, according to the editors of the Washington, D.C., *Evening Star*, offered Japan the chance for survival, "which, in the opinion of a good many Americans, is more than they deserve." They added that if the Japanese rejected it, the United States should use every means available "to destroy them as quickly as possible."[35]

Some commentary conveyed disappointment that the declaration did not blame Hirohito for Japanese aggression. Columnist Hanson W. Baldwin, who criticized the "hands off" policy toward Hirohito, likened making a distinction between the emperor and Japanese militarists akin to separating Siamese twins. Honorable peace, he said, meant nothing to leaders who held values "completely foreign and utterly repugnant to all we fight for."[36] Columnist Gladstone Williams suggested amending the proclamation to say that Hirohito was accountable for ending the war.[37] The editors of the *St. Louis Post-Dispatch* argued that the declaration implied that Hirohito could be removed from power.[38] However, the radio commentator H.V. Kaltenborn claimed that despite the omission of any direct reference to the emperor, the Allies intended to allow the Japanese to keep the emperor.[39]

Yet another part of the complex mosaic of issues that confronted U.S. leaders in the war's final months was the potential for using atomic weapons. A Target Committee composed of Army Air Forces officers, civilian advisers, scientists from the Manhattan Project, and representatives of Gen. Leslie Groves, who supervised the program, compiled a list of potential targets and presented its recommendations to Stimson. The committee members agreed that the bomb should be used in a manner that impressed as many Japanese as possible and was "sufficiently spectacular for the importance of the weapon to be internationally recognized when publicity on it is released." These goals made it certain that the weapon would be dropped over a city. Tokyo was deemed an unsuitable target because it was "practically rubble."[40]

The committee appraised the ancient city of Kyoto, long a cultural and intellectual center in Japan, as an enticing target because the people there would be "better able to appreciate the significance of the weapon." This observation apparently presumed the survival of suitably awestruck inhabitants. It was decided that Hirohito's palace possessed "a greater fame than any other target but is of least strategic value." The committee also discussed the potential of an incendiary raid immediately following the atomic attack. Members decided that the risk of radioactivity from the blast of "the gadget" warranted additional study before they considered this option further.[41]

In a conversation with Stimson in late May, General Marshall mentioned dropping the bomb over a military objective, such as a large naval base. If results proved inconclusive, he proposed warning the Japanese to evacuate certain cities before using the bomb over an urban area. "Every effort should be made to keep our record of warning clear," Marshall said. "We must offset by such warning methods the opprobrium which might follow from an ill considered employment of such force."[42] Apparently, it was the only time Marshall made the suggestion.

Stimson, with Truman's approval, organized the Interim Committee to discuss the bomb's use and issues concerning the postwar control of atomic power. Headed by Stimson it included his assistants Harvey Bundy and George Harrison; Vannevar Bush, the director of the U.S. Office of Scientific Research and Development; Karl T. Compton, a physicist and the president of the Massachusetts Institute of Technology; James B. Conant, a noted chemist and the president of Harvard University; Under Secretary of the Navy Ralph A. Bard; and Assistant Secretary of State William L. Clayton. Truman chose James Byrnes as his personal representative to the committee. Marshall and General Groves met with the committee as well.[43]

Over the course of several meetings, the members concurred with the guidelines established by the Target Committee. Marshall proposed inviting two prominent Soviet representatives to witness the first test explosion of the atomic bomb scheduled for July. Byrnes strongly objected to sharing any information with the Soviets. He preferred using the bomb without warning, a recommendation that the Interim Committee endorsed. Committee members agreed that the optimal target was a large war plant located near workers' houses.[44]

Numerous scientists working for the Manhattan Project conveyed their distress about dropping the bomb without prior notice. Dr. James Franck, a Nobel prize-winning chemist, chaired a committee of scientists from the Metallurgical Laboratory in Chicago that produced a report opposed to direct unannounced use of the bomb on Japan.[45] Leo Szilard, another physicist associated with the scientists working in Chicago, traveled to Byrnes's home in South Carolina in May 1945 in a fruitless attempt to convince him that the bomb should not be used against Japan.[46] Two navy officials also expressed concern about the Interim Committee's findings. Ralph Bard, the navy's representative on the committee, dissented from surprise use of the bomb. Lewis Strauss, special assistant to Secretary of the Navy James Forrestal, proposed a demonstration of the weapon over a forest in Japan.[47]

The Interim Committee appraised several Japanese cities as potential targets.[48] General Groves deemed Kyoto the most attractive because it was the largest of the listed cities and thus, he believed, better suited to demonstrate the damage the atomic bomb caused when dropped over a major urban area. All the cities were described as militarily important. Yet when Stimson objected to the inclusion of Kyoto because of its historical and cultural importance, Groves contended that such a large city "must be involved in a tremendous amount of war work even if there were but few large factories." Although Hiroshima was the location of a local army headquarters and a large port, Groves considered it "not nearly as satisfactory" a target as Kyoto. After talking with General Arnold, Marshall, and finally Truman, Stimson succeeded in having Kyoto removed from the list.[49]

By mid-July, the first atomic bomb was ready to be tested. Manhattan Project officials detonated it shortly after dawn on July 16, 1945, at the Alamagordo base of the Army Air Forces, in New Mexico's Tularosa Valley. The explosion produced a dazzling flash visible for 250 miles. An ominous column of smoke and ash rapidly moved upward to form an enormous mushroom-shaped cloud. Within thirty seconds, a blast of hot wind buffeted observers six miles away who then heard a prolonged roar.

Truman received the initial reports of the test shortly after his arrival at his quarters in Babelsburg, Germany, for the Potsdam Conference. The first brief messages indicated that the results had surpassed expectations, and subsequent communiques confirmed this. The news heartened Truman. Although it did not make him immediately discount Soviet participation in the war, he undoubtedly recognized that the war might now be ended without Soviet assistance.[50]

At this time, a faction within the Japanese government sought to end the war. Scholarly descriptions of the inner workings of Japan's government are reminiscent of novelist Edith Wharton's depiction of elite society in nineteenth-century New York City. Japanese leaders, like Wharton's characters in *The Age of Innocence*, interacted in "an atmosphere of faint implications and pale delicacies," an environment that resembled "a kind of hieroglyphic world, where the real thing was never said or done or even thought, but only represented by a set of arbitrary signs."[51] Scholars have noted the concept of "haragei," which was a tendency by Japanese government officials to hint at their true thoughts rather than openly espouse them. Such ambiguities have complicated the task of assessing the motives of various Japanese leaders.[52]

Appointed Japan's premier in April 1945, the retired admiral Baron Kantaro Suzuki gradually accepted the notion of endeavoring to conclude the war in an honorable fashion, which meant avoiding unconditional surrender. One of the ironies of the Pacific War is that despite American intransigence on the issue of the emperor, Hirohito and his closest advisers decisively influenced events in Japan that contributed to ending the war. Suzuki faced staunch opposition from both hard-line army and navy leaders, but he succeeded in having the more moderate Shigenori Togo appointed as foreign minister, in the hope that he might help end hostilities.[53]

Suzuki and Togo thought that the Soviet Union might mediate an agreement ending the war. Former premier Koki Hirota, the onetime ambassador to the Soviet Union, held inconclusive discussions with the Soviet ambassador to Japan. The end-the-war faction hoped to entice the Soviets with offers of territorial concessions in Asia. With the exception of Togo, nobody considered the possibility that the Allies had already undercut these overtures with previously arranged territorial compensations made at the Yalta Conference.[54]

In June, Japan's Supreme Council for the Direction of the War approved an army plan that advocated mass resistance to an Allied invasion, even though supporting memorandums made clear that Japan lacked the resources to continue the war. Only Togo questioned the proposal. Japan's cabinet endorsed the plan, and on June 8 Hirohito listened to it silently.[55]

With Hirohito's approval, Togo appointed Prince Funimaro Konoye as a special envoy to the Soviet Union, but the Soviets refused Konoye entry into the country. By July 12, the Japanese ambassador in Moscow, Naotake Sato, had received instructions from Tokyo to inform the Soviet government that Japan wanted to end the war on terms other than unconditional surrender. The Soviets rebuffed Sato's requests for a meeting with foreign minister V.M. Molotov, saying that Molotov was too busy preparing for the Allied conference at Potsdam. Sato conducted unproductive talks with other Soviet officials. When he did meet Molotov on August 7, the wily foreign minister presented the Soviet Union's declaration of war on Japan.[56]

Stalin informed Truman about the Japanese overtures at Potsdam, two days after the release of the Potsdam Declaration. Truman already knew about the Japanese diplomatic maneuvers. Because American cryptanalysts had previously cracked the Japanese diplomatic codes, American officials read intercepts of these messages.[57]

Disputes among Japan's leadership about the appropriate reply to the Potsdam Declaration ensued after the pronouncement's release. Togo and Suzuki favored a moderate rejoinder, but hard-line militarists advocated rejection of the statement. These disagreements resulted in the release to the Japanese press of Suzuki's preference for "moku-satsu," or withholding comment. Because of its varied interpretations, the term could be defined as not responding, as Suzuki intended; ignoring the declaration; or treating it with contempt, which was the manner in which the Japanese press reported the official reply. Suzuki subsequently issued a statement that Japan intended to continue the war.[58]

In the American media, Japan's unfavorable answer to the pronouncement prompted disagreement. Those who deemed the Potsdam statement a satisfactory explanation of terms believed that there was no alternative to Japan's destruction.[59] The columnist Barnet Nover said that Japan's reply disproved the claims that defining terms of surrender "would have the same effect on Japan that the blast of Joshua's trumpet had on the walls of Jericho."[60]

The editors of the *Washington Post* preferred that the United States carefully consider its options, reasoning that the Allies should continue trying to drive a wedge between the Japanese people and their leaders.[61] The editors of the *Chicago Daily Tribune* said that creative diplomacy could still resolve the war. "The situation as it exists is made to order for diplomatic action," they wrote, arguing that peace could be achieved on the basis of the fact that Japan could not win the war and the United States could not lose it.[62] Likewise, the *New Republic* did not deem Japan's rejection of the Potsdam terms as proof of the declaration's failure. Its editors thought that U.S. leaders should allow more time for Japanese moderates to gain support for peace.[63]

Events proceeded quickly. Truman had already approved the use of the two available atomic bombs. On August 6, 1945, shortly before 8:15 A.M., the B-29 bomber "Enola Gay" released an atomic bomb over the city of Hiroshima. Approximately forty-five seconds later a searing flash marked the bomb's detonation above the city, most of which was destroyed by the concussive blast and blistering heat. An estimated 130,000 inhabitants died instantly, some literally vaporized. Thousands more died later from shock, burns, and radiation poisoning. Truman described Hiroshima as a military base. "Although Hiroshima was a naval base," Admiral Leahy wrote in his diary, "it is probable that the destruction of civilian life was terrific." He noted that some scientists had predicted the area would be uninhabitable for several years.[64]

Two days later the Soviet Union declared war on Japan, and Soviet armies invaded Manchuria. "If they continue to fight in the face of the overwhelming odds that are against them," said columnist Gladstone Williams about the Japanese, "then civilization will have lost nothing in the destruction that awaits them."[65] On August 9, an atomic bomb was dropped over the city of Nagasaki, killing another seventy thousand.

Just prior to the bombing of Nagasaki, the Japanese Supreme Council convened to reconsider the Potsdam Declaration. Several military leaders still opposed peace on the basis of the conditions issued at Potsdam. When Hirohito met with the Supreme Council on August 9, he indicated his preference for accepting the Potsdam terms, with the added stipulation that the throne be preserved. The following day, the Japanese government conveyed its agreement with the terms, provided they did not "comprise any demand which prejudices the prerogatives of His Majesty as a Sovereign Ruler." It was, according to Stimson, "the very single point that I feared would make trouble."[66]

Further discussion over the conditions of surrender had continued within the Truman administration after the Potsdam Conference.[67] On August 8, before the dropping of the second atomic bomb, Stimson had presented Truman with two position papers on the potential usefulness of the emperor in achieving Japan's surrender. Stimson compared proper methods of punishing a dog to the manner in which the Japanese should be treated.[68]

Others, however, remained staunchly opposed to altering unconditional surrender. In a cable to Truman, Sen. Richard B. Russell (D-Ga.) urged continued pounding of Japan with more atomic bombs and incendiary attacks until "they are brought groveling to their knees." He opposed any concession about Hirohito. In his reply, Truman described Japan as "a terribly cruel and uncivilized nation in warfare," calling the Japanese "beasts" but adding that he did not think the United States should act in a similar fashion. He lamented "wiping out whole populations because of the 'pigheadedness' of the leaders" and said that although he intended to save American lives, "I also have a humane feeling for the women and children in Japan."[69]

When Truman met with his top advisers on August 10, James Byrnes argued against deviating from unconditional surrender. He claimed that accepting conditions would mean the "crucifixion of the President." Henry Stimson said that preserving the emperor would facilitate the occupation of Japan, help secure the surrender of outlying Japanese forces, and prevent the Soviets from exerting more influence on the war's outcome. James Forrestal proposed drafting a compromise reply that reconciled these differences. Byrnes and his staff worked out an answer which stipulated that the emperor's authority was subject to the supreme commander of the Allied powers. It emphasized the section of the Potsdam Declaration which had decreed that the people of Japan would ultimately determine their form of government. British, Chinese, and Soviet agreement came rapidly, and the message was delivered to Japan via Switzerland.[70]

Japanese leaders discussed the proposal for three days, with some members of the Supreme Council still opposed to acceptance. U.S. aircraft dispersed leaflets over Tokyo that contained the text of the Japanese offer and the Allied reply. Fearful of revolts from junior army and navy officers who wanted to continue the war, Marquis Koichi Kido urged Hirohito to end the impasse. After he convened a meeting with the cabinet, Hirohito instructed his ministers to accept the Allied reply and to prepare a script for him to make an unprecedented broadcast to the Japanese nation. Several assassination attempts on Kido, Suzuki, and other government leaders occurred in the following days. A group of radical army officers even tried to confiscate and destroy the taped transcripts of Hirohito's speech to prevent its broadcast.[71]

As Americans anxiously awaited a resolution to the war, politicans voiced their opinions about the final terms. "Damn the emperor—he's a war criminal and I'd like to see him hung up by his toes," declared Sen. Tom Stewart (D-Tenn.), conveying the imagery of a lynching. "If the Japs are allowed to keep their fantastic god-Emperor system," warned Sen. Brien McMahon (D-Conn.), "we may get an armistice and not an end to the war." No terms of any kind," said Sen. William Langer (R-N.Dak.). "That means that the Emperor ought to be treated like Hitler," he added. Sen. Elbert D. Thomas (D-Utah), chairman of the Military Affairs Committee and formerly a missionary in Japan, remarked, "I don't see why anybody should want to fight a war over an emperor." Several Republican senators affirmed their support for allowing the Japanese to preserve an imperial system that functioned under Allied control.[72]

Newspapers formerly opposed to conditional surrender, such as the *Los Angeles Times* and the *St. Louis Post-Dispatch*, now endorsed permitting the Japanese to keep the emperor as long as he followed Allied orders.[73] Other editorials, however, resolutely opposed this course of action. The editors of the *Cleveland Plain Dealer* blamed Hirohito and Shintoism for Japan's aggression. Muslims did not revolt when the sultan of Turkey was "deposed and politically manhandled" after World War I, the editors argued. They regarded those events as comparable because "the Arab world is every bit as fanatical as the Japanese."[74]

In spite of ongoing arguments about the emperor's fate, Japan's acceptance of terms on August 14, 1945, provoked jubilation in the

United States. Some complained that the settlement resembled a compromise, but others considered it a wise decision. Soldiers in the Pacific discounted continuing the war merely to depose the emperor.[75] On September 2, aboard the battleship *USS Missouri* in Tokyo Bay, General MacArthur, now appointed supreme commander of the Allied powers in Japan, presided over the formal Japanese surrender.

The news of the atomic bomb nearly overshadowed Japan's capitulation. Citizens expressed overwhelming approval of the bomb's use.[76] Yet the public's mood was described as a "strangely dazed" sense of relief.[77] One editorial viciously mocked "the whining, sniveling protest of the Japanese at the inhuman quality of the atomic bomb." Although they admitted that the terrific destruction was unsettling, the editors of the *Atlanta Constitution* argued that the results produced "grim satisfaction that Japan finally tastes some of the horror she showed the world."[78] An editorial in the *Washington Post* said that most citizens received the news about the bomb "not with exultation but with a kind of bewildered awe." "It was wonderful to think of what the Atomic Age might be, if man were strong and honest," *Time* concluded. "But at first it was a strange place, full of weird symbols and the smell of death."[79]

Dissent about the bomb's use appeared immediately. The White House and newspapers across the country received hundreds of letters and telegrams criticizing the decision to drop the bomb. Anne Ford, the publicity director of a major publishing company, said that she had never written to a president before, but the destruction of Hiroshima compelled her to do so. "I think it is a disgrace that America should be involved in such a diabolical thing," she wrote.[80] When Dr. Harold Jacobson of Columbia University, a low-level scientist in the Manhattan Project, composed an article for the International News Service that described the lingering effects of radiation, the government swiftly pressured him to recant.[81] Newspapers published letters both supportive and critical of the bomb. Some Americans feared that the United States' claim to leadership as a humane, Christian nation had been permanently damaged.[82]

As part of their later justification for using the bomb, Truman and Byrnes said that an invasion of Japan would have resulted in half a million American casualties. Subsequent research cast doubt on these claims.[83] Truman apparently began citing these figures to correspond with those publicized by Stimson after the war. In January 1953, just before he left office, Truman responded to an inquiry from James L. Cate, a history professor at the University of Chicago who was one of the editors and authors of the official history of the Army Air Forces in World War II. Cate had written Truman about the timing of the order that authorized the dropping of the atomic bombs, which was issued one day prior to the release of the Potsdam Declaration. In his hand-written draft reply, Truman recounted that General Marshall had told him that a landing near Tokyo would result in a minimum of 250,000 American casualties and an equal number of Japanese.[84]

Truman's assistants, Kenneth W. Hechler and David D. Lloyd, reviewed his response. Hechler recommended revising the casualty figure upward to conform with those cited in Stimson's book *On Active Service in Peace And War*. In that work, Stimson said that he was told an invasion of Japan would result in one million American casualties. Hechler reasoned that it was important that the figures correspond. Lloyd admitted that Truman's calculations sounded more plausible, but he suggested changing the wording to read that Marshall "expected a minimum of a quarter of a million casualties and possibly a much greater number—as much as a million." Truman's reply to Cate included the proposed alterations.[85]

It is inconceivable that Truman would have approved any operation expected to result in half a million casualties.[86] Although Truman and others later exaggerated the casualty estimates of 1945, it is also true that for Truman—and other leaders such as Stimson—the use of the atomic bomb was preferable to an invasion regardless of the casualty estimates. Truman's postwar claims ignored the decisions reached at the meeting of June 18, 1945, where he approved the invasion plans for Kyushu but not those for Honshu. The fact that projections of one million American casualties appeared in the media in 1945 probably contributed to the later acceptance of Truman's and Stimson's figures. In a diary entry composed after a meeting with Stimson during the Potsdam Conference, Truman indicated that the bomb would be used so that it did not target women and children. It is difficult to understand why he would believe this, especially after he approved the idea of dropping the bomb over a city. As historian Barton J. Bernstein has said, the comments were probably self-deception.[87]

In general, scholars have concurred that because unconditional surrender hindered a peace settlement even after the use of two atomic bombs and the Soviet Union's declaration of war, the bombs were not absolutely necessary because the United States accepted a conditional surrender. Disputes among historians persist over a variety of issues related to the use of atomic bombs: questions of morality, the decision-making process, and the motives of U.S. leaders.[88]

Unconditional surrender proved to be an amazingly resilient policy that did not change despite the fact that Marshall, Stimson, McCloy, Grew, and Forrestal favored clarification of terms. The Potsdam Declaration restated the conditions of earlier pronouncements without mentioning the newly developed atomic bomb. Japanese leaders did not know that the threatened destruction entailed force beyond incendiary bombing or invasion. Initially, the Potsdam pronouncement received favorable comment on the home front. Praised for its firmness by those who equated any alteration of unconditional surrender to appeasement, it also temporarily satisfied many people who wanted the United States to issue more exact terms.

The discussions among U.S. leaders about unconditional surrender and the disposition of the emperor took place in forums isolated from public input. In retrospect, Grew's proposals for seeking a political solution to hostilities appear more sensible than the assumption that an ultimatum must be accompanied by militarily induced shocks. Grew preferred clarification of terms to an ultimatum, and he considered the destructive firebombing of Japanese cities and the invasion of Okinawa sufficient demonstrations of American determination. His proposals combined the concern about Soviet influence in the Far East with a more astute evaluation of Japan, although he at times overestimated the influence of Japanese moderates.[89] But Grew was by nature a cautious man who preferred compromise to assertive debate. Although he met daily with Truman, acting as a stand-in for the secretary of state weakened his influence, and at times Truman became impatient with him. Grew's temporary status probably contributed to the lack of detailed discussion between him and Stimson about how the atomic bomb might influence the timing of a warning to Japan.[90]

Of course, there is no assurance that the war would have ended before it did had a guarantee been provided to Japan about the emperor's status. Hirohito remained supportive of the war throughout most of 1945, even though Prince Konoye had pleaded with the emperor to sue for peace in February 1945.[91]

Stimson later said that Truman and Byrnes resisted a specific guarantee about the emperor because "too many people were likely to cry shame."[92] However, he never explained why assurance about the emperor appeared abhorrent in July and acceptable in August. Stimson also simplified opinion on these issues, presenting Truman and Byrnes as captives of a potentially vengeful citizenry.

In an evaluation of the Potsdam Declaration one author later said that "domestic politics had overwhelmed diplomatic initiative."[93] More accurately, discriminating evaluations of domestic opinion and politics overcame statesmanship. Truman, influenced by Byrnes, opted for a declaration that listed Allied conditions for surrender but avoided any pledge about the emperor—the point most likely to influence the Japanese. Several commentaries on the home front regarded the Potsdam announcement as a precursor to further diplomacy that could end the war. For Truman, it was the first and final gesture before using atomic weapons.

Certainly, James Byrnes exaggerated the political dangers of offering assurance that the Japanese could preserve their monarchy. Eventually, the United States allowed retention of the emperor under the condition that he obey Allied dictates. Truman then faced the rhetorical task of explaining that a conditional surrender really constituted an unconditional capitulation.

The combination of Allied insistence on Japan's immediate unconditional surrender and the continued resistance by the Japanese prolonged the Pacific War. Nearly all Americans dreaded invading Japan. But keeping the admirable and understandable desire to quickly end the war bound to the policy of unconditional surrender propelled U.S. leaders toward a strategy of invasion, a prospect that appalled nearly everyone who pondered it. By June 1945, American leaders had information that certain Japanese leaders wanted to end the war. With the invasion of Kyushu scheduled for November 1, 1945, there was certainly ample time to explore options that might have prevented the destruction of Hiroshima and Nagasaki.

Conclusion

In retrospect, one is struck by the abundance of contradictions on the home front in the final months of the Pacific War. The government urged continued support for the war with appeals to patriotism and by exploiting atrocity reports. The Treasury Department even promoted Admiral Halsey's frivolous ambition to ride Hirohito's horse through the streets of Tokyo in "Let's Get the Admiral His Horse!" advertisements.[1] Such exhortations emphasized the importance of achieving a timely victory. Yet numerous commentators, government officials, and military leaders warned the public to expect a prolonged conflict. Advertisers reflected the ambivalence of the time by lamely endorsing the war effort while simultaneously extolling the impending bonanza of postwar consumerism.

The persistence of wartime stereotypes about the Japanese revealed interesting dichotomies in the war's last months. Commentators who characterized the Japanese as irrational also expressed consternation at Japan's continued resistance. Various military leaders and numerous commentators talked of defeating the Japanese mentality. Indeed, some observers on the home front, in calling for the destruction of the Japanese monarchy and Shintoism, advocated a crusade, a war fought to establish new political orders and alter cultures.[2]

An editorial from *Life*, published just prior to Japan's surrender, claimed that the Japanese "remain psychologically undefeated. The Japanese mind—so closed yet keen, so antlike yet inspired—is a sort of feudal atom which the 20th Century must find a way to split."[3] By comparing the process of understanding the Japanese to the splitting of atoms, the editorial implied that the former constituted as vast an endeavor as the latter.

The editors of the *St. Louis Post-Dispatch* also regarded the enigma of Japanese thought as a postwar challenge. They contended that "all kinds of Oriental superstitions" would complicate the democratization of Japan. Still, the editors remained optimistic that the Japanese would eventually adopt democratic principles. "The Japs," the editorial concluded, "are great imitators."[4]

Looking back, one must regret the pervasive ignorance about Japan. Even laudable, earnest efforts by military intelligence to learn more about the Japanese occurred, as the historian Michael Sherry later said, in an "intellectual, cultural, and bureaucratic void," absent of standards "by which to distinguish racial from situational sources of Japanese behavior."[5] An army intelligence report from mid-1944 lamented that a captured handbook for Japanese troops on sustaining morale, written by General Tojo, had never been translated. The report acknowledged that "in many instances the belief in certain features of Japanese morale seems to have established itself simply by constant repetition of a statement originally based on very flimsy evidence." It concluded that the effort to "relate the actions of the Japanese to Western philosophy" had caused the Allies to "alternate between overestimating and underestimating" the Japanese.[6]

A few commentaries offered more enlightened views of the Japanese, but the stereotypical images prevalent throughout the war overshadowed attempts to distinguish between the Japanese people and their leaders. Given the appalling rampages of looting and raping by Japanese forces in China, the misery imposed upon tens of thousands of Asians and prisoners of war who toiled in forced labor for the Japanese, and the abuse and murder of Allied prisoners of war, it is not surprising that Americans evinced little sympathy for Japan. Moreover, the lingering bitterness from Pearl Harbor, aggravated by atrocities committed against American troops in particular, combined with racial prejudices to give the Pacific War a unique character. After V-E Day the government and the media sustained the perception that all Japanese virtually thought as one. Logically, then, the deaths of any Japanese gained vengeance for previous wrongs.

With the exception of a handful of specialists within the State Department and the Office of War Information, few people knowledgeable about Japan held influential positions. The psychological warfare analysts working for civilian and military agencies compiled some of the most thorough and balanced assessments of the Japanese, but these studies had limited influence.[7]

American leaders who held more reasonable views of the Japanese did not express them publicly. After his return from Japan in 1942, Joseph Grew frequently spoke out against underestimation of the Japanese. By 1943 he began distinguishing between Japanese leaders and the people of Japan.[8] Yet he continued to describe all Japanese, regardless of gender or age, as dangerously unique fanatics. His public statements undercut more thoughtful public opinion that was in accord with his efforts to modify American war aims.[9] Henry Stimson, like

Grew, regretted the vitriol directed toward Hirohito during the war, but neither of them ever publicly denounced it.[10]

Casualties and the war's length remained the foremost concerns on the home front. People expressed a preference for sparing the lives of American soldiers even at the risk of protracting the war. Yet there was also ample evidence of the restlessness that indicated a desire for a rapid termination of the war.

Numerous commentators hoped that technology would minimize casualties. By 1945 most Americans had accepted mass destruction in warfare, as indicated by the limited criticism of incendiary bombing. Yet tolerance of technology was still constrained by certain standards, as evidenced by the debate over chemical warfare. Supporters of incendiary bombing and exponents of chemical warfare often said that these strategies might convince the Japanese that they must surrender or be annihilated. Others urged the government to denounce references to extermination.

Commentators speculated on the war's length, assessed strategies for ending the war, and critiqued the policy of unconditional surrender. In some instances, the letters from citizens offered ideas more imaginative than the policies pursued by the U.S. government. But the diversity of opinion on the home front had little impact on American leaders. Admittedly, the multitude of views made the task of evaluating them difficult. It is important, however, to recall the scope of opinion at the time.

In their day-to-day tasks American leaders remained largely removed from the opinions of commentators and citizens. Overall, the consideration given the home front centered around influencing the public and securing its approval for particular policies, rather than evaluating and responding to expressed views. There was little effort to distinguish between public opinion, composed of initial responses or impulses, and what Daniel Yankelovich has called "public judgment," which consists of more measured conclusions derived from deliberate, thoughtful consideration of issues.[11] Nevertheless, spirited debate occurred over the major issues of strategy and diplomacy. With the exception of not knowing about the atomic bomb, Americans had access to fairly accurate accounts of pending policies and varied evaluations of those plans.

American leaders faced the dilemma that a strategy of siege would save American lives but possibly extend the war beyond public patience; assault might end the war more quickly but at the cost of prohibitive casualties. Several commentators and many citizens considered unconditional surrender an obstacle to ending the war and suggested that more definite terms might prompt a Japanese surrender without additional military operations.

Truman's remark on June 18, 1945—that he believed he could not change public opinion on unconditional surrender but remained receptive to congressional action on the issue—was not an example of inspired leadership. He did not encourage Congress to evaluate the policy, let alone alter it. Despite the voluminous amount of mail from citizens who wanted terms for Japan cogently explained, the politicians who criticized unconditional surrender—mainly Republicans—did not initiate an organized effort to change it.

Simultaneously, various military leaders advocated clarifying unconditional surrender, but disagreements over the ideal moment to do so delayed the process. The ferocity of the battle for Okinawa made General Marshall and Henry Stimson reluctant to issue a statement until the island was secured. Afterward, several leaders regarded Okinawa as a shaky platform from which to call for Japan's capitulation.[12] One can understand these concerns. Yet the logic implied that casualty rates rather than military progress determined policy. A surrender statement released during the Okinawa campaign, whose eventual outcome was never really in doubt, or immediately following could have noted the immense Japanese losses, emphasized Allied military superiority, reiterated the destructive impact of bombing and blockade, allowed a constitutional monarchy that pledged to renounce aggression, and reaffirmed without sounding defeatist the Allied commitment to achieving Japan's surrender.

The refusal to modify terms narrowed options and made escalation of the war more likely. Militarily, Japan was comparable to a besieged fortress, a situation usually regarded as fitting for offering the beleaguered incentive to surrender. "The United States," the author Paul Kecskemeti later observed, "acted as if the problem were that of defeating Japan, when in fact the problem was to avoid an unnecessary last battle *after* Japan was defeated."[13] One cannot claim with certainty that had the Potsdam Declaration contained a specific reference about preserving the emperor, Japan would have surrendered. Recent scholarship has noted the differing views among Japanese leaders about whether to continue the war, the sluggish pace of decision-making within the Japanese government, and a desire by certain Japanese to win additional conditions beyond preservation of the emperor.[14] An offer to make a concession about Hirohito might have encouraged the Japanese toward further bargaining—precisely what unconditional surrender was intended to avoid.

However, the knowledge that several Japanese leaders, most notably Hirohito, were discussing surrender could have prompted more imaginative policy by the United States. A guarantee to preserve the imperial institution would have provoked dissent, but it would not have ruined Truman politically. With regard to the Pacific War, it appeared that unconditional surrender mattered more to citizens while the war raged. When peace became a reality, objections to altering unconditional surrender became less important.[15] The public was not implacably opposed to allowing Japan to keep its imperial system. Even the columnist Gladstone Williams, who produced some of the most virulent anti-Japanese rhetoric during the war, accepted Hirohito remaining on the throne while following Allied commands.[16]

The evidence suggests that fear of a negotiated peace was more of a concern among American leaders, and several of them worried that the public would support a negotiated settlement to the war. Yet in the aftermath of Hiroshima, people such as Truman, Stimson, and Byrnes argued that part of the rationale in using the atomic bomb was that Americans would have vehemently opposed diplomatic efforts to end the war. The content of the media and the letters from citizens indicate that many Americans would have welcomed diplomacy. Not all of those who favored more concise terms wanted to bargain with Japan. The evidence indicates that there was substantial support for terms that provided the Japanese with incentive to surrender, terms that went beyond the threat of further destruction.

After Japan's negative response to the Potsdam pronouncement, several commentaries urged that American leaders allow the Japanese more time to consider it before the United States launched an invasion. Had the atomic bombs not been dropped so soon after the Potsdam statement's release, it is likely that the declaration would have received more critical scrutiny in the United States. Instead, the news of the bombs replaced evaluation of the Potsdam terms. When the war ended, Truman insisted that the Japanese surrender was unconditional. Certainly many people recognized this claim as untruthful but that did not prevent them from rejoicing over the war's conclusion.

The possession of atomic weapons placed American leaders in a unique position. A nation had never before possessed the power to inflict such tremendous ruination with so little risk to itself. The bomb's unparalleled, indiscriminate destructive power made it an unconventional weapon. Yet discussion about its use, for the most part, reflected conventional thought.

The idea of combining atomic bombing with incendiary raids recalled contingency plans for chemical warfare, which had proposed the dispersal of toxins over cities amidst incendiary bombing.[17] The members of the Target and Interim Committees discussed impressing as many Japanese as possible by dropping the bomb over an urban area. This, too, resembled contingency plans for chemical warfare that had suggested that the dispersal of chemical agents over Japanese cities would panic *all* Japanese. The instigation of widespread panic in Japan, which was mentioned in connection with incendiary bombing, chemical warfare, and the bomb, never occurred. Insulated from military blows, Japanese leaders, the people these strategies presumably were intended to affect the most, remained largely unconcerned about the plight of civilians.

For historians, the use of the atomic bomb remains the source of one of the great historiographical debates in recent U.S. history. Authors have belabored the issue to the point that it appears there is little left to say. As Michael Sherry has cogently explained, a variety of reasons—which influenced different individuals to varying degrees—determined the use of atomic weapons: the hope for quick victory, the desire to spare American lives and avoid an invasion, the intent to end the war before the Soviet Union contributed to Japan's defeat, thoughts of intimidating the Soviet Union, the visceral hatred of the Japanese.[18]

The idea of using all available weaponry retains its appeal among certain observers. During the Gulf War the conservative columnist and commentator Cal Thomas revived several Pacific War motifs, urging that the Allied coalition use tactical nuclear weapons against Iraqi forces in order to shorten the war and save lives. Because the Iraqi dictator Saddam Hussein would not hesitate to use such weapons if he could, according to Thomas the Allies should not feel remorse in using them. He also suggested that Allied aircraft disperse leaflets over Kuwait demanding that Iraqi troops surrender immediately or face death from tactical nuclear weapons.[19]

For most historians, scholarship had debunked the postwar "official" explanation of the decision to use atomic weapons put forth by Truman, Stimson, and others.[20] Surprisingly, in the years after World War II, several commanders weakened these justifications. Rear Adm. Ellis M. Zacharias, a captain in naval intelligence during the war, argued as early as 1946 that the bombs were unnecessary.[21] Gen. Dwight D. Eisenhower, Adm. William Leahy, and Adm. Ernest King also later criticized the decision to use the bomb.[22]

These critiques had little impact on public memory.[23] To many Americans, the standard explanations remained trustworthy. Then, in the context of the backlash against "politically correct" thinking, the events surrounding the end of the Pacific War suddenly became contentious for the public. Controversy erupted in 1994 over the content of a forthcoming exhibition at the Smithsonian Institution commemorating the fiftieth anniversary of the atomic bombing of Hiroshima. Members of Congress and veterans organizations complained that early drafts of the scripts for the display panels in the exhibit were pro-Japanese. Veterans groups argued that the use of atomic bombs prevented an invasion, thereby saving up to one million American lives.

After officials from the Smithsonian announced further revisions in the scripts, historians plunged into the dispute. In a letter criticizing the proposed alterations, a group of scholars accused Smithsonian officials of "historical cleansing." They denounced the removal of documents such as Under Secretary of the Navy Ralph Bard's memo objecting to unannounced use of the atomic bomb, as well as statements by Leahy and Eisenhower reflecting their opinion that the bombings were unnecessary.[24]

In a critique of the planned display, columnist Charles Krauthammer described the use of atomic bombs as preferable to an invasion of Japan. His comments, as well as the arguments of organizations such as the American Legion, proved the continued widespread acceptance of the belief that U.S. options in 1945 were either invading Japan or using atomic bombs. Krauthammer suggested that Americans "let the Japanese commemorate the catastrophe they brought on themselves."[25]

Of course, Japanese leaders also bear responsibility for the war's duration. Hard-line Japanese militarists endorsed Japan's futile, suicidal defense, ignoring the fact that Japan had lost the war. Meanwhile, the United States clung to the policy of unconditional surrender, even though all of Truman's top advisers, with the exception of James Byrnes, favored changing it. Devotion to unconditional surrender helped drive U.S. leaders toward the strategy most of them, and many ordinary citizens, wanted to avoid—an invasion of Japan.

Ignorance of and prejudice toward their enemies influenced the decisions made by both Japanese and Americans during the Pacific War. The Japanese have had a particularly difficult time in admitting their responsibility for the war and their part in wartime atrocities. For instance, groups of Asian women have organized protests to draw attention to the anguished suffering they endured after being forced into Imperial Army brothels and repeatedly raped.[26]

Yet it is important that Americans remember the intolerance that so influenced their attitudes toward the Japanese. To recall the events in the final months of the Pacific War as merely the inevitable punishment that the Japanese brought upon themselves simplifies and distorts history. Despite the pervasive hatred of the Japanese in 1945, commentators and citizens engaged in extensive debate about the war that evaluated options beyond escalating the conflict.

The use of atomic weapons has overshadowed the fact that prior to Hiroshima numerous commentaries discussed ending the war by means other than force. In the aftermath of the bomb, the media largely ignored the discourse that occurred on the home front during the war's last months. The continued clamor for revenge against the fanatical Japanese coexisted with considerable opposition to chemical warfare and abundant support for revising surrender terms. The American hostility toward Japan did not make dropping the bombs inevitable. Having used the most powerful weapon in their arsenal, American leaders became more receptive to altering their terms, a move that many Americans had advocated months earlier.

Notes

Introduction

1. *Chicago Tribune*, 23 February 1990, p. 2.
2. The Buick advertisement was not the only automobile advertisement of the time to exploit anti-Japanese sentiment. Pontiac and Oldsmobile, divisions of General Motors, also produced television and print advertisements that contained anti-Japanese messages. See Clarence Page, "Bigotry to Sell Cars Sells America Short," *Chicago Tribune*, 20 July 1990. Two years later, a Chevrolet dealer in Latrobe, Pennsylvania, offered people the opportunity to smash a Honda Civic with a sledgehammer for one dollar, with proceeds donated to the United Auto Workers; "U.S. Blue-Collar Employees Want Respect for Hard Work," *Indiana Daily Student*, 6 February 1992, p. 5.
3. Rauch, *The Roosevelt Reader*, 301.

1 War Half Won

1. "The Hard Road to Tokyo," *St. Louis Post-Dispatch*, 19 May 1945, p. 4A.
2. "AP's False Flash on Nazi Surrender Excites Nation to Brief Celebration," *Newsweek*, 7 May 1945, 77-78; "False Alarm," *Time*, 7 May 1945, 19-20. The cities where newspapers reported the German surrender prematurely included Houston, Omaha, New Orleans, Atlanta, Knoxville, Tenn., Nashville, St. Louis, Chicago, Minneapolis, Cleveland, and New York.
3. Landstrom, *Associated Press News Annual*, 211. Contrary to the Allied intention of a joint announcement of Germany's unconditional surrender on 8 May, Edward Kennedy, chief of the Associated Press staff in France, reported the signing twenty-four hours before the official pronouncement, which resulted in his disaccreditation as a war correspondent by the Army and fomented a sharp editorial controversy in the American press.
4. "Chief Cities Take Victory in Stride," *New York Times*, 8 May 1945, p. 5; "City Quietly Hears News of Surrender," *Atlanta Constitution*, 8 May 1945, p. 4; "Churches Filled with Thankful," ibid., p. 8; "Citizens Show Caution about Letdown on War," *Los Angeles Times*, Extra, 8 May 1945, p. 8; "War Is Not Over," *Wall Street Journal*, 8 May 1945, p. 6; "Nation, World Rejoice; City Takes News in Stride," *Indianapolis Star*, 8 May 1945, pp. 1, 3, 12; "City Waits for Official Word to Celebrate," *St. Louis Post-Dispatch*, 7 May 1945, pp. 1, 10; "Report from the Nation," *New York Times*, 13 May 1945, p. 6E.
5. "D.C. Takes Peace News Calmly, Plans Quiet VE Celebration," *Washington Post*, 8 May 1945, pp. 1, 15; Anne Hagner, "VE Gets Staid Greeting Here: 1—War Policy of U.S. Due Today," ibid., 9 May 1945, pp. 1, 4; "Thanksgiving Is VE Theme at Worship," ibid., p. 5.

6. Nichols, *Washington Despatches 1941-1945*, 560.

7. "Chicago Turns to Next Step: Lick the Japs," *Chicago Daily Tribune*, 8 May 1945, pp. 1, 10; "Chief Cities Take Victory in Stride," *New York Times*, 8 May 1945, p. 5; "At Home: A Nation Rededicated," *Newsweek*, 14 May 1945, 44-45. For individual remembrances of VE Day see Hoopes, *Americans Remember the Home Front*, 343-45; Perrett, *Days of Sadness, Years of Triumph*, 415; Paul Gallico, "What We Talked About," in *While You Were Gone*, ed. Goodman, 61.

8. Meyer Berger, "City's Celebration Chilled by Mayor," *New York Times*, 8 May 1945, p. 7; Frank S. Adams, "Wild Crowds Greet News in City while Others Pray," ibid., pp. 1, 7.

9. Berger, ibid.

10. *Congressional Record*, Appendix, 79th Cong. 1st sess., 1945, pt. 11: A2341. The remarks were made by William L. Nelson, former representative from Missouri, in a speech before the Kiwanis Club of Columbia, Missouri, on V-E Day.

11. Litoff and Smith, *Since You Went Away*, 78; see also idem, *Dear Boys*, 234-35, for another account of the restrained response to V-E Day.

12. Announcement from author's collection.

13. *Public Papers of the Presidents: Harry S. Truman*, 43-48, hereafter cited as *Truman Public Papers*; Truman, *Memoirs*, 1: 206-7; "Truman, Churchill Proclaim Defeat of Nazis, Call for Unrelenting War to Finish Japan," *Washington Post*, 9 May 1945, pp. 1, 2; "At Home: A Nation Rededicated," *Newsweek*, 14 May 1945, 45.

14. *Truman Public Papers*, 48-50; Truman, *Memoirs*, 1: 206-7; "Truman, Churchill Proclaim Defeat of Nazis, Call for Unrelenting War to Finish Japan," *Washington Post*, 9 May 1945, pp. 1, 2; "At Home: A Nation Rededicated," *Newsweek*, 14 May 1945, 45; Hagner, "VE Gets Staid Greeting Here," *Washington Post*, 9 May 1945, pp. 1, 4.

15. Useful sources of information on Truman's background and life are Hamby, *Man of the People*, McCullough, *Truman*, Ferrell, *Harry S. Truman: A Life*. See also Ferrell, *Harry S. Truman: His Life on the Family Farms*, and idem, *Choosing Truman*.

16. McCullough, *Truman*, 339; Donovan, *Conflict and Crisis*, 18.

17. William D. Leahy Diaries, 12 April 1945, pp. 55, microfilm reel 3, Library of Congress, (LC). Secretary of the Navy James Forrestal also initially doubted Truman's ability to be president. See Hoopes and Brinkley, *Driven Patriot*, 204; Buell, *Master of Seapower*, 490.

18. Sledge, *With the Old Breed*, 201.

19. Adams, *Witness to Power*, 282-83.

20. "Washington Notes," *New Republic*, 14 May 1945, 676.

21. U.S. Department of Commerce, *Statistical Abstract of the United States 1944-45*, 17.

22. "Dictation Queen," *Chicago Daily Tribune*, 13 May 1945, p. 18.

23. Larry Wolters, "Don't Fence Me In' Leads All Radio Song Hits," ibid., 10 July 1945, p. 10.

24. Gardner, *The Year That Changed the World 1945*, 189.

25. *Chicago Daily Tribune*, 18 May 1945, p. 21; *St. Louis Post-Dispatch*, 20 June 1945.

26. Terkel, *"The Good War."* There is a growing historical literature devoted to countering the idea of World War II as strictly a "good war." These works have emphasized the horrors of combat and the plethora of problems on the American home front such as racial tensions, societal disruption, and juvenile delinquency. Fussell, *Wartime*, helped encourage this reappraisal; see Polenberg, "The Good War?" 295-322, which lauds Fussell. See also the criticisms of Fussell's approach in Marwil, "Paul Fussell's Wars," 431-52, and Cameron, *American Samurai*, 243, 245-46, 248-49, 255-56, 261-62, 265, 267-69, 272. See also Adams, *The Best War Ever*, and O'Neill, *A Democracy at War*.

27. Polenberg, *War and Society*, 132-33; Winkler, *Home Front U.S.A.*, 25-37.

28. Harris, Mitchell, and Schechter, *The Homefront*, 68, 70, 75, 80.

29. See O'Neill, *A Democracy at War*, chap. 18, for a discussion of the slide in morale that began in 1944.

30. "Burglars Get Meat, Whisky, Cigarettes, $315 in Theft," *St. Louis Post-Dispatch*, 2 July 1945, p. 8A; "A Burglar in Springfield Gets 2 Packs of Cigarettes," *Chicago Daily Tribune*, 17 July 1945, 2. The second article covered the ransacking of a man's home in Springfield, Illinois, where only two packs of cigarettes turned up missing.

31. Polenberg, *War and Society*, 136-38; Merrill, *Social Problems on the Home Front*, 233-34.

32. Gallup, *The Gallup Poll*, 1: 488.

33. Landstrom, *Associated Press News Annual*, 234-36. For examples of coverage of Gertie see "Gertie the Duck" and accompanying photographs in the Pictures section of the *St. Louis Post-Dispatch*, 17 June 1945, p. 10. See also the photo essay, "'Gertie the Great' Hatches Her Eggs on Milwaukee Bridge," *Life*, 18 June 1945, 37, 38, 40; *Newsweek*, 4 June 1945, 34-35. The feature in *Life* magazine noted that birth certificates were mailed to Gertie's "address" from Milwaukee City Hall, poems written for her arrived at the bridge tender's shanty for several days, and she received two Mother's Day cards.

34. Landstrom, *Associated Press News Annual*, 233.

35. "ODT Puts 5-Day Limit on Train Reservations," *St. Louis Post-Dispatch*, 30 June 1945, p. 1.

36. "Sleepers Barred after July 15 to Civilians on Trips in 450-Mi. Radius," ibid., 7 July 1945, pp. 1, 3A; "91 Pct. of Soldiers in Day Coaches Instead of Pullmans; Boxcar Diners," ibid., p. 3A.

37. "5 Extra Carloads to Ease Shortage of Toilet Tissue," ibid., 5 July 1945, p. 3A.

38. "Pink Panties Not Worn by Detroit Men," *Washington Post*, 21 July 1945, p. 3.

39. "Soap, He Says! 1,000 Women Mob Druggist," *Chicago Daily Tribune*, 15 July 1945, p. 1.

40. Landstrom, *Associated Press News Annual*, 233.

41. "Vegetable Diet Indicated for U.S. by August," *Chicago Daily Tribune*, 24 May 1945, p. 19.

42. "20 Pct. Meat Cut for Restaurants Ordered By OPA," *St. Louis Post-Dispatch*, 7 June 1945, p. 11A.

43. "OWI Tells Home Front What It Can Do to Help in War against Japan," ibid., 2 July 1945, p. 8A.

44. "America's Midsummer Mood: War Weary, Restless, Irksome," *Newsweek*, 23 July 1945, 23-24.

45. Lingeman, *Don't You Know There's A War On?*, 134.

46. Minutes of Meeting Held by Joint Chiefs of Staff (JCS) and Heads of Civilian War Agencies, 27 February 1945, p. 4, JCS Decimal File 1942-1945, CCS 334 JCS (2-2-45) (Meetings-186th-194th), box 196, Record Group (RG) 218.

47. Landstrom, *Associated Press News Annual*, 232.

48. Nichols, *Washington Despatches 1941-1945*, 558.

49. Arnold, *Global Mission*, 559.

50. "Grew Puts Stress on Fight in Pacific," *New York Times*, 9 May 1945, p. 6.

51. *Congressional Record*, 79th Cong. 1st sess. 1945, 91, pt. 4: 4304-05, 4307, 4312-14.

52. Ibid., 4305.

53. See the remarks of Luther A. Johnson (D-Tex.), George H. Bender (R-Ohio), and A. Leonard Allen (D-La.) in ibid., 4306, 4309.

54. Ibid., 4305, 4311.

55. "Japan Feels the Blow." *Washington Post*, 5 May 1945, p. 8.

56. "And Now Japan" and "On the Home Front," *New York Times*, 8 May 1945, p. 18. See also the editorial "Out of Great Tribulation—Triumph," reprinted from the *New York Sun*, 8 May 1945, in *Congressional Record*, Appendix, 79th Cong. 1st sess., 1945, 91, pt. 11: A2355. The editorial was introduced into the *Congressional Record* by Sen. H. Alexander Smith of New Jersey on 17 May 1945.

57. "This Day of Victory," *St. Louis Post-Dispatch*, 7 May 1945, p. 2B.

58. *Time*, 14 May 1945, 15.

59. *Washington Post*, 8 May 1945, pp. 3, 9.

60. See Macy's advertisement in *New York Times*, 8 May 1945, p. 9; see also the Bloomingdale's display on p. 13 and advertisements on pp. 4, 14.

61. *Chicago Daily Tribune*, 8 May 1945, pp. 14-15; see also the advertisement for the Evans Fur Company, p. 2.

62. *Indianapolis Star*, 8 May 1945, p. 11.

63. *Harrisburg* (Illinois) *Daily Register*, 8 May 1945, p. 5; sec. 2, p. 2; sec. 4, p. 2. Several of these advertisements are examples of displays designed by advertising agencies and then offered for sale to local businesses across the country; see *Advertising and Selling* 38 (June 1945): 37.

64. *Harrisburg* (Illinois) *Daily Register*, sec. 2, p. 4; sec. 3, p. 3. Hirohito never vowed that Japanese troops would march down Pennsylvania Avenue, but this powerful imagery had been used in director Frank Capra's 1942 propaganda film "Prelude to War," which contained a scene of victorious Japanese marching on Pennsylvania Avenue in Washington. See Dower, *War without Mercy*, 16-17.

65. *Harrisburg* (Illinois) *Daily Register*, sec. 4, pp. 3, 4, 6.

66. "On to Tokyo Clubs Formed to Stay on Job till Japs Quit," *St. Louis Post-Dispatch*, 15 May 1945, p. 9A.

67. Sherwood, "I Can't Make Your Party, Pete," 24.

68. David Lawrence, "Pacific Morale Seen Hurt by V-E Parades," *Evening Star*, 7 June 1945, p. A-10; idem, "'Global War' Phrase Recalled by Observer," ibid., 23 June 1945, p. A-8.

69. Lingeman, *Don't You Know There's a War On?*, 355. "America's Midsummer Mood: War Weary, Restless, Irksome," *Newsweek*, 23 July 1945, 23.

70. "Exhibit Here Will Afford Public Glimpse of Dream Trains Designed for Postwar Era," *Washington Post*, 7 May 1945, p. 1B.

71. Doherty, *Projections of War*, 245, mentions that newsreel footage of the celebrations of Monday, 7 May 1945, was shown in theaters by Wednesday, 9 May.

2 Images of the Enemy

1. Summary of the average American's knowledge of Japan at the beginning of the war, according to an Army Air Forces publication; *Impact*, III (Sept.-Oct. 1945), 3.

2. Pyle, *Last Chapter*, 5.

3. Polenberg, *War and Society*, 38, 135; Blum, *V Was for Victory* 7, 8, 46.

4. Dower, *War without Mercy*, 34-35; Sherry, *The Rise of American Air Power*, 244-45.

5. "Public Thinks Germans Less Cruel Than Japs," *Los Angeles Times*, 10 June 1945, pt. 1, p. 4; "Jap People Responsible?" *Atlanta Constitution*, 10 June 1945, p. 9-C; Gallup, *The Gallup Poll*, 1: 508-9.

6. Dick, *The Star-Spangled Screen*, 230-36; Doherty, *Projections of War*, 133-39.

7. Allan Nevins, "How We Felt about the War," in *While You Were Gone*, ed. Goodman, 13. Reiterating the theme that warfare against the Japanese was the equivalent of

fighting Indians, Gen. George C. Kenney of the Army Air Forces said in a letter of January 1943, "We have to get back to the days when we learned how to fight the Indians in the woods and eventually beat them at their own game"; Arnold, *Global Mission*, 382. Johnson, *American Attitudes toward Japan, 1941-1975*, 17-21, argued that initial Allied defeats and American disdain for jungle warfare also contributed to feelings of hatred for the Japanese.

8. Dower, *War without Mercy*, chap. 7, explores attitudes toward the Japanese as part of a historical tradition of whites distinguishing themselves from nonwhite peoples. See also Cameron, *American Samurai*, 89-97, which discusses American attitudes toward Chinese and Japanese before World War II. Among the works that study the relationship between racism and perceptions of American Indians, blacks, and Asians are Berkhofer, *The White Man's Indian*; Drinnon, *Facing West*; Gossett, *Race*; Jordan, *White over Black*; S.C. Miller, *The Unwelcome Immigrant*; Isaacs, *Images of Asia*; S.C. Miller, *"Benevolent Assimilation"*; Wu, *The Yellow Peril*.

9. "On to Tokyo and What?" *Life*, 21 May 1945, 32.

10. Dower, *War without Mercy*, 148-54, further explores the comparisons of Japanese to American Indians in the context of Western encounters with native Indian peoples throughout history.

11. Ibid., 8-9, 81. A popular slang expression for Japanese troops among American marines was "Jape," a combination of Jap and ape; see Pyle, *Last Chapter*, 23.

12. Luvaas, *Dear Miss Em*, 271.

13. Dower, *War Without Mercy*, 28-29. See also Cameron, *American Samurai*, chap. 3, which examines the influence of the idea of the Japanese as the "Other" on the attitudes of American marines during the campaign on Guadalcanal.

14. Dower, *War without Mercy*, 36.

15. The *Washington Post* printed the phrase on its masthead on 11 December, 1941. A song of the same title was quickly produced and the expression became well-known. One account credits the Office of Production Management with coining the phrase and placing it across the top of mimeographed orders; see Lingeman, *Don't You Know There's a War On?*, 211-12.

16. "WAR!" *St. Louis Post-Dispatch*, 8 December 1941, p. 2C; "Sponsor of Undeclared War," ibid., 11 December 1941, p. 2C. Adm. William D. Leahy referred to the "Japanese assassins" when he reflected upon Pearl Harbor in his memoirs (*I Was There*, 438).

17. "Japan's Perfidy Unites the American People," *Chicago Daily Tribune*, 8 December 1941, pp. 1, 14.

18. "Way of the Jap," *Washington Post*, 10 December 1941, p. 16; "Americans Are One for War," *Indianapolis Star*, 9 December 1941, p. 10; "The U.S. at War," *Time*, 15 December 1941, 17. After the war, *Impact*, the Army Air Forces' pictorial magazine, combined the reasoning that the Japanese were illogical with the profane when it described the American response to Pearl Harbor as "You dumb bastards"; see *Impact*, 3 (Sept.-Oct.1945), 3.

19. See the speech delivered over the four major radio networks by Chief of Staff Adm. William D. Leahy in *Congressional Record*, Appendix, 79th Cong., 1st sess., 1945, 91, pt. 11:A2178; Leahy, *I Was There*, 365.

20. *Congressional Record*, 79th Cong., 1st sess., 1945, 91, pt. 4: 4305, 4308.

21. *Congressional Record*, Appendix, 79th Cong., 1st sess., 1945, 91, pt. 11: A2341. The speaker was William L. Nelson of Missouri.

22. "On to Tokyo and What?" *Life*, 21 May 1945, 32. See also the editorial "Pearl Harbor's Harvest," *Evening Star*, 27 May 1945, p. C-2.

23. "Atomic Doom from Skies," *Indianapolis Star*, 7 August 1945, p. 10.

24. Harold Streeter, "Bypassed Japs Problem Child of Pacific War," *Washington Post*, 13 May 1945, sec. 2, p. 3. In a similar vein the *Chicago Defender*, 26 May 1945, p. 10, published a series of photographs captioned, "24th Infantry Goes Jap-Hunting on 'Conquered Saipan.'"

25. "The Pacific: War without Quarter," *Newsweek*, 14 May 1945, 43. An editorial, ("Okinawa's General Dies," *New York Herald Tribune*, 20 June 1945, p. 18), called Buckner "a fighter in name, appearance and courage—ready to hunt Japanese in the same way he hunted with the dogs of his beloved Kentucky kennels."

26. Henry, "Frontal Assault," 132. See also the comments of Vice Adm. Marc A. Mitscher, in "Japs Must Be Burned Out Cave by Cave, Mitscher Says," *Washington Post*, 22 June 1945, p. 8.

27. Fletcher Pratt, "Nature of Jap Fighter Requires Re-Training and Re-Equipment of Yanks Being Sent from Europe," *St. Louis Post-Dispatch*, 24 June 1945, p. 3B.

28. Fred Hampson, "GI.S Who Fought in Europe To Find New Kind of Foe," ibid., 7 May 1945, p. 3.

29. "Final Plunge to Heart Of Japan Is On, Halsey Says," ibid., 25 July 1945, pp. 1, 2. Halsey was famous for his motto "Kill Japs, kill Japs, kill more Japs" and often described Japanese as "yellow bastards" and "yellow monkeys." He once remarked to a press conference his belief in a "Chinese proverb" that the Japanese were a result of mating between "female apes" and Chinese criminals; see Dower, *War Without Mercy*, 79, 85. Correspondent Robert Sherrod later recalled a typical Halsey address as focusing on the theme, "We're going to show these yellow bastards what God damn fools they were for starting this thing" (*On to Westward*, 238-42). After the capture of the island of Peleliu in October 1944, Halsey's congratulatory message to the troops ashore complimented them for exterminating "11,000 slant-eyed gophers"; see Cameron, *American Samurai*, 1. In July 1945, Halsey was quoted as saying, "We are drowning and burning the bestial apes all over the Pacific, and it is just as much pleasure to burn them as drown them," and at an off-the-record dinner for newspapermen in August 1945, he purportedly said, "I hate Japs. I'm telling you men that if I met a pregnant Japanese woman, I'd kick her in the belly"; see photograph of Halsey with these accompanying quotations in *politics* 2 (Aug. 1945): 226. An editorial in the journal *Crisis*, published by the National Association for the Advancement of Colored People, lamented Halsey's inability to resist calling the Japanese "monkeys"; (see "Now for V-J Day!" June 1945, 161).

30. See Dower, *War Without Mercy*, 89-91 on the use of hunting metaphors during the war. Even historians have compared combat with Japanese forces to hunting. Herbert Feis described Japanese on Okinawa being "hunted with mortar and fire" (*The Atomic Bomb*, 3).

31. E. Jones, "To the Finish: A Letter from Iwo Jima," 50, 51, 53. Hollywood films and newsreels presented dead enemy soldiers much more explicitly than dead Americans during the war. Only in the war's later years did government and military censors allow footage of wounded or dead Americans to be shown, and Japanese corpses were usually depicted in more detailed fashion than dead Germans. "Fury in the Pacific," released in March 1945, was one of the combat report films shown in theaters during the war. It covered combat on the island of Peleliu and ended with a series of "wipes" over the screen as the camera lingered over Japanese corpses, thus doubly wiping out the enemy. The freeze-frame ending was a close shot of a dead, bespectacled Japanese soldier with "The End" superimposed; see Doherty, *Projections of War*, 57, 246, 261-62.

32. "Peace Feelers Seen as Japs' Towns Are Lost," *Washington Post*, 6 July 1945, p. 3.

33. *Atlantic Monthly*, June 1945, 27.

34. *Newsweek*, 11 June 1945, 26.

35. *Fortune*, June 1945, 241.

36. *Life*, 11 June 1945, 20.

37. Ibid., 18 June 1945, 106.

38. *Washington Post*, 24 June 1945, p. 2.

39. "Farm Agency Tips to Wipe Out Jap Beetle," ibid., 5 July 1945, p. 2.

40. "2,000 Traps Placed in State to Mop Up Japanese Beetles," *Atlanta Constitution*, 20 June 1945, p. 3.

41. Notes on JCS 115th Meeting, 21 September 1943, Japanese Atrocities-Reports of by Escaped Prisoners, ABC 383.6 Japan (17 Aug 42), sec. 1, box 393, RG 165. The warning was issued after Secretary of War Henry Stimson and Secretary of the Navy Frank Knox advised Roosevelt that the story should be suppressed. In 1943 the U.S. government did announce that Japan had condemned to death several American fliers, and also released translated passages from a diary recovered from a dead Japanese soldier that described the beheading of a captured airman. Those sentenced to death had participated in the first bombing raids on Japan, led by Lt. Col. James Doolittle in April 1942. Launched from aircraft carriers off the coast of Japan, the attacks on Tokyo and other cities inflicted minor damage but provided a psychological boost on the American home front. The torture and trial of the captured airmen became the basis for the film "The Purple Heart" released in 1944; Dower, *War Without Mercy*, 48-51. The Office of War Information (OWI), created in June 1942 and headed by the commentator Elmer Davis, initially continued the policy of its predecessor, the Office of Facts and Figures (OFF). Under the direction of author and poet Archibald MacLeish, OFF stipulated that atrocities committed by the Axis powers should be attributed to enemy regimes and their political ideologies rather than national or racial characteristics of enemies. Although OWI officially disapproved of racial epithets, derogatory terms often appeared in OWI literature and posters that frequently portrayed the enemy, especially the Japanese, as less than human; see Tobin, "Why We Fight," 94-95. Tobin noted that author Philip Wylie and pollster Hadley Cantril, both of whom worked for the OWI, disagreed with the policy and considered hatred of enemy people an inevitable and unifying event for a population at war (95-97). See also Jones, "The U.S. Office of War Information," 199-201, and Lloyd, "American Society and Values," 85, 94, 100.

42. At the time a ship carrying Japanese nationals who were in the United States when war was declared was en route to Portugal where they were to be exchanged for interred American and British citizens arriving on a Japanese ship; Corbett, *Quiet Passages*, is an interesting account of this and subsequent exchanges of internees. See JCS 504, Japanese Atrocities-Reports of by Escaped Prisoners, 17 September 1943, Formerly Top Secret Correspondence of Secretary of War Stimson ("Safe File") July 1940-September 1945, Japan (After 7/41), box 8, RG 107; Roosevelt's letter is in Enclosure "A" and the reply memo is in Enclosure "B" of the document, hereafter cited as Stimson "Safe File."

43. Memorandum for the Secretary of War, 8 October 1943, Memorandum for the Chief of Staff, 8 October 1943, Stimson "Safe File'" Japan (After 7/41), box 8, RG 107. Stimson was especially concerned about the effect that publicizing atrocities might have on the Imperial Japanese Army, since it held most American POWs. He characterized the Japanese Army as "a quite distinct and independent entity both in its mentality and power from the rest of the Japanese government and the people."

44. Secret Priority Message from Operations Division, WDGS, 6 October 1943, instructing theater commanders to suppress the release of atrocity accounts; Memorandum for General Marshall from the White House, 13 October 1943, informing Marshall that Roosevelt approved further study of the issue; Memo from Tenth Army Air Force, 11 November 1943, and Secret Memo from Operations Division, WDGS, 26 November

1943, instructing that the circulation of the memo be suppressed, are all located in ABC 383.6 Japan (17 Aug 42), sec. 1, box 393, RG 165. The description released by the headquarters of the Tenth Army Air Force was based on the experiences of Maj. William E. Dyess of the Army Air Forces, the same officer who had sold the option on his story to the *Chicago Daily Tribune*. Extract from Minutes, CCS 125th Meeting, 29 October 1943, item 6, where Admiral Leahy noted the complaints of the OWI, and Elmer Davis's letter of 24 December 1943 are contained in JCS 504/2, 27 December 1943, in the same location.

45. JPS 276/2, 3 January 1944, and JPS 276/3, 10 January 1944, both entitled Publication or Circulation of Stories Regarding Japanese Atrocities, deal with this issue and contain the comments of the Joint Staff Planners. Extract from Minutes, JCS 142nd Meeting, 18 January 1944, item 5, contains comments from the Joint Chiefs and their agreement to recommend to Roosevelt the release of atrocity information. Memorandum for the Record, 20 January 1944, notes that Roosevelt approved the recommendation and Elmer Davis indicated he would release the accounts the week of 23 January 1944. All documents are located in ABC 383.6 Japan (17 Aug 42), sec. 1, box 393, RG 165.

46. Memorandum for the President: Enemy Reprisals against American Airmen, 22 January 1944, Central Decimal Files October 1942-May 1944, Warfare 385-D, box 591, RG 18.

47. "And Now Japan," *New York Herald Tribune*, 8 May 1945, p. 14.

48. One of the most widely publicized incidents was the beheading of sixteen Americans, including eleven Baptist missionaries and a nine-year-old boy, by Japanese troops on Panay in the Philippines in December 1943. The group apparently eluded capture for two years before their location was disclosed by a captured Filipino guerrilla tortured by the Japanese; "Jap Beheading of 12 in Baptist Group Reported," *Chicago Daily Tribune*, 2 June 1945, p. 3 (this article did not mention that the Filipino was tortured but said that he "betrayed" the missionaries); "Japs Behead Family of Three from Altadena," *Los Angeles Times*, 3 June 1945, pp. 1, 7; "Japs Behead 16 from U.S.; Story by Eyewitness," *Chicago Daily Tribune*, 7 June 1945, p. 10; Richard Bergholz, "Witness Tells Executions of 16 Americans by Japs," *Los Angeles Times*, 6 June 1945, p. 4; "11 U.S. Missionaries Beheaded by Foe," *New York Times*, 2 June 1945, p. 5; "Missionaries Beheaded by Japs," *St. Louis Post-Dispatch*, 2 June 1945, p. 1B. A concurrent account told of the execution of an American educator working as a school superintendent and Boy Scout commissioner in the Philippines; see "Scout Master Killed Defying Japs in Silence," *Chicago Daily Tribune*, 12 June 1945, p. 1.

49. Several press accounts concerned the abuse of marines captured on Wake Island in December 1941. The well-remembered fighting on Wake Island boosted public morale in the gloomy opening weeks of the war when the small command held out for several days against a larger Japanese force; see "2 Wake Survivors Escape Japanese, Tell of Surrender," *New York Times*, 21 July 1945, p. 1; "Two Wake Marines Escape Japs, Tell of Fall of Isle, Mistreatment," *St. Louis Post-Dispatch*, 21 July 1945, p. 2A; "2 Survivors Tell of Wake Surrender," *Washington Post*, 21 July 1945, pp. 1, 2.

50. "Marine Tells of Seeing Friends Beheaded in Japanese War Camp," *New York Times*, 13 May 1945, p. 4; "Saw Comrades Beheaded by Jap Captors," ibid., 13 May 1945, p. 12.

51. For accounts by formerly captive fliers see "Indian Saves Jap-Tortured U.S. Airman," *Atlanta Constitution*, 23 May 1945, p. 3; "Charges Japs, Stung by B-29's, Abuse Captives," *Chicago Daily Tribune*, 12 June 1945, p. 2; "St. Louisan Captured by Japs Tells of Death March in Burma Jungle," *St. Louis Post-Dispatch*, 9 July 1945, pp. 1, 7. On American POWs being moved to bombed areas see "Americans Moved to Bomb Zones," *Los Angeles Times*, 1 August 1945, p. 1; "Nips Put U.S. POW's under Own Bombs," *Atlanta Consti-

tution, 1 August 1945, p. 1; "Japs Keep Yank Prisoners in Areas Subject to Bombing," *Washington Post*, 1 August 1945, p. 9. Reports from the Domei News Agency, the mouthpiece of the Japanese government, argued that no area of Japan was safe from American bombers and accused the United States of bombing shrines, schools, temples, historic sites, and hospitals. "Even if a prisoner of war camp should be established on the summit of Mount Fuji, it eventually would be the target of the American bombers," one commentator said over Radio Tokyo. See "U.S. Invasion on Big Scale Will Win, Japs Admit," *Chicago Daily Tribune*, 5 August 1945, p. 2; "All Japan Unsafe for Prisoners, Tokyo Replies," *Los Angeles Times*, 5 August 1945, p. 4; "B-29 'Chutists Strafed by Japs in Kobe Attack," *St. Louis Post-Dispatch*, 6 June 1945, pp. 1, 2A; McDougall, "I Was Tortured by the Japs," 17, 99-102, 104. After torpedoing the Liberty ship *Jean Nicollet*, Japanese crewmen on a submarine murdered seventy-seven survivors by clubbing, stabbing, and shooting them in the water. This incident and others were protested by the U. S. government; see U.S. Department of State, *Foreign Relations of the United States, Diplomatic Papers*, 1944, "Protests by the United States against Attacks by Japanese Naval Forces on Survivors of Torpedoed American Merchant Vessels," 5: 1175-77; hereafter cited as *FRUS*. See also Noell, "My Japanese Jailer," 18-19, 105-6, in which Noell, an Army Air Corps medical officer, recounted his captivity in the Philippines by the Japanese. The account focused on a cruel Japanese officer "motivated by a strong inferiority complex," who commanded one of the prison labor details. For the Japanese attack on an Army hospital see John M. Carlisle, "Japanese Attack American Hospital in Celebration of Hirohito's Birthday," *Atlanta Constitution*, 29 May 1945, p. 1; for the report of the bayoneting of Allied prisoners by Koreans see "Japs Force Koreans to Massacre Americans in Bayonet Practice," ibid., 27 June 1945, p. 1. On Japanse POW camps see Walter Simmons, "Bones of Yanks Tell Infamy of Jap Prison Camp," *Chicago Daily Tribune*, 30 May 1945, pp. 1, 2; Richard Bergholz, "150 Skeletons Found at Jap Prison Camp," *St. Louis Post-Dispatch*, 4 June 1945, pp. 1, 4A; "Sealing Mindanao," *Newsweek*, 18 June 1945, 39.

52. "Dutch Charge Japs Burn Slave Laborers Alive," *Los Angeles Times*, 4 July 1945, p. 1; "Ill Slaves Burned by Foe on Borneo," *New York Times*, 4 July 1945, p. 2; "Japanese Employ Chinese as Detonators of Bombs," ibid., 12 May 1945, p. 4; "Japanese Terrorists Behead Okinawans," ibid., 28 May 1945, p. 3. "Japanese Massacre on Luzon Revealed," ibid., 18 July 1945, p. 5; "Japs Butcher 2,000 Filipinos and Burn Homes," *Chicago Daily Tribune*, 18 July 1945, p. 4. Additional reports recounted Japanese soldiers and sailors killing their own wounded as well as killing Japanese civilians. See "80,000 of Own Men Slain by Japanese," *New York Times*, 24 June 1945, p. 3; "Japanese Slay Thousands of Their Wounded," *Los Angeles Times*, 24 June 1945, p. 1; "If Wounded, Die," *Newsweek*, 2 July 1945, 34; "Japanese Civilians Massacred by Own Troops on Panay," *St. Louis Post-Dispatch*, 23 May 1945, p. 2A; "Blasted by Sub, Jap Transport Kills Own Men," *Chicago Daily Tribune*, 3 June 1945, p. 9.

53. The photograph appeared in *Life*, 14 May 1945, 97, and letters concerning the picture were printed in ibid., 4 June 1945, 2. General Arnold sent a copy of the photograph to Secretary of War Stimson nearly a year earlier with a memo stating that during the Hollandia campaign in 1944, graves of headless Americans were discovered. Stimson kept the photographs, which are in Stimson "Safe File," July 1940-September 1945, Japan (After Dec. 7), box 8, RG 107. The photograph was widely reprinted in newspapers. The *New York Herald Tribune* published it before *Life*, on 12 May 1945, p. 5. The same photograph, captioned "This Is the Enemy in the Pacific," appeared in the *St. Louis Post-Dispatch*, 11 May 1945, p. 1, and in the *Chicago Daily Tribune* on 12 May 1945, p. 3.

54. "The Atlantic Report on the World Today: The Pacific War," *Atlantic Monthly*, May 1945, 11.

55. Lamott, "What Not to do with Japan," 585.

56. Macdonald, "A Japanese Badoglio?" 161; George S. Schuyler, "Views and Reviews," *Pittsburgh Courier*, 19 May 1945, p. 7.

57. "Now for V-J Day!" *Crisis*, June 1945, 161.

58. "Yanks Burned Alive by Japs, Letter Reveals," *Washington Post*, 4 August 1945, p. 2.

59. An interesting dichotomy existed with regard to atrocities. Although reported atrocities were exploited by the government to sustain support for the war, Hollywood films avoided the ignominy of the Bataan death march and only hinted at it in scenes that depicted it more as a voluntary recessional; see Dick, *The Star-Spangled Screen*, 132-34.

60. Dower, *War without Mercy*, 42.

61. Bruner, *Mandate from the People*, 151.

62. Macdonald, "A Japanese Badoglio?" 161.

63. Army Talk, Orientation Fact Sheet, 12 May 1945, 3; Plans and Operations Division "ABC" Decimal File 1942-1948, ABC 384 Japan (3 May 44), sec. 1-B, box 428, RG 319.

64. "Shift to the Pacific," *New York Times*, 12 May 1945, p. 12.

65. Dower, *War without Mercy*, chaps. 5-6, especially 94-97, 122-135; Johnson, *The Japanese through American Eyes*, chap. 1, Minear, "Wartime Studies," 36-59.

66. Gill Robb Wilson, "U.S. Superiority in Pacific Analyzed," *New York Herald Tribune*, 13 June 1945, p. 4.

67. "The Upside-Down Japanese Mind: It Makes Our Defeat Seem Easy," *Newsweek*, 25 June 1945, 36.

68. Ibid., 11 June 1945, 48.

69. Pakenham, "The Japanese Mentality as a Factor in War," ibid., 11 June 1945, 48.

70. Ibid.

71. Dick, *The Star-Spangled Screen*, 179-82, discusses the distinctions Hollywood films made between rape by Germans and rape by Japanese. The latter, in keeping with views of the Japanese as subhuman, was portrayed as bestial, more a form of perversion than an act of violence.

72. Dower, *War without Mercy*, 46, mentions face slapping. The Japanese atrocities committed in Nanking shocked world opinion at the time, and even German observers condemned the Japanese army in an official report as "bestial machinery"; see Toland, *The Rising Sun*, 56. Authors have sometimes referred to the sack of Nanking in sexual terms; Hersey, *Into the Valley*, xxviii, called it "the orgiastic Japanese rape of Nanking." Doenecke and Wilz, *From Isolation to War, 1931-1941*, 67, referred to the event as "an orgy of looting and murder." In a January 1943 letter to General Arnold, Gen. George Kenney, the Army Air Forces commander under MacArthur, called the Japanese "a low order of humanity" and asserted, "He is far better off in the army, where he is comparatively well-fed and clothed, than as a half-starved coolie at home. At home, he can't indulge in his Mongol liking for looting, arson, massacre, and rape. In the army, he can look forward to all four"(*Global Mission*, 382).

73. Pakenham, "Mother and Father to Japanese—the Army," 44.

74. Pakenham, "With His Trick Mind, the Japanese Fools Himself," 33.

75. "Japanese Are Open to Terms Minus Threats, Says Domei," *New York Times*, 23 July 1945, pp. 1, 4.

76. "Japan: Peace of Mind," *Newsweek*, 14 May 1945, 62. In another example of unreality, Radio Tokyo broadcast a news release from Domei, the official government news agency, about a "Bomb America" rally held in Tokyo by the "Society for Bombing America"; "Jap 'Bomb America' Society Has Meeting," *Los Angeles Times*, 19 July 1945, p. 1.

77. See Harold Smith, "B-29 Raids Help Jap Wrestlers Groan Louder," *Chicago Daily Tribune*, 24 May 1945, p. 4; "It'll Suit Japan If We Just Go Home," *Atlanta Constitution*, 3 June 1945, p. 10; "Hirohito Must Be Hungry; He's Planting Rice!" *Chicago Daily Tribune*, 24 June 1945, p. 3; "Japs to Build Planes of Wood, Milk, Soybeans!" ibid., 23 July 1945, p. 5; "Hirohito Horse Just a Western Stock Animal," ibid., 11 August 1945, p. 5.

78. Webber, *Retaliation*, 93-126, 133-49, 167-73, is an interesting account of the development of the balloons and lists known landings in the United States and Canada. Balloons were recovered as far south as Texas and as far east as Michigan. The accidental death of the six people in Oregon is described on pp. 93-98, an event disclosed by the War Department after the initial release of information about the balloons. Radio commentators H.V. Kaltenborn and Raymond Gram Swing discussed the balloons in their broadcasts of 22 May 1945 (Papers of H.V. Kaltenborn, file 3, box 175, State Historical Society of Wisconsin [SHSW]; Papers of Raymond Gram Swing, box 26, LC). For contemporary accounts see "Jap Balloon Bomb Explosion Kills Six Persons in Oregon," *Washington Post*, 1 June 1945, p. 1; "Jap Balloon Bomb Claims 6 Lives in Oregon," *Chicago Daily Tribune*, 1 June 1945, p. 11. One newspaper criticized the army for withholding information about the balloons, saying earlier disclosure might have saved lives; see "A Major News Bungle by the Army," *Los Angeles Times*, 24 May 1945, sec. 2, p. 4. In a meeting with the Joint Chiefs of Staff in late March, Byron Price, director of the Office of Censorship, complained that he was having difficulty preventing the release of information about the balloons and said that if the press could not be given convincing reasons to withhold the information, it was doubtful that news of any injuries or serious damage caused by a balloon could be withheld; Minutes of Meeting Held by Joint Chiefs of Staff and Heads of Civilian War Agencies, 27 March 1945, pp. 1-2, JCS Decimal File, CCS 334 JCS (2-2-45) (Meetings 186th-194th), box 196, RG 218. There was concern that the balloons carried disease-causing organisms and constituted a form of bacteriological warfare; see "Potentialities of New Developments in Warfare," Memo for the Chief of Staff, 26 May 1945, Henry H. Arnold Papers, Official Decimal File 1938-1946, SAS 385 Japan, box 115, LC, and George W. Merck, "Activities of the United States in the Field of Biological Warfare," a report that Merck, special consultant on biological warfare, compiled for Secretary of War Stimson, pt. 2, p. 6, in entry 488, box 182, Dr. G.W. Merck's File, RG 165. See also Bernstein, "America's Biological Warfare Program," 307-08, and Larsen, "War Balloons over the Prairie," 103-15.

79. "Piloted Balloons Will Blast U.S., Japs Say," *Washington Post*, 5 June 1945, p. 3; "Japan Threatens Mass Bombing of U.S. from Piloted Balloons," *New York Herald Tribune*, 5 June 1945, pp. 1, 2. Although the *Washington Post* described the balloons in a condescending manner, its editors were initially confused about the balloons' point of origin and speculated that they were launched from submarines. "But can the Japanese afford to employ submarines on such a fool's errand?" the paper queried ("Great Balloon Mystery," 27 May 1945, p. 4B). A subsequent article confirmed that they were launched in Japan; "Fire Balloons Drifting to U.S. Start in Japan," ibid., 30 May 1945, pp. 1, 3. An article in the *New York Times* related the basic principles of how the balloons operated in a regular column on scientific matters; see Waldemar Kaempffert, "Science in Review" column, "Japanese Balloons Reaching America Employ Principles That Have Long Been Known," 10 June 1945, p. E9.

80. "Japan's 'Unique Originations,'" *New York Herald Tribune*, 5 June 1945, p. 18.

81. "The Balloon Bomb," *Evening Star*, 26 May 1945, p. A-6, was published before any casualties had resulted from the balloons.

82. "Naval Bombardment of Jap Soil Warns Foe Final Blow Is Near," *Newsweek*, 23 July 1945, 34, 36.

83. "Military Review," *New Republic*, 23 July 1945, 93-94.

84. "Japan under Gunfire," *Evening Star*, 15 July 1945, p. C-2.

85. Robert Quillen, "Is Jap a Jap for All Tha'?" *Atlanta Constitution*, 22 June 1945, p. 8.

86. Ibid. Quillen's column revived the kind of "once a Jap always a Jap" thinking that was used to justify the relocation of Japanese Americans to detention camps earlier in the war; see Dower, *War without Mercy*, 80-81.

87. "What's Wrong with the Japs? Their Women, Says Admiral," *Los Angeles Times*, 15 July 1945, p. 1. Sherrod, *On to Westward*, 243, described McCain's hat as "a mechanic's cap topped by a black headband and a gold-encrusted visor."

88. Wylie, *Generation of Vipers*.

89. "Shift to the Pacific," *New York Times*, 12 May 1945, p. 12.

90. See Feist, "Bats Away," 93-94, and Couffer, *Bat Bomb*, written by a participant in the project.

3 How Long Will This War Last?

1. Leahy, *I Was There*, 367.

2. Judge Samuel I. Rosenman, special counsel to President Roosevelt, later recalled that after 1943 Roosevelt often worried about public complacency about the war (*Working with Roosevelt*, 388). In 1944, Secretary of the Navy James Forrestal feared that Allied military successes would prompt public demands for a relaxing of wartime restrictions; see Millis, *The Forrestal Diaries*, 3. For more examples of concern about sustained public support for the war in 1943-1944 see Brower, "The Joint Chiefs of Staff and National Policy," 199-200, 202-10. See Gluck, *Rosie the Riveter Revisited*, 141-42, for other recollections of decreasing enthusiasm for the war by 1944.

3. The problem was initially raised in Memorandum for General Marshall, from Lt. Gen. Brehon Somervell, 27 November 1944; also see the Joint Chiefs' memo to Roosevelt, Prohibition of Public Statements by Government Officials on Early Termination of the War, undated, and the White House memo, 1 December 1944. All three documents are in Combined Chiefs of Staff Decimal File 1942-1945, CCS 000.7 (11-28-44), box 8, RG 218. For further evidence of General Marshall's concerns about public morale dropping after Germany's defeat, see Brower, "Sophisticated Strategist," 326.

4. Perry, "*Dear Bart*," 249.

5. Matloff, *Strategic Planning for Coalition Warfare 1943-1944*, 5; Brower, "Sophisticated Strategist," 321; Pogue, *George C. Marshall: Statesman 1945-1959*, 6.

6. Baldwin, "America at War," 540. Baldwin had published a similar observation in the *New York Times*: "Strategically the situation on the various 'fronts' in the Pacific means that Japan has lost the war—but we have not yet won it"("Blows to Crush Japan Are Now Foreshadowed," 20 May 1945, p. E5).

7. "Japanese Resistance," *Evening Star*, 18 May 1945, p. A-8.

8. Moley, "Attacking the Jap Mentality," 92.

9. Army Talk, Orientation Fact Sheet, 12 May 1945, 2-3, Plans and Operations Division "ABC" Decimal File 1942-1948, ABC 384 Japan (3 May 44), sec. 1-B, box 428, RG 319.

10. Minutes of Meeting Held by Joint Chiefs of Staff and Heads of Civilian War Agencies, 22 May 1945, JCS Decimal File 1942-1945, CCS 334 JCS (2-2-45)(Meetings 186th thru 194th), box 196, RG 218.

11. William D. Leahy Diaries, 1 January 1945, p. 2, microfilm reel 3, LC.

12. Arnold, *Global Mission*, 576, 580.

13. "Grew Puts Stress on Fight in Pacific," *New York Times*, 9 May 1945, p. 6.

14. *Congressional Record*, Appendix, 79th Cong., 1st sess., 1945, 91, pt. 11:A2178. Leahy, *I Was There*, 364-65. See also the V-E Day remarks of Adm. King, 8 May 1945, Speech, Article, and Book File, 1908-1953, May-September 1945, box 28, Ernest J. King Papers, LC.

15. "Japs Will Fight Even in Tokyo's Ruins, U.S. Told," *Chicago Daily Tribune*, 14 July 1945, p. 3; "Japan Won't Quit, Patterson Reports," *Washington Post*, 14 July 1945, p. 2.

16. See the comments of Reps. Luther A. Johnson (D-Tex.) and George H. Bender (R-Ohio); *Congressional Record*, 79th Cong., 1st sess., 1945, 91, pt. 4: 4306. See also the remarks of Rep. Aime J. Forand (D-R.I.) on p. 4312.

17. "If We Expect a Long War, Let's Act That Way!" *Saturday Evening Post*, 7 July 1945, 108.

18. "A Day of Victory—And Rededication," *Atlanta Constitution*, 8 May 1945, p. 10.

19. "Palmer Warns Nips Set for Murderous Combat," *Los Angeles Times*, 8 May 1945, pt. 2, p. 1; "Palmer Warns No Easy Way Open to Beat Japs," ibid., 17 May 1945, p. 5.

20. "Americanism Rally Pledges to Crush Japs," *Chicago Daily Tribune*, 21 May 1945, p. 9.

21. Ibid., 27 June 1945, p. 1.

22. "Target for Now," *New York Times*, 9 June 1945, p. 12. The *Boston Daily Record* previously expressed similar sentiments on V-E Day when it stated that with Germany's defeat Americans could turn their attention exclusively to "our war." *Congressional Record*, Appendix, 79th Cong., 1st sess., 1945, 91, pt. 11:A2179.

23. Baldwin, "America at War," 542. See also, idem, "Japan's Plight Grave," *New York Times*, 20 June 1945, p. 10.

24. Fletcher Pratt, "Nature of Jap Fighter Requires Re-Training and Re-Equipment of Yanks Being Sent from Europe," *St. Louis Post-Dispatch*, 24 June 1945, p. 3B.

25. "Eyes to the East," *Newsweek*, 18 June 1945, 21.

26. Jack Steele, "Army Expects Long Campaign against Japan," *New York Herald Tribune*, 10 May 1945, p. 13. See Skates, *The Invasion of Japan*, chap. 5, for an explanation of redeployment plans and the point system devised by the War Department to demobilize troops with long service overseas.

27. Baldwin, "America at War," 539. Journalist Fletcher Pratt contended that troops transferred to the Pacific would have to be retrained to fight Japanese who "started out at the age of six learning to fight dirty"("Nature of Jap Fighter Requires Re-Training and Re-Equipment of Yanks Being Sent from Europe," *St. Louis Post-Dispatch*, 24 June 1945, p. 3B.)

28. Somervell, "The Biggest Moving Job in History," 24-25, 94, 96, 98.

29. "Japan Held Capable of Long War; Many of Industries Are Still Intact," *New York Times*, 27 May 1945, p. 4.

30. "Japan's Growing Crisis," *New York Times*, 28 May 1945, p. 18. Swing mentioned the FEA report in his broadcast of May 28, 1945; "We still need to think first that we are at war. We need to appreciate that it is a difficult war, and may well be a long and extremely costly war. Until that war is won, everything else is secondary"(Script of broadcast for 28 May 1945, p. 3, Raymond Gram Swing Papers, LC).

31. Gallup, *The Gallup Poll*, 516; "Average American Thinks War Will Last Another 12 Months," *Washington Post*, 20 July 1945, p. 3.

32. "U.S. War Leaders Still Base Plans on Japs Fighting till End Of 1946," *St. Louis Post-Dispatch*, 19 July 1945, p. 2A; "Navy Thumbs Nose at Kamikazes," *Los Angeles Times*, 11 July 1945, pt. 2, p. 4.

33. Gayn, "Terror in Japan," 59. Fighting men in the Pacific concocted slogans expressive of their hopes for when the war might end. The more optimistic stuck with

"Home alive by '45." New mottoes included "Out of the sticks in '46," "From hell to heaven in '47," and "Golden Gate by '48." See "Numbers Game," *Time*, 4 June 1945, 35.

34. "Patch Echoes Warning," *Washington Post*, 3 August 1945, p. 13.

35. Gen. George C. Marshall condemned speculation about when Japan might quit or whether Russia would enter the war at a meeting of the Joint Chiefs in May 1945; Minutes of Meeting Held by the Joint Chiefs of Staff and Heads of Civilian War Agencies, 22 May 1945, JCS Decimal File 1942-1945, CCS 334 JCS (2-2-45) (Meetings 186th thru 194th), box 196, RG 218.

36. "A Day of Victory-And Rededication," *Atlanta Constitution*, 8 May 1945, p. 10.

37. "Target for Now," *New York Times*, 9 June 1945, p. 12.

38. *Congressional Record*, 79th Cong., 1st sess., 1945, 91, pt. 4: 4304, 4305, 4308, 4311, 4313-4315. Others who reiterated the theme in remarks on V-E Day included Philip J. Philbin (D-Mass.), J. Vaughan Gary, (D-Va.), and Raymond S. Springer (R-Ind.).

39. Ibid., 4309, 4313.

40. "The Big Job Ahead in Beating Japan," *St. Louis Post-Dispatch*, 17 May 1945, p. 2B.

41. An article about the war in the *St. Louis Post-Dispatch* observed, "The world's No. 1 military question now is whether Japan can be beaten quickly, or will fight on until she is overrun by United States armies and occupied"(Ibid.).

42. Broadcast of May 7, 1945, p. 1, folder 1, box 175, H.V. Kaltenborn Papers, SHSW.

43. "Japs May Quit within 90 Days, House Is Told," *Chicago Daily Tribune*, 15 June 1945, p. 3.

44. David Lawrence, "Japan May Surrender within Six Months," *Evening Star*, 17 July 1945, p. A-6.

45. Harold Streeter, "U.S. War Chiefs Doubt Japs Will Fight to End," *St. Louis Post-Dispatch*, 20 May 1945, p. 3D; idem, "Japs Expected to Yield When Home Isles Fall," *Chicago Daily Tribune*, 20 May 1945, p. 7.

46. Hanin, "War on Our Minds," 195-97.

47. *Fortune*, June 1945, 259.

48. Caterpillar Tractor Company, *Saturday Evening Post*, 3 June 1944, 87; Chrysler, *Saturday Evening Post*, 24 June 1944, 35. See the advertisement, "Those doggoned kids!" in *Time*, 5 July 1943, 49, depicting a colonel who admired the resolution of his men who persistently labored on an abandoned French tank until it again sputtered and ran. Produced by a group of electric companies, the advertisement contained an unsubtle hint that consumers would be provided cheaper energy by the private sector, and that government power producers such as the Tennessee Valley Authority were counter to the American way. Faith in American technological predominance also influenced military analyses. An Army Air Forces evaluation of Japanese pilots said that their lack of mechanical instruction "makes difficult the transition from a ricksha to a modern day fighter or bomber." Few Japanese had ever driven a car, and the report deemed this deficiency more detrimental than their lack of flight training, concluding that "the superior, more intelligent, faster thinking aggressive attitude" of American pilots, combined with "their much higher level of mechanical experience and aptitudes," made them better fliers; "Japanese Air Force Pilot Training Programs," Memo from Gen. T.D. White to Arnold, 13 July, 1944, Official Decimal File 1938-1946, file 97, box 43, Henry H. Arnold Papers, LC (White was assistant chief of the Air Staff Intelligence).

49. *Saturday Evening Post*, 12 June 1943, inside cover; ibid., 15 May 1943, inside cover.

50. *Atlanta Constitution*, 6 May 1945, p. 10-A. Graphic footage of Japanese burned by flamethrowers appeared in newsreels too; see Doherty, *Projections of War*, 228, 246.

51. "And Now Japan," *New York Times*, 8 May 1945, p. 18.

52. "A Moment for Taking Stock," *Commonweal*, 1 June 1945, 155.

53. *Congressional Record*, 79th Cong. 1st sess., 1945, 91 pt. 4: 4309.

54. George Connery, "Army Set to Unleash Final, Fiery Attack on Enemy in Far East," *Washington Post*, 13 May 1945, sec. 2, pp. 1, 3.

55. *New York Herald Tribune*, 10 May 1945, p. 24.

56. "Special Message to the Congress on Winning the War With Japan," *Truman Public Papers*, 83, 96.

57. "The Task Ahead," *New York Times*, 2 June 1945, p. 14.

58. "Army Promises 1,000 B-29's a Day Will Raid Japan," *St. Louis Post-Dispatch*, 22 June 1945, p. 8A.

59. "Japan and Surrender," *Evening Star*, 26 July 1945, p. A-10. Similar sentiments were expressed in an editorial that stated, "The only question is how much destruction and punishment the Jap war lords will be able to compel their people to endure before they accept unconditional surrender("Navy Thumbs Nose at Kamikazes," *Los Angeles Times*, 11 July 1945, pt. 2, p. 4).

60. Harold Streeter, "U.S. War Chiefs Doubt Japs Will Fight to End," *St. Louis Post-Dispatch*, 20 May 1945, p. 3D.

61. "Japan's Invasion Jitters Grow," *Los Angeles Times*, 30 June 1945, sec. 2, p. 4.

62. "It Is Reason or Ruin for Japs," *Indianapolis Star*, 24 May 1945, p. 10.

63. Gladstone Williams, "End in '45 Possible But Improbable," *Atlanta Constitution*, 26 May 1945, p. 4; quotation from idem, "Next Twelve Months to Tell the Story," ibid.

64. Idem, "Japan Faces Doom, May Seek Peace," ibid., 16 May 1945, p. 6.

65. "For Japan to Choose," *Evening Star*, 27 July 1945, p. A-4.

66. "Palmer Warns Nips Set for Murderous Combat," *Los Angeles Times*, 8 May 1945, pt. 2, p. 1.

67. *Congressional Record*, 79th Cong., 1st sess., 1945, 91, pt. 4: 4310.

68. "Jap Psychology," *Evening Star*, 19 May 1945, p. A-8.

69. "The Defeat of Japan," *Fortune*, June 1945, 113.

70. Jesse F. Steiner, "Can Japan's Millions Take It till the End?" *New York Times Magazine*, 15 July 1945, p. 6.

71. "Inside Japan," *Washington Post*, 12 June 1945, p. 8. See also Barnet Nover, "Which Way Japan?" ibid., 12 May 1945, p. 8; and "Crescendo of Doom," ibid., 11 July 1945, p. 8.

72. "A Day of Victory—And Rededication," *Atlanta Constitution*, 8 May 1945, p. 10.

73. *Congressional Record*, 79th Cong., 1st sess., 1945, 91, pt. 4: 4314.

74. James Lindsley, "Japs Must Surrender or Die—Adm. Sherman," *St. Louis Post-Dispatch*, 26 June 1945, p. 2A. Apparently annoyed at the survival of isolated and by-passed Japanese soldiers, General Arnold, commander of the Army Air Forces, requested the devising of "'Buck Rogers' ideas, unorthodox plans, unorthodox equipment or un-orthodox techniques" to "quickly and effectively exterminate those garrisons" ("Extermi-nation of By-passed Jap Garrisons in South Pacific," directive from Arnold, 25 May 1945, file 67, box 42, Henry H. Arnold Papers, LC).

75. "'Los Angeles' Own' Exterminating Japs," *Los Angeles Times*, 5 July 1945, pt. 2, p. 1.

76. Merlo Pusey, "Japan Can Surrender," *Washington Post*, 9 May 1945, p. 11.

77. "Meditation," *New York Times*, 17 June 1945, p. E5.

78. Jones, "Japan's Secret Weapon," 44.

79. "Letters to The Star; Total Destruction Demanded," *Evening Star*, 23 May 1945, p. A-8.

80. Sherrod, *Tarawa*, 147-49.

81. "Prisoners on Okinawa," *New York Herald Tribune*, 25 June 1945, p. 16.

82. "The Japanese Answer," *New York Times*, 10 May 1945, p. 22.

83. "And Now Japan," ibid., 8 May 1945, p. 18.

84. "Military Review," *New Republic*, 7 May 1945, 627.

85. Brooks Atkinson, "The Vast Job in the Vast Pacific," *New York Times Magazine*, 13 May 1945, p. 11. For similar points of view see "Japan's Growing Crisis," *New York Times*, 28 May 1945, p. 18; "The Task Ahead," ibid., 2 June 1945, p. 14.

86. Pakenham, "How the Jap Learns to Fight as He Does," 47.

87. Ibid.

88. Pakenham, "Does the Jap Soldier Have a Breaking Point?" 35. This article appeared in an issue of *Newsweek* that displayed a bespectacled Japanese soldier on the cover with the words, "The Jap: How Long Can He Take It?"

89. McGurn, "How Good Is the Jap GI?" 120-22, 206-7.

90. Noble, "Give the Devils Their Due," 18-19, 95-96.

91. Quotation, "with remarkable docility," from Steiner, "Can Japan's Millions Take It till the End?" *New York Times Magazine*, 15 July 1945, p. 6; see also Seeman, "Life in Japan Today," 7-15.

92. Steiner, "Can Japan's Millions Take It till the End?" 37.

93. Roger W. Babson, "Japan's Collapse?" *Washington Post*, 11 June 1945, p. 4B.

94. Maj. George Fielding Eliot, "How Long—Japan?" *Evening Star*, 18 May 1945, p. A-8; idem, "Campaign of Devastation," ibid., 2 June 1945, p. A-8; idem, "Jap Reaction Studied," ibid., 19 June 1945, p. A-8; idem, "How Long Can Japs Last?" ibid., 29 June 1945, p. A-6.

95. Eliot, "Dark Ways of Jap Mind Unknown Factor in War," *Los Angeles Times*, 23 July 1945, pt. 1, p. 6.

96. Dower, *War Without Mercy*, 56.

4 Visions of Abundance

1. Sevareid, "Super-Dupering the War," 9.

2. Polenberg, *War and Society*, 135; Blum, *V Was for Victory*, 100; Lingeman, *Don't You Know There's a War On?*, 292-93.

3. Tobin, "Why We Fight," 146-51, quotation, 151.

4. The Royal Typewriter Company proclaimed the war's objective was to quickly usher in the day when one could "once more walk into any store in the land and buy anything you want!"(Fox, *Madison Avenue Goes to War*, 34). In 1944 Alcoa Aluminum announced, "The very essence of what we are fighting for lies in the beautiful fact that these new products will be *candidates* for your dollar . . . no more, and no less"(*Better Homes and Gardens*, September 1944, 79).

5. Fox, *Madison Avenue Goes to War*, 37.

6. See advertisements for the Rohr Aircraft Corp., in *Atlantic*, July 1945, 29, and ibid., May 1945, 31. See also the advertisement for Chesebrough Manufacturing Co., which bluntly asked, "Are you worth dying for?" (*Collier's*, 23 June 1945, 6).

7. For threads see the Belding Corticelli advertisement, *New York Times*, 3 June 1945, p. 58. For an example of the importance of boxes in the war effort, see advertisement for the Gaylord Container Corp., *Newsweek*, 4 June 1945, 83. International Telephone and Telegraph claimed that its broadcasting equipment beamed "verbal blockbusters" to Japan; see ibid., 25 June 1945, 94.

8. See the advertisement for the Broderick and Bascom Rope Co., *Time*, 9 July 1945, 74. See also the display for the Jones and Lamson Machine Co., *New Yorker*, 19 May 1945,

43, and the advertisement entitled "A Strange Sort of Prayer" published by the Young and Rubicam advertising agency, *Newsweek*, 28 May 1945, 30.

9. As early as 1942 some advertisers mentioned that improved consumer products would be available when the war ended, and by mid-1944 advertisements for postwar products became more numerous. See Blum, *V Was for Victory*, 100-101; see also Westbrook, "Fighting for the American Family," in Fox and Lears, *The Power of Culture*, 213-15. By mid-1944, Ford, Remington Rand, and W.A. Schaeffer were promoting postwar cars, typewriters, and pens, respectively; see Fox, *Madison Avenue Goes to War*, 34.

10. Advertisement for Kinsey Distilling, *New Yorker*, 23 June 1945, 61.

11. See *Fortune*, May 1945, 164. See also the display for Everglaze Chintz, *House Beautiful*, June 1945, 23.

12. Advertisement for General Electric, *Saturday Evening Post*, 5 May 1945, 5.

13. *Life*, 9 July 1945, 87.

14. Examples of advertisements focused on the hauling of war-related cargo are those for the Norfolk and Western in *Newsweek*, 14 May 1945, 18, and ibid., 18 June 1945, 105, and the Southern Pacific, *Time*, 9 July 1945, 49. The Atchison, Topeka, and Santa Fe concentrated on the war but promised better passenger service and more efficient freight service after the war; see Santa Fe advertisement in *New Yorker*, 21 July 1945, 53. The Chicago, Milwaukee, St. Paul, and Pacific marked the tenth anniversary of its fleet of Hiawatha streamliners, which were then still "on the warpath." But when the war ended, the Milwaukee Road promised improvements in service; *Newsweek*, 11 June 1945, 13. See also the advertisement for new passenger cars by Edward G. Budd Manufacturing Co., in ibid., 14 May 1945, 48, and the advertisement for new diesel locomotives by the Electro-Motive Division of General Motors in ibid., 21 May 1945, 13. For a brief overview of advertising by railroads during World War II, see Nelson, "Serving the Nation," 45-47.

15. As early as April 1942, Republic Steel described the war effort as a transcendent advance toward technologically improved products designed to shape "a better world, of new products, new ideas, and new ideals"(*Saturday Evening Post*, 18 April 1942, 109). See Bendix advertisement, *House Beautiful*, May 1945, 44. The theme that the application of wartime technological advances to consumer products would produce superior goods after the war had been mentioned in advertisements in 1944 too; see Sherry, *The Rise of American Air Power*, 125-26. Advertisers used this theme in the 1950s as well, when a variety of companies claimed that developments in weaponry would benefit American consumers; see Whitfield, *The Culture of the Cold War*, 74-75.

16. Raymond Rubicam, "Advertising," in *While You Were Gone*, ed. Goodman, 444.

17. *American Magazine*, May 1945, 153.

18. *Life*, 21 May 1945, 51.

19. Revere Copper and Brass, *Newsweek*, 7 May 1945, 48. See also the streamlined mower in the advertisement for Bohn Aluminum and Brass, *Fortune*, May 1945, 173.

20. See the Capehart and Farnsworth advertisements in *Newsweek*, 7 May 1945, 30; also the Belmont Radio advertisement in *American Magazine*, July 1945, 107.

21. Advertisement for Allen B. DuMont Laboratories, *House Beautiful*, May 1945, 14.

22. See the Crosley advertisement, *Parents' Magazine*, June 1945, 79.

23. Argus cameras, *Fortune*, May 1945, 169; Schlitz beer, *Life*, 28 May 1945, 109; Firestone tires, *Saturday Evening Post*, 14 July 1945, 47.

24. Anheuser-Busch, *Fortune*, July 1945, 246.

25. See Ford advertisement, *Newsweek*, 7 May 1945, 47.

26. *New Yorker*, 19 May 1945, 13; *Atlantic*, May 1945, 1; ibid., July 1945, 1.

27. *Saturday Evening Post*, 26 May 1945, 71.

28. *Life*, 21 May 1945, 109.

29. *Saturday Evening Post*, 14 July 1945, 75. See also the advertisements for Pan American World Airways in *Newsweek*, 25 June 1945, 2, and Douglas Aviation in *Time*, 16 July 1945, 63.

30. See Goodyear advertisements in *Saturday Evening Post*, 2 June 1945, 34-35, and *Life*, 25 June 1945, 54-55.

31. *Saturday Evening Post*, 11 August 1945, 45.

32. *Life*, 7 May 1945, 110; *Newsweek*, 21 May 1945, 51.

33. Galvin Manufacturing Corp., *Cosmopolitan*, May 1945, 14.

34. Articles in various magazines reinforced this message. See, for instance, Herrmann, "The Things They Never Tell You," May 1945, 58-59, in which the author praises marriage and criticizes various negative perceptions of it spread by "Gloom Girls."

35. *Life*, 7 May 1945, 23.

36. Text quoted is from ibid., 4 June 1945, inside cover; see also, "Speaking of Pictures," ibid., 14 May 1945, 12-13.

37. *House Beautiful*, May 1945, 54; *Parents' Magazine*, June 1945, 97.

38. *House Beautiful*, May 1945, 2.

39. May, *Homeward Bound*, 60-68, 71; Gluck, *Rosie the Riveter Revisited*, 15-17; Hartmann, *The Home Front and Beyond*, 189, 199-200, 204; Rupp, *Mobilizing Women for War*, chaps. 4-6.

40. For an example of this type of illustration, see the advertisement for Frigidaire in *Good Housekeeping*, July 1945, 80.

41. See the advertisement for Revere Copper and Brass, *Saturday Evening Post*, 12 May 1945, 89, and the Hotpoint advertisement in *Parents' Magazine*, May 1945, 85. A brochure entitled "Kelvinator in the Home of Your Dreams" touted a variety of decorative themes for kitchens, all designed to provide a "gay, light-hearted postwar kitchen"(*Life*, 11 June 1945, inside cover).

42. Crosley Corp., *Saturday Evening Post*, 11 August 1945, 70.

43. *Parents' Magazine*, June 1945, 78.

44. Mullins Corp., ibid., June 1945, 54.

45. American Gas Assoc., ibid., July 1945, 57.

46. Ibid., May 1945, 95.

47. See the Frigidaire advertisement, *Good Housekeeping*, July 1945, 80; see also the General Electric advertisements in ibid., June 1945, 95, and ibid., May 1945, 79.

48. Ibid., July 1945, 108.

49. See advertisements for American Kitchens in *Parents' Magazine*, May 1945, 98, and in *Newsweek*, 4 June 1945, 115.

50. *Parents' Magazine*, June 1945, 91.

51. Ibid., July 1945, 38.

52. Landers, Frary, and Clark, makers of Universal appliances; ibid., June 1945, 101.

53. Westinghouse advertisement, *House Beautiful*, August 1945, 12. See also the Roper advertisement in *Good Housekeeping*, May 1945, 211.

54. *Collier's*, 12 May 1945, 10; *Parent's Magazine*, July 1945, 53. See also the Westinghouse advertisement, *Life*, 4 June 1945, 12.

55. *Collier's*, 12 May 1945, 9.

56. Breines, *Young, White, and Miserable*, 103-04, discusses these traits in advertising directed at women in the 1950s. Two examples of streamlined bathrooms can be found in Briggs advertisements in *House and Garden*, May 1945, 99, and ibid., July 1945, 95. The Briggs company promised postwar bathroom fixtures would be better than ever yet available to the most modest budget.

57. Kohler advertisement, *House Beautiful*, July 1945, 17.

58. Ibid., August 1945, 79.

59. American Radiator and Standard Corp., *House and Garden*, August 1945, 25; Crane, *Parents' Magazine*, July 1945, 48.

60. *Life*, 25 June 1945, inside cover.

61. Advertisement for Nairn linoleum, *Parents' Magazine*, August 1945, 16.

62. Herrmann, "The Things They Never Tell You," May 1945, 58-59.

63. See, for example, the York advertisement where a GI enjoys an atypical meal of meat, potatoes, and peas courtesy of York refrigerators, in *Newsweek*, 7 May 1945, 71. Certain illustrations supportive of the seventh war bond drive conveyed some sense of the nature of combat in the Pacific; see the International Paper Co. advertisement in *Advertising and Selling*, June 1945, 11. In the late 1960s sculptor Edward Keinholz addressed the commercialization of combat in his work "The Portable War Memorial," in which the famous image of marines raising the American flag on Iwo Jima is incongrously placed amidst the trappings of a hotdog stand; see Marling and Wetenhall, *Iwo Jima*, 202-4. The weekly casualty lists published in newspapers, newsreels, and published accounts of ongoing battles in the Pacific starkly contrasted with the stylized combat presented in advertisements. Film critic James Agee said that the graphic footage of combat on Iwo Jima amounted to pornography; see Fielding, *The American Newsreel 1911-1917*, 293-94.

64. Ibid., 28 May 1945, 55. Eugene B. Sledge's vivid memoir of combat in the Pacific made clear that night was often more terrifying than daylight, because Japanese soldiers frequently used the cover of darkness to infiltrate American lines(Sledge, *With the Old Breed*, 82-83).

65. Advertisement for Kelly-Springfield tires, *Saturday Evening Post*, 21 July 1945, 35. See also the advertisement for the Allison division of General Motors, *Newsweek*, 25 June 1945, inside cover.

66. *Evening Star*, 10 May 1945, p. A-7.

67. Advertisement for Cris-Craft Corp., *Fortune*, May 1945, 24.

68. *Atlantic*, August 1945, 30.

69. See Nash advertisement, *Life*, 7 May 1945, 17; see also the Nash advertisement in *Newsweek*, 9 July 1945, inside cover.

70. *Newsweek*, 14 May 1945, inside cover; ibid., 9 July 1945, inside cover.

71. Advertisement for Caterpillar, ibid., 14 May 1945, 71.

72. Bausch and Lomb, ibid., 21 May 1945, 8.

73. Ibid., 18 June 1945, 65.

74. Ibid., 18 June 1945, 75.

75. Caterpillar Tractor Co., *Collier's*, 5 May 1945, 58.

76. Binsse, "The House You'll Live In," 350. A caustic, earlier critique of advertising methods, from which the chapter-opening quotation was taken, was Sevareid, "Super-Dupering the War," 9-10.

77. Yoder, "I Just Want to Be a Customer," 11, 102-03.

78. Marchand, *Advertising the American Dream*.

79. See Cowan, *More Work for Mother*, chap. 6; see also Strasser, *Never Done*.

80. See Corn, *The Winged Gospel*, 12; see also pp. 65-68, where the author explains that during World War II the airplane came to be viewed more as an instrument of destruction. See chap. 10, for a discussion of the idea of widespread ownership of private planes that was being promoted at the end of World War II and the efforts to develop hybrid automobile/airplanes.

81. Bemis Brothers Bag Co., *Newsweek*, 21 May 1945, 4.

82. Ewen, *Captains of Consciousness*, 39.

83. Ibid., pt. 3, chap. 6, discusses how women in the 1920s were also portrayed as benefiting from new technologies when new devices such as electric vacuum cleaners were depicted as liberating for the "new woman."

84. Advertisement for Department of Water and Power, *Los Angeles Times*, 11 June 1945, p. 8.

85. Glough, "Home Should Be Even More Wonderful Than He Remembers It," 29. For more on this theme see Hartmann, "Prescriptions for Penelope," 223-39.

86. Will V. Neely, "Clean Up Your House, Warns GI Correspondent, to Our Erring, Lonely War Wives," *Pittsburgh Courier*, 19 May 1945, p. 10.

87. Severo and Milford, *The Wages of War*, 283-84.

88. Cameron, *American Samurai*, 204-07.

89. Fox, *Madison Avenue Goes to War*, 76-79.

90. Mullins Manufacturing Corp., *House Beautiful*, August 1945, 107.

91. Douglas, *Where the Girls Are*, 56.

92. Doherty, *Projections of War*, 169.

5 Okinawa

1. "Okinawa, Preview of Japan," *New York Herald Tribune*, 7 June 1945, p. 18.

2. Smith, *Triumph in the Philippines*, chaps. 22-23, 26-29, 32, Conclusion.

3. Appleman, et al., *Okinawa*, 7, 9-10.

4. Ibid., *Okinawa*, 9; G. Kerr, *Okinawa*, chaps. 9-11.

5. Spector, *Eagle against the Sun*, 532.

6. Frank and Shaw, *Victory and Occupation*, 39-56; Nichols and Shaw, *Okinawa*, 49-53; Toland, *The Rising Sun*, 770-71. Ushijima lost the elite Ninth Division, which was transferred to the Philippines at the end of 1944. He suffered an earlier blow in June 1944 when the submarine *USS Sturgeon* torpedoed and sank a Japanese troop transport carrying all 6,000 men of the forty-fourth Brigade to Okinawa. Only about 600 Japanese survived.

7. Belote and Belote, *Typhoon of Steel*, 18, 24; Feifer, *Tennozan*, 237-38; Sherrod, *On to Westward*, 259. Buckner earned this sobriquet because of his fondness for Alaska, where he had recently purchased a farm to which he eagerly anticipated retiring after the war.

8. Belote and Belote, *Typhoon of Steel*, 73-74.

9. Spector, *Eagle against the Sun*, 534-35.

10. Within the caves and bunkers of one typical position that measured 2,500 yards by 4,500 yards, the Japanese stocked sixteen grenade launchers, nearly 130 machine guns, seven antitank guns, several mortars and howitzers, additional artillery, and a minefield; see Frank and Shaw, *Victory and Occupation*, 49.

11. Ibid., 533; Appleman et al., *Okinawa*, 255-57, 441-42.

12. Sledge, *With the Old Breed*, 223.

13. Gordon Cobbledick, "Cries of Dying Spoil V-E Day for Okinawa," *Chicago Daily Tribune*, 9 May 1945, p. 1.

14. Homer Bigart, "U.S. Wins Okinawa Crest on Seventh Try, Marines Strike Downhill for Naha," *New York Herald Tribune*, 20 May 1945, p. 1; idem, "German Artillerists Reported," ibid., 19 May 1945, p. 1; Appleman et. al., *Okinawa*, 317-18.

15. Feifer, *Tennozan*, 277; Nichols and Shaw, *Okinawa*, 176-84.

16. Spector, *Eagle against the Sun*, 536-37; Appleman et al., *Okinawa*, 362, 364, Morison, *History of United States Naval Operations*, 14: 273-80, chaps. 11-16. Japanese air attacks became particularly heavy in late May, as the Japanese conducted sorties against the fleet and Okinawa. There were nearly nine hundred air raids against American ground forces and airfields on Okinawa, the highest total of any campaign in the Pacific, but the Japanese lost an estimated four thousand planes; see Appleman et al., *Okinawa*, 361-62.

17. For the effects of the rains upon operations and morale see Appleman et al., *Okinawa*, 366, 422; Nichols and Shaw, *Okinawa*, 197-98; Sledge, *With the Old Breed*, 214-15,

224-25; Hynes, *Flights of Passage*, 234-35; Murray Lewis, "Okinawa: Nightmare of Rain and Death," in *Semper Fidelis*, ed. O'Sheel and Cook 106-08.

18. Feifer, *Tennozan*, 300-06; Sledge, *With the Old Breed*, 265-66.

19. Manchester, *Goodbye Darkness*, 359-60.

20. Feifer, *Tennozan*, 269.

21. Herman Kogan, "You Still Living?" in *Semper Fidelis*, ed. O'Sheel and Cook, 159.

22. Sledge, *With the Old Breed*, 253.

23. Ibid., 258-59.

24. Potter, *Nimitz*, 368, 373-75, certainly sanitized Nimitz' remarks to Buckner; it is hard to believe that Nimitz would have used the adjective "stupid" to describe the destructive Japanese suicide raids. For more on the controversy about additional landings on Okinawa, see ibid., 375; Nichols and Shaw, *Okinawa*, 55, 142-43; Frank and Shaw, *Victory and Occupation*, 51; Spector, *Eagle against the Sun*, 535; Belote and Belote, *Typhoon of Steel*, 213-14; O'Neill, *A Democracy at War*, 413-14. See also Robert Trumbull, "Geiger Sees Japan Ripe for Invasion," *New York Times*, 7 July 1945, pp. 1, 3.

25. Appleman et al., *Okinawa*, 462-63; "Perfect Invasion Defense, Tokyo Says," *Washington Post*, 15 June 1945, p. 2.

26. Appleman et al., *Okinawa*, 465, 467; Cameron, *American Samurai*, 170.

27. Appleman et al., *Okinawa*, 456, 461.

28. Ibid., 472-73.

29. Ibid., 473; the observation about U.S. Navy casualties is in Cameron, *American Samurai*, 168. Cameron also pointed out that naval casualties at Okinawa nearly equaled those suffered in the Atlantic throughout the entire war.

30. Cameron, *American Samurai*, 187-89.

31. Robin Coons, "Jap Suicide Weapons Give Only Empty Glory," *Atlanta Constitution*, 27 May 1945, p. 6A; idem, "Japs' Suicidal 'Divine Wind' Is Mostly Hot Air," *St. Louis Post-Dispatch*, 27 May 1945, p. 3D. The headlines of the same article in different newspapers are indicative of the dismissive attitude regarding kamikazes; see also "Mitscher Scoffs at Suicide Planes," *New York Times*, 6 June 1945, p. 3, and "Spaatz Scorns Suicide Corps," ibid. Even after the war General Arnold, commander of the Army Air Forces, denigrated kamikaze pilots. Describing his visit to Okinawa in late June 1945, he later wrote: "From what I saw as we flew around the Island, the Kamikaze suicide planes had an easy time finding targets when they came down to Okinawa because there were innumerable ships of all kinds everywhere. All the Japanese had to do, once near Okinawa, was to close their eyes and put the noses of their planes down, and they would be almost sure to hit a ship every time"(*Global Mission*, 571). Arnold ignored the absurdity of comparing his aerial approach to Okinawa with that of Japanese pilots, who contended with American planes and a curtain of antiaircraft fire that downed the majority of the kamikazes.

32. "Japanese Etch Grim War Plans with Suicide as National Weapon," *Newsweek*, 11 June 1945, 43-44, 46; Halsey quote on 43.

33. Coons, "Japs' Suicidal 'Divine Wind' Is Mostly Hot Air," *St. Louis Post-Dispatch*, 27 May 1945, p. 3D.

34. "Suicide Raids," *Washington Post*, 6 June 1945, p. 10.

35. Hersey, "Kamikaze," 68-75; quotation is from 68.

36. "To Meet the Kamikaze," *New York Times*, 7 July 1945, p. 10.

37. "'Kamikaze' and the Navy," *Evening Star*, 2 June 1945, p. C-2.

38. Worden, "Kamikaze," 17, 77. This essay, and others, also ridiculed the rocket-propelled suicide craft first used by the Japanese at Okinawa, which Americans quickly dubbed the "Baka" or stupid bomb. One officer described the weapon as "a typical Jap idea. Take a German invention, add one Jap." The remark harkened back to the sentiment

that the Germans had somehow designed the attack on Pearl Harbor and compelled the Japanese to execute the plan, which was believed too complex for the Japanese to have devised and carried out on their own; see Dower, *War without Mercy*, 37, n. 10, 324. For another example of condescending reporting about the Japanese rocket-propelled kamikazes see Lardner, "Japs in Flying Caskets Go V-Bombs One Better," 46.

39. "Japs Reported Using Women as Pilots of Suicide Planes," *St. Louis Post-Dispatch*, 13 June 1945, p. 1; "3 Women Shot Down in U.S. Planes, Tokyo Radio Claims," ibid., 2 July 1945, p. 8A. Radio Tokyo speculated that a shortage of American airmen prompted the enlistment of women; it claimed the women were clothed "in smart outfits which may have been designed by Walt Disney because they were so natty"("See Jap Trick in Claim U.S. Girls Fly in Combat," *Chicago Daily Tribune*, 4 July 1945, p. 2).

40. Broadcast of 28 May 1945, p. 1; H.V. Kaltenborn Papers, folder 3, box 175, SHSW.

41. James, *The Years of MacArthur*, 2: 732-33. In 1944, during a meeting with President Roosevelt in Hawaii, MacArthur persuasively argued that American forces should next liberate the Philippines rather than bypass them and attack Formosa as advocated by Admiral Nimitz. When Roosevelt questioned MacArthur about losses in a campaign to capture Luzon, MacArthur said that casualties would not be any heavier than those of previous operations; "The days of frontal attack are over. Modern infantry weapons are too deadly, and direct assault is no longer feasible. Only mediocre commanders still use it. Your good commanders do not turn in heavy losses"(Potter, *Nimitz*, 318). Still, as his primary biographer D. Clayton James has made clear, MacArthur did not always reject the tactic of frontal assault.

42. Homer Bigart, "Tactics Called Conservative," *New York Herald Tribune*, 29 May 1945, p. 2.

43. David Lawrence, "Critics in Capital Hit Okinawa 'Mistakes,'" *Evening Star*, 30 May 1945, p. A-8.

44. Idem, "Writer Calls for Truth on Okinawan 'Fiasco,'" ibid., 4 June 1945, p. A-6.

45. Homer Bigart, "Nimitz Upholds Army Tactics, Denies 'Fiasco' on Okinawa," *New York Herald Tribune*, 17 June 1945, pp. 1, 2. Nimitz mistakenly referred to the Lawrence articles as appearing in the *Washington Post*, rather than the *Evening Star*; "Nimitz Defends Okinawa Campaign," *New York Times*, 17 June 1945, p. 3; "Backs Tactics of Buckner in Campaign," *Chicago Daily Tribune*, 17 June 1945, p. 1; Harold Smith, "Nimitz Sets Precedent in Blasting Critic," *Chicago Daily Tribune*, 18 June 1945, p. 2. The Smith piece speculated that Lawrence might have believed that some rivalry existed between the various branches of service at higher levels but dubiously contended that the correspondents who had accompanied landing forces on numerous operations in the Pacific "have encountered only complete harmony at the top."

46. Potter, *Nimitz*, 375-76.

47. See Spector, *Eagle against the Sun*, 314-17, and Potter, *Nimitz*, 305-9, for accounts of the controversy over this earlier imbroglio in which the press also became involved.

48. Bigart, "Nimitz Upholds Army Tactics, Denies 'Fiasco' on Okinawa," *New York Herald Tribune*, 17 June 1945, pp. 1, 2. Bigart observed, "This writer covered the Italian campaign during the Anzio and Cassino actions, and he knows what a fiasco is."

49. Bigart received a Pulitzer Prize in 1946 for his reporting in the Pacific. Kluger, *The Paper*, 363-74, contains a summary of Bigart's career but barely mentions this controversy. Wade, *Forward Positions*, xi-xvi, discusses Bigart's wartime reporting and prose style but does not include his most controversial pieces about the Okinawan campaign.

50. Nimitz conjectured that Gen. Alexander A. Vandegrift, commandant of the marines, may have leaked information to Bigart. Vandegrift denied the charge, but he

did tell King that he considered Buckner's tactics laborious and costly; see Vandegrift, *Once a Marine*, 291; Potter, *Nimitz*, 375-76.

51. "Statement by Lawrence," *New York Herald Tribune*, 17 June 1945, p. 2; "Nimitz Defends Okinawa Campaign," *New York Times*, 17 June 1945, p. 3. Belote and Belote, *Typhoon of Steel*, 152, singled out Homer Bigart as one reporter who consistently filed dispatches that displayed a thorough understanding of military tactics and the problems of cracking Japanese defensive positions.

52. "The Okinawa Controversy," *New York Herald Tribune*, 18 June 1945, p. 16.

53. W. Pratt, "A Reply to the Okinawa Critics," 36.

54. Hanson W. Baldwin, "Okinawa in Retrospect," *New York Times*, 13 July 1945, p. 2.

55. Maj. George Fielding Eliot, "Okinawa—Gettysburg," *Evening Star*, 22 June 1945, p. A-6; "Okinawa Casualties," ibid., 25 June 1945, p. A-8.

56. David Lawrence, "Discussion of Losses on Okinawa Urged," ibid., 22 June 1945, p. A-6. Lawrence subsequently referred to the campaign on Okinawa several times, faulting the military for its practice of concealing mistakes rather than critically evaluating instances of strategic blundering to avoid repeating them in future campaigns ("Few Military Leaders Know Real War Story," ibid., 5 July 1945, p. A-12). He reaffirmed his belief in Okinawa's strategic importance, even though he disapproved of the tactics for capturing it ("Iwo, Okinawa Bases Seen Justifying Cost," ibid., 7 July 1945, p. A-7). Later he reiterated his criticisms of the covering up of mistakes by the military—and the problem of rivalries between services—which he also believed contributed to the manner in which the campaign on Okinawa was fought("Baldwin Article Cited on Okinawa Battle," ibid., 23 July 1945, p. A-8).

57. "Letters to the Star; Questions Critic's Qualifications to Judge Okinawa Campaign," ibid., 8 June 1945, p. A-6; "Letters to the Star; Mr Lawrence Criticized," ibid., 25 June 1945, p. A-8.

58. "To the Last Line," *Time*, 18 June 1945, 34.

59. "Results on Okinawa," *New York Times*, 25 June 1945, p. 16; R.L. Prattis, "Do We Want to Pay the Price to Exterminate the Japanese People?" *Pittsburgh Courier*, 23 June 1945, p. 7 (Prattis was the newspaper's executive editor).

60. "The End on Okinawa," *Evening Star*, 22 June 1945, p. A-6.

61. Bruce Rae, "Okinawa Is a Lesson for Invasion of Japan," *New York Times*, 27 May 1945, p. E3.

62. "After Okinawa, What?" *Christian Century*, 9 May 1945, 574. It is noteworthy that this journal, which often faulted the reasoning that considered all Japanese implacable enemies, implied the same in this editorial; "Okinawa Is Captured," ibid., 4 July 1945, 779; Hanson W. Baldwin, "End in Sight on Okinawa," *New York Times*, 4 June 1945, p. 4.

63. Broadcast of 28 May 1945, p. 3, box 26, Raymond Gram Swing Papers, LC.

64. "To Say Japs Are Fanatics Understatement, Says Lt. Bell," *Atlanta Constitution*, 24 June 1945, p. 7A.

65. "Results on Okinawa," *New York Times*, 25 June 1945, p. 16.

66. "Through Japan's Door," *Washington Post*, 22 June 1945, p. 14.

67. Portions of the original editorial were reprinted in "Looking on the Face of War," *Christian Century*, 18 July 1945, 829. The original editorial was written shortly after the conclusion of the campaign on Okinawa.

68. Barnet Nover, "Victory on Okinawa," *Washington Post*, 23 June 1945, p. 6.

69. "Increasing Tempo in Pacific," *Los Angeles Times*, 5 July 1945, pt. 2, p. 4.

70. Kaltenborn discussed Okinawa in broadcasts on 10, 17, 21, 28 May and 21, 22, 26 June 1945. Quotations are from pp. 1, 5 of his broadcast of 21 June 1945, folder 6, box 175, H.V. Kaltenborn Papers, SHSW.

71. Ibid., broadcast of 26 June 1945, pp. 4-7.

72. *Chicago Daily Tribune,* 7 June 1945, p. 1.

73. "Target for Now," *New York Times,* 9 June 1945, p. 12.

74. "Prediction of Cars to Come," *New York Herald Tribune,* 28 June 1945, p. 18.

75. Even General Buckner admitted this in early May; see H.V. Kaltenborn broadcast of 10 May 1945, p. 2, in which he cited Buckner as saying that the original estimates of the Japanese garrison predicted sixty thousand Japanese troops on Okinawa (folder 1, box 175, H.V. Kaltenborn Papers, SHSW).

76. Appleman et al., *Okinawa,* 103; Nichols and Shaw, *Okinawa,* 20-21.

77. For an excellent account of the controversial circumstances surrounding Rosenthal's photograph, as well as various meanings attributed to it over the years, see Marling and Wetenhall, *Iwo Jima.*

78. Ibid., *Iwo Jima,* 94-96.

79. The postwar film most often associated with heroism in the Pacific War was "Sands of Iwo Jima," from 1949, starring John Wayne; see ibid., chap. 7, and Doherty, *Projections of War,* 272-74.

80. Cameron, *American Samurai,* 166.

81. Ibid., 188-89.

82. Timing of Proposed Demand for Japanese Surrender, 29 June 1945, Stimson "Safe File," Japan (After 7/41), box 8, RG 107.

6 The Sinister Cloud

1. Mandelbaum, *The Nuclear Revolution,* 47.

2. Rosenman, *Public Papers and Addresses,* Vol. 6, *The Constitution Prevails,* 320-21; Brown, *Chemical Warfare,* 124-25. Roosevelt admitted, however, that defensive necessities mandated the study of chemical warfare.

3. Letter from Frank Knox to Cordell Hull, 14 January 1942, and letter from Henry L. Stimson to Cordell Hull, 18 February 1942, both contained in JCS 731, 25 February 1944, Communication from Apostolic Delegate in Washington Regarding Use of Poison Gas by Japanese Forces; Knox's letter is in Enclosure "B," p. 4, Stimson's letter is in Enclosure "C," pp. 5-6, CCS 441.5 (8-27-42), sec. 3, box 427, RG 218.

4. *Complete Presidential Press Conferences,* 19: 363-64. After Japanese forces invaded China there were numerous reports of their use of poison gas, and by 1941 the Chinese claimed over one thousand gas attacks by Japanese troops. One confirmed instance of Japanese dispersal of mustard gas in significant quantities occurred in fighting at Ichang in October 1941. American intelligence deemed many of the Chinese reports specious but considered several as confirmed. See Tab "A," Condensed Statement of Information Available Concerning Japanese Use of War Gas attached to letter from Gen. William N. Porter, chief of Chemical Warfare Service, to Gen. H.H. Arnold, 7 January 1944, which listed then-available reports of Japanese use of poisonous gases in China; Central Decimal File, October 1942-May 1944, Warfare 385-D, box 591, RG 18. For further discussion of evidence of Japan's deployment of chemical agents in China, see *The Problem of Chemical and Biological Warfare,* I:147-52; Spiers, *Chemical Warfare,* 97-103; van Courtland Moon, "Chemical Weapons and Deterrence," 30. The Japanese army also tested biological agents against civilians and soldiers in China and conducted experiments on prisoners of war, possibly including some Americans. Later, charges were made that the U.S. government concealed its knowledge of these activities, and the Japanese scientists and officers involved escaped prosecution in exchange for turning over their records to the United States; see Powell, "Japan's Germ Warfare," 2-17; idem, "A Hidden Chapter in

History," 44-52; Williams and Wallace, *Unit 731*; S. Harris, *Factories Of Death*. A book published in 1944 accused the Japanese of extensive experimentation in biological warfare; see Newman, *Japan's Secret Weapon*.

5. van Courtland Moon, "Chemical Weapons and Deterrence," 12-14. Although the document implied that the Allies would resort to chemical warfare only in response to an attack by an Axis power, first use of poison gas by the Allies was not prohibited.

6. *Complete Presidential Press Conferences*, 21: 362-63. Rosenman, *Public Papers and Addresses*, Vol. 12, *The Tide Turns*, 242-43. At the behest of the Joint Chiefs of Staff, the army composed radio bulletins to be broadcast in the event the Allies launched a retributive chemical attack. They described the use of poison gas as an "inhuman method of warfare" and a "crime against civilization"; Notes on JCS 61st Meeting 9 February 1943, Air Force-Plans Project Central Decimal File 1942-1954, 471.6 (8-28-42), box 299, RG 341. The Joint Staff Planners were directed to prepare the broadcasts after correspondence between General Marshall and Admiral King; JCS 176/3, Allied Chemical Warfare Program, 6 February 1943, contains the proposed announcements, in Air Force-Plans Project Central Decimal File 1942-1954, 471.6 (8-28-42), box 299, RG 341.

7. On the development of CWS see Bernstein, "Why We Didn't Use Poison Gas in World War II," 42. The annual budget for the Chemical Warfare Service averaged $1.5 million during the 1930s, and its personnel numbered roughly five hundred. By 1942 it received $1 billion and its personnel included more than sixty thousand. Summaries of biological warfare developments are contained in Merck, Activities of the United States in the Field of Biological Warfare, a report prepared for Secretary of War Stimson, in entry 488, Biological Warfare Reference File, Dr. G.W. Merck's File, box 182, RG 165.

8. USCWC 91/3, Report of Readiness for Chemical Warfare as of 1 July 1944, 2 September 1944, p. 49, Subject Series 1942-1945, 334.8, box 140A, RG 175.

9. The study, Selected Aerial Targets for Retaliatory Gas Attack on Japan-April 1944, was prepared by the assistant chief of Air Staff Intelligence and is mentioned in a cable from Chief of Staff to Theater Commanders OPD 385 CWP, 13 July 1943, which is contained in Report of Readiness for Chemical Warfare, pp. 85-86; the list of cities is in USCWC 142, Performance of Responsibility for Carrying Out a Coordinated Anglo-American Chemical Warfare Procurement and Supply Program; both are located in Subject Series 1942-1945, 334.8 Chemical Warfare Committee, box 140A, RG 175. The listed cities included Tokyo, Osaka, Nagoya, Yokohama, Kobe, Yawata, Wakamatsu, and Kawasaki; also listed were thirty targeted German cities.

10. JPS 392 19 February 1944 Preparation of a Plan for Retaliatory Air Chemical Warfare against the Japanese, annex, pt. 1, sec., 1, p. 6; Gas Attacks from the Air, and annex, pt. 3, sec., 3, pp. 27-28, in CCS 470.6 (2-19-44), box 475, RG 218. In early 1945 chemical warfare contingency plans stated, "Strategic gas attack against Japanese cities which contain densely populated areas and are the location of important military installations and war production plants and facilities will constitute the initial target areas selected for attack by Army Air Forces, Pacific Ocean Areas"(Chemical Warfare Theater Plan United States Army Forces, Pacific Ocean Areas Revised as of 1 February, 1945, sec. 3, p. 2, Operations Division Decimal File 1945, OPD 385 TS (21 Feb 45), Theater Plans for Chemical Warfare-POA, box 166, RG 165.

11. A persistent gas is one that remains effective for more than ten minutes after dispersal, while a nonpersistent agent dissipates more quickly. The primary persistent gas, mustard, is a slowly evaporating liquid that can be sprayed or spread by explosives. Breathing it can be fatal, and it will permeate any porous clothing causing burning blisters particularly on joints, hands, and scrotum. It adheres to any surface and under the right conditions can remain effective for several days or even weeks. An example of a

deadly nonpersistent agent is phosgene, which chokes victims to death by burning out the respiratory tract, causing body fluids to flood the injured lungs.

12. SPCWC 470.6, 6 December 1943, Report from William H. Porter, Chief of CWS, to Joint Committee on New Weapons and Equipment, Joint Chiefs of Staff; Subject: Present State of Development of Toxic Gases, pp. 1-7; CCS 441.5 (8-27-42), sec. 3, box 427, RG 218. Porter theorized on the effectiveness of the use of mustard gas at Betio atoll during the campaign to capture Tarawa in 1943. He said that 900 tons of mustard gas, as compared with the 3,000 tons of high explosives fired, probably would have killed the entire Japanese garrison. After four days American forces could have landed with little opposition, "at the cost of slight casualties from residual mustard contamination," which Porter regarded as "insignificant compared with those recorded for the actual operation in the Battle for Betio Island"; see Annex A, pp. 1-3, of this report.

13. Report of Chemical Warfare Service Conference, 10-13 October 1944, appendix 2, Chemical Warfare Service Miscellaneous Series 1942-1945, 337 Chemical Warfare Service, box 170, RG 175.

14. van Courtland Moon, "Chemical Weapons and Deterrence," 14-15. Fearful of the vulnerability of Britain and the Indian subcontinent to retaliation by the Axis if the United States initiated chemical warfare, the British requested that retaliation occur only by order of the Combined Chiefs of Staff after approval by the governments of the United States, United Kingdom, and Commonwealth nations. In April 1944, the Joint Chiefs accepted this proposal; see ibid., 15-16. See also JCS 176/7, 27 January 1944, Allied Chemical Warfare Policy, CCS 441.5 (8-27-42), sec. 3, and CCS 106/14, Allied Chemical Warfare Program, 25 April 1944, CCS 441.5 (8-27-42), sec. 4, both in box 427, RG 218.

15. JIC MFI81, 21 July 1944, Joint Intelligence Committee Memorandum for Information no. 81, Japanese Battle Morale, p. 13, Plans Project Decimal File 1942-1945, Pd 330.11 Japan (7-21-44), box 385, RG 341.

16. Memorandum no. 1, 4 May 1943, Air Force-Plans Project Central Decimal File 1942-1954, 471.6 (8-28-42), box 299, RG 341.

17. JCS 176/7, 27 January 1944, Allied Chemical Warfare Policy, Appendix "A," pp. 5-6, CCS 441.5 (8-27-42), sec. 3, box 427, RG 218.

18. A report by the Joint Staff Planners cautioned that if chemical warfare spread, the United States would probably be obligated to provide protective equipment on a massive scale for Chinese civilians and the Chinese army; JPS 484/1, 8 July 1944, Joint Staff Planners, Implications of Retaliatory Chemical Warfare Against the Japanese, pp. 1-6, CCS 441.5 (8-27-42), sec. 3, box 427, RG 218. The Joint Chiefs recognized the problem in directive JCS 825/3, which contained the quoted passages; see JCS 825/3, 29 August, 1944, Capabilities of Implementing a Decision to Initiate Retaliatory Chemical Warfare Against the Japanese, 25-26, in same location.

19. SIPRI, 1: 288. Japan never ratified the Geneva Protocol of 1925.

20. Because of the relative autonomy of Japanese commanders and the lack of centralized decision-making regarding overall Japanese military strategy, Allied intelligence generally considered spontaneous use of poison gas by order of a local commander the most likely scenario should the Japanese use gas at all; see Memorandum for Information no. 56, Axis Capabilities and Intentions, Gas Warfare, Report by the Combined Intelligence Committee, 5 April 1943, enclosure "B," pp. 2-5, CCS 441.5 (8-27-42), sec. 1, box 426, RG 218. For more information on the complexities of Japanese military decision-making, see van Courtland Moon, "Chemical Weapons and Deterrence," 28-29. There were reports that Japanese forces used toxic smoke on Guadalcanal in January 1943 and suspicion that Japanese troops had buried gas mines in the Philippines; see Condensed Statement of Information Available Concerning Japanese Use of War Gas, p. 1, Tab "A,"

attached to a letter from Gen. William N. Porter, Chief of Chemical Warfare Service, to Gen. H.H. Arnold, 7 January 1944, Central Decimal Files October 1942-May 1944, Warfare 385-D, box 591, RG 18. Sixth Army Headquarters suspected that Japanese troops had buried gas mines beneath some streets in the Philippine city of Davao; see World War II Operations Reports 1940-1948 Special File, War Department Adjutant General's Office, USAFFE Board Report no. 241, Possible Use of Poison Gas Mines by Japanese, 31 March 1945, E427, RG 407. Japan accused the United States of using gas shells on Bataan, a charge General MacArthur denied, and of using gas during combat on Attu in the Aleutian islands in 1943. Japanese army documents captured in 1944 showed that Imperial Headquarters had informed units in the field that American forces had used gas at Attu and in New Guinea; see Kendrick Lee, *Gas Warfare*, a booklet prepared for the War Department contained in Editorial Research Reports, vol. 2, 1943, CCS 441.5 (8-27-42) B.P. (Bulky Package) Chemical Warfare Program, box 427, RG 218.

21. Jacobs, *War Gases*, described poison gas as more a threat than an effective weapon; Waitt, *Gas Warfare*, said gas was potentially decisive.

22. Milliman, "The Truth about Poison Gas," 15; Kearney, "Don't Let Poison Gas Panic You," 33.

23. Marshall, "We Are Ready with Gas," 21.

24. "Colleges Advised to Keep Basic Aim," *New York Times*, 7 February 1943, p. 37. The speaker was Dr. C.P. Rhoads, director of Memorial Hospital and assistant director of the Committee on Treatment of War Gas Casualties.

25. Waitt, "Poison Gas in This War," pp. 563-64.

26. "The Last Weapon," *Time*, 25 May 1942, 71-72.

27. Fuqua, "The Case for Gas as a Humane Weapon," 25.

28. "We Should Gas Japan," *New York Daily News*, 20 November 1943.

29. "We Should Have Used Gas at Tarawa," *Times-Herald*, 20 December 1943; "You Can Cook 'Em Better with Gas," ibid., 1 February 1944, p. 12.

30. Hanson W. Baldwin, "A War without Quarter Forecast in Pacific," *New York Times*, 30 January 1944, p. E3. Baldwin's article elicited response from the Japanese government, which used various channels to communicate its claim to the State Department that Japanese forces had not used poison gas in China and would refrain from using it as long as the United States did. Japanese protestations were made through the Special Envoy of the Japanese Government to the Holy See and communicated via a letter to Secretary of State Cordell Hull from the Apostolic Delegate in Washington, D.C., dated 15 February 1944. After consultation with the Joint Chiefs, Hull's response of 30 March 1944 said that the United States stood by Roosevelt's declaration of 8 June 1943 that the United States would only use gas in retaliation for first use by Japan; see JCS 731, 25 February 1944, Communication from Apostolic Delegate in Washington Regarding Use of Poison Gas by Japanese Forces, CCS 441.5 (8-27-42), sec. 3, box 427, RG 218.

31. Lindley, "Thoughts on the Use of Gas in Warfare," 24.

32. Cousins, "The Poison Gas Boys," 12.

33. "Should the U.S. Use Gas?," *Time*, 3 January 1944, 15.

34. Mandelbaum, *The Nuclear Revolution*, 47. In 1944 General Porter, head of the Chemical Warfare Service, remarked, "Once Germany is out of the war, the advantage in gas warfare will rest with the United Nations, and no legal international complications will exist" ("Gas Warfare in the Pacific Theaters," attached to letter from Gen. William N. Porter to Gen. H.H. Arnold, 7 January 1944, Central Decimal File October 1942-May 1944, Warfare 385-D, box 591, RG 18.

35. "You Can Cook Them Better with Gas," *Chicago Daily Tribune*, 11 March 1945, p. 18.

36. Tests of aerial spraying in March 1945 indicated that mixing the substance with oil prevented it from freezing during transport and helped disguise the true nature of the spray. Merck and Porter both said that the chemicals were not fatal when ingested. The concept was still being evaluated in June, and the Joint Staff Planners recommended informing commanders in the Pacific about the developments to learn their opinions about using it against bypassed garrisons. The use of these substances against crops in Japan was studied, but the Joint Staff Planners noted that a conventional aerial assault against the means of distributing and storing food would be more effective than attacking crops. See JCS 1371/1, Policy on the Use of Chemical Agents for the Destruction of Japanese Food Crops, 1 June 1945, ABC 475.92 (25 Feb 44), sec. 1-C, box 578, RG 319, which contains a concise summary of these plans, including all of General Porter's memos and a chronological account of the development of the chemical mixture; in the same location see also Memorandum for the Assistant Secretary WDGS, Policy on the Use of Chemical Agents for the Destruction of Japanese Food Crops, 6 June 1945. See also Memorandum for Record: Destruction of Crops by "LN" Chemicals, 9 March, by the Joint Chiefs of Staff; Memo for Mr. Merck, 9 March 1945, from Gen. J.E. Hull; Memorandum for Mr. George W. Merck, undated, from Chief of Staff; Memorandum for Gen. George C. Marshall, undated, Destruction of Crops by "LN" Chemicals, from George W. Merck; Memorandum for the Secretary of War, 5 March 1945, Destruction of Crops by Chemicals, from Myron C. Cramer; undated summary of the characteristics of "LN" chemicals; all in Operations Division Decimal File 1945, OPD 385 TS, box 166, RG 165. Perhaps these plans were in part a response to General Arnold's previously cited memo requesting new methods of exterminating Japanese garrisons on bypassed islands; "Extermination of By-passed Jap Garrisons in South Pacific," directive from General Arnold, 25 May 1945, file 67, box 42, Henry H. Arnold Papers, LC. See also Bernstein, "America's Biological Warfare Program," 308-10.

37. Memorandum from V.E. Bertrandias to Gen. H.H. Arnold, 29 May 1945, Official Decimal File 1938-1946, file SAS 385 Japan, box 115, Henry H. Arnold Papers, LC; Memorandum for General Arnold from R.P. Proctor, undated, in same file, summarized Bertrandias's plan.

38. Memorandum from John A. Samford to V.E. Bertrandias, 4 June 1945, Official Decimal File 1938-1946, SAS Japan 385, box 115, Henry H. Arnold Papers, LC. In the same file is a memorandum that served as a kind of cover letter for a report, "Development of Tactics and Techniques for Dissemination of Chemicals from Aircraft for Crop Destruction," which said that the development and production of crop-destroying chemicals was continuing and sufficient stocks existed to destroy 20,000 acres. Experiments were being conducted by the Special Projects Branch of the Chemical Warfare Service at its facility in Terre Haute, Indiana. At least one person on the home front advocated a similar plan, Rep. Frank Boykin (D-Ala.), who sent a letter to the White House that he had received from a close friend suggesting the spraying of defoliants on Japanese rice crops after the fashion of crop dusting methods used to control boll weevils. Boykin endorsed the idea: "I think this is a great suggestion and might do what all of the right thinking people of this earth want, the quick ending of the killing of our men" (Letter from Harry F. Barkerding to Sen. Burnett R. Maybank, 23 July 1945; letter from Rep. Frank Boykin to Mr. Matthew Connely, Secretary to the President, 25 July 1945, Papers of Harry S. Truman, Official File, OF 190-Misc. 1945, box 662, Harry S. Truman Library, [HSTL]. See also Bernstein, "America's Biological Warfare Program," 309-10.

39. Arnold conferred with MacArthur in Manila during a tour of the Pacific. Summarizing the conversations in his diary Arnold quoted MacArthur as saying, "Can see no reason why we should not use gas right now against Japan proper. Any kind of gas.

Sees no reason for gassing Japs in by-passed areas" (Arnold Journals 1945, 6-24 June Trip to Pacific, Entry for 17 June, box 272, Henry H. Arnold Papers, LC).

40. Stilwell's memo, submitted to General Marshall, contained several points for deliberation in planning an invasion of Japan. He suggested limiting the use of poison gas to military targets rather than civilians. General Arnold sent a memo to Marshall commenting on Stilwell's proposals; see ABC Japan (3 May 44), sec. 1-B, box 428, RG 165. The memo is also in Official Decimal File 1938-1946, file 114, box 44, Henry H. Arnold Papers, LC; SAS Japan 385, box 115 in the same file, contains Stilwell's letter and a memo from Brig. Gen. Lauris Norstad of the Army Air Forces, dated 28 May 1945, in which Norstad acknowledged ongoing consideration and study of the strategic and tactical use of gas against Japan by the Army Air Forces and the Chemical Warfare Service.

41. Brophy and Fisher, *Organizing for War*, 86.

42. Ibid., 86-87.

43. Ibid., 87; van Courtland Moon, "Chemical Weapons and Deterrence," 22. For more on the SPHINX tests see van Courtland Moon, "Project SPHINX," 303-23.

44. Memorandum of Conversation with General Marshall 29 May 1945, Stimson "Safe File," July 1940-September 1945, folder S-1, box 12, RG 107. Marshall later claimed that British fear of German retaliation had stymied serious discussion of using poison gas on Okinawa; Lilienthal, *The Journals of David E. Lilienthal*, 2:199.

45. Memorandum for the Chief of Staff: 15 June 1945, from J.J.McC., ABC 475.92 (25 Feb 44), sec. 1-C, box 578, RG 319.

46. Memorandum, attached to A.J. Goodpaster's memo for General Lincoln, in Plans and Operations Division "ABC" Decimal File 1942-1948, ABC 381 Strategy Section Papers (7 Jan 43) (SS 387), box 370, RG 319.

47. Memorandum for General Lincoln, 4 June 1945, SS 387, Use of Gas Warfare against the Japanese, ibid.

48. Col. Max S. Johnson reiterated that SS 387 was *"highly theoretical"*; see Memorandum for General Lincoln, 20 June 1945, from M.S.J.; ABC 475.92 (25 Feb 44), sec. 1-C, box 587, RG 319. See also the comments of Col. A.J. Goodpaster in Memorandum for the Chief, Strategy Section, OPD, 3 June 1945, in Plans and Operations Division "ABC" Decimal File 1942-1948, file ABC 381 Strategy Section Papers (7 Jan 43) (SS 387), box 370, RG 319.

49. Memorandum by the Chief of Staff, U.S. Army, undated, Operations Division Decimal File 1945, OPD 385 TS, sec., 1, box 166, RG 165. The memorandum said that Chiang Kai-shek should eventually be advised, although it did not say that his approval was necessary to initiate offensive chemical warfare. (This memo is undated but was probably issued on June 20 or June 21, since accompanying memos bear those dates).

50. van Courtland Moon, "Chemical Weapons and Deterrence," 22-23; Brophy and Fisher, *Organizing for War*, 87-88. Memo dated 5 July 1945 from Gen. J.E. Hull noted that after further discussion the Joint Chiefs decided to delay making a decision on preparation for chemical warfare: "Admiral King felt that we should not make an early decision in regard to the further production of gas" (Operations Division Decimal File 1945, OPD 385 TS, 3 July 1945, sec. 1, RG 165). The Navy was never enthusiastic about chemical warfare; for earlier evidence of Navy attitudes see Memorandum no. 1, 4 May 1943, Plans Project Central Decimal File 1942-1954, file 471.6 (8-28-42), box 299, RG 341. In an informal conversation with journalists in 1944, King indicated tentative support for using gas but said he believed the American public would not tolerate it. Most of the assembled reporters disagreed and argued that the public would support using any weapon against the Japanese. With Germany still in the war, King noted that use of gas might bring retaliation upon Britain as well as Japanese retaliation against China; Perry, *"Dear Bart,"* 249.

51. Memorandum for General Marshall, 20 June 1945, Operations Division Decimal File 1945, file OPD 385 TS, sec., 1, box 166, RG 165. Leahy had expressed his opposition to biological warfare during a conversation with Roosevelt in July 1944 enroute to Honolulu for a meeting with General MacArthur and Admiral Nimitz (*I Was There*, 439-40).

52. Undated memo to Generals Eaker, Annders, and Norstad, file 151, box 45, Henry H. Arnold Papers, LC.

53. Change in Chemical Warfare Policy, Operations Division Executive Files 1940-1945, file 5, item 21A, tab 60, box 32, RG 165 (the memo is undated but located in a group labeled "10 July 1945 edition").

54. van Courtland Moon, "Chemical Weapons and Deterrence," 23; Brophy and Fisher, *Organizing for War*, 88.

55. Change in Chemical Warfare Policy, Operations Division Executive Files 1940-1945, file 5, item 21A, tab 60, box 32, RG 165 (the document is not dated but is bound in a group labeled "10 July 1945 edition").

56. Cantril, *Public Opinion 1935-1946*, 249. These polls were conducted by the American Institute of Public Opinion, which usually used a sample of three thousand.

57. Col. Frederic Palmer, "Poison Gas for Kamikazes," *Evening Star*, 24 July 1945, p. A-6.

58. Maj. George Fielding Eliot, "Gas against the Japanese," *Evening Star*, 6 June 1945, p. A-10. Eliot published another essay in the August issue of *Popular Science Monthly*, which featured photographs of dead Japanese soldiers charred by flamethrowers and mangled by shell fire to accentuate his contention that killing with poison gas was not worse than death by conventional weapons (Should We Gas the Japs?," 49-53).

59. Paulding, "Poison Gas," 229-30.

60. "Letters to the Star; Readers Differ on Use of Gas in War against the Japs," *Evening Star*, 11 June 1945, p. A-6; "Letters to the Star; Opposes Use of Poison Gas," ibid., 14 June 1945, p. A-12. The Socialist leader Norman Thomas later recalled that when he debated Major Eliot about foreign policy in 1940, Eliot did not even mention Japan in his appraisal of the global situation. When Thomas, who said that the United States was more likely to be brought into the war by Japan than Germany, inquired about the omission, Eliot replied that it was deliberate because Japan could be defeated in a few weeks (*What Is Our Destiny*, 16-17).

61. Broadcast of 15 June 1945, p. 2, box 26, Raymond Gram Swing Papers, LC.

62. "Blood, Gas and Morality," *Time*, 18 June 1945, 30.

63. Gladstone Williams, "Is Gas the Answer to a Quick Peace?" *Atlanta Constitution*, 13 June 1945, p. 6.

64. "We Can't Use Poison Gas," ibid., 30 June 1945, p. 4.

65. "Mawkish Religion?" written by M.L. Fairfax of Atlanta, in "The Pulse of the Public," *Atlanta Constitution*, 7 July 1945, p. 4; "Poison Gas," written by George Trawick of Douglas, Georgia, ibid., 10 July 1945, p. 6.

66. Spiers, *Chemical Warfare*, 87; Kleber and Birdsell, *Chemicals in Combat*, 652. Bernstein argues that Roosevelt's declared opposition to the initiation of chemical warfare narrowed Truman's options ("Why We Didn't Use Poison Gas," 45).

67. Gen. Albert C. Wedemeyer concluded an agreement with Chiang Kai-shek stipulating that chemical weapons would be used in China only on a tactical scale and placed certain restrictions on the dispersal of gas, although any use of it in areas occupied by the Japanese certainly would have resulted in the deaths of Chinese civilians; Memorandum to Chief of Staff, U.S. Army, 21 May 1945, Operations Division Decimal File 1945, OPD 385 TS, sec., 1, box 166, RG 165.

68. Leahy, *I Was There*, 79.

69. See Kleber and Birdsell, *Chemicals in Combat*, 651-52. Supply problems sometimes bordered on the ridiculous. One such example occurred when the Chemical Warfare Service in the Southwest Pacific received a shipment of twenty thousand gas masks for horses in a theater where horses were extremely rare(Ibid., 255). Mustard gas was particularly troublesome to move and store because it contained unstable impurities that frequently caused dangerously high levels of pressure within storage cylinders. If not vented, slow leaks or sudden showers of mustard gas sometimes resulted; see Brophy, Miles, and Cochrane, *The Chemical Warfare Service*, 386-87.

70. Complete preparedness for chemical warfare had not been achieved at the time Japan surrendered. See van Courtland Moon, "Chemical Weapons and Deterrence," 24-25; JCS 825/4, 7 October 1944, Capabilities of Implementing a Decision to Initiate Retaliatory Chemical Warfare against the Japanese, CCS 441.5 (8-27-42), sec. 5, box 427: JCS 825/5, 5 March 1945, Theater Plans for Chemical Warfare, CCS 441. 5 (8-27-42), sec. 5, box 427; JCS 825/6, 13 June 1945, Theater Plans for Chemical Warfare, CCS 441.5 (8-27-42), sec. 6, box 428; JCS 825/8, 6 July 1945, Availibility and Production of Chemical Munitions, CCS 441.5 (8-27-42), sec 6, box 428, all in RG 218. See also Brophy and Fisher, *Organizing for War*, 85.

71. See JPS 484/6, Theater Plans for Chemical Warfare, 4 June 1945, Plans and Operations Division Decimal File 1942-1948, ABC 475.92, (25 Feb 44), sec. 1-C, box 578, RG 319, which summarizes previous directives. It recommended moving the necessary stocks for retaliatory chemical warfare to forward positions by 1 November 1945, but since previous dates had been altered it is doubtful that compliance with this deadline would have been achieved. It also stipulated that the shipments were not to hinder the transport of other supplies for the planned invasion of Japan. For documents pertaining to the quantity and allotment of chemical warfare stocks, see Memorandum for Admiral Leahy, 21 June 1945, Operations Division Executive Files, File 10, item 64, box 59, RG 165; and Chemical Warfare Theater Plan United States Army Air Forces, Pacific Ocean Areas Revised as of 1 February, 1945, Annex A, p. 21, Operations Division Decimal File 1945, OPD 385 TS, (21 Feb 45), Theater Plans for Chemical Warfare-POA; the memo OPD 385 CWP (12 Mar 45); TS 385, sec., 1, and the series of memos in OPD 385 TS, (20 June 45); all in box 166, RG 165. See also Brown, *Chemical Warfare*, 265-66.

72. Kleber and Birdsell, *Chemicals in Combat*, 653-54.

73. See Mandelbaum, *The Nuclear Revolution*, 39, for further observations about repugnance toward chemical warfare. For an interesting analysis of American response to poison gas during World War I and after, see Slotten, "Humane Chemistry or Scientific Barbarism?" 476-98.

74. Employment of Gas Report of the Chief of the Chemical Warfare Service, undated. This report, along with the plans for DOWNFALL, OLYMPIC, and CORONET, are contained in a folder labeled "Operations against the Japanese," prepared by the Strategic Logistics Branch, Planning Division, 5 July 1945, Office Of The Commanding General Control Division 1942-1946 Operational Summaries, part. 1, tab 1-H, box 690, RG 160. The report said that phosgene would be the primary gas dispersed against civilians, and cyanogen chloride, a more recently developed gas, would be used against troops because it could penetrate Japanese gas masks. The report stated that use of gas could reduce American casualties by one-third to one-half.

75. Mandelbaum, *The Nuclear Revolution*, 47.

7 Assault or Seige

1. Pratt, "The War in the Pacific," 738.
2. Ferrell, *Off the Record*, 47.

3. Skates, *The Invasion of Japan*, 43-44. See also E. Miller, *War Plan Orange*, for details on the Navy's prewar contingency plans for conflict against Japan.

4. Skates, *The Invasion of Japan*, 9-11, 14, 34-35. Dividing the command in the Pacific between General MacArthur and Admiral Nimitz also hampered long-term planning. For background on the decision to designate separate commands, see Hayes, *The History of the Joint Chiefs of Staff*, 96-102.

5. *FRUS, Conferences at Washington, 1941-1942, and Casablanca, 1943*, 727.

6. The Joint Chiefs of Staff had previously discussed unconditional surrender, but Roosevelt had not specifically requested their advice in formulating the policy; see Skates, *The Invasion of Japan*, 14-17. For background on unconditional surrender see O'Connor, *Diplomacy for Victory*, and Armstrong, *Unconditional Surrender*. For a discussion of the relationship between unconditional surrender and public opinion, see Chase, "Unconditional Surrender Reconsidered," 366-80. See also Villa, "The U.S. Army, Unconditional Surrender, and the Potsdam Proclamation," 69-70.

7. Skates, *The Invasion of Japan*, 36.

8. A Strategic Plan for the Defeat of Japan, JWPC 15, 5 May 1943, Combined Chiefs of Staff Decimal File 1942-1945, CCS 381 (4024-43), sec. 6, pt. 1, box 311, RG 218.

9. CPS 83, 8 August 1943, Appreciation and Plan for the Defeat of Japan, Geographic File 1942-1945, CCS 381 (8-25-42), sec. 6, box 648, RG 218; see part 10 of this document, Basic Doctrine and Conclusions, Concept and Outline Plan, pp. 60-67.

10. For remarks by Army Air Forces and Navy strategists see Appreciation and Plan for the Defeat of Japan, Combined Chiefs of Staff Decimal File 1942-1945, CCS 334 Combined Staff Planners (5-6-43), box 184, RG 218.

11. JCS 924, 30 June 1944, Operations against Japan Subsequent to Formosa, Geographic File 1942-1945, CCS 381 Pacific Ocean Area (6-10-43), sec. 5, box 683, RG 218.

12. American military planners first proposed the defeat of Japan within one year of Germany's capitulation in 1943; see The Defeat of Japan within Twelve Months after the Defeat of Germany, Combined Staff Planners, 25 October 1943, Geographic File 1942-1945, CCS 381 Japan (8-25-42), sec. 8, box 648, RG 218. See also CPS 86/2, The Defeat of Japan within Twelve Months after the Defeat of Germany, contained within JCS 564, 4 November 1943, in ABC Files, ABC 381 Japan (8-27-42), sec. 6, box 352, RG 165. For acceptance of the concept see CCS 417/3, 11 July 1944, Over-All Objective in the War Against Japan, and Extract Minutes, CCS 167th Meeting, 14 July 1944, ABC Files, ABC 381 Japan (8-27-42), sec. 6, box 352, RG 165. At the Cairo Conference of December 1943, Allied military leaders agreed "to invade Japan proper *if this should prove necessary*"; see Corrigendum to J.C.S. 925/15 Pacific Strategy, 26 April 1945, Enclosure, 243, Geographic File 1942-1945, CCS 381 Pacific Ocean Area (6-10-43), sec. 12, box 687, RG 218. When Franklin Roosevelt met with Stalin and Churchill at Yalta he intimated his hope that Japan would surrender before an invasion. See William D. Leahy Diaries, 8 February 1945, p. 24, microfilm reel 3, LC. Leahy also believed Japan could be defeated without an invasion; see entry for 24 July 1944, p. 66.

13. JCS 924/4, 6 September 1944, Operations for the Defeat of Japan, 1944-45, Enclosure, p. 124, ABC Files, ABC 381 Japan (8-27-42), sec. 7, box 353, RG 165. Both Admiral King and General Arnold were still expressing reservations about invasion and they believed that siege would defeat Japan; see King memorandum, JCS 924/6, Operations for the Defeat of Japan, 3 November 1944, Arnold memorandum, JCS 924/7, same heading, 6 November 1944, and memorandum of telephone conversation between Brig. Gen. Frank Roberts and Rear Adm. D.B. Duncan, of 3 November 1944, all in same file. The Navy initially preferred an invasion of the southern island of Kyushu or the main island Honshu, while the Army argued that the northernmost, less heavily defended island of

Hokkaido could be seized with fewer casualties. At first, General MacArthur's staff expressed preference for attacking Hokkaido, as did General Henry Arnold of the Army Air Forces. Admiral King disagreed and repeatedly stressed that Hokkaido's lack of suitable anchorages and distance from established naval bases in the Ryukyus made an assault there impractical. For more on this see Memorandum from Headquarters, United States Army Forces, Pacific Ocean Areas Office of the Commanding General to Commander-in-Chief Pacific Ocean Areas, 27 September 1944; JCS 924/7, 3 November 1944, Operations for the Defeat of Japan, and Notes on JPS 179th Meeting, 16 November 1944, which summarizes further discussions among the Joint Chiefs about invading Japan. All of these documents are in ABC Files, ABC 381 Japan (8-27-42), sec. 7, box 353, RG 165. See also Memo, Future Operations in the Pacific, 23 September 1944, Operations Division Executive Files 1940-1945, file 2, item 11, box 12, RG 165, in which King proposed other operations rather than an invasion. See also Vander Linde, "'Downfall,'" 48-51.

14. JCS 924/5, 27 October 1944, Operations for the Defeat of Japan, 1944-45, Enclosure, p. 132, ABC Files, ABC 381 Japan (8-27-42), sec. 7, box 353, RG 165.

15. The controversial Gen. William L. "Billy" Mitchell had described Japan as a particularly attractive target for incendiary attack because of the prevalence of wooden structures in its cities; see Schaffer, *Wings of Judgment*, 25, and Sherry, *The Rise of American Air Power*, 31, 58-59. In 1919 a marine officer suggested incendiary bombing Japan with seaplanes launched from ships; see Spector, *Eagle against the Sun*, 503. Two committees composed of military specialists and civilians had studied the potential for incendiary bombing of Japan earlier in the war, and the Army Air Forces conducted several experimental incendiary raids against Japanese cities in 1944; see Schaffer, *Wings of Judgment*, 107-27, and Sherry, *The Rise of American Air Power*, 226-36. Memorandums and plans for the first incendiary raids and information on various targeted cities are located in Office of the Commanding General Numeric File 1944-1945, file 11, Plans for Incendiary Attacks, and file 18, Target Selection, box 101, RG 18.

16. The Japanese lacked sophisticated searchlights and possessed few radar-controlled antiaircraft guns like those used against Allied bombers in Europe. The paucity of Japanese pilots trained for night fighting, and the scarcity of fighter craft suited for it, also made Japanese cities more vulnerable to nocturnal bombing; see Schaffer, *Wings of Judgment*, 126, 128-137; Sherry, *The Rise of American Air Power*, 269-292.

17. Craven and Cate, *The Army Air Forces in World War II*, 5:618-23, 627-43, 653.

18. JCS 1232, 17 January 1945, Memorandum for Joint Chiefs of Staff, contains King's proposals. Memo for Record, 6 March 1945, Informal Comment on Conversation Taking Place in the Chief of Staff's Office This Morning, records General Wedemeyer and General Hull's objections to King's proposition. They both feared that King's proposed operations would delay the invasion of Kyushu, which they wanted launched as soon as possible after the capture of Okinawa. Both documents are located in ABC Files, ABC 384 Pacific (1-17-43), sec. 7, box 455, RG 165.

19. Memorandum for the Chief of Staff, 27 March 1945, from Gen. J.E. Hull, ABC Files, ABC 384 Pacific (1-17-43) sec. 9, box 457, RG 165.

20. Lincoln's comments are in Memorandum for General Bessell, 14 April 1945, ABC Files, ABC 384 Pacific (1-17-43), sec. 9, box 457, RG 165. For more on Lincoln's views see Brower, "Sophisticated Strategist," 324-35. The Joint Staff Planners also advocated invading Japan and objected to peripheral attacks along the Chinese coast. The arguments between army and navy strategists can be followed in the minutes of meetings of the Joint Staff Planners; see Minutes of Meeting Held 10 March 10-16 March 16 1945 (listed collectively as 192d Meeting), Combined Chiefs of Staff Decimal File 1942-1945, CCS 334 Joint Staff Planners (9-11-44), box 213, RG 218. In these sessions the naval representatives con-

tinually supported operations along the coast of China, while army strategists favored more definite planning for an invasion of Kyushu and deemed the proposed operations in the Chusan Archipelago counterproductive. General Lincoln's comments touched on the desirability of Soviet participation in the war against Japan. For more views on this topic see U.S. Department of Defense, *The Entry of the Soviet Union into the War against Japan*, 38-44, 50-52.

21. JIC 266/1, 18 April 1945, *Defeat of Japan by Blockade and Bombardment*, Geographic File 1942-1945, CCS 381 Japan (4-6-45), box 640, RG 218.

22. Corrigendum to JCS 924/15, Pacific Strategy, 26 April 1945, Geographic File 1942-1945, CCS 381 Pacific Ocean Area (6-10-43), sec. 12, box 687, RG 218.

23. Top Secret Outgoing Message, Joint Chiefs of Staff to MacArthur, Nimitz, Arnold, no. WARX 87938 CM-OUT-87938, 25 May 1945, Geographic File 1942-1945, CCS 381 Pacific Ocean Area (6-10-43), sec. 13, box 687, RG 218.

24. Brower, "Sophisticated Strategist," 328.

25. Schaffer, *Wings of Judgment*, 172, said, "Truman's initial reflections on ending the war led him to give highest priority to minimizing U.S. losses." McCoy, *The Presidency of Harry S. Truman*, 36, wrote, "Speed dictated most of the thinking of Truman and his advisers."

26. Truman, *Memoirs*, 1:17, 235-36.

27. JPS 697/D, 14 June 1945, Details of the Campaign against Japan, Plans and Operations Division "ABC" Decimal File 1942-1948, (TS) ABC 384 Japan (3 May 44), sec. 1-B, box 428, RG 319. U.S. Department of Defense, *The Entry of the Soviet Union into the War against Japan*, 76. Leahy's memo, dated 14 June 1945, is printed in Sherwin, *A World Destroyed*, 335-36; the quotation appears on p. 336. Leahy described Truman as an attentive listener who concealed his own thoughts, and he believed Truman shared his preference for a longer war if it meant fewer casualties (*I Was There*, 385).

28. *Truman Public Papers*, 45.

29. Messages to MacArthur sent on 15 and 18 June, MacArthur's casualty estimates, and his reply to Marshall are in Operations Division Decimal File 1945, folder OPD 704 TS, sec. 1, box 178, RG 165. In a memo prepared for Truman prior to the meeting of 18 June the Joint War Plans Committee estimated that an invasion of southern Kyushu followed by a landing on the Tokyo Plain in March 1946 would result in total casualties of 193,500, of which an anticipated 40,000 would be killed. If all of Kyushu were taken prior to invading Honshu, casualties were projected at 220,000 with 46,000 killed. See JWPC 369/1, Details of the Campaign Against Japan, 15 June 1945, p. 7, Plans and Operations Division "ABC" Decimal File 1942-1948, file ABC 384 Japan (3 May 44), sec. 1-B, box 428, RG 319. Casualty estimates from Admiral Nimitz's staff apparently arrived after the 18 June meeting. They anticipated forty-nine thousand casualties in the first thirty days of OLYMPIC and predicted total naval casualties would be roughly equal to those suffered during the battle for Okinawa; see JCS 1388/1, 20 June 1945, Proposed Changes to Details of the Campaign against Japan, Plans and Operations Division "ABC" Decimal File 1942-1948, file ABC 384 Japan (3 May 44), sec. 1-B, box 428, RG 319.

30. Skates, *The Invasion of Japan*, 79-80. Marshall's staff revised MacArthur's casualty estimates downward by about twenty thousand. General Lincoln, Marshall's chief strategist, claimed that MacArthur's figures reflected planning for the worst-casualty scenario for purposes of planning evacuation of wounded and sending in of replacements; see Brower, "Sophisticated Strategist," n. 37, 329-30.

31. Extracted from Minutes of Meeting Held at the White House 18 June 1945 at 1530, Geographic File 1942-1945, CCS 381 Japan (6-14-45), sec. 1, box 640, RG 218. See also JWPC 369/1, Details of the Campaign against Japan, 15 June 1945, a report prepared by

the Joint War Plans Committee prior to the meeting that summarizes the views of the Joint Chiefs; and Memorandum for the Chief of Staff, Amplifying Comments on Planners' Paper for Presentation to the President, undated, from Gen. J.E. Hull; both in Plans and Operations Division "ABC" Decimal File 1942-1948, file ABC 384 Japan (3 May 44), sec. 1-B, box 428, RG 319.

32. See "At Last Some Japs Are Giving Up but Bloody War Still Lies Ahead," *Newsweek*, 2 July 1945, 30. This article noted that American casualties on Okinawa were roughly half the number of Japanese defenders, and therefore if three million Japanese soldiers were stationed in the Japanese home islands, an invasion of Japan would mean American losses of up to 1.5 million men. A concurrent article stated, "The arithmetic is deadly simple: if one American must be killed for every two Japanese killed, that would mean 500,000 American casualties to defeat the million men the Japanese are known to have under arms for the defense of their home islands"; see "Military Review," *New Republic*, 2 July 1945, 37-38. *Life* referred to the possibility of one million American casualties if Japan were invaded; see "Japan—An Opportunity For Statesmanship," 16 July 1945, 22. As noted in a previous chapter, reporter Kyle Palmer of the *Los Angeles Times* predicted similar losses before the war ended. See also "Why Prolong the War against Japan?" *Catholic World*, August 1945, 422.

33. Cantril, *Public Opinion 1935-1946*, 1073, 1185. In a poll conducted by the American Institute of Public Opinion (AIPO) in May 1945, 79 percent of the respondents favored taking time and saving lives as opposed to ending the war quickly with higher casualties. A survey conducted by *Fortune* magazine (June 1945, 266) showed slightly over one-third of those polled preferred strategies that would save lives, but possibly lengthen the war; see Cantril, *Public Opinion 1935-1946*, 1073. In an AIPO poll from late June, 27 percent of the respondents advocated an invasion, while 58 percent wanted to wait until the Army Air Forces and the navy have "beaten them down and starved them out"; see Cantril, *Public Opinion 1935-1946*, 1185.

34. In a cable to Marshall before the meeting of 18 June, General Arnold supported the capture of Kyushu to acquire additional air bases; Japan could then be bombed into submission. See Arnold, *Global Mission*, 566-67.

35. William D. Leahy Diaries, 18 June 1945, p. 98, microfilm reel 3, LC.

36. "Log of the First Year of B-29 Raids," *New York Times*, 10 June 1945, p. E5. Hollywood war films also tended to emphasize aerial warfare over ground combat throughout the war; see Doherty, *Projections of War*, 104-5.

37. LeMay later wrote that he did not "shed any tears for uncounted hordes of Japanese who lie charred in that acrid-smelling rubble. The smell of Pearl Harbor fires is too persistent in our own nostrils" (*Mission with LeMay*, 12); Schaffer, *Wings of Judgment*, 153, 154. The Army Air Forces, and its commander General Arnold, retained a keen interest in public relations throughout the war. Press releases, clippings from editorials relating to the bombing campaigns, news items, and even cartoons from newspapers around the country were compiled and saved; see Office of the Chief of Air Staff Scientific Advisory Group, 1941-August 1947, 1st and 2d B-29 Raids, box 2, RG 18.

38. As Michael Sherry later observed, the American public entered World War II with "an impoverished legacy of concern about air war"; the remoteness not only of aerial warfare but of the war itself made incendiary bombing more acceptable, keeping the war removed and offering the possibility of quick, clean victory (*The Rise of American Air Power*, 74-75).

39. *Chicago Daily Tribune*, 29 May 1945, p. 1.

40. "Fire in the Night," *Time*, 2 July 1945, 26. An exception to the customary ignoring of civilian casualties occurred when an Army Air Forces officer estimated that 500,000

and perhaps as many as 1.5 million people had been killed in Tokyo alone by mid-June; "Jap Millions Believed Dead in B-29 Raids," *Los Angeles Times*, 14 June 1945, p. 1.

41. For different perspectives on why the Army Air Forces gradually forsook precision bombing in Europe even before the most destructive bombing of Japan, see Schaffer, *Wings of Judgment*, chap. 5, and Crane, *Bombs, Cities, and Civilians*, chaps. 7 and 8.

42. "Wreckage of Tokyo," *Evening Star*, 31 May 1945, p. A-10.

43. Report to Dr. Edward L. Bowles, Office of Secretary of War, from Dr. D.T. Griggs of Advisory Specialist Group, Far East Air Forces for information of Col. F.M. Dean and General Arnold, 18 July 1945, Official Decimal File, 1938-1946, file 41, box 41, Henry H. Arnold Papers, LC.

44. "Japs to Limit Population of Cities in Future (Aided by Yank Raids)," *St. Louis Post-Dispatch*, 21 June 1945, p. 1. A similar article referred to a piece published in a Japanese newspaper that noted a shortage of scrap iron in Japan; see "JAPS NEED SCRAP, B-29's 'Converting' Their Plants to It," *St. Louis Post-Dispatch*, 21 July 1945, p. 2A.

45. "Air Force Day Especially Significant in West," *Los Angeles Times*, 31 July 1945, pt. 2, p. 4.

46. Jack Tarver, "Keep 'Em Frying," *Atlanta Constitution*, 25 May 1945, p. 10. Toward the end of the war Tarver produced a brief column under the heading "The Japs' Trouble Is: They're So Perishable," in which he noted, "I don't know about Japanese menus. But over here you don't get a choice of vegetables with an ultimatum" (Ibid., 12 August 1945, p. C-10). Other sources noted the importance of fire as a weapon. In early August, *Newsweek* published photographs of a Japanese soldier burning to death after being sprayed by a flamethrower, which were captioned; "One Jap's fate is a nation's if the Berlin ultimatum goes unheeded by Tokyo" (6 August 1945, 20).

47. For an overview of public attitudes about American bombing during the war with examples of earlier criticism of it, see, Hopkins, "Bombing and the American Conscience during World War II," 451-73.

48. "One Million Bombs," *Washington Post*, 16 May 1945, p. 8.

49. "Fire in Japan," *New York Herald Tribune*, 9 June 1945, p. 10.

50. "They Ask Us to Spare the Japs," ibid., 22 June 1945, p. 14.

51. Sherry, *The Rise of American Air Power*, 141-42, 292.

52. "The Atlantic Report on the World Today: The Pacific War," *Atlantic Monthly*, July 1945, 11.

53. Schaffer, *Wings of Judgment*, 137.

54. Painton, "Why We Must Bomb Japanese Cities," 82-84.

55. LeMay mentioned the dispersal of industries throughout residential areas as justification for burning civilian areas, although he maintained that the Army Air Forces did not indiscriminately bomb civilian areas (*Mission with LeMay*, 349, 384, 425). Schaffer contains remarks by LeMay as well as other Army Air Forces commanders who defended the destruction of civilian areas (*Wings of Judgment*, 151-52). The comments of Colonel Klaberer are in "Jap Millions Believed Dead in B-29 Raids," *Los Angeles Times*, 14 June 1945, p. 1.

56. Schaffer, *Wings of Judgment*, 142.

57. "Japan's Total War Compels Total Defeat," *Life*, 11 June 1945, 53.

58. "Jap Surrender Seen," *Washington Post*, 7 July 1945, p. 2. Ingram was to the Atlantic what Admiral Halsey was to the Pacific: aggressive although not always wise and ever quotable. Admiral King, chief of Naval Operations, considered Ingram "part erratic genius and part court jester," according to author Ladislas Farrago. Ingram caused a stir in January 1945, when without consulting the Joint Chiefs he announced to the press that the East Coast was imminently threatened from attack by German rockets launched from submarines; see Farrago, *The Tenth Fleet*, 11-12.

59. Broadcast of 6 July 6 1945, p. 5, folder 7, box 175, H.V. Kaltenborn Papers, SHSW.

60. Seeman, "Life in Japan Today," 12-15. Seeman's beliefs were shared by others. William M. McGovern, a member of the Office of Strategic Services, (OSS) and a political scientist, explorer, and war correspondent, served on the Army Air Forces' Committee of Operations Analysts earlier in the war and strongly advocated large-scale incendiary attacks upon Japanese cities for similar reasons, saying the Japanese tended to panic and were terrified of fire (Schaffer, *Wings of Judgment*, 118). In its August 1945 issue, *Impact*, the secret Army Air Forces magazine published during the war, described the effectiveness of dropping napalm upon Japanese soldiers: "Observers reported that the Japs who weren't killed were almost scared to death. Prisoners said that, when planes began dropping napalm, they became too frightened to do anything but run for cover—a futile gesture, because the intense heat soon forced them from whatever protection they sought. They deserted their foxholes to run around like nervous chickens" (p. 49).

61. Moley, "Attacking the Jap Mentality," 92, cited Compton Pakenham as the source of his information.

62. In another example of the pervasiveness of the belief that the Japanese were prone to panic, General MacArthur told Secretary of the Navy James Forrestal in 1945 that the trait was shared by other "Orientals." Whenever their basic strategy was thwarted, according to MacArthur, "Orientals" panicked; see Hoopes and Brinkley, *Driven Patriot*, 201.

63. "Fighting Fire with Fire," *Indianapolis Star*, 16 July 1945, 8. "What Is the Score?" a letter from Robert T. Bean of Glendora, California, to *Time*, 6 August 1945, 10, 12, was an exception and argued that those who protested the "obliteration bombing" of Japanese cities were trying to alert the public that American military leadership was "running wild as it perpetrates one of the most terrible massacres of civilians in human history." The issue in which the letter appeared bore the date that the atomic bomb was dropped on Hiroshima.

64. "Blazing Tokyo Symbolizes Doom That Awaits Every Big Jap City," *Newsweek*, 4 June 1945, 41-42; "The Levelling Of Tokyo," *Christian Century*, 6 June 1945, 667.

65. "Ministers Ask for Statement of Japanese War Aims," *Christian Century*, 27 June 1945, 747.

66. "A Statement on Our Policy toward Japan," *Christianity and Crisis* 5, no. 11 (25 June 1945); Papers of Harry S. Truman, Official File, OF 197 Misc. (1945-1946), box 685, HSTL. See also "What Is Military Necessity?" i, 2 July 1945, 80.

67. McNeal, *Harder Than War*, 65-70. Until the dropping of the atomic bombs, the few statements condemning bombing pertained to bombing in Europe.

68. Broadcast of 30 May 1945, pp. 4-5, folder 3, box 175, H.V. Kaltenborn Papers, SHSW.

69. LeMay, *Mission with LeMay*, 373; Schaffer, *Wings of Judgment*, 138-39.

70. "Gen. Arnold Says Japs Can't Take Bombings," *Washington Post*, 10 May 1945, p. 2.

71. Joseph Hanlon, "Superfortress Chief Thinks B-29's Can Wipe Out Japanese Industry; Cites Ruin of Five Major Cities," *St. Louis Post-Dispatch*, 20 June 1945, p. 1B.

72. "Guesses and Explosives," *Time*, 30 July 1945, 27.

73. Lindesay Parrott, "Shortages Blight Japan's Air Power," *New York Times*, 16 July 1945, p. 5.

74. "Invasion of Japan in Overwhelming Force Promised," *St. Louis Post-Dispatch*, 30 July 1945, p. 2A.

75. *Chicago Daily Tribune*, 14 July 1945, p. 1.

76. This was Rear Adm. DeWitt C. Ramsey, chief of staff to Adm. Raymond A. Spruance. "Crushing Invasion of Japan Planned," *New York Times*, 30 July 1945, p. 3.

77. "Crescendo of Doom," *Washington Post*, 11 July 1945, p. 8.

78. "Japan Can Be Bombed Out of War, Says Gen. Giles," *St. Louis Post-Dispatch*, 28 July 1945, p. 3A.

79. Lindesay Parrott, "Arnold Sees Japan Razed in 18 Months," *New York Times*, 19 June 1945, p. 5.

80. Al Dopking,"B-29s Will Be Lacking Targets by Christmas, Augurs Air Boss LeMay," *Washington Post*, 22 July 1945, p. 2B.

81. Memorandum for the Secretary of War, from Robert A. Lovett, 31 July 1945, Stimson "Safe File," Aircraft Air Corps General, box 1, RG 107.

82. Gayn, "Terror in Japan," 11-12, 59.

83. Broadcast of 21 June 1945, pp. 3-5, box 26, Raymond Gram Swing Papers, LC.

84. "The Real Air War Begins," *New York Times*, 15 May 1945, p. 18. For a restatement of the same views see the editorial, "Strategic Bombing of Japan," ibid., 30 May 1945, p. 18.

85. "LeMay Tells Japanese People Where 'Superforts' Will Hit," ibid., 28 July 1945, pp. 1, 3.

86. When he proposed the leaflet campaign, LeMay called it "a powerful psychological weapon which can be used to convince the Japanese people and certain articulate minority groups of our own people that our Air Force policy is aimed at destruction of the war-making industrial capacity of Japan and not at the Japanese people" (Priority Message from Headquarters, 21st Bomber Command, Guam to War Department, 16 July 1945, Headquarters 20th Air Force Office of the Commanding General Numeric File 1944-1945, file 12 Psychological Warfare, box 101, RG 18.

87. David Lawrence, "Japan Believed Here on Verge of Collapse," *Evening Star*, 1 August 1945, p. A-10. Sen. Richard B. Russell (D-Ga.) echoed Lawrence's criticism in a telegram to Truman in early August, urging Truman to halt "this showmanship" because he believed the Japanese would place American prisoners within the warned cities (Telegram from Richard B. Russell to the President, 7 August 1945, Papers of Harry S. Truman, Official File, OF 197 Misc. [1945-1946], box 685, HSTL).

88. *Evening Star*, 4 August 1945, p. 1.

89. John Shirley Hurst, "Babe Ruth and Air Power," in "What Goes On," *Washington Post*, 30 July 1945, p. 2.

90. "Through Japan's Door," ibid., 22 June 1945, p. 14.

91. "Letters to the Star," "'Rush' to the Orient," *Evening Star*, 24 July 1945, p. A-6.

92. Gill Robb Wilson, "The Air World" column; "Air Power May Force Japan to Quit," *New York Herald Tribune*, 28 May 1945, p. 10; idem, "The Air World," column; "Saturation Bombing Missed at Okinawa," ibid., 27 June 1945, p. 6; W. Pratt, "Can Air Power Bring Tokyo to Terms?" 48; idem, "Summarizing Japan's Military Position," 44.

93. Maj. George Fielding Eliot, "Blockade and Assault," *Evening Star*, 14 May 1945, p. A-8; Selden Menefee, "Blockade of Japan," in "Pacific Affairs," *Washington Post*, 21 July 1945, p. 5; T. Johnson, "Doom over Japan," 236-41.

94. "Blockade of Japan," *New York Times*, 9 May 1945, p. 22; "The Roads to Tokyo," ibid., 26 May 1945, p. 14.

95. E. Jones, "Japan's Secret Weapon," 44-47.

96. Maj. George Fielding Eliot, "Kinkaid Discusses Jap War," *Evening Star*, 5 July 1945, p. A-12.

97. Hailey, "The War Converges on Japan," 599.

98. Memo from J.W. Stilwell for JCS, Official Decimal File 1938-1946, SAS Japan 385, box 115, Henry H. Arnold Papers, LC.

99. Brooks Atkinson, "The Vast Job in the Vast Pacific," *New York Times Magazine*, 13 May 1945, p. 32; Bruce Rae, "Okinawa Is a Lesson for Invasion of Japan," *New York Times*, 27 May 1945, p. E3.

100. "'Damage on Our Side Is Light,' Says Jap Radio," *Chicago Daily Tribune*, 15 July 1945, p. 9; "Perfect Invasion Defense, Tokyo Says," *Washington Post*, 15 June 1945, p. 2; "Nip Spokesman Sees 'Ghastly Landing' by Yanks in Japan," *Los Angeles Times*, 19 June 1945, p. 2; "Japs Claim to Have Vast Underground Defense System," *St. Louis Post-Dispatch*, 6 June 1945, p. 2A.

101. Barnet Nover, "Road of Surrender," *Washington Post*, 31 July 1945, p. 8. For specific examples see "Tokyo Calls Japan Fortress of Caves," *New York Times*, 7 June 1945, p. 3; "Japanese Women Are Told to Fight," ibid., 17 June 1945, p. 4; "Tokyo Previews Japan's Invasion; Pictures Suicide Defense Blows," ibid., 3 July 1945, p. 3; "Enemy Says Forts Will Girdle Japan," ibid., 5 July 1945, p. 2; "Waiting," *Time*, 9 July 1945, 39. *Time* regularly discussed the content of such broadcasts, including the most recent one mentioned in this article, during which a Japanese spokesman proclaimed; "The sooner the enemy comes, the better for us, for our battle array is complete."

102. Barnet Nover, "Hungry Japan," *Washington Post*, 14 July 1945, p. 4. General Kenney also speculated that a shortage of food might cause Japan's surrender; see Lindesay Parrott, "Kenney Says Japan Faces Food Dearth," *New York Times*, 9 June 1945, p. 3.

103. *Chicago Daily Tribune*, 23 June 1945, p. 1.

104. For comments by Gen. Joseph Stilwell see "Landing Necessary, Stilwell Says," *New York Times*, 7 July 1945, p. 3; see also "Gen. Stilwell Thinks Air Force to Lose Bets on Length of War," *Washington Post*, 7 July 1945, p. 2. See also the comments of Maj. Gen. Archibald V. Arnold, commander of the Seventh Army Division, who said he spoke as "an old foot soldier" when he told reporters that only an invasion of Japan would end the war; "Okinawa Leader Sees Need of Invading Japan," *Los Angeles Times*, 14 July 1945, pt. 2, p. 1. Lt. Gen. Holland Smith predicted the war would end within six months but refused to respond to queries that he expound on the necessity of an invasion; see "'Howlin' Mad' Smith Gives Japs 6 Months," *St. Louis Post-Dispatch*, 28 July 1945, pp. 1, 3.

105. "No. 1 Priority," *Time*, 21 May 1945, 28.

106. "Landing on Japan 'Easy,' Barbey Says," *New York Times*, 15 July 15, 1945, p. 2; "Invasion of Japan Easy, Barbey Says," *Washington Post*, 15 July 1945, p. 2. Barbey, a veteran commander of the Seventh Amphibious Force, served under General MacArthur in the southwest Pacific, where he conducted over fifty amphibious operations.

107. Robert Trumbull, "Geiger Sees Japan Ripe for Invasion," *New York Times*, 7 July 1945, pp. 1, 3; "U.S. Can Invade Japan 'With No Trouble' at Any Time, Geiger Says," *St. Louis Post-Dispatch*, 7 July 7, p. 2A. Maj. Gen. William H. Gill, commander of the Thirty-Second Infantry Division in the Philippines, also said American troops had the advantage of greater intelligence; see "Japan Likely to Use Caves for Defense," *Washington Post*, 15 July 1945, p. 2.

108. Broadcast of 21 June 21 1945, p. 1, folder 6, box 175, H.V. Kaltenborn Papers, SHSW. Raymond Gram Swing contended that any bases established in China would only be used to assist in the invasion of Japan; see broadcast of 21 June 1945, p. 5, box 26, Raymond Gram Swing Papers, LC. Maj. George Fielding Eliot also regarded any landings in China as secondary to the main assault on Japan; see "Next Pacific Landing," *Evening Star*, 23 June 1945, p. A-8.

109. "Increasing Tempo in Pacific," *Los Angeles Times*, 5 July 1945, pt. 2, p. 4.

110. "Tokyo Reports More War Plants Are Being Moved to Manchuria," *St. Louis Post-Dispatch*, 29 June 1945, p. 2A; "New Suicide Weapons Will Amaze World, Tokyo Says," ibid., 28 June 1945, p. 14A; "Japs Brag New Suicide Weapon Will Save Isles," *Chicago Daily Tribune*, 29 June 1945, p. 2; "Japs Boast of Double Sure Hit Secret Weapon," ibid., 22 July 1945, p. 6.

111. In March 1945 Gen. Albert C. Wedemeyer said that an invasion of Japan must be launched as soon as possible to prevent the Japanese from redeploying their armies to

Manchuria and Korea; Minutes of Meeting on 7 March 1945, 191st Meeting, Combined Chiefs of Staff Decimal File 1942-1945, CCS 334 Joint Staff Planners (9-11-44), box 213, RG 218; Conference with Commanding General, U.S. Forces in China Theater, JCS 192d Meeting, 13 March 1945, JCS Decimal File 1942-1945, CCS 334 JCS (2-2-45) (Meetings 186th thru 194th), box 196, RG 218. A report by the Joint Intelligence Committee, (JIC 259/1, Industrial War-Making Potential of Japan, 29 March 1945) concluded that if the Japanese began transferring industries to Manchuria by 1 March 1945, it would require several years for the move to have any impact upon the war; see Plans Project Central Decimal File 1942-1954, PD 381 Japan (20 Mar 45), box 386, RG 341. See also Robert E. Smith, "Army, Navy Deny Japs Can Move War Plants," *Washington Post*, 1 July 1945, p. 3M; "No Safe Place," ibid., 2 July 1945, p. 8. The *Washington Post* believed the stories should be seriously considered but doubted that the transfer of industry to Manchuria would prolong the war. The *Los Angeles Times* scoffed at the reports and said that Japan lacked the ships to achieve a massive relocation of its industry ("Japan's Invasion Jitters Grow," 30 June 1945, sec. 2, p. 4). Commentator H.V. Kaltenborn also doubted that Japan could successfully transfer industries to China; broadcast of 29 June 1945, pp. 1-2, folder 6, box 175, H.V. Kaltenborn Papers, SHSW. See comments of Rep. Mike Mansfield (D-Mont.), in "Jap Prison Treatment of Americans Shows Improvement," *Washington Post*, 10 July 1945, p. 5.

112. Gladstone Williams, "Japs Show Signs of Desperation," *Atlanta Constitution*, 4 July 1945, p. 6.

113. Hanson W. Baldwin, "Blows to Crush Japan Are Now Foreshadowed," *New York Times*, 20 May 1945, p. E5; idem, "Problems of Supply Dominant in Far East," ibid., 17 June 1945, p. E5; idem, "Japan's Industrial Power," ibid., 22 June 1945, p. 2; idem "Main Battle for Oil Now Joined in Pacific," ibid., 8 July 1945, p. E5.

114. Idem, "1,000 Plane Blows Daily Is Prospect for Japan," ibid., 3 June 1945, p. E3.

115. Idem, "Japan's Main Defense Is Her Powerful Army," ibid., 22 July 1945, p. E5; "Air Lessons of Europe Used in Bombing Japan," ibid., 15 July 1945, p. 4B.

116. *Fortune*, June 1945, 266.

117. "Doomsday Picture," *Evening Star*, 19 July 1945, p. A-13.

8 Unconditional Surrender

1. "Japan Rejects," *New York Times*, 30 July 1945, p. 18.

2. Sigal, *Fighting to a Finish*, 88, 92, 95; Skates, *The Invasion of Japan*, 252-53.

3. Truman, *Memoirs*, 1:42. Truman noted the approval he received when he reiterated the policy of unconditional surrender during his first address to Congress as president: "I was applauded frequently, and when I reaffirmed the policy of unconditional surrender the chamber rose to its feet." He said that any capitulation was compelled by the victor in a war, "whether the surrender terms by conditional or unconditional," and observed that unconditional surrender did not guarantee that future generations would remember a war as a victory, citing the War of 1812 as proof that a defeat could be portrayed as a triumph. "If there is any reason for unconditional surrender," he wrote, "it is only the practical matter of taking over a defeated country and making its control easier." He rejected the notion of requiring unconditional surrender "for moral or educational purposes" (see pp. 208-10).

4. Butow, *Japan's Decision to Surrender*, 103-11; Sigal, *Fighting to a Finish*, 26-86, especially 59-64; Bernstein, "Understanding the Atomic Bomb and the Japanese Surrender," 241-44. Alperovitz, *The Decision to Use the Atomic Bomb*, chaps. 18, 23.

5. Frederick Kuh, "Jap Peace Bid Is Reported," *Washington Post*, 9 May 1945, pp. 1, 6. Numerous letters to the White House and the State Department mentioned the

Kuh article and asked if it was accurate. See also Alfred Wagg, "Latest Rumor on Jap Peace: Within 10 Days," *Chicago Daily Tribune*, 22 May 1945, p. 3; Washington Notes, *New Republic*, 21 May 1945, 708; "Admissions of Defeat by Nipponese," *Atlanta Constitution*, 26 May 1945, p. 4; "Wave Of Peace Feelers From Japs Rumored," *Chicago Daily Tribune*, 18 May 1945, p. 5; George Axelsson, "Stockholm Hears Tokyo Peace Tale," *New York Times*, 16 June 1945, p. 3. For an account of the actual peace feelers that prompted these stories see Sigal, *Fighting to a Finish*, 26-86.

6. "No Diversion from This Job!" *Los Angeles Times*, 18 May 1945, sec. 2, p. 4. This point of view was similar to one expressed by the former ambassador to Japan, Joseph Grew, in a speech he delivered in 1943. He asserted that jujitsu, the Japanese art of self-defense, offered hints about Japanese military tactics. "The essence of this art," Grew explained, "it that by letting the adversary take the initiative and by giving way and simulating defeat the adversary may be lulled into dropping his guard; then when the adversary has advanced too far and is off balance, he is destroyed by a quick recovery and a lightning attack where he is weakest" (*Turbulent Era*, 2: 1396-97).

7. "'Annoyed' Japs Deny Stories of Peace Feelers Have Basis," *Washington Post*, 20 May 1945, p. 2; "New Jap Moves Arouse Peace Talk in Capital," *Chicago Daily Tribune*, 20 May 1945, p. 8. See also the comments of Japanese government spokesmen in "Japs Again Deny Seeking Way Out of War; Tokyo Radio Blames 'Rumors' on Allies," *Washington Post*, 20 June 1945, p. 5.

8. For the text of the Cairo Declaration see U.S. Department of State, *Bulletin*, 9 (4 Dec. 1943):393. See also "Now Japan," *Washington Post*, 9 May 1945, p. 10. Halsey's racist and derogatory statements about the Japanese during the war were widely reported, and most Americans were familiar with his motto, "Kill Japs, kill Japs, kill more Japs." Paul V. McNutt, chairman of the War Manpower Commission, gained notoriety in April 1945 when he told an audience in Chattanooga, Tennessee, that he favored "the extermination of the Japanese in toto." Asked if he meant the military or the people of Japan, he said the latter, "for I know the Japanese people." A few days later he said the opinion was his own and not that of the government. In his speech, McNutt had stressed the necessity of ending the war quickly with minimal casualties. The former high commissioner of the Philippines, McNutt said he departed from his prepared remarks "out of an overwhelming anxiety to complete the war in the Pacific against an enemy whose fanatic disregard for human values became familiar to me during the years I lived in the Pacific"; see "McNutt for Erasing Japanese," *New York Times*, 6 April 1945, p. 5, and "M'Nutt Explains Speech," ibid., 13 April 1945, p. 10.

9. "Mr. Grew on Peace," *Washington Post*, 13 July 1945, p. 14; see also, "Fatal Phrase," ibid., 11 June 1945, p. 11. At times, the *Washington Post* employed stereotypes to make its point. In one editorial that again criticized comments by individuals who had spoken in favor of exterminating the Japanese, the editors said that because the Japanese were "phenomenally submissive" and "much more obedient than children in our own country," the United States should employ "verbal warfare" to convince Japanese leaders that America did not intend to annihilate Japan ("Inside Japan," 12 June 1945, p. 8).

10. "Power v. Statesmanship," *Time*, 16 July 1945, 13.

11. "On to Tokyo and What?" *Life* 21 May 1945, 32; "Japan—An Opportunity for Statesmanship," ibid., 16 July 1945, 22-23.

12. Hanson W. Baldwin, "Ideas Can Fight Japan," *New York Times*, 18 July 1945, p. 4.

13. Walter Lippmann, "Terms for Japan," *St. Louis Post-Dispatch*, 16 July 1945, p. 3B.

14. Gladstone Williams, "We Should Define Our Surrender Terms," *Atlanta Constitution*, 7 June 1945, p. 8.

15. Broadcasts of 28 June 1945, p. 3, file 6; 11 July 1945, pp. 5-6, file 8; 17 July 1945, pp. 5-10, file 8; all in box 175, H.V. Kaltenborn Papers, SHSW.

16. Broadcast of 6 June 1945, p. 1, box 26, Raymond Gram Swing Papers, LC.

17. Norman Thomas, "Mr. Thomas Says Hard Terms Imposed on Japan Prolong War," in "Letters to the Times," *New York Times*, 21 May 1945, p. 18; see also idem, "Terms for Japan Suggested," ibid., 24 July 1945, p. 22 (these opinions were previously expressed in Thomas's book, *What Is Our Destiny?*). See also Chatfield, "Norman Thomas," in *Peace Heroes in Twentieth Century America*, ed. DeBenedetti, 105-17.

18. Letter from the Fellowship of Reconciliation to the Honorable Harry S. Truman, 9 May 1945, 740.00119 PW/5-945; letter from Women's International League for Peace and Freedom, California State Branch, to Hon. Harry S. Truman, 25 May 1945, 740.00119 PW/5-2545; both in Department of State (DOS) 1945-1949 Central Decimal File, box 3923, RG 59.

19. Letter from Matthew Woll, Second Vice President of the American Federation of Labor to Hon. Harry S. Truman, 5 July 1945, 740.00119 PW/7-545; DOS 1945-1949 Central Decimal File, box 3923, RG 59.

20. Stanley Washburn, "Understanding Asked," in "Letters to the Times," *New York Times*, 8 July 1945, p. 8E. Washburn's views and those of Bishop Tucker of New York, with whom he conferred, are also contained in a letter that Washburn wrote to Joseph Grew on 22 June 1945, Stimson "Safe File," Japan folder, RG 107. See also Moley, "Attacking the Jap Mentality," 92; "Japanese Peace Terms," *Evening Star*, 20 July 1945, p. A-4.

21. "A Moment for Taking Stock," *Commonweal*, 1 June 1945, 155; "Definite Terms for Japan," ibid., 15 June 1945, 203-4 (quotation is from 203); "Japan and the Far East," ibid., 29 June 1945, 251.

22. Howard, "America, Japan, and Russia," 547-49 (Howard had lived in Japan from 1916-1921, working as a correspondent for American and British newspapers); Morley, "What Unconditional Surrender Means," 857-58; "Why Prolong the War against Japan?" 421-25. McNeal, *Harder Than War*, 51-52, discusses worries among American Catholic hierarchy about the spread of communism.

23. "Why Prolong the War Against Japan?" 421-25. George S. Schuyler, associate editor of the *Pittsburgh Courier*, raised similar concerns: "Now, not satisfied with pulling in our belts to feed 12,000,000 Europeans indefinitely, we are out to destroy Japanese economic life so we will have to feed them also!" (Views and Reviews, 19 May 1945, p. 7).

24. "After Okinawa, What?" *Christian Century*, 9 May 1945, 574-75.

25. An Open Letter to the President of the United States of America, 22 June 1945, Papers of Harry S. Truman, Official File, OF 197 Misc. (1945-1946), box 685, HSTL.

26. "A Statement on Our Policy toward Japan," *Christianity and Crisis*, 25 June 1945, in Papers of Harry S. Truman, Official File, OF 197 Misc. (1945-1946), box 685, HSTL. Bishop Malcolm E. Peabody of Syracuse, New York, son of Rev. Endicott Peabody, founder and headmaster of the prestigious Groton School, wrote the White House in support of the editorial; see letter of 6 July 1945, and reply from William D. Hasset, one of Truman's personal secretaries, of 11 July in the same file. Mrs. Endicott Peabody sent Truman the copy preserved in his files and indicated her sympathy with its rationale; her letter of 3 July 1945 is also in the same file.

27. "Declare War Aims, Churchmen Urge," *New York Times*, 18 June 1945, p. 5. Many of the signers of the declaration had called for a halt to the bombing of Germany in 1944 and protested the bombing of monuments in Italy. The letter was sent on behalf of the Postwar World Council, and several of the signers were listed in a brief article; see "Postwar Council Asks President to Define Terms for Japan," *Christian Century*, 4 July 1945, 794.

28. "Ministers Ask for Statement of Japanese War Aims," *Christian Century*, 27 June 1945, 747. For an example of an unfavorable response see "The Gentlemen Are in Error," *Atlanta Constitution*, 4 July 1945, p. 6.

29. "They Ask Us to Spare the Japs," *New York Herald Tribune*, 22 June 1945, p. 14.

30. "Plea to Spare the Japanese," ibid., 29 June 1945, p. 12.

31. Rev. Russell J. Clinchy, "Negotiated Peace Barred," in "Letters to the Times," *New York Times*, 21 June 1945, p. 18.

32. Albert Joseph McCartney, "Pacifist Group Scored," in ibid., 27 June 1945, p. 18.

33. "What Is Military Necessity?" *Time*, 2 July 1945, 80.

34. Robert Quillen, "Plea for Japan Is Unjustified," *Atlanta Constitution*, 5 July 1945, p. 10.

35. "A Petition to the President," *Christian Century*, 27 June 1945, 750-51; the petition was printed on p. 762. See letter from Paul Hutchinson to President Harry C. (*sic*) Truman, 9 July 1945, DOS 1945-1949 Central Decimal File, 740.00119 PW/7-945, box 3923, RG 59. William D. Haslett, secretary to the president, sent the letter to the State Department. The petition was also printed in *Christian Advocate*, a Methodist newsletter; see Rev. John Evans, "Petition Seeks Definition of Terms to Japs," *Chicago Daily Tribune*, 7 July 1945, p. 10. Satisfied with the terms of the Potsdam Declaration, the editors of *Christian Century* did not present the petition, which contained over fifteen thousand signatures ("Terms for Japan," 8 August 1945, 902-3).

36. "An Act of Mercy," *Chicago Daily Tribune*, 10 July 1945, p. 10.

37. *Congressional Record*, Appendix, 79th Cong., 1st sess., 1945, 91, pt.12:A3254, A3255.

38. In his letter to Grew, Bishop Welch called the petition's purpose "admirable" but so detailed that it struck him as "almost absurd." However, he did say that he hoped Truman would clarify terms. See letter from the Committee for Overseas Relief to the Honorable Joseph C. Grew, of 12 July 1945, and the letter from Joseph C. Grew to Bishop Welch of 18 July 1945, in DOS 1945-1949 Central Decimal File, box 3923, RG 59.

39. The White House sent most of the letters received there to the State Department, which composed brief replies that bore the signature of Erle R. Dickover, chief of the Division of Japanese Affairs. The records of the State Department at the National Archives are rather disorganized, and certainly not all of the letters received from citizens about clarifying unconditional surrender were preserved. Several members of Congress turned over similar letters to the State Department and mentioned that they were receiving a considerable amount of mail on the subject; see for example, letter from Sen. Henrik Shipstead (R-Minn.), 7 July 1945, DOS 1945-1949 Central Decimal File, 740.00119 PW/7-745, box 3923, RG 59. In a letter to General MacArthur's staff, Joseph Grew said that letters and telegrams from citizens all over the country were demanding clarification of terms of surrender; see letter to Lt. Gen. Robert C. Richardson, 25 May 1945, DOS 1945-1949 Central Decimal File, 740.00119 PW/5-1645, box 3923, RG 59. Records at the Truman Library pertaining to this topic are also incomplete, but logs summarizing correspondence received at the White House list dozens of letters from May, June, and July, calling for clarification of unconditional surrender. These included letters that suggested completely dropping the term and a few that requested a halt to the bombing of Japanese cities. Some letters were signed by several people, such as one from a man in Fergus Falls, Minnesota, that bore seventeen signatures in support of clearly defined terms. Only a few letters staunchly supported unconditional surrender. See Papers of Harry S. Truman, General File, Unconditional Surrender, box 2492, HSTL.

40. Letter from Mrs. David L. Lares to Sen. Henrik Shipstead of Minnesota, 7 July 1945, DOS 1945-1949 Central Decimal File, 740.00119 PW/7-745, box 3923, RG 59. Senator Shipstead sent the letter addressed to him to the State Department and in his cover letter noted that he was receiving "a number of letters on this subject, and shall greatly appreciate your comments."

41. Letter from Mrs. Priscilla Hopkins to Rep. Karl LeCompte, 23 July 1945, DOS 1945-1949 Central Decimal File, 740.00119 PW/7-2645, box 3923, RG 59.

42. Letter from Miss Lottie B. Owen to Hon. Harry S. Truman, 17 May 1945, DOS 1945-1949 Central Decimal File, 740.00119 PW/5-1745, box 3923, RG 59.

43. Letter from Mrs. Marie E. Osborne to President Harry S. Truman, 21 May 1945, DOS 1945-1949 Central Decimal File, 740.00119 PW/5-2145, box 3923, RG 59.

44. Letter from E. Lewis B. Curtis and Catharine S. Curtis, 14 May 1945, and letter from Elizabeth T. Johnson, 30 May 1945, both in Papers of Harry S. Truman, Official File, file OF 197 Misc. (1945-1946), box 685, HSTL.

45. Telegram from Dr. Edwin O. Kennedy to the Honorable Harry S Truman, 23 May 1945, DOS 1945-1949 Central Decimal File, 740.00119 PW/7-345, box 3923, RG 59.

46. Letter from Gullie B. Goldin to Honorable Harry S. Truman, 7 May 1945, DOS 1945-1949 Central Decimal File, 740.00119 PW/5-745, box 3923, RG 59.

47. Letter from Merlin G. Miller to His Excellency Harry S. Truman, 19 June 1945, 740.00119 PW/7-545, DOS 1945-1949 Central Decimal File, box 3923, RG 59.

48. Letter from Ruth P. Whitcomb to President Harry S. Truman, 25 July 1945, DOS 1945-1949 Central Decimal File, 740.00119 PW/7-2545, box 3923, RG 59.

49. Letter from James R. Ware to the President, 18 May 1945, DOS 1945-1949 Central Decimal File, 740.00119, PW/5-1845, box 3923, RG 59.

50. Hermens, "Peacemaking 1945," 123-29; quote is from 123. Hermens was an associate professor of politics at Notre Dame University.

51. The growing criticism of unconditional surrender was partly politically motivated. Sen. Robert A. Taft (R-Ohio), grew increasingly concerned that Truman would outspend Roosevelt's New Deal and by June 1945 was criticizing Truman publicly about domestic policy; Donovan, Conflict and Crisis, 62.

52. Congressional Record-Senate, 79th Cong., 1st sess., 1945, 91, pt. 6: 7129-30. Senate Majority Leader Alben W. Barkley (D-Ky.) questioned the wisdom of a unilateral declaration, since unconditional surrender was an Allied policy. White said that an Allied statement that clarified terms would be fine. See also "Surrender Statement Urged As Step to Make Japs Give Up," St. Louis Post-Dispatch, 2 July 1945, p. 2A.

53. Congressional Record-Senate, 79th Cong., 1st sess., 1945, 91, pt. 6: 7437-39. Taft, who had three sons in service in the Pacific, feared the cost of invading Japan and met with Truman shortly after Roosevelt's death in the hope of persuading the new president to reconsider applying unconditional surrender to Japan. Taft was even willing to concede Formosa to Japan; see Patterson, Mr. Republican, 301-02. For contemporary accounts of Capehart's statements and responses to them, see William Moore, "Capehart Asks U.S. Give Exact Terms for Japs," Chicago Daily Tribune, 13 July 1945, p. 2; "Senator Says Jap Peace Bids Should Be Made Public," St. Louis Post Dispatch, 24 June 1945, p. 2A; "Grew in Reply to Senator Denies Tokyo Peace Bid," ibid., 29 June 1945, p. 1B. Rep. Clare Hoffman (R-Mich.) supported Capehart; "Peace Rumors Bring Demand U.S. Tell Terms," Washington Post, 4 July 1945, p. 4; "Barkley Hits Capehart's Terms for Jap Surrender," ibid., 13 July 1945, p. 10. A businessman from Indianapolis wrote to Rep. George W. Gillie (R-Ind.) in support of Capehart. The man opposed compromise with Japan but said that everyone he knew endorsed finding a way to end the war; see letter from F.T. Holliday, W.J. Holliday and Co., Steel Industrial Supplies, Indianapolis, to Hon. George W. Gillie, 7 July 1945, DOS 1945-1949 Central Decimal File, PW 740.00119 PW/7-1345, box 3923, RG 59. Pickett, Homer E. Capehart, summarizes Capehart's background and his conservative outlook but does not mention his stance regarding unconditional surrender. Truman once referred to Capehart, who made his money from the manufacture of radios and jukeboxes, as "a pro-

moter gone political." In his diary, Truman sarcastically summarized a meeting with Capehart and three other senators who had recently returned from visiting Europe; see Ferrell, *Off the Record*, 48.

54. "Terms for Japan," *New York Times*, 4 July 1945, p. 12, argued that terms were sufficiently defined, while "Surrender Terms," *Evening Star*, 4 July 1945, p. A-8, said that White's proposal deserved serious and thorough evaluation.

55. Lindley, "The Jap Does Have a Choice," 31. For an example of White, Capehart, Wherry, and other senators who requested clarification of terms being labeled "soft peace" advocates, see Gladstone Williams, "Soft-Peace Advocates Render a Disservice," *Atlanta Constitution*, 28 July 1945, p. 4. Ernest K. Lindley, in "Terms for Japan," *Washington Post*, 25 July 1945, p. 9, again argued that further defining terms did not constitute an attempt to secure a "soft peace."

56. "After Okinawa, What?" *Christian Century*, 9 May 1945, 575.

57. "Power v. Statesmanship," *Time*, 16 July 1945, 13.

58. Letter from Robert Gray Taylor to Secretary James F. Byrnes, 6 July 1945, DOS 1945-1949 Central Decimal File, 740.00119 PW/7-645, box 3923, RG 59.

59. Dorothy Thompson, "A Pessimistic View of Our World Aims—Or Lack of Them," *St. Louis Post-Dispatch*, 20 July 1945, p. 3B.

60. Letter from David Frederick, Director of War Programs, Domestic Branch, to Archibald MacLeish, 3 July 1945, DOS 1945-1949 Central Decimal File, 740.00119 PW/7-345, box 3923, RG 59.

61. Text of Department of State release no. 547, 10 July 1945 is in DOS 1945-1949 Central Decimal File, 740.00119 PW/7-1345, box 3923, RG 59. "Navy Thumbs Nose at Kamikazes," *Los Angeles Times*, 11 July 1945, pt. 2, p. 4; Lansing Warren, "Grew Denies Any Tokyo Bid; Sees Tale as Divisive Tactic," *New York Times*, 11 July 1945, pp. 1, 2; "Grew Says Japs Have Not Made Any Peace Bid," *St. Louis Post Dispatch*, 10 July 1945, pp. 1, 3; "U.S. Brushes Jap Peace Feelers Aside," *Washington Post*, 11 July 1945, pp. 1, 2. Grew's statements were correct. As mentioned, the reports of Japanese peace initiatives were based on sketchy information gathered from contacts made by individual Japanese without authority of the Japanese government; Butow, *Japan's Decision to Surrender*, 103-11, and Sigal, *Fighting to a Finish*, 59-64.

62. *Congressional Record-Senate*, 79th Cong., 1st sess., 1945, 91, pt 6:7437.

63. Broadcast of 10 July 1945, p. 8, file 8, box 175, H.V. Kaltenborn Papers, SHSW.

64. "Mr. Grew on Peace," *Washington Post*, 13 July 1945, p. 14.

65. "Tokyo Denies Peace Rumors; Will Fight On," *Washington Post*, 13 July 1945, p. 2.

66. Letter from Ernest Caldecott, Minister, First Unitarian Church, Los Angeles, to Hon. Joseph C. Grew, 12 July 1945, DOS 1945-1949 Central Decimal File, PW/7-1245, box 3923, RG 59.

67. Letter from W.H. Rayner, University of Illinois, College of Engineering, Department of Civil Engineering, to Hon. Joseph C. Grew, 13 July 1945, DOS 1945-1949 Central Decimal File, 740.00119 PW/7-1345, box 3923, RG 59.

68. Letter from Paul E. Johnson to Mr. Joseph C. Grew, 15 July 1945, DOS 1945-1949 Central Decimal File, 740.00119 PW/7-1545, box 3923, RG 59.

69. The student did not type his name and the signature is illegible, but the letter was sent from Loyola Medical School in Chicago; see letter to Mr. Grew, 21 July 1945, DOS 1945-1949 Central Decimal File, 740.00119 PW/7-2145, box 3923, RG 59.

70. "The Peace Rumors," *New York Times*, 19 July 1945, p. 22.

71. "Unconditional Surrender—Another Victory," *Atlanta Constitution*, 8 May 1945, p. 10.

72. David Lawrence, "Japs Seen Watching Trend in U.S. Press," *Evening Star*, 14 July 1945, p. A-8.

73. *Congressional Record*, Appendix, 79th Cong., 1st sess., 1945, 91, pt. 12: A2821.

74. Japanese propaganda broadcasts, widely reported in the American press, often reinforced this belief. See, for example, "Nomura Attacks Our Peace Terms," *New York Times*, 9 July 1945, p. 3, which summarized a Radio Tokyo broadcast that included portions of an article written for a Tokyo newspaper by Adm. Nomura Kichisaburo, Japan's special envoy to the United States when the war began. He was quoted as saying, "Japan's set method in this war has been and is to take the heaviest toll of the enemy so as to make the enemy realize his folly." Opposing views on the issue are exemplified in the July radio discussion between Paul Hutchinson, managing editor of *Christian Century*, who endorsed clarification of terms, and Owen Lattimore, professor at Johns Hopkins University (later targeted as a communist by Sen. Joseph McCarthy), who opposed any deviation from unconditional surrender; see *The University of Chicago Round Table* "Terms or Unconditional Surrender for Japan?" 1-17.

75. Gladstone Williams, "No Reason Now to Redefine Terms," *Atlanta Constitution*, 16 July 1945, p. 6.

76. Idem. "Soft-Peace Advocates Render a Disservice," ibid., 28 July 1945, p. 4.

77. Pakenham, "With His Trick Mind, the Japanese Fools Himself," 33; idem, "The Divine Dummy: How Jap Leaders Rule," 38.

78. Barnet Nover, "Terms for Japan," *Washington Post*, 12 July 1945, p. 10.

79. "The Fortune Survey," *Fortune*, June 1945, 266. Slightly more than 84 percent of those polled opposed accepting any Japanese offer of surrender that did not allow American occupation of Japan, but the survey did not ask about clarification of unconditional surrender; 33.3 percent favored winning the war quickly, while 43 percent wanted to take more time if it meant saving lives.

80. Gallup, *The Gallup Poll*, 1:511-12; 5 percent identified General Tojo as the emperor, while others offered the names Hari-Kari, Yokohama, and Fujiyama.

81. "Job as Doorman among Ideas on What to Do with Hirohito," *Evening Star*, 7 May 1945, p. B-1. Suggested positions included having Hirohito serve as porter at the American Embassy or doorman at U.S. Army Headquarters in Tokyo.

82. "Hirohito and the Horse," *Atlanta Constitution*, 9 June 1945, p. 4. The emperor's white horse garnered considerable attention in the war's final months, mainly due to Admiral Halsey's vow to ride the stallion through the streets of Tokyo. Halsey received numerous letters that endorsed his plan, as well as bags of oats and offers of elaborate saddles. One man wrote Halsey that he intended to manufacture figurines of the admiral astride Hirohito's mount; see Subject File, The Emperor's White Horse 1945-46 and Undated, box 40, William F. Halsey Papers, LC. It was reported that the stallion, reputed to be an Arabian thoroughbred, was actually a western stock animal purchased in California; see "Hirohito Horse Just a Western Stock Animal," *Chicago Daily Tribune*, 11 August 1945, p. 5.

83. Fleisher, *What to Do with Japan*, 32-33, quotation from 33; Johnstone, *The Future of Japan*, 96-100.

84. "Terms for Japan," *New Republic*, 30 July 1945, 119-20.

85. Broadcast of 25 June 1945, pp. 1-3; box 26; quotations from broadcast of 13 July 1945, p. 3, box 27; in Raymond Gram Swing Papers, LC. Swing did say that if any American official advocated retention of the emperor, it was "high time to re-examine his credentials."

86. Ernest Lindley, "Vote on the Emperor," *Washington Post*, 16 July 1945, p. 7.

87. "Peace Feelers," *Chicago Daily Tribune*, 10 May 1945, p. 18.

88. James L. Wright, "Is Jap Peace Possible without Occupation?" *Atlanta Constitution*, 25 June 1945, pp. 1, 9.

89. "Conditional Surrender," *Washington Post*, 19 May 1945, p. 6; "Mikado," ibid., 30 May 1945, p. 8. The editors denied being among the ranks of "appeasers" by suggesting Hirohito's retention.

90. Merlo Pusey, "Japan Can Surrender," ibid., 9 May 1945, p. 11.

91. Gladstone Williams, "Hirohito Should Be Held Responsible," *Atlanta Constitution*, 3 August 1945, p. 8.

92. "Let Japanese Keep Hirohito, Say Three Republican Senators," *St. Louis Post-Dispatch*, 28 July 1945, p. 2A.

93. Letter from Mrs. Ruth Miller to Sen. Brien McMahon, 13 July 1945, DOS 1945-1949 Central Decimal File, 740.00119 PW/7-1345, box 3923, RG 59.

94. "The God-Emperor," *Time*, 21 May 1945, 33-36; quotations from 33, 36.

95. Robert Quillen, "Let Hirohito Keep His Job?" *Atlanta Constitution*, 8 May 1945, p. 10. Newspapers had reported Grew favored retaining the emperor, although Grew denied this during hearings before the Senate Foreign Relations Committee on his appointment as under secretary of state in 1944 (*Turbulent Era*, 2:1415-19).

96. *Congressional Record*, Appendix, 79th Cong., 1st sess., 91, pt. 12:A3479; Freeman's letter was originally published in the *Seattle Times*.

97. Records of DOS Relating to World War II, 1939-1945, PW/7-1645, microfilm roll 250, RG 59; taken from a column by James R. Young, *Seattle Times*, 12 July 1945, cited in a 16 July 1945 memo from S. Shephard Jones to Joseph Grew about public opinion regarding the emperor.

98. Sun Fo, "The Mikado Must Go, Says Chinese Leader, If Peace Is to Last," *Washington Post*, 29 July 1945, p. 1B.

99. Thomas L. Stokes, "We Have No Use for the Emperor," *Atlanta Constitution*, 15 August 1945, p. 9.

100. Mark Sullivan, "Hirohito's Future," *Washington Post*, 16 July 1945, p. 6. Historian Julius W. Pratt had expressed similar thoughts in 1944 when he asserted that Hirohito should not be a target of propaganda, since he was a symbol largely controlled by militarists: "It is not contended that he should be deliberately safeguarded from bomb or bullet" ("The Treatment of the Japanese Emperor," paper for the Council on Foreign Relations, PWC-147, 4 April 1944, DOS Documents of the Post-War Programs Committee, microfilm roll 2, RG 59).

101. "Bombs for the Mikado," *St. Louis Post-Dispatch*, 28 May 1945, p. 2B. For earlier examples of discussion about whether Hirohito's palace should be bombed, see Hopkins, "Bombing and the American Conscience during World War II," 471.

102. Herbert R. Hill, "As I See It," *Indianapolis News*, 7 May 1945, p. 6. One of those diplomats was Joseph Grew, who believed targeting the emperor's residence would merely increase Japanese resolve (*Turbulent Era*, 2:1411-12). See Sherry, *The Rise of American Air Power*, 301-4, for public reaction to fires spreading apparently unintentionally to the imperial grounds during raids in May 1945.

103. *Congressional Record*, Appendix, 79th Cong. 1st sess., 91, pt. 12: A2870, "Bombing the Sun God" was printed in the *Charleston* (W.Va.) *Gazette* on 6 June 1945.

104. Records of DOS Relating to World War II, 1939-1945, PW/7-1645, microfilm roll 250, RG 59; taken from an editorial, "The Fate of Hirohito," *Dayton News*, 7 July 1945, cited in a 16 July 1945 memo to Joseph Grew regarding public opinion about the emperor.

105. Herbert R. Hill, "As I See It," *Indianapolis News*, 7 May 1945, p. 6. Rep. Frank Boykin (D-Ala.) sent to the White House a letter he had received in which a friend proposed that the government announce that no shrines would be allowed in Japan after the

war. Boykin's friend reasoned this would halt kamikaze attacks because he heard a report that claimed the motivation for those who joined aerial suicide squadrons was to be memorialized as a hero in a shrine; see letter from Jack Danciger to Hon. Frank Boykin, 4 June 1945, Papers of Harry S. Truman, Official File, OF 197 Misc. (1945-1946), box 685, HSTL.

106. Holton, "The Japanese Mind," 743.

107. Letter from Rev. J. Gordon Holdcroft of the Independent Board for Presbyterian Foreign Missions, to the Secretaries of State, War, and the Navy, Senators of the United States of America and Members of the House of Representatives, 28 July 1945, 740.00119 PW/7-2845; and letter from Clarence F. McCall to the Hon. Joseph Grew, 27 July 1945, 740.00119 PW/7-2745, both in DOS 1945-1949 Central Decimal File, box 3923, RG 59. O. Gaylord Marsh, a retired consul general who had worked and resided in Japan, sent a letter to Truman that said veneration of Hirohito had to be stopped in order to salvage the souls of the Japanese people; see letter from O. Gaylord Marsh to President Harry S. Truman, 25 July 1945, DOS 1945-1949 Central Decimal File, 740.00119 PW/7-2545, box 3923, RG 59.

108. Letter from Joseph C. Grew to Rev. J. Gordon Holdcroft, August 1945 (exact date illegible), DOS 1945-1949 Central Decimal File, 740.00119 PW/7-2845, box 3923, RG 59; see also Grew, *Turbulent Era*, 2:1414-15. A March 1944 memo by the State Department's Interdivisional Area Committee on the Far East recommended that occupation forces permit freedom of worship in Japan but maintain close supervision of nationalist Shinto shrines dedicated to military heroes, which the report distinguished from older shrines dedicated to deities; see "Japan: Freedom Of Worship," 15 March 1944, in *FRUS, 1944*, 5:1207-08.

109. "Report Truman Urged to Tell Terms to Japs," *Chicago Daily Tribune*, 24 July 1945, p. 1; "Statement of Terms to End War Urged," *Washington Post*, 24 July 1945, p. 3. Wherry said he did not know who originally drafted the letter, but he provided copies for reporters.

110. "Magnuson Urges Japanese Be Told There Is No Hope of Easy Terms," *St. Louis Post-Dispatch*, 24 July 1945, p. 2A. Sen. Warren G. Magnuson (D-Wash.) countered that a slackening in the war effort rather than the policy of unconditional surrender threatened to prolong the conflict.

111. "Peril in Keeping Hirohito," ibid., 25 July 1945, p. 2B; see also "Bargaining With Japan," *New York Times*, 25 July 1945, p. 22.

9   Resolution

1. Harry Truman's comment to the sailors of the cruiser *USS Augusta* seated near him after he received word of the dropping of the atomic bomb on Hiroshima (*Memoirs*, 1:421).

2. See documents of the Interdivisional Country and Area Committee, "Japan: Political Problems: The Institution of the Emperor," originally drafted on 3 March 1944, final draft date 9 May 1944; the report was also revised by the Interdivisional Area Committee on the Far East and was composed by Dr. George H. Blakeslee, Hugh Borton, Joseph Ballantine, Eugene Dooman, Erle Dickover, and Alger Hiss (quotation is taken from a related document, "Japan: Policy in Regard to Propaganda Treatment of the Institution of the Emperor," 27 June 1944, p. 2); DOS Documents of the Interdivisional Country and Area Committee, 1943-1946, T1221, microfilm reels 1 and 3, RG 59. The Committee on Post-War Programs favored a peace document signed by the emperor; see "Japan: Terms of Surrender: Underlying Principles," memorandum prepared by the Committee on Post-War Pro-

grams, 13 November 1944, in *FRUS, 1944*, 5:1277, 1283. The Interdivisional Area Committee proposed allowing the emperor limited direction of certain administrative functions after the war; see "Japan: Political Problems: The Institution of the Emperor," memorandum prepared by the Interdivisional Area Committee on the Far East, 9 May 1944, in *FRUS*, 1944, 5:1250-54.

3. Quotation is from Corrigendum to JCS 924/15 Pacific Strategy, 26 April 1945, Enclosure, p. 244, Geographic File 1942-1945, CCS 381 Pacific Ocean Area (6-10-43), sec. 12, box 687, RG 218. Villa ("The U.S. Army, Unconditional Surrender, and the Potsdam Declaration," 81-83) studied reports of the Joint Intelligence Staff from April 1945, the early drafts of which were deemed unacceptable by the State Department because they diverted too far from unconditional surrender.

4. JIC 266/1, 18 April 1945, Defeat of Japan by Blockade and Bombardment, p. 4, Geographic File 1942-1945, CCS 381 Japan (4-6-45), box 640, RG 218.

5. JCS Memo 390, Unconditional Surrender of Japan, 29 April 1945, pp. 1-3, Geographic File 1942-1945, CCS 387 Japan (4-6-45), box 655, RG 218. See also JIC 268/1, Unconditional Surrender of Japan, 25 April 1945, ABC 387 Japan (15 Feb 45), sec. 1-A, box 504, RG 165.

6. Corrigendum to JCS 924/15 Pacific Strategy, 26 April 1945, pp. 244-45, Geographic File 1942-1945, CCS 381 Pacific Ocean Area (6-10-43), sec. 12, box 687, RG 218.

7. In his letter dated 25 May 1945, Col. Juluis Klein, a member of Gen. Robert C. Richardson, Jr.'s staff, told Merrill C. Meigs, vice president of the Hearst Corp., that he "persuaded" Richardson to give him "a very interesting draft which he prepared while coming back from Manila." Klein suggested that Meigs show the ultimatum to Truman. On 2 June, Meigs wrote to Matthew J. Connelly, one of Truman's secretaries, explaining that he and Klein had formerly worked together in the newspaper business and he asking Connelly to pass the statement on to Truman if he thought it appropriate; see Papers of Harry S. Truman, Official File, OF 197 Misc. (1945-1946), box 685, HSTL. Grew also received a copy of the later draft and in his reply reiterated his earlier statements, which he hoped had been passed on to General MacArthur. Draft sent to Grew, dated 28 April 1945, and Grew's reply of 9 May 1945, are in Records of DOS Relating to World War II, 1939-1945, PW/4-2845, microfilm reel 248, RG 59; the later draft, with Grew's reply, is in DOS 1945-1949 Central Decimal File, 740.00119 PW/5-1645, box 3923, RG 59. There is no indication that Truman directly responded to the proposed ultimatum, but it may have contributed to his antipathy toward MacArthur. Just a few days after the letter would have been shown to Truman by Connelly, assuming he did so, Truman made sarcastic references to MacArthur in his diary. Summarizing activities that occurred during a cruise on the presidential yacht with advisers including Connelly, Truman noted discussion over "what to do with Mr. Prima Donna, Brass Hat, Five Star MacArthur" (Ferrell, *Off the Record*, 47). MacArthur's later attempt to undercut Truman and the State Department by issuing a belligerent statement intended to induce North Korean forces to enter armistice negotiations during the Korean War influenced Truman's decision to relieve him as overall commander of the United Nations forces.

8. Copies of Hoover's papers and a cover letter from Truman dated 9 June 1945, are in Stimson "Safe File," Japan (After 7/41), box 8, RG 107. See also Wilson, "Herbert Hoover's Plan for Ending the Second World War," 84-102, for background information about Hoover's proposals.

9. Memorandum, 4 June 1945, Stimson "Safe File," Japan (After 7/41), box 8, RG 107.

10. Memorandum of Comments on 'Ending the Japanese War,' 14 June 1945; accompanying Memorandum for the Secretary of War from Chief of Staff, 15 June 1945, states that Marshall was in substantial agreement with the evaluations; both are in Stimson

"Safe File," Japan (After 7/41), box 8, RG 107. Stimson noted the receipt of Hoover's proposals in his diary and characterized them as "interesting, rather dramatic and radical" (Henry L. Stimson Diaries, 16 May 1945, p. 2, microfilm reel 9, Indiana University Library [IUL]). Joseph Grew's thoughts about clarifying unconditional surrender supported the position of the Joint Chiefs of Staff. In his summary of Hoover's proposals Grew emphasized that the war against Japan was both a military and intellectual endeavor, and that military occupation of Japan was a necessary precondition to the fostering of democratic tendencies among the Japanese; see Memorandum for the President, 13 June 1945, Stimson "Safe File," Japan (After 7/41), box 8, RG 107.

11. In 1944 Grew had published a best-selling book, *Ten Years in Japan,* based on the diaries he kept while ambassador there. It was an unusual work for the time because it included portrayals of reasonable and intelligent Japanese leaders as well as bellicose militarists. See S. Johnson, *The Japanese through American Eyes,* 55-56, for a brief evaluation of Grew's book. In his public statements Grew always endorsed unconditional surrender, but published reports that he favored allowing the Japanese to retain the emperor prompted sharp questioning by members of the Senate Foreign Relations Committee when Grew was appointed under secretary of state in 1944. Grew contended that the issue "should be left fluid until we get to Tokyo," but he acknowledged privately that unconditional surrender would be difficult to achieve unless the Japanese were assured they could preserve their present dynasty (*Turbulent Era,* 2:1417). See also Giovannitti and Freed, *The Decision to Drop the Bomb,* 71.

12. Grew had written Secretary of State Cordell Hull in 1944, saying that more specific terms that included retention of the emperor might prompt Japan's surrender prior to an invasion (*Turbulent Era,* 2:1408-15, 1417, 1419, 1445-46). See also Sigal, *Fighting to a Finish,* 96-102. The statement that Grew gave to Truman, which was the rough draft of a message prepared by a subcommittee of the State-War-Navy Coordinating Committee, can be found in Memorandum by Joseph C. Grew, 28 May 1945, Papers of Harry S. Truman, Official File, OF 3234, box 1753, HSTL; Grew, *Turbulent Era,* 2:1423, 1428-34; *FRUS, 1945,* 6:545-47.

13. Among those opposed to Grew's ideas who did not know about the bomb was Elmer Davis, the director of the Office of War Information. Stimson's further remarks to Marshall after the meeting indicated that he preferred waiting to release a statement near to the time when the atomic bomb would be ready; see Stimson Diaries, 29 May 1945, pp. 2-3, microfilm reel 9, IUL; Millis, *The Forrestal Diaries,* 66; Grew, *Turbulent Era,* 2:1434; *FRUS, 1945,* 6:548-49; Memorandum of Conversation with General Marshall 29 May 1945, Stimson "Safe File," folder S-1, box 12, RG 107. For Elmer Davis' objections see Giovannitti and Freed, *The Decision to Drop the Bomb,* 95. Historians have disagreed about Grew's knowledge of the atomic bomb. Sigal, *Fighting to a Finish,* 115, and Skates, *The Invasion of Japan,* 235, contend that Grew knew nothing about it, while Feis, *The Atomic Bomb,* 19 n. 7, Sherry, *The Rise of American Air Power,* 304-5, and Alperovitz, *The Decision to Use the Atomic Bomb,* chap. 4, believe he did know about its development. Minutes of previous meetings of the Committee of Three show that Grew, Stimson, and Forrestal discussed the atomic bomb prior to 29 May; see Minutes of Meeting of the Committee of Three, 1 May 1945, and 8 May 1945, Stimson "Safe File," box 3, RG 107. James Forrestal's diary for 8 May recounted that Stimson informed Forrestal and Grew about the formation of the Interim Committee; Millis, *The Forrestal Diaries,* 54.

14. Letter from Joseph C. Grew to Judge Samuel I. Rosenman, 16 June 1945, Stimson "Safe File," Japan (After 7/41), box 8, RG 107; Grew, *Turbulent Era,* 2:1424, 1435-37. See also Alperovitz, *The Decision to Use the Atomic Bomb,* 60, 62-3 on the mystery surrounding Truman's decision to postpone a clarifying statement.

15. Sherwin, *A World Destroyed*, 41-42; Skates, *The Invasion of Japan*, 241.

16. Henry L. Stimson Diaries, 13 May 1945, p. 3, microfilm reel 9, IUL. See also Millis, *The Forrestal Diaries*, 52, 55, 56; Grew, *Turbulent Era*, 2:1455-57; and U.S. Department of Defense, *The Entry of the Soviet Union*, 70-71.

17. Henry L. Stimson Diaries, 19 June 1945, p. 1, microfilm reel 9, IUL.

18. Ibid., 10 May 1945, p. 5, microfilm reel 9, IUL. Stimson mentioned discussing with Marshall the delay of an invasion "until after we had tried S-1." Page 2 of the 15 May 1945 entry contains the quotation "until after my secret is out" and the remark about the remaining uncertainties of the war; the 26 June 1945 entry contains the quotation about a warning after possible use of S-1. In his talks with Truman, Stimson expressed his belief that possession of the bomb would also strengthen the United States' bargaining position with the Soviet Union. Using card-playing analogies he called the weapon a "royal flush" and a "master card"; see his entries for 14 May 1945 and 15 May 1945, p. 1. See also Hewlett and Anderson, *A History of the United States Atomic Energy Commission*, 1:350.

19. Villa, "The U.S. Army, Unconditional Surrender, and the Potsdam Proclamation," 84-86. The initial drafts of the study were reviewed by the Joint Intelligence Committee and the State-War-Navy Coordinating Committee; see JCS 1340/2, Immediate Demand for the Unconditional Surrender of Japan, 9 June 1945, Geographic File 1942-1945, CCS 387 Japan (5-9-45), box 655, RG 218. Memos for Leahy, King, and Arnold about the document are in the file, and Leahy's contains a handwritten notation at the bottom in which he stated his preference for waiting until Okinawa was captured. Stimson's views are contained in Memo for the Chief of Staff from McCloy, 20 May 1945, ABC 387 Japan (15 Feb 45), sec. 1, box 504, RG 165; the views of Military Intelligence Division are in Memo for Asstistant Chief of Staff OPD, from Maj. Gen. Clayton Bissell, 15 May 1945, in same file. In the earlier draft of JCS 1340/2, a naval strategist argued that the Japanese could make the United States look bad by pointing out the severity of American naval losses and claiming a smaller Japanese army successfully held off a larger American force; see JCS 1340/1, 9 May 1945, in Geographic File 1942-1945, CCS 387 Japan (5-9-45), box 655, RG 218.

20. JCS 1340/2 Immediate Demand for the Unconditional Surrender of Japan, 9 June 1945, Geographic File 1942-1945, CCS 387 Japan (5-9-45), box 655, RG 218. The Joint Chiefs, Stimson, Grew, and Forrestal all expressed concern about morale on the home front during the war's final months. When Stimson presented his version of a warning statement for Japan to Grew and Forrestal during a meeting in June, all of them agreed that if Japan responded negatively to such a pronouncement, it could help unify public opinion and check what they perceived to be a "deterioration of will" among Americans; see Minutes of Meeting of the Committee of Three, 26 June 1945, Stimson "Safe File," Committee of Three, box 3, RG 107.

21. Memorandum for Colonel Stimson, 28 May 1945; Memorandum for the Chief of Staff, 30 May 1945, Stimson "Safe File," Japan (After 7/41), box 8, RG 107. At the Committee of Three meeting on 12 June, Stimson said he did not object to dropping the phrase unconditional surrender if the United States could still accomplish all of its strtegic objectives; see Minutes of the Meeting of the Committee of Three, 12 June 1945, Stimson "Safe File," Committee of Three, State, War, Navy Minutes of Meetings, box 3, RG 107.

22. Memorandum for Colonel Stimson, 28 May 1945, from J.J.McC. (John J. McCloy); Memorandum for the Chief of Staff, 30 May 1945, from Secretary of War; in Stimson "Safe File," Japan (After 7/41), box 8, RG 107. Memo from Chief of Staff to Secretary of War 7 June 1945, ABC 387 Japan (15 Feb 45), sec. 1, box 504, RG 165; Memo for Secretary of

War, 9 June 1945, from Chief of Staff, Stimson "Safe File," Japan (After 7/41), box 8, RG 107 (only last sentence and quotation are based on this memo).

23. The report added that exact terms could possibly end the war "before too many of our Allies are committed there and have made substantial contributions toward the defeat of Japan"; see Terms of Japanese Surrender, undated, but included in sheaf labeled 10 July edition, in OPD Executive Files 1940-1945, file 5, item 21A, tab 62, box 32, RG 165. The reference to excluding other powers may apply to both Britain and Russia. In the same file is a document which concluded that the United States should seek Soviet participation in the war against Japan. Although Churchill desired that the British have as large a role as possible in the Pacific, the Joint Chiefs were less than enthused at the prospect. Admiral King consistently opposed it, and even Marshall advised Truman that British participation "in some ways would constitute an embarrassment." King considered Russian participation desirable, but not indispensable. See Extracted from Minutes of Meeting Held at the White House, 18 June 1945, at 1530, JCS Decimal File, CCS 334 JCS Meetings (2-2-45), (Meetings 186th-194th), box 196, RG 218.

24. Extracted from Minutes of Meeting Held at the White House, 18 June 1945, at 1530, Geographic File 1942-1945, CCS 381 (6-14-45), sec. 1, box 640, RG 218. For McCloy's comments see Bird, *The Chairman*, 244-47; see also Alperovitz, *The Decision to Use the Atomic Bomb*, 67-72 for a discussion of the evidence concerning McCloy's proposal. Summarizing the meeting in his diary, Admiral Leahy wrote, "It is my opinion at the present time that a surrender of Japan can be arranged with terms that can be accepted by Japan and that will make fully satisfactory provision for America's defense against future trans-Pacific aggression" (William D. Leahy Diaries, 18 June 1945, p. 99, microfilm reel 3, LC).

25. Brower, "Sophisticated Strategist," 332-35; Villa, "The U.S. Army, Unconditional Surrender and the Potsdam Declaration," 87-89.

26. Memorandum for the Secretary, Interpretation of Japanese Unconditional Surrender, 6 July 1945, DOS 1945-1949 Central Decimal File, 740.00119 P.W./7-645, box 3923, RG 59; in the same file is a nearly identical memo from MacLeish to Dean Acheson, dated 5 July. See also *FRUS, Conference of Berlin*, 1:895-97, 900-1; Giovannitti and Freed, *The Decision to Drop the Bomb*, 186. Acheson later regretted his views (*Present at the Creation*, 112-13). Although Acheson was acting as a kind of liaison between the State Department and Congress, he described his objection to retention of the emperor in terms of his own belief that Hirohito was a weak leader who had been manipulated by the military. He did not cite congressional or public opinion.

27. Memorandum for the President, Proposed Program for Japan, along with an explanatory cover letter are in Stimson "Safe File," Japan (After 7/41), box 8, RG 107; see also Henry L. Stimson Diaries, 2 July 1945, microfilm reel 9, IUL. Stimson's proposal, like those that Grew had proposed to Truman, was influenced by plans prepared by the State-War-Navy Coordinating Committee's Subcommittee on the Far East in early 1945; see Borton, *American Presurrender Planning for Postwar Japan*, 24.

28. Henry L. Stimson Diaries, 2 July 1945, microfilm reel 9, IUL.

29. Messer, *The End of an Alliance*, 3, 7-9, 67-70; Robertson, *Sly And Able*, 390-95; Alperovitz, *The Decision to Use the Atomic Bomb*, 196-200.

30. Hull reiterated his view in a subsequent telegram to Byrnes; Messer, *The End of an Alliance*, 8-9, 73; Hull, *The Memoirs of Cordell Hull*, 2:1593-94; *FRUS, Conference of Berlin*, 2:1267-68. In his study of Byrnes, David Robertson, who believes Byrnes did fear a negative reaction from Congress and the public if the U.S. made a guarantee about the emperor, argued that Byrnes "trusted Hull's political judgment implicitly, as only one secretary of state who had run successfully for elective office could trust another former secretary who had also spent time on the Democratic party stumps. (Stimson had never

run for public office.)" Actually, Stimson was the unsuccessful Republican candidate for the governorship of New York in 1910. Perhaps Byrnes sought Hull's advice as a fellow southerner and someone outside the eastern establishment background of Stimson; see Robertson, *Sly And Able*, 418-19. Alperovitz, *The Decision to Use the Atomic Bomb*, 307-8, downplays Hull's influence on Byrnes; see idem, ibid., chaps. 24-25 regarding Truman's and Byrnes's decision to omit any reference to Hirohito from the Potsdam Declaration.

31. "Proclamation Calling for the Surrender of Japan," in *FRUS, Conference of Berlin*, 2:449-50. See also Alperovitz, *The Decision to Use the Atomic Bomb*, 232-38, 241-47, 271-75, 298-303, 310-12 concerning Truman's and Byrnes's decision to omit any direct reference to the emperor from the Potsdam Declaration.

32. "Buzzes with Peace Speculation," *New York Times*, 28 July 1945, p. 3.

33. "Japan," *Life*, 6 August 1945, 20; "Terms to Japan," *Washington Post*, 27 July 1945, p. 14; Ernest K. Lindley, "People Laud Ultimatum for Japan," ibid., 29 July 1945, p. 5B; "Surrender or Be Destroyed," *Los Angeles Times*, 27 July 1945, pt. 2, p. 4; "Attention, Tokyo!" *Time*, 6 August 1945, 32.

34. David Lawrence, "Surrender by Japan in Sight, Says Writer," *Evening Star*, 27 July 1945, p. A-4.

35. "Domei's Reply," ibid., 28 July 1945, p. A-6.

36. Hanson W. Baldwin, "Terms for Japan," *New York Times*, 23 July 1945, p. 18.

37. Gladstone Williams, "Hirohito Should Be Held Responsible," *Atlanta Constitution*, 3 August 1945, p. 8.

38. "Hirohito in the Potsdam Statement," *St. Louis Post-Dispatch*, 28 July 1945, p. 4A.

39. Broadcast of 26 July 1945, p. 10, file 9, box 175, Papers of H.V. Kaltenborn, SHSW.

40. Correspondence ("Top Secret") of the Manhattan Engineer District 1942-1946, Subseries I, Top Secret Manhattan Project Files, file 5, Events Preceding and Following the Dropping of the First Atomic Bombs at Hiroshima and Nagasaki, Notes on Initial Meeting of Target Committees, 27 April 1945, p. 4, microfilm reel 1; Memorandum for Maj. Gen. L.R. Groves, Summary of Target Committee Meetings on 10 and 11 May 1945, p. 6, both in RG 77.

41. Correspondence ("Top Secret") of the Manhattan Engineer District 1942-1946, Subseries I, Top Secret Manhattan Project Files, file 5, Events Preceding and Following the Dropping of the First Atomic Bombs at Hiroshima and Nagasaki, Memorandum for Maj. Gen. L.R. Groves, Summary of Target Committee Meetings on 10 and 11 May 1945, p. 6, microfilm reel 1, RG 77.

42. Memorandum of Conversation with General Marshall 29 May 1945, pp. 1-2, Stimson "Safe File," folder S-1, box 12, RG 107. See Alperovitz, *The Decision to Use the Atomic Bomb*, 172 on why Marshall did not press this suggestion.

43. Hewlett and Anderson, *A History of the United States Atomic Energy Commission*, 1:344-45.

44. Ibid., 353-61; Messer, *The End of an Alliance*, 87-88; Robertson, *Sly and Able*, 398. Sherwin, *A World Destroyed*, 206-9, summarizes the decisions of the Interim Committee and its discussion about a demonstration drop of the weapon. Alperovitz, *The Decision to Use the Atomic Bomb*, 163-67, sees the work of the Interim Committee as approving a decision already made by Truman and Byrnes. Although Stimson chaired the Interim Committee, in a 1946 letter Truman cited Byrnes's work on the committee but did not mention Stimson; see idem, ibid., 173-74.

45. Hewlett and Anderson, *A History of the United States Atomic Energy Commission*, 1:365-70; Giovannitti and Freed, *The Decision to Drop the Bomb*, 145-46; Sherwin, *A World Destroyed*, 210-15, 217 (see pp. 323-33 for the views of the dissenting scientists, the Franck Report). The objections of various scientists to the use of the bomb have helped sustain

lingering suspicions about their motives, which were revived in 1994 by the publication of the memoirs of a former Soviet intelligence officer (Sudoplatov and Sudoplatov with Schechter and Schechter, *Special Tasks*, which claimed that many of the top Manhattan Project scientists supplied information about the project to the Soviet Union). See Powers, "Were the Atomic Scientists Spies?," 10-14, 16-17, which exposes the numerous flaws of this book.

46. See Roberston, *Sly and Able*, 399-406, for a good account of Szilard's meeting with Byrnes.

47. Sherwin, *A World Destroyed*, 307-8, contains Bard's views; for Strauss's see *Men and Decisions*, 192-93; see also Giovannitti and Freed, *The Decision to Drop the Bomb*, 145.

48. The order listing several targeted cities that were not to be attacked by conventional bombing raids unless otherwise instructed was issued on 3 July 1945; see Eyes Only from JCS to MacArthur, Nimitz, Arnold, 3 July 1945, War Department General and Special Staffs, OPD Executive Files 1940-1945, file 2, item 11, box 12, RG 165.

49. Groves, *Now It Can Be Told*, 273-75, quotations from 274, 275; Henry L. Stimson Diaries of 1 June 1945, p. 1, microfilm reel 9, IUL; Schaffer, *Wings of Judgment*, 143-46. See also Cary, "The Sparing of Kyoto, Mr. Stimson's 'Pet City,'" 337-347.

50. Henry L. Stimson Diaries of 21, 22, 23, 24, July 1945, microfilm reel 9, IUL. William D. Leahy now believed that Soviet participation was unnecessary, although in April 1945 he had considered it beneficial; see Leahy Diaries, 5 April, 29 July 1945, microfilm reel 3, LC. See also Sherwin, *A World Destroyed*, 223-24 and 308-14, which contains the text of General Groves's report sent to Stimson at Potsdam. On Truman's and Byrnes's attitudes about Soviet participation see Messer, *The End of an Alliance*, 102-7; Ferrell, *Off the Record*, 53, 54; idem, *Dear Bess*, 519, 520; also see Messer, "New evidence on Truman's decision," 50-56. Truman did remark that he preferred knowing if the bomb worked before journeying to Potsdam, and both Stimson and Byrnes hoped it would give the United States an advantage. But Truman's letters and diary entries indicate a genuine reluctance about attending rather than a resolve to force a confrontation with Stalin; see Maddox, *From War to Cold War*, 77-78, which cites remarks that Truman made about wishing the bomb was ready; see also Sherwin, *A World Destroyed*, 222, 225. For Truman's thoughts see Ferrell, *Off the Record*, 49, and idem, *Dear Bess*, 517-20, 522. See also Robertson, *Sly and Able*, 420-422, for insight into Byrnes's thoughts about Soviet participation.

51. Edith Wharton, *The Age of Innocence* (New York: Scribner Classic/Collier Edition, 1986), 17, 45.

52. Butow, *Japan's Decision to Surrender*, 70-71. Butow's work remains a classic account, but more recent scholarship has refined some of his assumptions; see Bix, "Japan's Delayed Surrender," 197-203; see also Bernstein, "Understanding the Atomic Bomb and the Japanese Surrender," 238-41.

53. Butow, *Japan's Decision to Surrender*, 58-72. Sigal, *Fighting to a Finish*, 45-49, characterized Suzuki as a consensus politician who was initially noncommittal about ending the war.

54. Butow, *Japan's Decision to Surrender*, 84-87, 90-92, 121-23; Sigal, *Fighting to a Finish*, 49-59.

55. Butow, *Japan's Decision to Surrender*, 93-102; Sigal, *Fighting to a Finish*, 64-71.

56. Butow, *Japan's Decision to Surrender*, 124-28; Sigal, *Fighting to a Finish*, 71-86. Togo-Sato exchanges are in *FRUS, Conference of Berlin*, 1:874-81.

57. Secretary of the Navy James Forrestal summarized the Togo-Sato exchanges in his diary (Millis, *The Forrestal Diaries*, 74-76), and Strauss related that he and Forrestal read them together (*Men and Decisions*, 188-89). The Togo-Sato exchanges are among the ULTRA and MAGIC intercepts; see SRS 1692 MAGIC no. 1170, 8 June 1945; SRS 1726

MAGIC no. 1204, 12 July 1945; SRS 1727 MAGIC no. 1205, 13 July 1945, box 15; and SRS 1728 MAGIC no. 1206, 14 July 1945; SRS 1732 MAGIC no. 1210, 17 July 1945, box 7; all in RG 457. See Alperovitz, *The Decision to Use the Atomic Bomb*, chap. 18, on Truman's knowledge of the intercepted messages.

58. Butow, *Japan's Decision to Surrender*, 145-49; Sigal, *Fighting to a Finish*, 147-153. See also Kawai, "*Mokusatsu*, Japan's Response to the Potsdam Declaration," 409-14.

59. "The Ultimatum," *New York Times*, 28 July 1945, p. 10; "The Japanese Emperor," ibid., 31 July 1945, p. 18.

60. Barnet Nover, "Road of Surrender," *Washington Post*, 31 July 1945, p. 8.

61. "Japan on the Spot," ibid, 1 August 1945, p. 8.

62. "Ultimatum to Japan," *Chicago Daily Tribune*, 30 July 1945, p. 10.

63. "Japan Rejects," *New Republic*, 6 August 1945, 152.

64. William D. Leahy Diaries, 8 August 1945, p. 140, microfilm reel 3, LC. In his entry for 9 August, Leahy noted Japanese reports of 100,000 civilians killed at Hiroshima.

65. Gladstone Williams, "Japs Facing Momentous Decision," *Atlanta Constitution*, 9 August 1945, p. 10.

66. Butow, *Japan's Decision to Surrender*, 160-76; Henry L. Stimson Diaries, 10 August 1945, p. 2, microfilm reel 9, IUL; Sigal, *Fighting to a Finish*, 224-45.

67. Sigal, *Fighting to a Finish*, 245-49.

68. Henry L. Stimson Diaries of Memorandum of Conversation with the President, 8 August 1945, included with his entry for 9 August, microfilm reel 9, IUL. Sherry, *The Rise of American Air Power*, 348, said that Stimson's remarks reflected his "genteel, unself-conscious racism."

69. Cable to the President, 7 August 1945, and Truman's reply of 9 August 1945, Papers of Harry S. Truman, Official File 196-197 Misc., OF 197 Misc., (1945-1946), box 685, HSTL.

70. Byrnes's remark quoted in Bernstein, "The Perils and Politics of Surrender," 5. See also Millis, *The Forrestal Diaries*, 83-85. Henry L. Stimson Diaries, 10 August 1945, microfilm reel 9, IUL; Sigal, *Fighting to a Finish*, 245-56.

71. Butow, *Japan's Decision to Surrender*, chaps. 9, 10; Sigal, *Fighting to a Finish*, 256-81.

72. C.P. Trussell, "Many Congressmen Are Hostile to Any Leniency to Hirohito," *New York Times*, 11 August 1945, p. 8; "Washington Views Are Split on Jap Conditional Surrender," *Washington Post*, 11 August 1945, pp. 1, 2; "Hated Hirohito Finds Little Love Wasted on Him," *Atlanta Constitution*, 11 August 1945, p. 2; "Senators Divided on Retention of Hirohito on Japanese Throne," *St. Louis Post-Dispatch*, 10 August 1945, 1C; "What of the Emperor?" *Atlanta Constitution*, 11 August 1945, 1945, p. 4; Sterling Slappey, "Atlanta Divided on Hirohito, Peace Terms, Future of Japs," ibid., 12 August 1945, pp. 1, 2.

73. "The Japanese Surrender Offer," *Los Angeles Times*, 11 August 1945, pt. 2, p. 4; "The Jap Peace Offer," *St. Louis Post-Dispatch*, 10 August 1945, p. 2C; "Hirohito as a Stooge," ibid., 12 August 1945, p. 2D.

74. "Hirohito, War Criminal," *St. Louis Post-Dispatch*, 14 August 1945, p. 2B.

75. "This Peace Is No Sell-Out," *Washington Post*, 13 August 1945, p. 8; "GI's in Pacific Go Wild with Joy; 'Let 'Em Keep Emperor,' They Say," *New York Times*, 11 August 1945, pp. 1, 4.

76. In a Gallup poll from August 1945, 85 percent of the respondents approved using atomic bombs against Japanese cities, while only 10 percent disapproved (*The Gallup Poll*, 1:521-522). In a poll conducted by *Fortune* in September 1945, 54 percent of those queried supported the use of two bombs, and 23 percent of the respondents said the United States should have used even more atomic bombs before Japan surrendered.

Only 5 percent opposed using atomic bombs at all, and 14 percent endorsed the idea of a demonstration drop over an unpopulated region to display a bomb's power, then dropping it over a city only if Japan did not surrender; see Mueller, *War, Presidents, and Public Opinion*, 172.

77. "The Peril of Victory," *New Republic*, 20 August 1945, 203.

78. "—and Murder Whiles I Smile,'" *Atlanta Constitution*, 9 August 1945, p. 8. Some of the final propaganda from Japan claimed that the Japanese possessed an atomic bomb which they intended to use against the United States; see "Japs Threaten To Use Weapon Like Atom Bomb," *Chicago Daily Tribune*, 10 August 1945, p. 1; "Nip Radio Claims Allies Stole Bomb, Vows Revenge with 'Atom' Weapon," *Atlanta Constitution*, 10 August 1945, p. 1; "Benevolent Japs Won't Use 'Atom Weapon' on U.S. Civilians," *Washington Post*, 10 August 1945, p. 3. For an account of Japanese efforts to develop atomic weapons see Wilcox, *Japan's Secret War*.

79. "The Haunted Wood," *Washington Post*, 7 August 1945, p. 8. "A Strange Place," *Time*, 20 August 1945, 29.

80. Papers of Harry S. Truman, Official File 692, Misc., Civilian Control of Atomic Energy (X)-692 A Misc., folder 692-A, Misc. (Apr.-Oct. 1945), box 1527, HSTL. This folder contains numerous letters and telegrams pertaining to the atomic bomb, including Anne Ford's letter of 9 August 1945.

81. Harold Jacobson, "Death Will Saturate Bomb Targets for 70 Years, Atomic Expert Says," *Atlanta Constitution*, 8 August 1945, pp. 1, 3. The same article appeared in the *Washington Post*; see idem, "Area Struck by Atomic Bomb Is Saturated with Death for 70 Years, Scientist Reveals," 8 August 1945, p. 1. "Bombs' Radioactivity Does Not Last— Physicist," *Atlanta Constitution*, 9 August 1945, p. 2, and "Atom Bomb's Death Rays Fade Rapidly," *Washington Post*, 9 August 1945, pp. 1. 2, resulted from Jacobson's retraction after pressure from the War Department and relentless questioning by the FBI. For more on this episode see Boyer, *By the Bomb's Early Light*, 188.

82. For examples see letters in "The Pulse of The Public," *Atlanta Constitution*, 11 August 1945, p. 4; "Letters to the Editor," *Washington Post*, 12 August 1945, p. 4B, and 17 August 1945, p. 14; and "Two Atomic Bombs," ibid., 23 August 1945, p. 10; "Views on Moral Aspects of Bomb by St. Louisans," *St. Louis Post-Dispatch*, 8 August 1945, pp. 1B, 6B; "Letters to the Star," *Evening Star*, 16 August 1945, p. A-8; letter "Ye Fools and Blind," *Time*, 27 August 1945, 2. See also Boyer, *By the Bomb's Early Light*, which analyzes response to the bomb, especially chaps. 16-19.

83. Truman, *Memoirs*, 1:417; Byrnes, *Speaking Frankly*, 262; Miles, "Hiroshima," 121-40; Bernstein, "A Postwar Myth," 38-40.

84. Letter from James L. Cate to the President, 6 December 1952 and Truman's draft reply of 31 December 1952, Student Research File (B File), Decision to Drop the Atomic Bomb, file 7, box 1, HSTL.

85. Memorandum for Mr. Lloyd, 2 January 1953, Memorandum for the President, 6 January 1953, and Truman's reply to Cate of 12 January 1953 are in same file cited above; Stimson and Bundy, *On Active Service in Peace and War*, 619.

86. Miles, "Hiroshima," 137.

87. Bernstein, "Understanding the Atomic Bomb and the Japanese Surrender," 257-58.

88. Walker, "The Decision to Use the Bomb," 97-114; Sherwin, *A World Destroyed*, 236-37.

89. Bix, "Japan's Delayed Surrender," 199.

90. Heinrichs, *American Ambassador*, 371, 384-85; Giovannitti and Freed, *The Decision to Drop the Bomb*, 150-51; Grew, *Turbulent Era*, 2:1517-19. Robert H. Ferrell has argued that Truman also blamed Grew, in part, for the controversy that erupted when Truman signed

an order restricting lend-lease in early May 1945, a move that angered the Soviets; see *Harry S. Truman: A Life*, 199.

91. Bix, "Japan's Delayed Surrender," 201-03.

92. Stimson and Bundy, *On Active Service in Peace and War*, 626.

93. Sigal, *Fighting to a Finish*, 140.

Conclusion

1. See advertisement in *New Yorker*, 26 May 1945, 61.

2. Walzer, *Just and Unjust Wars*, 113-14.

3. "The Meaning of Victory," *Life*, 27 August 1945, 34.

4. "Hirohito as a Stooge," *St. Louis Post-Dispatch*, 12 August 1945, p. 2D.

5. Sherry, *The Rise of American Air Power*, 247.

6. JIC MFI81, 21 July 1944, Joint Intelligence Committee, Memorandum for Information No. 81 Japanese Battle Morale, Plans Project Central Decimal File 1942-1954, Pd 330.11 Japan (7-21-44), pp. 2, 8, box 385, RG 341.

7. Sparagana, "The Conduct and Consequences of Psychological Warfare," 11-20. See Leighton, *Human Relations in a Changing World*, introduction, and part 2, chaps. 2, 3 for an overview of the work of the Office of War Information's Foreign Morale Analysis Division.

8. Heinrichs, *American Ambassador*, 362-66.

9. Grew even used animalistic imagery in reference to the Japanese; describing them as being "somewhat like sheep in following leaders" and comparing the relationship between the emperor and his subjects to that of a queen bee and a hive (*Turbulent Era*, 2:1387-91, 1394, 1418-19). See also "Japan: The Institution of the Emperor," statement read by Grew at meeting of the Committee on Post-War Programs, 28 April 1944, DOS Documents of the Post-War Programs Committee, PWC-146, microfilm reel 2, RG 59. See also Grew's comments to Stimson and others in mid-June about Japanese resistance; Minutes of the Meeting of the Committee of Three, 19 June 1945, Stimson "Safe File," Committee of Three, box 3, RG 107.

10. Henry L. Stimson Diaries, 18 June 1945, p. 1, and 10 August 1945, p. 2, microfilm reel 9, IUL.

11. Yankelovich, *Coming to Public Judgment*, 5-6.

12. Villa, "The U.S. Army, Unconditional Surrender, and the Potsdam Declaration," 85-87.

13. Kecskemeti, *Strategic Surrender*, 208.

14. Bix, "Japan's Delayed Surrender," 214-25; Bernstein, "Understanding the Atomic Bomb and the Japanese Surrender," 238-41.

15. Hikins, "The Rhetoric of 'Unconditional Surrender' and the Decision to Drop the Atomic Bomb," 380, 389, 397.

16. Gladstone Williams, "Expediency Dictates Keeping of Emperor," *Atlanta Constitution*, 13 August 1945, p. 6.

17. Memorandum for General L.R. Groves, Summary of Target Committee Meetings on 10 and 11 May 1945, p. 6, Correspondence ("Top Secret") of the Manhattan Engineer District 1942, Subseries 1, Top Secret Manhattan Project Files, file 5, Events Preceding and Following the Dropping of the First Atomic Bombs at Hiroshima and Nagasaki, microfilm reel 1, RG77.

18. Sherry, "Guilty Knowledge," p. 11.

19. Cal Thomas, "Shorten the War with Nuclear Bombs," *St. Louis Post-Dispatch*, 7 February 1991, p. 3C.

20. The two most influential official explanations of the use of the bomb were Truman, *Memoirs*, Vol. 1, *Year of Decisions*, and Henry L. Stimson, "The Decision to Use the Atomic Bomb," *Harper's*, February 1947, 97-107.

21. Zacharias, *Secret Missions*; see also idem, "The A-Bomb Was Not Needed," 25-29; idem, "How We Bungled The Japanese Surrender," 12-14, 16-19, 21.

22. Eisenhower, *Crusade in Europe*, 443; Leahy, *I Was There*, 441; King and Whitehill, *Fleet Admiral King*, 623. After the war, Leahy and King also disputed the idea that the only alternative to the atomic bomb was an invasion of Japan; see Leahy, *I Was There*, 259. Although he supported the plans for invading Kyushu in 1945, King later argued that siege would have defeated Japan without an invasion; see Buell, *Master of Seapower*, 490-91, and King and Whitehill, *Fleet Admiral King*, 598. Gen. Albert Wedemeyer, who had favored an invasion of Kyushu in 1945, later said that the idea of landing in Japan was a mistake (*Wedemeyer Reports*, 250). See Alperovitz, *The Decision to Use the Atomic Bomb*, chaps. 26-28 on the views of various military leaders regarding the bomb.

23. Bernstein, "Understanding the Atomic Bomb and the Japanese Surrender," 265-67.

24. Letter sent to Dr. Ira Michael Heyman, secretary of the Smithsonian, 11 November 1994; copy in author's collection. The controversy produced a voluminous amount of material. For starters see Winkler, "50 Years Later, the Debate Rages Over Hiroshima," pp. A-10, A-18-A-19; Thelen, "History after the *Enola Gay* Controversy," 1029-35; Kohn, "History and Culture Wars," 1036-1063; Harwit, "Academic Freedom in 'The Last Act,'" 1064-1082; Sherwin, "Hiroshima as Politics and History," 1085-1093; Linenthal, "Struggling with History and Memory," 1094-1101.

25. Charles Krauthammer, "Beware Revisionism about Hiroshima," *St. Louis Post-Dispatch*, 21 August 1994, p. 3B; see also the editorial "A Politically Correct Enola Gay?" ibid., 29 August 1994, p. 3B. See Walker, "History, Collective Memory, and the Decision to Use the Bomb," 319-28, for an interesting evaluation of the ways in which various sources have shaped collective memory of the reasons the atomic bombs were used; see also Lifton and Mitchell, *Hiroshima in America*, parts 1-3, and Alperovitz, *The Decision to Use the Atomic Bomb*, chaps. 35-48.

26. Buruma, *The Wages of Guilt*.

Sources

Archival Sources

NATIONAL ARCHIVES, WASHINGTON, D.C.

Record Group 18, Records of the Army Air Forces
    Central Decimal File October 1942-May 1944
    Office of the Commanding General Numeric File 1944-1945
Record Group 38, Records of Naval Intelligence through 1946
Record Group 59, Records of the U.S. Department of State (DOS)
    1945-1949 Central Decimal File
    Minutes of Meetings of the Interdivisional Area Committee on the Far East, 1943-1946, microfilm
    Minutes of Meetings of the State-War-Navy Coordinating Committee (SWNCC), 1944-1947, microfilm
    Minutes of Meetings of the Subcommittee for the Far East, 1945-1947, microfilm
    Records of the Department of State (DOS) Relating to World War II, 1939-1945, microfilm
    State Department (DOS) Documents of the Interdivisional Country and Area Committee, 1943-1946, microfilm
    State Department (DOS) Documents of the Post-War Programs Committee, microfilm
    State-War-Navy Coordinating Committee (SWNCC) and State-Army-Navy-Air Force Coordinating Committee (SANACC) Decimal Subject Files, 1944-1949, microfilm
Record Group 77, Records of the Office of the Chief of Engineers
Record Group 94, Records of the Adjutant's General's Office
    World War II Operations Reports 1940-1948 Special File
Record Group 107, Records of the Office of the Secretary of War
    Formerly Top Secret Correspondence of Secretary of War Stimson ("Safe File") July 1940-September 1945
Record Group 160, U.S. Army Service Forces, Records of the Office of The Commanding General Control Division, 1942-1946
    Operational Summaries
Record Group 165, Records of the War Department General and Special Staffs
    Combined Chiefs of Staff (CCS) Decimal File 1942-1945
    Dr. G.W. Merck's File

General and Special Staffs Geographic File 1942-1945
OPD File OLYMPIC
Operations Division (OPD) Decimal File 1945
Operations Division (OPD) Executive Files 1940-1945 (ABC Files)
Operations Division (OPD) Project Decimal File Strategy and Policy Group, OPD
Strategy Section Papers
Record Group 218, Records of the U.S. Joint Chiefs of Staff (JCS) and the Combined Chiefs of Staff (CCS)
Combined Chiefs of Staff (CCS) Decimal File 1942-1945
Geographic File 1942-1945
Joint Chiefs of Staff (JCS) Decimal File 1942-1945
Record Group 226, Records of the Office of Strategic Services
Record Group 243, Records of the U.S. Strategic Bombing Survey
Record Group 319, Records of the U.S. Army Staff Plans and Operations Division
Plans and Operations Division (OPD) "ABC" Decimal File 1942-1948
Record Group 341, Records of Headquarters, U.S. Air Force
Plans Project Central Decimal File 1942-1954
Record Group 353, Records of the Intra and Inter-Departmental Committees
Record Group 407, Records of the War Department Adjutant General's Office
Record Group 457, Japanese Intercepts, ULTRA and MAGIC

WASHINGTON NATIONAL RECORDS CENTER, SUITLAND, MARYLAND

Record Group 175, Records of the Chemical Warfare Service
General Administrative Series 1942-1945
Miscellaneous Series 1942-1945
Subject Series 1942-1945

LIBRARY OF CONGRESS, WASHINGTON, D.C.

Henry H. Arnold Papers
Ira C. Eaker Papers
Herbert Feis Papers
William F. Halsey Papers
Ernest J. King Papers
Frank Knox Papers
William D. Leahy Diaries, microfilm
William D. Leahy Papers
Curtis LeMay Papers
Carl Spaatz Papers
Raymond Gram Swing Papers

STATE HISTORICAL SOCIETY OF WISCONSIN, MADISON

H.V. Kaltenborn Papers

HARRY S. TRUMAN LIBRARY, INDEPENDENCE, MISSOURI

Papers of Eben A. Ayers
Papers of Harry S. Truman, General File and Official File

President's Secretary's Files
Student Research File (B File)

Indiana University Library, Bloomington

Henry L. Stimson Diaries, microfilm

Wartime Magazine Articles and Editorials

"After Okinawa, What?" *Christian Century*, 9 May 1945, 574-75.

"America's Midsummer Mood: War Weary, Restless, Irksome." *Newsweek*, 23 July 1945, 23-24.

"AP's False Flash on Nazi Surrender Excites Nation to Brief Celebration." *Newsweek*, 7 May 1945, 77-78.

"At Home: A Nation Rededicated." *Newsweek*, 14 May 1945, 44-45.

"The Atlantic Report On The World Today: The Pacific War." *Atlantic*, May 1945, 8, 11, 13.

"At Last Some Japs Are Giving Up but Bloody War Still Lies Ahead." *Newsweek*, 2 July 1945, 30.

"Atom Cracking May Be World Cracking." *Christian Century*, 25 July 1945, 851-52.

"Atomic Bomb Loosed against Japan." *Christian Century*, 15 August 1945, 923.

"Attack by Fire." *Time*, 4 June 1945, 35.

"Attention, Tokyo!" *Time*, 6 August 1945, 32-34.

"Baptist Missionaries Killed by Japanese in Philippines." *Christian Century*, 20 June 1945, 738.

"Blazing Tokyo Symbolizes Doom That Awaits Every Big Jap City." *Newsweek*, 4 June 1945, 41-42.

"Blood, Gas and Morality." *Time*, 18 June 1945, 30.

"Bloody Luzon." *Time*, 6 August 1945, 31.

"The Bomb." *Atlantic Monthly*, July 1945, 8, 11, 13.

"The Bomb." *Time*, 20 August 1945, 21.

"Cherry Blossom." *Newsweek*, 18 June 1945, 42.

"Cigars and Bombs." *Time*, 21 May 1945, 28-29.

"Define Terms for Japan." *Commonweal*, 15 June 1945, 203-04.

"Down with the Gumbatsu!" *Time*, 18 June 1945, 30.

"Eyes to the East." *Newsweek*, 18 June 1945, 21.

"False Alarm." *Time*, 7 May 1945, 19-20.

"Far Greater Fury." *Newsweek*, 7 May 1945, 49.

"Fire in the Night." *Time*, 2 July 1945, 26.

"The God Emperor." *Time*, 21 May 1945, 33-36.

"Guesses and Explosives." *Time*, 30 July 1945, 27.

"How Effective Is 2%?" *Time*, 16 July 1945, 22.

"Hurly-Burly Thoroughfare." *Time*, 6 August 1945, 29.

"If We Expect a Long War, Let's Act That Way!" *Saturday Evening Post*, 7 July 1945, 108.

"If Wounded, Die." *Newsweek*, 2 July 1945, 34.

"Japan." *Life*, 6 August 1945, 20.

"Japan: Double Feature." *Newsweek*, 18 June 1945, 40.

"Japanese Etch Grim War Plans with Suicide as National Weapon." *Newsweek*, 11 June 1945, 43-44, 46.

"Japan and the Far East." *Commonweal*, 29 June 1945, 251.

"Japan Foresees Victory in Suicide for Beaten People of Homeland." *Newsweek*, 18 June 1945, 39.

"Japan—An Opportunity for Statesmanship." *Life*, 16 July 1945, 22-23."

"Japan: Peace of Mind." *Newsweek*, 14 May 1945, 62.

"Japan Rejects." *New Republic*, 6 August 1945, 152.

"Japan's Total War Compels Total Defeat." *Life*, 11 June 1945, 53-59.

"The Job before Us." *Fortune*, June 1945, 113.

"The Last Weapon." *Time*, 25 May 1942, 71-72.

"The Levelling of Tokyo." *Christian Century*, 6 June 1945, 667.

"Looking on the Face of War." *Christian Century*, 18 July 1945, 829.

"Look out for Gas." *Time*, 15 June 1942, 23.

"The Meaning of Victory." *Life*, 27 August 1945, 34.

"Military Review." New Republic, 7 May 1945, 627.

———. *New Republic*, 2 July 1945, 37-38.

———. *New Republic*, 23 July 1945, 93.

"Ministers Ask for Statement of Japanese War Aims." *Christian Century*, 27 June 1945, 747.

"A Moment for Taking Stock." *Commonweal*, 1 June 1945, 155.

"My God!" *Time*, 20 August 1945, 28.

"Naval Bombardment of Jap Soil Warns Foe Final Blow Is Near." *Newsweek*, 23 July 1945, 34, 36.

"No. 1 Priority." *Time*, 21 May 1945, 28.

"Numbers Game." *Time*, 4 June 1945, 35.

"Okinawa: The End." *Newsweek*, 2 July 1945, 30.

"Okinawa Is Captured." *Christian Century*, 4 July 1945, 779.

"Okinawa: Times Square." *Newsweek*, 9 July 1945, 38.

"On to Tokyo and What?" *Life*, 21 May 1945, 32.

"The Pacific: War without Quarter." *Newsweek*, 14 May 1945, 42-43.

"The Peril of Victory." *New Republic*, 20 August 1945, 203-4.

"The Periscope." *Newsweek*, 21 May 1945, 27-28, 30.

"A Petition to the President." *Christian Century*, 27 June 1945, 750-51.

"Postwar Council Asks President To Define Terms for Japan." *Christian Century*, 4 July 1945, 794.

"Power vs. Statesmanship." *Time*, 16 July 1945, 13.

"Recent Events." *Catholic World*, June 1945, 272.

"Sealing Mindanao." *Newsweek*, 18 June 1945, 40.

"Short Cut?" *Time*, 13 August 1945, 22.

"Should the U.S. Use Gas?" *Time*, 3 January 1944, 15.

"A Strange Place." *Time*, 20 August 1945, 29.

"Terms for Japan." *New Republic*, 30 July 1945, 119-20.

"Terms for Japan." *Christian Century*, 8 August 1945, 902.

"To the Last Line." *Time*, 18 June 1945, 32, 34.

"Unconditional Surrender Defined for Japan." *Christian Century*, 1 August 1945, 875.

"The Upside-Down Japanese Mind: It Makes Our Defeat Seem Easy." *Newsweek*, 25 June 1945, 36.
"U.S. Looks into One-War Future for Outline of Home-Front Pattern." *Newsweek*, 21 May 1945, 33-40, 43.
"Victory in Europe." *New Republic*, 14 May 1945, 659-60.
"Waiting." *Time*, 9 July 1945, 39.
"Washington Notes." *New Republic*, 14 May 1945, 676.
———. *New Republic*, 21 May 1945, 708.
"What Is Military Necessity?" *Time*, 2 July 1945, 80.
"Why Are We Having a New Liquor Holiday?" *Christian Century*, 11 July 1945, 804.
"Why Prolong the War Against Japan?" *Catholic World*, August 1945, 421-25.
"Words Are Weapons." *Time*, 6 August 1945, 28.

Selected Other Sources

Acheson, Dean. *Present at the Creation: My Years in the State Department*. New York: W.W. Norton, 1969.

Adams, Henry. *Witness to Power: The Life of Fleet Admiral William D. Leahy*. Annapolis, Md.: Naval Institute Press, 1985.

Adams, Michael C.C. *The Best War Ever: America and World War II*. Baltimore: Johns Hopkins Univ. Press, 1994.

Adams, Valerie. *Chemical Warfare, Chemical Disarmament*. Bloomington: Indiana Univ. Press, 1990.

Allen, Louis. "The Campaigns in Asia and the Pacific." *Journal of Strategic Studies* 13 (March 1990): 162-92.

Allen, Thomas B., and Norman Polmar. *Code-Name Downfall: The Secret Plan to Invade Japan—And Why Truman Dropped The Bomb*. New York: Simon and Schuster, 1995.

Alperovitz, Gar. *Atomic Diplomacy: Hiroshima, and Potsdam: The Use of the Atomic Bomb and American Confrontation with Soviet Power*. New York: Simon and Schuster, 1965.

———. "More on atomic diplomacy." *Bulletin of the Atomic Scientists* 41 (Dec. 1985): 35-39.

———. *The Decision to Use the Atomic Bomb: And the Architecture of an American Myth*. New York: Alfred A. Knopf, 1995.

Anderson, Karen. *Wartime Women: Sex Roles, Family Relations, and the Status of Women during World War II*. Westport, Conn: Greenwood Press, 1981.

Appleman, Roy E., James M. Burns, Russell A. Gugeler, and John Stevens. *Okinawa: The Last Battle*. Washington, D.C.: Historical Division, Department of the Army, 1948.

Armstrong, Anne. *Unconditional Surrender: The Impact of the Casablanca Policy upon World War II*. New Brunswick, N.J.: Rutgers Univ. Press, 1961.

Arnold, H.H. *Global Mission*. New York: Harper, 1949.

Astor, Gerald. *Operation Iceberg: The Invasion and Conquest of Okinawa in World War II*. New York: Donald I. Fine, 1995.

Baldwin, Hanson W. "America at War: Victory in Europe." *Foreign Affairs* 23 (July 1945): 527-42.

Baldwin, Hanson W. *Great Mistakes of the War*. New York: Harper, 1949.

Barnet, Richard J. *The Rockets' Red Glare: When America Goes to War—The Presidents and the People*. New York: Simon and Schuster, 1990.

Batchelder, Robert C. *The Irreversible Decision: 1939-1950*. Boston: Houghton Mifflin, 1961.

Bauer, K. Jack, and Alan C. (Alvin D.) Coox. "Olympic *vs.* Ketsu-Go." *Marine Corps Gazette* 49 (Aug. 1965): 32-44.

Behr, Edward. *Hirohito: Behind the Myth*. New York: Villard Books, 1989.

Belote, James, H. and William M. Belote. *Typhoon of Steel: The Battle for Okinawa*. New York: Harper and Row, 1970.

Bennett, W. Lance. *Public Opinion in American Politics*. New York: Harcourt Brace Jovanovich, 1980.

Berkhofer, Robert F. *The White Man's Indian: Images of the American Indian from Columbus to the Present*. New York: Alfred A. Knopf, 1978.

Bernstein, Barton J. "The Atomic Bomb and American Foreign Policy, 1941-1945: An Historiographical Controversy." *Peace and Change* 2 (Spring 1974): 1-16.

———. "Roosevelt, Truman, and the Atomic Bomb: A Reinterpretation." *Political Science Quarterly* 90 (Spring 1975): 23-69.

———. *The Atomic Bomb: The Critical Issues*. Boston: Little, Brown, 1976.

———. "The Perils and Politics of Surrender: Ending the War with Japan and Avoiding the Third Atomic Bomb." *Pacific Historical Review* 46 (Feb. 1977): 1-27.

———. "Radiological Warfare: The Path Not Taken." *Bulletin of the Atomic Scientists* 41 (Aug. 1985): 44-49.

———. "Why We Didn't Use Poison Gas in World War II." *American Heritage* 36 (Aug.-Sept. 1985): 40-45.

———. "A Postwar Myth: 500,000 U.S. Lives Saved." *Bulletin of the Atomic Scientists* 42 (June/July 1986): 38-40.

———. "The Birth of the U.S. Biological-Warfare Program." *Scientific American* 256 (June 1987): 116-21.

———. "America's Biological Warfare Program in the Second World War." *Journal of Strategic Studies* 11 (Sept. 1988): 292-317.

———. "Seizing the Contested Terrain of Early Nuclear History: Stimson, Conant, and Their Allies Explain the Decision to Use the Atomic Bomb." *Diplomatic History* 17 (Winter 1993): 35-72.

———. "The Atomic Bombings Reconsidered." *Foreign Affairs* 74 (Jan./Feb. 1995): 135-52.

———. "Understanding the Atomic Bomb and the Japanese Surrender: Missed Opportunities, Little-Known Near Disasters, and Modern Memory." *Diplomatic History* 19 (Spring 1995): 227-73.

Berry, Henry. *Semper Fi, Mac: Living Memories of the United States Marines in World War II*. New York: Arbor House, 1982.

Binsse, Harry Lorin. "The House You'll Live In." *Commonweal*, 27 July 1945, 350-52.

Bird, Kai. *The Chairman: John J. McCloy, The Making of the American*. New York: Simon and Schuster, 1992.

Bix, Herbert P. "Japan's Delayed Surrender: A Reinterpretation." *Diplomatic History* 19 (Spring 1995): 197-225.

Blair, Clay Jr. *Silent Victory: The U.S. Submarine War against Japan.* New York: Bantam Books, 1985.

Bland, Larry I., ed. *George C. Marshall Interviews and Reminiscences for Forrest C. Pogue.* Rev. ed. Lexington, Va.: George C. Marshall Research Foundation, 1991.

Blum, John Morton. "The G.I. in the Culture of the Second World War." *Ventures* 8 (Spring 1968): 51-56.

———. *V Was for Victory: Politics and American Culture during World War II.* New York: Harcourt Brace Jovanovich, 1976.

Borton, Hugh. *American Presurrender Planning for Postwar Japan.* New York: East Asian Institute, Columbia University, 1967.

Bosworth, R.J.B. *Explaining Auschwitz and Hiroshima: History Writing and the Second World War 1945-1990.* London: Routledge, 1993.

Boyer, Paul. *By the Bomb's Early Light: American Thought and Culture at the Dawn of the Atomic Age.* New York: Pantheon Books, 1985.

Breines, Wini. *Young, White, and Miserable: Growing Up Female in the Fifties.* Boston: Beacon Press, 1992.

Brinkley, David. *Washington Goes to War.* New York: Alfred A. Knopf, 1988.

Brophy, Leo P., and George J.B. Fisher. *The Chemical Warfare Service: Organizing for War.* Washington, D.C.: Office of the Chief of Military History, Department of the Army, 1959.

Brophy, Leo P., Wyndham D. Miles, and Rexmond C. Cochrane, *The Chemical Warfare Service: From Laboratory To Field.* Washington, D.C.: Office of the Chief of Military History, Department of the Army, 1959.

Brower, Charles F., IV. "The Joint Chiefs of Staff and National Policy: American Strategy and the War With Japan, 1943-1945." Ph.D. diss., Univ. of Pennsylvania, 1987.

———. "Sophisticated Strategist: General George A. Lincoln and the Defeat of Japan, 1944-45." *Diplomatic History* 15 (Summer 1991): 317-37.

Brown, Frederic J. *Chemical Warfare: A Study in Restraints.* Princeton: Princeton Univ. Press, 1968.

Bruner, Jerome S. *Mandate from the People.* New York: Duell, Sloan, and Pearce, 1944.

Buell, Thomas B. *Master of Seapower: A Biography of Fleet Admiral Ernest J. King.* Boston: Little, Brown, 1980.

Buruma, Ian. *The Wages of Guilt: Memories of War in Germany and Japan.* New York: Farrar, Strauss, and Giroux, 1994.

Butow, Robert J.C. *Japan's Decision to Surrender.* Stanford: Stanford Univ. Press, 1954.

Byrnes, James F. *Speaking Frankly.* New York: Harper, 1947.

———. *All in One Lifetime.* New York: Harper, 1958.

Calvocoressi, Peter, Guy Wint, and John Pritchard. *Total War: The Causes and Courses of the Second World War.* Rev. 2d ed. New York: Pantheon Books, 1989.

Cameron, Craig M. *American Samurai: Myth, Imagination, and the Conduct of Battle in the First Marine Division, 1941-1951*. Cambridge: Cambridge Univ. Press, 1994.

Campbell, D'Ann. *Women at War with America: Private Lives in a Patriotic Era.* Cambridge: Harvard Univ. Press, 1984.

Cant, Gilbert. *The Great Pacific Victory: From the Solomons to Tokyo.* New York: John Day, 1945.

Cantelon, Philip L., Richard G. Hewlett, and Robert C. Williams, eds. *The American Atom: A Documentary History of Nuclear Policies from the Discovery of Fission to the Present.* 2nd ed. Philadelphia: Univ. of Pennsylvania Press, 1991.

Cantril, Hadley, ed. *Public Opinion 1935-1946*. Princeton: Princeton Univ. Press, 1951.

Carter, April. *Peace Movements: International Protest and World Politics since 1945.* New York: Longman, 1992.

Cary, Otis. "The Sparing of Kyoto, Mr. Stimson's 'Pet City,'" *Japan Quarterly* 22 (Oct.-Dec. 1975): 337-47.

————. "Atomic Bomb Targeting—Myths and Realities." *Japan Quarterly* 26 (Oct.-Dec. 1979): 506-14.

Casdorph, Paul. *Let the Good Times Roll: Life at Home in America during World War II.* New York: Paragon House, 1989.

Cashman, Sean Dennis. *America, Roosevelt, and World War II.* New York: New York Univ. Press, 1989.

Chase, John L. "Unconditional Surrender Reconsidered." In *Essays on the History of American Foreign Relations.* Edited by Lawrence E. Gelfand. New York: Holt, Rinehart and Winston, 1972.

Chatfield, Charles. "Norman Thomas: Harmony of Word and Deed." In *Peace Heroes in Twentieth-Century America.* Edited by Charles DeBenedetti. Bloomington: Indiana Univ. Press, 1986.

————. *The American Peace Movement: Ideas and Activism.* New York: Twayne, 1992.

Clarke, Robin. *The Silent Weapons.* New York: David McKay, 1968.

Clinard, Marshall B. *The Black Market: A Study of White Collar Crime.* New York: Rinehart, 1952.

Cline, Ray S. *Washington Command Post: The Operations Division.* Washington, D.C.: Government Printing Office, 1951.

Coakley, Robert W., and Richard M. Leighton. *Global Logistics and Strategy, 1943-1945.* Washington, D.C.: Government Printing Office, 1968.

Coffey, Thomas M. *Iron Eagle: The Turbulent Life of General Curtis LeMay.* New York: Avon Books, 1988.

Columbia Broadcasting System. *From Pearl Harbor into Tokyo: The Story as Told by War Correspondents on the Air.* New York: Columbia Broadcasting System, 1945.

Complete Presidential Press Conferences of Franklin D. Roosevelt. Vols. 19-20, 1942; Vols. 20-21, 1943. New York: De Capo Press, 1972.

Cookson, John, and Judith Nottingham. *A Survey of Chemical and Biological Warfare.* New York: Monthly Review Press, 1969.

Corbett, P. Scott. *Quiet Passages: The Exchange of Civilians between the United States and Japan during the Second World War.* Kent, Ohio: Kent State Univ. Press, 1987.

Corn, Joseph J. *The Winged Gospel: America's Romance with Aviation, 1900-1950.* New York: Oxford Univ. Press, 1983.

Costello, John. *The Pacific War.* New York: Quill, 1982.

————. *Virtue under Fire: How World War II Changed Our Social and Sexual Attitudes.* New York: Fromm International 1987.

Couffer, Jack. *Bat Bomb: World War II's Other Secret Weapon.* Austin: Univ. of Texas Press, 1992.

Cousins, Norman. "The Poison Gas Boys." *Saturday Review of Literature,* 22 January 1944, 12.

Cowan, Ruth Schwartz. *More Work for Mother: The Ironies of Household Technology from the Open Hearth to the Microwave.* New York: Basic Books, 1983.

Craig, William. *The Fall of Japan.* New York: Dial Press, 1967; Penguin Books, 1979.

Crane, Conrad C. "The Evolution of American Strategic Bombing of Urban Areas." Ph.D. diss., Stanford Univ. 1990.

————. *Bombs, Cities and Civilians: American Airpower Strategy in World War II.* Lawrence: Univ. Press of Kansas, 1993.

Craven, Wesley Frank, and James Lea Cate, eds. *The Army Air Forces in World War II.* Vol. 5, The Pacific: Matterhorn to Nagasaki June 1944 to August 1945. Chicago: Univ. of Chicago Press, 1953.

Cray, Ed. *General of the Army George C. Marshall: Soldier and Statesman.* New York: W.W. Norton, 1990; Touchstone, 1991.

Davis, Kenneth S. *The American Experience of War 1939-1945.* London: Secker and Warburg, 1967.

DeBenedetti, Charles, ed. *Peace Heroes in Twentieth-Century America.* Bloomington: Indiana Univ. Press, 1986.

Desmond, Robert W. *Tides of War: World News Reporting 1931-1945.* Iowa City: Univ. of Iowa Press, 1984.

Dick, Bernard F. *The Star-Spangled Screen: The American World War II Film.* Lexington: Univ. Press of Kentucky, 1985.

Dockrill, Saki ed. From *Pearl Harbor to Hiroshima: The Second World War in Asia and the Pacific, 1941-45.* New York: St. Martin's Press, 1994.

Dod, Karl C. *The Corps of Engineers: The War against Japan.* Washington, D.C.: Office of the Chief of Military History, Department of the Army, 1966.

Doenecke, Justus D. *Not to the Swift: The Old Isolationists in the Cold War Era.* Cranbury, N.J.: Associate Univ. Press, 1979.

Doenecke, Justus D., and John E. Wilz. From *Isolation to War, 1931-1941.* 2nd ed. Arlington Heights, Ill.: Harlan Davidson, 1991.

Doherty, Thomas. *Projections of War: Hollywood, American Culture, and World War II.* New York: Columbia Univ. Press, 1993.

Donovan, Robert J. *Conflict and Crisis: The Presidency of Harry S Truman, 1945-1948.* New York: W.W. Norton, 1977.

Douglas, Susan J. *Where the Girls Are: Growing Up Female with the Mass Media.* New York: Times Books, 1995.

Dower, John W. *War without Mercy: Race and Power in the Pacific War.* New York: Pantheon Books, 1986.

Drea, Edward J. *MacArthur's Ultra: Codebreaking and the War against Japan, 1942-1945.* Lawrence: Univ. Press of Kansas, 1992.

Drinnon, Richard. *Facing West: The Metaphysics of Indian-Hating and Empire Building.* New York: New American Library, 1980.

Edoin, Hoito. *The Night Tokyo Burned.* New York: St. Martin's Press, 1987.

Eisenhower, Dwight D. *Crusade in Europe.* Garden City, N.Y.: Doubleday, 1948.

Eliot, George Fielding. "Should We Gas the Japs?" *Popular Science Monthly,* August 1945, 49-53.

Ellis, John. *Brute Force: Allied Strategy and Tactics in the Second World War.* New York: Viking Books, 1990.

Ewen, Stuart. *Captains of Consciousness: Advertising and the Social Roots of the Consumer Culture.* New York: McGraw-Hill, 1976.

Fahey, James J. *Pacific War Diary, 1942-1945.* New York: Boston: Houghton Mifflin, 1963; Berkley, 1973.

Farrago, Ladislas. *The Tenth Fleet.* New York: Drum Books, 1986.

Feifer, George. *Tennozan: The Battle of Okinawa and the Atomic Bomb.* New York: Ticknor and Fields, 1992.

Feis, Herbert. *The Atomic Bomb and the End of World War II.* Princeton: Princeton Univ. Press, 1966.

Feist, Joe Michael. "Bats Away." *American Heritage* 33 (April-May 1982): 93-94.

Ferrell, Robert H. *Harry S. Truman: His Life on the Family Farms.* Worland: High Plains, 1991.

———. *Choosing Truman: The Democratic Convention of 1944.* Columbia: Univ. of Missouri Press, 1994.

———. *Harry S. Truman: A Life.* Columbia: Univ. of Missouri Press, 1994.

Ferrell, Robert H., ed. *Off the Record: The Private Papers of Harry S. Truman.* New York: Penguin Books, 1982.

———. *Dear Bess: The Letters from Harry to Bess Truman, 1910-1959.* New York: W.W. Norton, 1983.

Fielding, Raymond. *The American Newsreel 1911-1967.* Norman: Univ. of Oklahoma Press, 1972.

———. *The March of Time, 1935-1951.* New York: Oxford Univ. Press, 1978.

Fleisher, Wilfrid. *What to Do with Japan.* Garden City, N.Y.: Doubleday, Doran, 1945.

Fox, Frank. *Madison Avenue Goes to War: The Strange Military Career of American Advertising 1941-1945.* Provo, Utah: Brigham Young Univ. Press, 1975.

Frank, Benis M. *Okinawa: The Great Island Battle.* New York: Elsevier-Dutton, 1978.

Frank, Benis M., and Henry I. Shaw, Jr. *History of U.S. Marine Corps Operations in World War II.* Vol. 5, *Victory and Occupation.* Washington, D.C.: Historical Branch, G-3 Division, Headquarters, U.S. Marine Corps, 1968.

Franklin, H. Bruce. "Fatal Fiction: A Weapon to End All Wars." *Bulletin of the Atomic Scientists* 45 (Nov. 1989): 18-24.

Freeman, Karen. "The Unfought Chemical War." *Bulletin of the Atomic Scientists* 47 (Dec. 1991): 30-39.

Fuqua, Stephen O. "The Case for Gas as a Humane Weapon." *Newsweek,* 25 May 1942, 25.

Fussell, Paul. *Thank God for the Atom Bomb and Other Essays.* New York: Summit Books, 1988.

———. *Wartime: Understanding and Behavior in the Second World War.* New York: Oxford Univ. Press, 1989.

Gallup, George H. *The Gallup Poll: Public Opinion 1935-1971.* Vol. 1, 1935-1948. New York: Random House, 1972.

Gardner, Brian. *The Year That Changed the World 1945.* New York: Coward-McCann, 1963.

Gayn, Mark. "Terror in Japan." *Collier's,* 16 June 1945, 11-12, 59.

Gilmore, Allison B. "In the Wake of Winning Armies: Allied Psychological Warfare against the Imperial Japanese Army in The Southwest Pacific Area during WWII." Ph.D. diss., Ohio State Univ., 1989.

Giovannitti, Len, and Fred Freed. *The Decision to Drop the Bomb.* New York: Coward-McCann, 1965.

Glough, Marion. "Home Should Be Even More Wonderful Than He Remembers It." *House Beautiful,* January 1945, 29.

Gluck, Sherna Berger. *Rosie the Riveter Revisited: Women, the War, and Social Change.* Boston: Twayne, 1987.

Gomer, Robert. "Japan's Biological Weapons: 1930-1945." *Bulletin of the Atomic Scientists* 37 (Oct. 1981): 43.

Goodman, Jack, ed. *While You Were Gone: A Report on Wartime Life in the United States.* New York: Simon and Schuster, 1946.

Gossett, Thomas F. *Race: The History of an Idea in America.* Dallas: Southern Methodist Univ. Press, 1963.

Grew, Joseph C. *Ten Years in Japan.* New York: Simon and Schuster, 1944.

———. *Turbulent Era: A Diplomatic Record of Forty Years 1904-1945.* Edited by Walter Johnson. Vol. 2. Boston: Houghton Mifflin, 1952.

Groves, Leslie R. *Now It Can Be Told: The Story of the Manhattan Project.* New York: Harper, 1962.

Hailey, Foster. "The War Converges On Japan." *Yale Review,* June 1945, 587-600.

Hamby, Alonzo. *Man of the People: A Life of Harry S. Truman.* New York: Oxford Univ. Press, 1995.

Hammond, Thomas T. "Atomic Diplomacy Revisited." *Orbis* 19 (Winter 1976): 1403-28.

Hanin, Eric Michael. "War on Our Minds: The American Mass Media in World War II." Ph.D. diss., Univ. of Rochester, 1976.

Harris, Mark Jonathon, Franklin D. Mitchell, and Steven J. Schechter. *The Homefront: America during World War II.* New York: G.P. Putnam's Sons, 1984.

Harris, Robert, and Jeremy Paxman. *A Higher Form of Killing: The Secret Story of Gas and Germ Warfare.* New York: Hill and Wang, 1982.

Harris, Sheldon H. *Factories of Death: Japan's Secret Biological Warfare Projects in Manchuria and China.* New York: Routledge, 1994.

Harrison, John A. "The USSR, Japan, and the End of the Great Pacific War." *Parameters* XIV (Summer 1994): 76-87.

Hartmann, Susan M. "Prescriptions for Penelope: Literature on Women's Obligations to Returning World War II Veterans." *Women's Studies* 5 (1978): 223-39.

———. *The Home Front and Beyond: American Women in the 1940's.* Boston: Twayne, 1982.

Harwit, Martin. "Academic Freedom in 'The Last Act'." *Journal of American History* 82 (December 1995): 1064-82.

Hayes, Grace P. *The History of the Joint Chiefs of Staff in World War II: The War Against Japan.* Annapolis, Md.: Naval Institute Press, 1982.

Heinrichs, Waldo H., Jr. *American Ambassador: Joseph C. Grew and the Development of the United States Diplomatic Tradition.* Boston: Little, Brown, 1966.

Henry, John. "Frontal Assault." *Cosmopolitan,* June 1945, 26, 128-33.

Hermens, Ferdinand. "Peacemaking 1945." *Catholic World,* May 1945, 123-29.

Herrmann, Helen Markel. "The Things They Never Tell You." *House Beautiful,* May 1945, 58-59.

Hersey, John. *Into the Valley: A Skirmish of the Marines.* New York: Alfred A. Knopf, 1943; Schocken Books, 1989.

Hersey, John. "Kamikaze." *Life,* 30 July 1945, 68-75.

Hersh, Seymour M. *Chemical and Biological Warfare: America's Hidden Arsenal.* New York: Anchor Books, 1969.

Hershberg, James. *James B. Conant: Harvard to Hiroshima and the Making of the Nuclear Age.* New York: Cambridge Univ.Press, 1994.

Hess, Gary R. *The United States at War, 1941-1945.* Arlington Heights, Ill: Harlan Davidson, 1986.

Hewlett, Richard G., and Oscar E. Anderson, Jr. *A History of the United States Atomic Energy Commission* Vol. 1, *The New World, 1939/1946.* University Park: Pennsylvania State Univ. Press, 1962.

Hikins, James W. "The Rhetoric of 'Unconditional Surrender' and the Decision to Drop the Atomic Bomb." *Quarterly Journal of Speech* 69 (Nov. 1983): 379-400.

Hodgson, Godfrey. *The Colonel: The Life and Wars of Henry Stimson 1867-1950.* New York: Alfred A. Knopf, 1990.

Holton, D.C. "The Japanese Mind." *New Republic,* 28 May 1945, 742-44.

Honey, Maureen. "Popular Magazines, Women, and World War II: The Use of Popular Culture as Propaganda." Ph.D. diss., Michigan State Univ., 1979.

———. *Creating Rosie the Riveter: Class, Gender, and Propaganda during World War II.* Amherst: Univ. of Massachusetts Press, 1984.

Hoopes, Roy. *Americans Remember the Home Front: An Oral Narrative.* New York: Hawthorn Books, 1977.

Hoopes, Townsend, and Douglas Brinkley. *Driven Patriot: The Life and Times of James Forrestal.* New York: Alfred A. Knopf, 1992.

Hopkins, George, E. "Bombing and the American Conscience during World War II." *Historian* 28 (May 1966): 451-73.

Hough, Frank O. *The Island War: The United States Marine Corps in the Pacific.* Philadelphia: J.B. Lippincott, 1947.

Howard, Harry Paxton. "America, Japan, and Russia." *Christian Century,* 2 May 1945, 547-49.

Howard, Michael. *Studies in War and Peace.* 1959. Reprint. New York: The Viking Press, 1972.

Hoyt, Edwin P. *Closing the Circle: War in the Pacific 1945.* New York: Van Nostrand Reinhold, 1982.

Hull, Cordell. *The Memoirs of Cordell Hull.* 2 vols. New York: Macmillan, 1948.

Hynes, Samuel. *Flights of Passage: Reflections of a World War II Aviator.* New York: Frederic C. Beil, 1988; Annapolis, Md.: Naval Institute Press, 1988.

Ienaga, Saburo. *The Pacific War, 1931-1945: A Critical Perspective on Japan's Role in World War II.* New York: Pantheon Books, 1978.

IMPACT: The Army Air Forces' Confidential Picture History of World War II. New York: James Parton, 1980.

Iriye, Akira. *Power and Culture: The Japanese-American War, 1941-1945.* Cambridge: Harvard Univ. Press, 1981.

Isaacs, Harold R. *Images of Asia: American Views of China and India.* New York: Harper, 1972.

Jacobs, Morris B. *War Gases: Their Identification and Decontamination.* New York: Interservice Publishers, 1942.

James, D. Clayton. *The Years of MacArthur.* Vol. 2, 1941-1945. Boston: Houghton Mifflin, 1975.

———. *A Time for Giants: Politics of the American High Command in World War II.* New York: Franklin Watts, 1987.

Johnson, Sheila K. *American Attitudes toward Japan, 1941-1975.* Stanford: Hoover Institution on War, Revolution and Peace, Stanford Univ., 1975.

———. *The Japanese through American Eyes.* Stanford: Stanford Univ. Press, 1988.

Johnson, Thomas M. "Doom Over Japan." *American Mercury,* August 1945, 236-41.

Johnstone, William C. *The Future of Japan.* New York: Oxford Univ. Press, 1945.

Jones, David Lloyd. "The U.S. Office of War Information and American Public Opinion during World War II, 1939-1945." Ph.D. diss., State Univ. of New York at Binghamton, 1976.

Jones, Edgar L. "To The Finish: A letter from Iwo Jima." *Atlantic Monthly,* June 1945, 50-53.

———. "Japan's Secret Weapon." *Atlantic Monthly,* July 1945, 44-47.

Jordan, Winthrop D. *White over Black: American Attitudes toward the Negro, 1550-1812.* Chapel Hill: Univ. of North Carolina Press, 1968.

Kawai, Kazuo. "Mokusatsu, Japan's Response to the Potsdam Declaration." *Pacific Historical Review* 19 (Nov. 1950): 409-14.

Kearney, Paul W. "Don't Let Poison Gas Panic You." *Good Housekeeping,* May 1943, 33, 215.

Kecskemeti, Paul. *Strategic Surrender: The Politics of Victory and Defeat.* Stanford: Stanford Univ. Press, 1958.

Keegan, John. *The Second World War.* New York: Viking, 1989; Penguin Books, 1990.

Kenney, George C. *General Kenney Reports: A Personal History of the Pacific War.* New York: Duell, Sloan, and Pearce, 1949; Washington, D.C.: Office of Air Force History, U.S. Air Force, 1987.

Kerr, E. Bartlett. *Flames over Tokyo: The U.S. Army Air Forces' Incendiary Campaign Against Japan 1944-1945.* New York: Donald I. Fine, 1991.

Kerr, George H. *Okinawa: The History of an Island People.* Rutland, Vermont: Charles E. Tuttle, 1958.

King, Ernest J., and Walter Muir Whitehill. *Fleet Admiral King: A Naval Record.* New York: W. W. Norton, 1952.

Kleber, Brooks E., and Dale Birdsell. *The Chemical Warfare Service: Chemicals in Combat.* Washington, D.C.: Office of the Chief of Military History, Department of the Army, 1966.

Kluger, Richard. *The Paper: The Life and Death of the New York Herald Tribune.* New York: Alfred A. Knopf, 1986.

Knightley, Phillip. *The First Casualty: From the Crimea to Vietnam: The War Correspondent as Hero, Propagandist, and Myth Maker.* New York: Harcourt Brace Jovanovich, 1975.

Kohn, Richard H. "History and the Culture Wars: The Case of the Smithsonian Institution's Enola Gay Exhibition." *Journal of American History* 82 (December 1995): 1036-63.

Laffin, John. *Americans in Battle.* New York: Crown, 1973.

Lamott, Willis Church. "What Not to Do with Japan." *Harper's,* June 1945, 585-91.

Landstrom, Russell. *The Associated Press News Annual:1945.* New York: Rinehart, 1946.

Lardner, John. "Japs in Flying Caskets Go V-Bombs One Better." *Newsweek,* 7 May 1945, 46.

Larsen, Lawrence H. "War Balloons over the Prairie: The Japanese Invasion of South Dakota." *South Dakota History* 9 (Spring 1979): 103-15.

Leahy, William D. *I Was There: The Personal Story of the Chief of Staff to Presidents Roosevelt and Truman Based on His Notes and Diaries Made at the Time.* New York: Whittlesey House, 1950.

Lears, Jackson. *Fables of Abundance: A Cultural History of Advertising in America.* New York: Basic Books, 1994.

Leff, Mark. "The Politics of Sacrifice on the American Home Front in World War II." *Journal of American History* 77 (March 1991): 1296-1318.

Leffler, Melvyn P. *A Preponderance of Power: National Security, the Truman Administration, and the Cold War.* Stanford: Stanford Univ. Press, 1992.

Leighton, Alexander H. *Human Relations in a Changing World: Observations in the Use of the Social Sciences.* New York: E.P. Dutton, 1949.

LeMay, Curtis E., with MacKinlay Kantor. *Mission with LeMay.* Garden City, N.Y.: Doubleday, 1965.

Lewin, Ronald. *The American Magic: Codes, Ciphers, and the Defeat of Japan.* New York: Penguin Books, 1983.

Libby, Justin H. "The Search for a Negotiated Peace." *World Affairs* 156 (Summer 1993): 35-45.

Lichtenstein, Nelson. "The Making of the Postwar Working Class: Cultural Pluralism and Social Structure in World War II." *Historian* 51 (Nov. 1988): 42-63.

Lifton, Robert Jay, and Greg Mitchell. *Hiroshima in America: Fifty Years of Denial.* New York: G.P. Putnam's Sons, 1995.

Lilienthal, David E. *The Journals of David E. Lilienthal.* Vol. 2, *The Atomic Energy Years 1945-1950.* New York: Harper and Row, 1964.

Lindley, Ernest K. "Thoughts on the Use of Gas in Warfare." *Newsweek,* 20 December 1943, 24.

———. "The Jap Does Have a Choice." *Newsweek,* 16 July 1945, 31.

Linenthal, Edward Taber. *Changing Images of the Warrior Hero in America: A History of Popular Symbolism.* New York: Edwin Mellen Press, 1982.

———. "Struggling with History and Memory." Journal of American History 82 (December 1995): 1094-1101.

Lingeman, Richard R. *Don't You Know There's a War On?: The American Home Front, 1941-1945.* New York: Perigee Books, 1980.

Lippmann, Walter. *Public Opinion.* 1922. Reprint. New York: Free Press, 1965.

Litoff, Judy Barrett, and David C. Smith eds. *Dear Boys: World War II Letters from a Woman Back Home.* Jackson: Univ. of Mississippi Press, 1991.

———. *Since You Went Away: World War II Letters from American Women on the Home Front.* New York: Oxford Univ. Press, 1991.

Lloyd, Charles David. "American Society and Values in World War II from Publications of the Office of War Information." Ph.D. diss., Georgetown Univ. 1975.

Love, Robert William, Jr. "Ernest Joseph King." In *The Chiefs of Naval Operations.* Edited by Robert William Love, Jr. Annapolis, Md.: Naval Institute Press, 1980.

Luvaas, Jay ed. *Dear Miss Em: General Eichelberger's War in the Pacific, 1942-1945.* Westport, Conn.: Greenwood Press, 1972.

Macdonald, Dwight. "A Japanese Badoglio?" *politics* 2 (June 1945): 161-63.

MacIsaac, David. *Strategic Bombing in World War Two: The Story of the United States Strategic Bombing Survey.* New York: Garland, 1976.

McCarthy, Richard. *The Ultimate Folly: War by Pestilence, Asphyxiation, Defoliation.* New York: Alfred A. Knopf, 1969.

McCoy, Donald R. *The Presidency of Harry S. Truman.* Lawrence: Univ. Press of Kansas, 1984.

McCullough, David. *Truman.* New York: Simon and Schuster, 1992.

McCune, Shannon. *Intelligence on the Economic Collapse of Japan in 1945*. Lanham, Md.: Univ. Press of America, 1989.

McDougall, John Alexander, Jr. "I Was Tortured By The Japs." *American Magazine*, May 1945, 17, 99-102, 104.

McFarland, Stephen. "Preparing for What Never Came: Chemical and Biological Warfare in World War II." *Defense Analyis* 2 (June 1986): 107-21.

McGill, Peter. "A Coverup for a Death Camp." *Maclean's* 98(20 May 1985): 32.

McGurn, Barrett. "How Good Is the Jap GI?" *Popular Science Monthly*, May 1945, 120-22, 206-7.

McNeal, Patricia. *Harder Than War: Catholic Peacemaking in Twentieth-Century America*. New Brunswick, N.J.: Rutgers Univ. Press, 1992.

Maddox, Robert James. *From War to Cold War: The Education of Harry S. Truman*. Boulder, Colo.: Westview Press, 1988.

———. *The United States and World War II*. Boulder, Colo.: Westview Press, 1992.

Magruder, J.H. "Epitaph for a Young Marine." *Saturday Evening Post*, 21 July 1945, 62.

Mahoney, Tom. "Words That Win Battles." *Popular Science Monthly*, June 1945, 121-23, 206-7.

Manchester, William. *Goodbye, Darkness: A Memoir of the Pacific War*. Boston: Little, Brown, 1979.

Mandelbaum, Michael. *The Nuclear Revolution: International Politics before and after Hiroshima*. Cambridge: Cambridge Univ. Press, 1981.

Manzo, Louis A. "Morality in War Fighting and Strategic Bombing in World War II." *Air Power History* 39 (Fall 1992): 35-50.

Marchand, Roland. *Advertising the American Dream: Making Way for Modernity*. Berkeley: Univ. of California Press, 1985.

Marling, Karal Ann, and John Wetenhall. *Iwo Jima: Monuments, Memories, and the American Hero*. Cambridge: Harvard Univ. Press, 1991.

Marshall, Jim. "We Are Ready with Gas." *Collier's*, 7 August 1943, 21, 59.

Marwil, Jonathan. "Paul Fussell's Wars." *Michigan Quarterly Review* (Summer 1990): 431-52.

Matloff, Maurice. *The War Department: Strategic Planning for Coalition Warfare 1943-1944*. Washington, D.C.: Office of the Chief of Military History, Department of the Army, 1959.

May, Elaine Tyler. *Homeward Bound: American Families in the Cold War Era*. New York: Basic Books, 1988.

Merrill, Francis E. *Social Problems on the Home Front: A Study of War-time Influences*. New York: Harper, 1948.

Meselson, Matthew. "The Myth of Chemical Superweapons." *Bulletin of the Atomic Scientists* 47 (April 1991): 12-17.

Messer, Robert L. *The End of an Alliance: James F. Byrnes, Roosevelt, Truman, and the Origins of the Cold War*. Chapel Hill: Univ. of North Carolina Press, 1982.

———. "New evidence on Truman's Decision." *Bulletin of the Atomic Scientists* 41 (Aug. 1985): 50-56.

Miles, Rufus E., Jr. "Hiroshima: The Strange Myth of Half a Million American Lives Saved." *International Security* 10 (Fall 1985): 121-40.

Milkman, Ruth. *Gender at War: The Dynamics of Job Segregation by Sex during World War II.* Urbana: Univ. of Illinois Press, 1987.

Miller, Edward S. *War Plan Orange.* Annapolis, Md.: Naval Institute Press, 1991.

Miller, Stuart Creighton. *The Unwelcome Immigrant: The American Image of the Chinese, 1785-1882.* Berkeley: Univ. of California Press, 1969.

———. *"Benevolent Assimilation:" The American Conquest of the Philippines, 1899-1903.* New Haven: Yale Univ. Press, 1982.

Milliman, Leonard. "The Truth about Poison Gas." *Collier's,* 26 September 1942, 14-15.

Millis, Walter, ed. *The Forrestal Diaries.* New York: Viking Press, 1951.

Minear, Richard H. "The Wartime Studies of Japanese National Character." *Japan Interpreter* 13 (Summer 1980): 36-59.

Moley, Raymond. "Attacking the Jap Mentality." *Newsweek,* 2 July 1945, 92.

Morison, Samuel Eliot. *History of United States Naval Operations in World War II.* Vol. 14, *Victory in the Pacific, 1945.* Boston: Little, Brown, 1960.

Morley, Felix. "What Unconditional Surrender Means." *Christian Century,* 25 July 1945, 857-58.

Mueller, John E. *War, Presidents, and Public Opinion.* New York: John Wiley, 1973.

Muir, Malcolm. "Memo." *Newsweek,* 21 May 1945, 25.

Nelson, Douglas. "Serving the Nation." *Trains* 54 (June 1994): 45-47.

Newman, Barclay Moon. *Japan's Secret War.* Current Pub., 1944.

Nichols, Chas. S., Jr., and Henry I. Shaw, Jr. *Okinawa: Victory in the Pacific.* Rutland, Vermont: Charles E. Tuttle, 1955.

Nichols, H.G., ed. *Washington Despatches 1941-1945: Weekly Political Reports from the British Embassy.* Chicago: Univ. of Chicago Press, 1981.

Noble, Harold J. "Give the Devils Their Due." *Saturday Evening Post,* 12 May 1945, 18-19, 95-96.

Noell, Livingston P., Jr. "My Japanese Jailer." *Saturday Evening Post,* 7 July 1945, 18-19, 105-6.

O'Connell, Robert L. *Of Arms and Men: A History of War, Weapons and Agression.* New York: Oxford Univ. Press, 1989.

O'Connor, Raymond G. *Diplomacy for Victory: FDR and Unconditional Surrender.* New York: W.W. Norton, 1971.

O'Neill, William L. *A Democracy at War: America's Fight at Home and Abroad in World War II.* New York: Free Press, 1993.

O'Sheel, Patrick, and Gene Cook, eds. *Semper Fidelis: The U.S. Marines in the Pacific 1941-1945.* New York: William Sloane, 1947.

Painton, Frederick C. "Why We Must Bomb Japanese Cities." *Reader's Digest,* May 1945, 82-84.

Pakenham, Compton. "The Japanese Mentality as a Factor in War." *Newsweek,* 11 June 1945, 48.

———. "Mother and Father to Japanese—the Army." *Newsweek,* 25 June 1945, 44.

————. "With His Trick Mind, the Japanese Fools Himself." *Newsweek,* 2 July 1945, 33.

————. "How the Jap Learns to Fight as He Does." *Newsweek,* 9 July 1945, 47.

————. "How the Jap Will Take Final Defeat." *Newsweek,* 16 July 1945, 40.

————. "The Divine Dummy: How Jap Leaders Rule." 23 July 1945, *Newsweek,* 23 July 1945, 38.

————. "Does the Jap Soldier Have a Breaking Point?" *Newsweek,* 30 July 1945, 35.

Pape, Robert A. "Why Japan Surrendered." *International Security* 18 (Fall 1993): 154-201.

Parrish, Thomas. *Roosevelt and Marshall: Partners in Politics and War.* New York: William Morrow, 1989.

Patterson, James T. *Mr. Republican: A Biography of Robert A. Taft.* Boston: Houghton Mifflin, 1972.

Paulding, C.G. "Poison Gas." *Commonweal,* 22 June 1945, 229-30.

Perrett, Geoffrey. *Days of Sadness, Years of Triumph: The American People 1939-1945.* New York: Coward, McCann, and Geohagen, 1973.

————. *A Country Made by War: From the Revolution to Vietnam—The Story of America's Rise to Power.* New York: Random House, 1989.

Perry, Glen C.H. *"Dear Bart": Washington Views of World War II.* Westport, Conn.: Greenwood Press, 1982.

Pickett, William B. *Homer E. Capehart: A Senator's Life, 1879-1979.* Indianapolis: Indiana Historical Society, 1990.

Pogue, Forrest C. *George C. Marshall: Organizer of Victory.* New York: Viking Press, 1973.

————. *George C. Marshall: Statesman 1945-1959.* New York: Viking Press, 1987.

Polenberg, Richard. *War and Society: The United States, 1941-1945.* Philadelphia: J.B. Lippincott, 1972.

————. "The Good War? A Reappraisal of How World War II Affected American Society." *Virginia Magazine of History and Biography* 100 (July 1992): 295-322.

Potter, E.B. *Nimitz.* Annapolis, Md.: Naval Institute Press, 1976.

Powell, John W. "Japan's Germ Warfare: The U.S. Cover-up of a War Crime." *Bulletin of Concerned Asian Scholars* 12 (Oct.-Dec. 1980): 2-17.

————. "A Hidden Chapter in History." *Bulletin of the Atomic Scientists* 37 (October 1981): 44-52.

Powers, Thomas. "Were the Atomic Scientists Spies?" *New York Review of Books,* 9 June 1994, 10-14, 16-17.

Pratt, Fletcher. "The War in the Pacific." *New Republic,* 28 May 1945, 737-39.

Pratt, William V. "Can Air Power Bring Tokyo to Terms?" *Newsweek,* 4 June 1945, 48.

————. "Summarizing Japan's Military Position." *Newsweek,* 11 June 1945, 44.

————. "A Reply to the Okinawa Critics." *Newsweek,* 2 July 1945, 36.

————. "Pacific Strategy: Japan Will Be Another Germany." *Newsweek,* 16 July 1945, 39.

Public Papers of the Presidents: Harry S. Truman: Containing the Public Messages, Speeches, and Statements of the President April 12, 1945 to December 31, 1945. Washington, D.C.: Government Printing Office, 1961.

Pyle, Ernie. *Last Chapter.* New York: Henry Holt, 1946.

Ramsdell, Daniel B. "Asia Askew: U.S. Best-Sellers on Asia, 1931-1980." *Bulletin of Concerned Asian Scholars* 15 (Oct.-Dec. 1983): 2-25.

Rauch, Basil, ed. *The Roosevelt Reader: Selected Speeches, Messages, Press Conferences, and Letters of Franklin D. Roosevelt.* New York: Holt, Rinehart, and Winston, 1964.

Reports of General MacArthur. Vol. 1, *The Campaigns of MacArthur in the Pacific.* Washington, D.C.: Government Printing Office, 1966.

Rhodes, Richard. *The Making of the Atomic Bomb.* New York: Simon and Schuster, 1986.

Robertson, David. *Sly and Able: A Political Biography of James F. Byrnes.* New York: W.W. Norton, 1994

Roeder, George H. Jr. *The Censored War: American Visual Experience during World War Two.* New Haven: Yale Univ. Press, 1993.

Roland, Alex. "Technology, Ground Warfare, and Strategy: The Paradox of American Experience." *Journal of Military History* 55 (Oct. 1991): 447-68.

Rose, Lisle A. *Dubious Victory: The United States and the End of World War II.* Kent, Ohio: Kent State Univ. Press, 1973.

Rose, Steven, ed. *CBW: Chemical and Biological Warfare.* Boston: Beacon Press, 1968.

Rosenman, Samuel I. *Working with Roosevelt.* New York: Harper, 1952.

Rosenman, Samuel I., ed. *The Public Papers and Addresses of Franklin D. Roosevelt.* Vol. 6, *The Constitution Prevails.* New York: Macmillan, 1941. Vol. 11, *Humanity on the Defensive.* New York: Harper, 1950. Vol 12, *The Tide Turns.* New York: Harper, 1950.

Rupp, Leila J. *Mobilizing Women for War: German and American Propaganda, 1939-1945.* Princeton: Princeton Univ. Press, 1978.

Sayle, Murray. "Did the Bomb End the War?" *New Yorker,* 31 July 1995, 40-64.

Sbrega, John J. *The War against Japan, 1941-1945: An Annotated Bibliography.* New York: Garland, 1989.

Schaffer, Ronald. *Wings of Judgment: American Bombing in World War II.* New York: Oxford Univ. Press, 1985.

Schaller Michael. *The American Occupation of Japan: The Origins of the Cold War in Asia.* New York: Oxford Univ. Press, 1985.

———. *Douglas MacArthur: The Far Eastern General.* New York: Oxford Univ. Press, 1989.

Seeman, Bernard. "Life in Japan Today." *American Mercury,* July 1945, 7-15.

Sevareid, Eric. "Super-Dupering the War," *Saturday Review of Literature,* 12 February 1944, 9-10.

Severo, Richard, and Lewis Milford. *The Wages of War: When American Soldiers Came Home—From Valley Forge to Vietnam.* New York: Touchstone, 1990.

Sherrod, Robert. *Tarawa: The Story of a Battle.* 1944. Reprint. Fredericksburg, Tex.: The Admiral Nimitz Foundation, 1973.

————. *On to Westward: War in the Central Pacific.* New York: Duell, Sloan, and Pearce, 1945.

Sherry, Michael S. *The Rise of American Air Power: The Creation of Armageddon.* New Haven: Yale Univ. Press, 1987.

————. "Guilty Knowlege." *New York Times Book Review,* 30 July 1995, pp. 11-13.

Sherwin, Martin J. *A World Destroyed: Hiroshima and the Origins of the Arms Race.* New York: Vintage Books, 1987.

————. "Hiroshima as Politics and History." *Journal of American History* 82 December 1995): 1085-93.

Sherwood, Robert. "I Can't Make Your Party, Pete." *Collier's,* 12 May 1945, 24.

Sigal, Leon V. *Fighting to a Finish: The Politics of War Termination in the United States and Japan, 1945.* Ithaca: Cornell Univ. Press, 1988.

Simon, Rita James. *Public Opinion in America: 1936-1970.* Chicago: Rand McNally, 1974.

Skates, John Ray. *The Invasion of Japan: Alternative to the Bomb.* Columbia: Univ. of South Carolina Press, 1994.

Sledge, E.B. *With the Old Breed at Peleliu and Okinawa.* Novato, Calif.: Presidio Press, 1981; New York: Oxford Univ. Press, 1990.

Slotten, Hugh R. "Humane Chemistry or Scientific Barbarism? American Responses to World War I Poison Gas, 1915-1930." *Journal of American History* 77 (Sept. 1990): 476-98.

Smith, Robert Ross. *Triumph in the Philippines.* Washington, D.C.: Center of Military History, Department of the Army, 1963.

Somervell, Brehon. "The Biggest Moving Job in History." *American Magazine,* July 1945, 24-25, 94, 96, 98.

Sparagana, Eleanor. "The Conduct and Consequences of Psychological Warfare: American Psychological Warfare Operations in the War against Japan, 1941-1945." Ph.D. diss., Brandeis Univ. 1990.

Spector, Ronald H. *Eagle against the Sun.* New York: Vintage Books, 1985.

Spiers, Edward M. *Chemical Warfare.* Urbana: Univ. of Illinois Press, 1986.

Steadman, John M. *The Myth of Asia.* New York: Simon and Schuster, 1969.

Stimson, Henry L. "The Decision to Use the Atomic Bomb." *Harper's* 194 (February 1947): 97-107.

Stimson, Henry L., and McGeorge Bundy. *On Active Service in Peace and War.* New York: Harper, 1947.

Stockholm International Peace Research Institute, (SIPRI). The Rise of CB Weapons. Vol. 1 of The Problem of Chemical and Biological Warfare, by Julian Perry Robinson with Milton Leitenberg. Stockholm: Almqvist and Wiksell, 1971.

Stone, I.F. *The War Years 1939-1945.* Boston: Little, Brown, 1988.

Strasser, Susan. *Never Done: A History of American Housework.* New York: Pantheon Books, 1982.

Strauss, Lewis L. *Men and Decisions.* Garden City, N.Y.: Doubleday, 1962.

Sudoplatov, Pavel and Anatoli Sudoplatov with Jerrold L. and Leona P. Schechter. *Special Tasks: The Memoirs of an Unwanted Witness—A Soviet Spymaster.* Boston: Little, Brown, 1994.

Takaki, Ronald. *Hiroshima: Why America Dropped the Atomic Bomb.* Boston: Little, Brown, 1995.

Tanaka, Yuki. "Poison Gas: The story Japan Would Like to Forget." *Bulletin of the Atomic Scientists* 44 (Oct. 1988): 10-19.

Terkel, Studs. *"The Good War": An Oral History of World War II.* New York: Pantheon Books, 1984.

Thelen, David. "History after the *Enola Gay* Controversy: An Introduction." *Journal of American History* 82 (December 1995): 1029-35.

Thomas, Norman. *What Is Our Destiny?.* Garden City, N.Y.: Doubleday, Doran, 1944.

Thorne, Christopher. *Allies of a Kind: The United States, Britain, and the War against Japan, 1941-1945.* New York: Oxford Univ. Press, 1978.

———. *Racial Aspects of the Far Eastern War of 1941-1945.* London: British Academy, 1982.

———. *The Issue of War: States, Societies, and the Far Eastern Conflict of 1941-1945.* New York: Oxford Univ. Press, 1985.

Tobin, Edward James. "Why We Fight: Versions of the American Purpose in World War II." Ph.D. diss., Univ. of Michigan, 1986.

Toland, John. *The Rising Sun: The Decline and Fall of the Japanese Empire 1936-1945.* New York: Bantam Books, 1971.

Truman, Harry S. *Memoirs by Harry S. Truman.* Vol. 1, *Year of Decisions.* Garden City, N.Y.: Doubleday, 1955.

Ugaki, Matome. *Fading Victory: The Diary of Admiral Matome Ugaki 1941-1945.* Translated by Masataka Chihaya. Edited by Donald M. Goldstein and Katherine V. Dillon. Pittsburgh: Univ. of Pittsburgh Press, 1991.

University of Chicago. The University of Chicago Round Table. no. 381, May-August 1945.

U.S. Congress. *Congressional Record: Proceedings and Debates of the 79th Congress, First Session.* Vol. 91, pt. 4, 7 May 1945 to 6 June 1945. Washington, D.C.: Government Printing Office, 1945.

———. *Congressional Record: Proceedings and Debates of the 79th Congress, First Session.* Vol. 91, pt. 5, 7 June 1945 to 30 June 1945. Washington, D.C.: Government Printing Office, 1945.

———. *Congressional Record: Proceedings and Debates of the 79th Congress, First Session.* Vol. 91, pt. 6, 2 July 1945 to 10 September 1945. Washington, D.C.: Government Printing Office.

———. *Congressional Record: Proceedings and Debates of the 79th Congress, First Session, Appendix.* Vol. 91, pt. 11, 23 March 1945 to 8 June 1945. Washington, D.C.: Government Printing Office, 1945.

———. *Congressional Record: Proceedings and Debates of the 79th Congress, First Session, Appendix.* Vol. 91, pt. 12, 11 June 1945 to 11 October 1945. Washington, D.C.: Government Printing Office, 1945.

U.S. Department of Commerce. *Statistical Abstract of the United States 1944-45.* Washington, D.C.: Government Printing Office, 1945.

U.S. Department of Defense. *The Entry of the Soviet Union into the War against Japan: Military Plans, 1941-1945.* Washington, D.C.: Government Printing Office, 1955.

U.S. Department of State. *Bulletin*. Vol. 9: 1943; Vol. 12: May-June 1945; Vol. 13: July-August 1945. Washington, D.C.: Government Printing Office, 1945.

———. *Foreign Relations of the United States*: Conference of Berlin (Potsdam). 2 vols. Washington, D.C.: Government Printing Office, 1960.

———. *Foreign Relations of the United States: Diplomatic Papers, 1944*. Vol. 5, The Near East; South Asia and Africa; The Far East. Washington, D.C.: Government Printing Office, 1965.

———. *Foreign Relations of the United States: The Conferences at Washington, 1941-1942 and Casablanca, 1943*. Washington, D.C.: Government Printing Office, 1968.

———. *Foreign Relations of the United States: Diplomatic Papers, 1945*. Vol. 6, The British Commonwealth; The Far East. Washington, D.C.: Government Printing Office, 1969.

Utgoff, Victor A. *The Challenge of Chemical Weapons: An American Perspective*. New York: St. Martin's Press, 1991.

van Courtland Moon, John Ellis. "Chemical Weapons and Deterrence: The World War II Experience." International Security 8 (Spring 1984): 3-35.

———. "Chemical warfare: A Forgotten Lesson." *Bulletin of the Atomic Scientists*, 45 (July/Aug. 1989): 40-43.

———. "Project SPHINX: The Question of the Use of Gas in the Planned Invasion of Japan." *Journal of Strategic Studies* 12 (Sept. 1989): 303-23.

van Creveld, Martin. *Technology and War: From 2000 b.c. to the Present*. New York: Free Press, 1989.

Vandegrift, A.A. *Once a Marine: The Memoirs of General A.A. Vandegrift*. New York: W. W. Norton, 1964.

Vander Linde, Dean Marvin. "'Downfall': The American Plans for the Invasion of Japan in World War II." Master's thesis, Michigan State Univ. 1987.

van der Vat, Dan. *The Pacific Campaign*. New York: Touchstone, 1992.

Villa, Brian L. "The U.S. Army, Unconditional Surrender, and the Potsdam Declaration." *Journal of American History* 63 (June 1976): 66-92.

Wade, Betsy, ed. *Forward Positions: The War Correspondence of Homer Bigart*. Fayetteville: Univ. of Arkansas Press, 1992.

Waitt, Alden H. *Gas Warfare: The Chemical Weapon, Its Use, and Protection Against It*. New York: Duell, Sloan, and Pearce, 1942.

Waitt, Alden H. "Poison Gas in This War." *New Republic*, 27 April 1942, 563-65.

Walker, J. Samuel. "The Decision to Use the Bomb: A Historiographical Update." *Diplomatic History* 14 (Winter 1990): 97-114.

———. "History, Collective Memory, and the Decision to Use the Bomb." *Diplomatic History* 19 (Spring 1995): 319-328.

Walzer, Michael. *Just and Unjust Wars*. 2d ed. New York: Basic Books, 1992.

The War Reports of General of the Army George C. Marshall, General of the Army H.H. Arnold, Fleet Admiral Ernest J. King. Philadelphia: J.B. Lippincott, 1947.

Webber, Bert. *Retaliation: Japanese Attacks and Allied Countermeasures on the Pacific Coast in World War II*. Corvallis: Oregon State Univ. Press, 1975.

Wedemeyer, Albert C. *Wedemeyer Reports!*. New York: Henry Holt, 1958.

Weekly, Terry M. "Proliferation of Chemical Warfare: Challenge to Traditional Restraints." *Parameters* 19, (Dec. 1989): 51-66.

Weigley, Russell F. *The American Way of War*. Bloomington: Indiana Univ. Press, 1977.

Weinberg, Gerhard L. *A World at Arms: A Global History of World War II*. New York: Cambridge Univ. Press, 1994.

Westbrook, Robert B. "Fighting for the American Family: Private Interests and Political Obligation in World War II." *In The Power of Culture: Critical Essays in American History*, edited by Richard Wightman Fox and T.J. Jackson Lears. Chicago: Univ. of Chicago Press, 1993.

Whitfield, Stephen J. *The Culture of the Cold War*. Baltimore: Johns Hopkins Univ. Press, 1991.

Wilcox, Robert K. *Japan's Secret War*. New York: William Morrow, 1985.

Williams, Peter, and David Wallace. *Unit 731: Japan's Secret Biological Warfare in World War II*. New York: Free Press, 1989.

Wilson, Joan Hoff. "Herbert Hoover's Plan for Ending the Second World War." *International History Review* 1 (Jan. 1979): 84-102.

Winkler, Allan M. *The Politics of Propaganda: The Office of War Information 1942-1945*. New Haven: Yale Univ. Press, 1978.

———. *Home Front U.S.A.: American during World War II*. Arlington Heights, Ill.: Harlan Davidson, 1986.

Winkler, Karen J. "50 Years Later, the Debate Rages over Hiroshima." *Chronicle of Higher Education* 21 April 1995, pp. A-10, A-18, A-19.

Winton, John. *ULTRA in the Pacific: How Breaking Japanese Codes and Cyphers Affected Naval Operations against Japan 1941-45*. Annapolis, Md.: Naval Institute Press, 1993.

Wittner, Lawrence. *Rebels against War: The American Peace Movement, 1941-1960*. New York: Columbia Univ. Press, 1969.

Worden, William L. "Kamikaze: Aerial Banzai Charge." *Saturday Evening Post*, 23 June 1945, 17, 77-78.

Wu, William F. *The Yellow Peril*. Hamden: Archon Books, 1982.

Wyden, Peter. *Day One: Before Hiroshima and After*. New York: Simon and Schuster, 1984.

Wylie, Philip. *Generation of Vipers*. New York: Rinehart, 1942.

Yankelovich, Daniel. *Coming to Public Judgment: Making Democracy Work in a Complex World*. Syracuse: Syracuse Univ. Press, 1991.

Yergin, Daniel. *The Prize: The Epic Quest for Oil, Money, and Power*. New York: Touchstone, 1993.

Yoder, Robert M. "I Just Want to Be a Customer." *Saturday Evening Post*, 5 May 1945, 11, 102-3.

Young, Roland. *Congressional Politics in the Second World War*. New York: Columbia Univ. Press, 1956.

Zacharias, Ellis M. *Secret Missions: The Story of an Intelligence Officer*. New York: G.P. Putnam's Sons, 1946; Paperback Library, 1961.

———. "The A-Bomb Was Not Needed," *United Nations World*, 3 (August 1949): 25-29.

———. "How We Bungled the Japanese Surrender," *Look, 6 June 1950, 12-14, 16-19, 21*.

Index

GAYLORD MG